THE CHINA-PAKISTAN AXIS

ANDREW SMALL

The China-Pakistan Axis

Asia's New Geopolitics

OXFORD
UNIVERSITY PRESS

OXFORD
UNIVERSITY PRESS

Oxford University Press is a department of the
University of Oxford. It furthers the University's objective
of excellence in research, scholarship, and education
by publishing worldwide.

Oxford   New York

Auckland   Cape Town   Dar es Salaam   Hong Kong   Karachi
Kuala Lumpur   Madrid   Melbourne   Mexico City   Nairobi
New Delhi   Shanghai   Taipei   Toronto

With offices in

Argentina   Austria   Brazil   Chile   Czech Republic   France   Greece
Guatemala   Hungary   Italy   Japan   Poland   Portugal   Singapore
South Korea   Switzerland   Thailand   Turkey   Ukraine   Vietnam

Oxford is a registered trade mark of Oxford University Press
in the UK and certain other countries.

Published in the United States of America by
Oxford University Press
198 Madison Avenue, New York, NY 10016

Library of Congress Cataloging-in-Publication Data is available for this title
Small, Andrew
The China-Pakistan Axis
Asia's New Geopolitics
ISBN 978-0-19-021075-5

Printed in India on acid-free paper

CONTENTS

ABBREVIATIONS

ANA	Afghan National Army
CENTO	Central Treaty Organization
CIA	Central Intelligence Agency
CICIR	Chinese Institute of Contemporary International Relations
CNPC	China National Petroleum Corporation
CPC	also CCP, Communist Party of China
ETIM	East Turkistan Islamic Movement
ETIP	East Turkistan Islamic Party
FATA	Federally Administered Tribal Areas
HIT	Heavy Industries Taxila
IAEA	International Atomic Energy Agency
IDCPC	International Department, Central Committee of the Communist Party of China
IED	improvised explosive device
ISI	Directorate for Inter-Services Intelligence
IMF	International Monetary Fund
IMU	Islamic Movement of Uzbekistan
JI	Jamaat-e-Islami
JuD	Jamaat-ud-Dawa
JUI	Jamiat Ulema-i-Islam
JUI-F	Jamiat Ulema-i-Islam (Fazlur Rehman group)
KGB	Committee for State Security
KKH	Karakoram Highway
LeT	Lashkar-e-Taiba
MCC	China Metallurgical Group Corporation

ABBREVIATIONS

NATO	North Atlantic Treaty Organization
NEO	non-combatant evacuation operation
NSA	National Security Agency
NSC	National Security Council
NSG	Nuclear Suppliers Group
NPT	Non-Proliferation Treaty (Treaty on the Non-Proliferation of Nuclear Weapons)
OIC	Organization of the Islamic Conference
PLA	People's Liberation Army
PLAN	People's Liberation Army Navy
PML	Pakistan Muslim League
PML-Q	Pakistan Muslim League (Quaid e Azam Group)
PML-N	Pakistan Muslim League (Nawaz)
POW	prisoner of war
PPP	Pakistan People's Party
PRC	People's Republic of China
PSA	Port of Singapore Authority
PTI	Pakistan Tehreek-i-Insaf
S&ED	U.S.-China Strategic and Economic Dialogue
SCO	Shanghai Cooperation Organization
SEATO	Southeast Asia Treaty Organization
SIGINT	Signals Intelligence
SSG	Special Services Group
TIP	Turkistan Islamic Party
TTP	Tehrek-i-Taliban Pakistan
UAV	unmanned aerial vehicle
UF6	uranium hexaflouride
WTO	World Trade Organization
ZTE	Zhongxing Telecommunication Equipment Organization

PROLOGUE

IN THE SHADOW OF THE RED MOSQUE[1]

"The Pakistanis love China for what it can do for them, while the Chinese love Pakistanis despite what they do to themselves."[2]

In the early hours of Sunday, June 24 2007, vigilante groups from Lal Masjid, the Red Mosque, raided a Chinese massage parlour and acupuncture clinic in sector F-8, one of Islamabad's wealthiest neighbourhoods.[3] Overpowering three Pakistani guards, the militants, including ten burqa-clad women armed with batons, entered the house and demanded that the workers there accompany them. When the seven Chinese staff and two Pakistani clients refused, they were beaten and forcibly abducted. The "vice and virtue" squad took their victims to the Jamia Hafsa madrassa, a short distance from the clinic, where a spokesman announced to local press that "this place was used as a brothel house and despite our warnings the administration failed to take any action, so we decided to take action on our own."[4]

For the Lal Masjid radicals it was a serious tactical error. The same band of militants had been involved in a similar episode a few months earlier, when they rounded off their assault on another brothel by kidnapping four policemen. But the involvement of Chinese citizens made the June 24 incident far graver a matter. The treatment of China's overseas nationals had become a subject of acute sensitivity for Beijing. In the eyes of the more assertive sections of the Chinese public it was a test of the Communist Party's backbone, as the mocking packages of calcium pills they sent to the foreign ministry attested.[5] The imprisonment of seven Chinese workers within spitting distance of the principal government institutions of a country that was supposed to be China's closest ally was a matter of serious embarrassment. China's president, Hu Jintao, would receive regular briefings from his diplomats in Pakistan as the drama of the next seventeen hours unfolded.[6]

The kidnappings set in motion a fateful chain of events that resulted, within weeks, in a bloody denouement at the mosque, and the irrevocable altering of the relationship between Pakistan's military and its militants. And while the showdown between the army and the extremist bastion in the nation's capital had been looming for some time, few would have anticipated the country that provided the final trigger for the confrontation. Not the United States, whose efforts to push Islamabad to crack down on domestic militancy were so often outmanoeuvred, but Pakistan's all-weather friend whose requests could not be ignored: China.

For all the challenges that Pakistan faced, early in 2007 things seemed to be looking up. Annual growth ran at nearly 7 per cent.[7] The inflow of foreign investment had doubled in each of the last three years,[8] and the Karachi Stock Exchange was one of the world's leading performers.[9] Three years of secret talks with India had brought the two sides tantalisingly close to a deal over Kashmir.[10] The strategic setback Pakistan faced in Afghanistan after 9/11, when it lost the government it had installed to a US invasion that it felt compelled to support, was being reversed by a resurgent Taliban. "Our boys", as they were once openly described by Pakistan's interior minister, had re-taken control over swathes of the south and east of Afghanistan.[11] Even better: despite the insurgency being led, armed and financed from Pakistan, the relationship with the United States remained strong. Pervez Musharraf, the president and chief of army staff, had recently completed a visit-cum-book-tour of the United States with an itinerary that would make any American politician envious.[12] His efforts to position Pakistan as a crucial ally in the war against global terrorism continued to bear fruit, not least in the flow of billions of dollars of military aid and vital arms transfers.

China had its own part to play in this upbeat picture. The new port at Gwadar—which Chinese companies had built and mostly paid for—had just been inaugurated, promising "the next Dubai" on the Makran coast and an energy transshipment corridor running from the Arabian Sea through to China's booming cities.[13] Coupled with plans to expand the Karakoram Highway, which spans the high mountain passes in North-East Pakistan and North-West China, and a host of new telecommunications and mining investments, there was now hope that Pakistan's prospects might be tied to China's extraordinary economic expansion. Beijing was even there to cushion the blow of the US-India civil nuclear agreement, announced in 2005. Not only was there a prospect of China giving Pakistan a matching deal—the expansion of the Chashma nuclear power plants—but the US-India move seemed to mark the end of any temptation for Beijing to take a more balanced approach in its relations with its two South Asian neighbours. Residual Pakistani anxieties about China being lured away by India's economic boom were instead superseded by the prospect of consolidating a new axis with the emerging superpower.

But a time-bomb was ticking in the heart of Pakistan's capital. Lal Masjid and the Jamia Hafsa madrassa are located only a few blocks from the Presidential Palace, and even closer to the headquarters of Pakistan's military intelligence service, the ISI. The first mosque to be built when Islamabad was established as the seat of government in Karachi's place, it had long been frequented by the city's senior generals and politicians.[14] Yet in the years leading up to 2007, it became the epicentre of Pakistan's fraught relationship with the extremist forces that its army both sympathised with and feared, part directed and part struggled to control. Lal Masjid's ties with militants were longstanding, but in the past those links had been largely state-supported. In the 1980s, the mosque acted as an important recruiting post for mujahideen in the anti-Soviet campaign, and welcomed fighters in transit to Afghanistan and Kashmir alike.[15] Its relationship with the Taliban and Al Qaeda burgeoned in the decade that followed. The mosque's founder, Muhammad Abdullah Ghazi, met and was professedly inspired by Osama Bin Laden during a trip to Kandahar in 1998 to "pay homage" to the Taliban's leader, Mullah Omar. Ghazi was accompanied by his son, Abdul Rashid, who would run the mosque with his elder brother, Abdul Aziz, following their father's murder barely months later. As journalist Zahid Hussain recounts,

At the end of the meeting… he picked up bin Laden's glass of water and drank from it. An amused bin Laden asked him the reason for his action, to which Abdul Rashid replied, "I drank from your glass so that Allah would make me a warrior like you".[16]

Tensions between Lal Masjid and the Pakistani government began after the decision by General Musharraf, Pakistan's army chief and president, to provide backing to the US invasion of Afghanistan, which the two brothers vocally denounced. In 2004, the delicate relationship between the two sides broke down when Abdul Rashid Ghazi issued a fatwa against the Pakistani army's operations in Waziristan, the hotbed of militancy in the tribal areas where Al Qaeda and Taliban fighters had fled after the invasion, declaring that "those killed in the battle against Pakistani forces are martyrs".[17] Seventy percent of the students at Lal Masjid and its affiliated seminaries, many of them hardened militants, were from the Federally Administered Tribal Areas (FATA) and North-West Frontier Province, the Pashtun-dominated territory that sits between Islamabad and the tribal regions.[18] Ghazi maintained close contact with the leaders of the insurgency. Soon afterwards, he was charged with a plot to blow up the president's house, the parliament building, and the army headquarters, before being bailed out by the federal minister for religious affairs, Ejaz ul Haq, a patron of the mosque and the son of the former army chief and Pakistani president, General Zia.[19] The deal that got Ghazi off the hook, in which he promised not to engage in anti-state activities, didn't hold for long.[20] By 2007, the mosque had become a near-insurrectionary enclave—a heavily armed, pro-Taliban HQ with its own sharia courts and "vice and virtue" groups that attacked music and DVD shops around the capital.[21] Yet it was to prove an even greater threat to the authority of the Pakistani state after the convulsive end of the Ghazis' reign.

The man on the spot as the kidnapping drama in Islamabad escalated was Luo Zhaohui, a young, self-confident ambassador on the rise, and a rarity in the Chinese foreign ministry both for his South Asia expertise and his towering height. He had taken up the post only recently, alongside his wife Jiang Yili, a fellow diplomat and scholar who had translated Benazir Bhutto's memoir into Chinese.[22] By the cautious standards of Chinese officials, he would play an unusually active role in the events that followed. Instead of leaving the task to the Pakistani government alone, Luo sought to use the influence of leading political figures that he knew had a direct channel to Abdul Rashid Ghazi. After speaking with Pakistan's Prime Minister, Shaukat Aziz, he met with Maulana Fazlur Rahman, the Opposition Leader, and former Prime Minister Shujaat

Hussain, the head of Musharraf's PML (Q) party, to seek their support for securing the freedom of the hostages. Rahman had long been the go-to guy for any dealings with this particular fringe of Pakistani political life but it was the PML chief—himself supposedly a user of the "clinic"—who was acting as chief government negotiator with the mosque's leadership, and fixed up the telephone call between Ghazi and the ambassador from his home.[23]

Abdul Rashid Ghazi was seen as a savvy operator, adept in dealing with the media and telling different political audiences what they wanted to hear. His handling of the Chinese was no different. He "assured [Luo] that they would be released soon" and allowed the ambassador to speak to the hostages.[24] Despite these promises, there were to be five hours of negotiation with senior police and administration officials, which Musharraf, who was then in Lahore, and Aziz monitored "minute by minute".[25] Deputy Commissioner Chaudhry Muhammad Ali and Senior Superintendent of Police Zafar Iqbal were reported to have "begged" for the release of the hostages, and given assurances about stopping mixed-sex massage parlours in future, before Ghazi finally relented.[26] "We released them in view of Pakistan-China friendship" he announced to a crowded press conference. "After receiving a number of complaints regarding 'sex business', our students and people of the area took an action that should have been taken by the government".[27] "We greatly respect Pakistan-China friendship but it doesn't mean that foreign women can come here and indulge in such vulgar activities. Even housewives used to tell us by phone that the centre charges Rs 1,000 for massage while by paying Rs 500, something else was also available", he said.[28] The Chinese women were released in burqas.[29]

The "near diplomatic disaster" with China still had further to run.[30] The kidnapping took place on the eve of high-level talks in Beijing with the Pakistani interior minister, as part of the preparation for the 2008 Olympics. Those talks would now be a great deal more uncomfortable. After giving his counterpart "an earful" in private,[31] Zhou Yongkang, China's public security minister, publicly declared on June 27 that "we hope Pakistan will look into the terrorist attacks aiming at Chinese people and organisations as soon as possible and severely punish the criminals".[32] A bracing phone call from Hu Jintao to President Musharraf followed similar lines, and was reinforced by senior PLA officials.[33] Word leaked out that in the course of its bilateral talks, China was attributing the instigation of the kidnappings to the influence of militants from China's Uighur minority at Lal Masjid.[34] Islamabad was not just being accused of being negligent in guaranteeing the security of Chinese citizens on Pakistan's soil but of tolerating terrorist threats to China itself.

Accounts of the crucial decision-making process in the Pakistani government vary. According to some, it was Chinese pressure itself that ultimately brought the siege about. Others suggest that in the debates over how to respond, China's concerns were used as a pretext by Musharraf and those around him who had long wanted to move against Lal Masjid anyway but had faced resistance to their previous demands for raids on the mosque.[35] Either way, in Musharraf's November speech justifying the action, China was at the forefront: "The Chinese, who are such great friends of ours—they took the Chinese hostage and tortured them. Because of this, I was personally embarrassed. I had to go apologize to the Chinese leaders, 'I am ashamed that you are such great friends and this happened to you'".[36]

On July 3, Pakistani security forces surrounded the Lal Masjid complex and the siege began. Seven days later, following several deadlines, hundreds of surrenders, and Abdul Aziz's attempt to flee the mosque disguised as a woman, they launched their final, decisive assault. At 4am on July 10, commandos from the Pakistani Army's Special Services Group stormed the compound. Islamabad shook to the sound of explosions as the battle began, the first time the Pakistani capital had ever experienced fighting on such a scale. The mosque and women's religious school in the centre of the city was by now a fortified enclave, protected by heavily-armed militants, and it took over twenty hours for the Pakistani forces to battle their way through the basements, bunkers and tunnels.[37] By the time the commando raid, Operation Silence, was over at least 103 people were dead. Some accounts place the numbers closer to several hundred.[38] Among the dead were many of the baton-wielding, burqa-clad female shock troops who had been dispensing vigilante justice around Islamabad. Of the 15 non-Afghan foreigners killed, 12 were Uighurs.[39] And among the Pakistanis was Abdul Rashid Ghazi himself, who died during the crossfire in the last standoff in the Jamia Hafsa madrassa's basement, shortly after giving his last telephone interview to Pakistan's Geo TV.

China did not have to wait long for the repercussions. Even as the siege was underway, an act of apparent retaliation saw three Chinese engineers at an auto-rickshaw factory in Peshawar murdered by gunmen shouting religious slogans.[40] Beijing was just getting used to being targeted by Baloch militants for its involvement in the Gwadar port development, but this was something altogether new. Belatedly, they moved to issue a public denial of any involvement, stating that "China did not push Pakistan for operations against the Red Mosque… It is the consistent policy of China not to meddle in the domestic affairs of other countries".[41] Few were convinced. More than a year later, following another kidnapping of Chinese workers, a Taliban spokesman was still citing "Chinese pressure to launch Operation Silence" at Lal Masjid as part of the rationale for seizing the engineers.[42] Luo Zhaohui himself would end up on a Taliban hit list. "The militants were offended", said one senior Peshawari journalist, "the feeling among them was that it would not have happened if the Chinese had not demanded action".[43] Pakistan was on its way to becoming the single most dangerous overseas location for Chinese workers.

Yet it was the consequences for Pakistan itself that were even more troubling for Beijing. The siege was a watershed moment for the country, the point after which the Pakistani government's delicate dance with the new wave of militants turned into open warfare. The assault on the mosque was used as a rallying cry by extremists, proof that the Pakistani military had betrayed them. A wave of violence and bombings convulsed Pakistan's major cities. Before July 2007 there had been only 42 suicide attacks in Pakistan. There were more than 47 in the remaining months of 2007 alone,[44] and in the year after the siege, 1,188 people were killed and 3,209 wounded.[45] Osama Bin Laden issued his first statement urging attacks on the Pakistani government.[46] Insurgents that had been reluctant to turn their focus away from Afghanistan were now snapping away at the hand that once fed them. The array of militant groups in the Federally Administered Tribal Areas (FATA) annulled their peace agreement with the Pakistani government and consolidated themselves into a new organisation—the Tehrik-i-Taliban-Pakistan. In less than two years, they would control territory within 60 miles of Islamabad.[47] One of the Pakistani army's crack corps had to be deployed to protect the Karakoram Highway, the principal land artery between China and Pakistan, which was believed to be under threat.[48] The economy, the stock exchange, and inward investment all plummeted and have never fully recovered. Neither did Musharraf. Within months, he would be swept away to be replaced by a new government led by Benazir Bhutto's widower, Asif Ali Zardari, a man Beijing found far less congenial to deal with. China's relationship with Pakistan has never been quite the same again.

INTRODUCTION

"Pakistan is China's Israel."

General Xiong Guangkai[1]

For decades, Beijing's secretive ties with Islamabad have run closer than most formal alliances. Founded on a shared enmity with India, China's backing to Pakistan has gone so deep that it was willing to offer the ultimate gift from one state to another: the materials that Pakistan's nuclear scientists needed to build the bomb. Pakistan acted as China's backdoor during its years of diplomatic isolation, the bridge between Nixon and Mao, and the front-line in Beijing's struggles with the Soviet Union during the late stages of the Cold War. Now, Pakistan is a central part of China's transition from a regional power to a global one. The country lies at the heart of Beijing's plans for a network of ports, pipelines, roads and railways connecting the oil and gas fields of the Middle East to the mega-cities of East Asia. Its coastline is becoming a crucial staging post for China's take-off as a naval power, extending its reach from the Indian Ocean to the Persian Gulf and the Mediterranean Sea. Penetration by Pakistan's intelligence services into the darkest corners of global jihadi networks are a vital asset to China as it navigates its growing interests in the Islamic world, and seeks to choke off support for the militant activities that pose one of the gravest threats to China's internal stability.

For Pakistan, China is the best potential ticket out of instability and economic weakness, the greatest hope that a region contemplating a

1

security vacuum after the West's withdrawal from Afghanistan can instead become an integral part of a new Silk Road. China has been Pakistan's diplomatic protector, its chief arms supplier, and its call of last resort when every other supposed friend has left it in the lurch. Virtually every important moment in Pakistan's recent history has been punctuated with visits by its presidents, prime ministers and army chiefs to Beijing, where the deals and deliberations have so often proved to have a decisive impact on the country's fate. Yet all of this now hangs in the balance. Pakistan is becoming the battleground for China's encounters with Islamic militancy, the country more than any other where China's rise has turned it into a target. As extremists at war with the Pakistani government train their sights on its increasingly powerful sponsor, this is the place where so many of Beijing's plans for the wider region, for its relationship with the Islamic world, for its counter-terrorism strategy, and for the stability of its western periphery could completely unravel.

Sino-Pakistani ties have proved remarkably resilient since their early, tentative days. Across the last few decades they have survived China's transition from Maoism to market economy, the rise of Islamic militancy in the region, and the shifting cross-currents of the two countries' relationships with India and the United States. Even developments that might have pulled the two sides apart have often ended up forcing them closer together. India's economic resurgence and the warming of New Delhi's ties with Washington could have tempted Beijing to contemplate a policy of equidistance in South Asia. Instead China has moved to bolster Pakistan further against the rise of a more potent rival. Concerns over growing unrest in the Muslim-majority province of Xinjiang, in China's far west, might have resulted in deepening tensions over Islamabad's dealings with extremist groups. It has instead led China to depend all the more heavily on Pakistani security forces. And while Chinese concerns about Pakistan's stability have undoubtedly stalled some commercial ventures, they have ultimately resulted in China doubling down on its economic support in order to help keep Pakistan's head above water.

At times, the continued vitality of a relationship that could have ended up as a quaint legacy of the 1960s is a puzzle to outside observers. It can seem thin, lacking the sense of cultural affinity or common values that so often help to underpin friendships and alliances. Pakistan looks to the

West and to the Islamic world as its reference points, not to the Middle Kingdom. Even the language—"all-weather friends", "deeper than the deepest ocean", "sweeter than honey"—can sound like protesting too much. And when the question posed is "What does Pakistan actually do for China?" the answers that come back are often a little lacklustre. Yet traditionally, the strength of the relationship has hinged on the fact that Beijing has rarely needed Pakistan to do anything vastly different from what it intends to do anyway. Just as advocates of deeper ties between Washington and New Delhi have argued that "American strategic generosity towards India [is] an investment in its own geopolitical well being,"[2] to be pursued regardless of any Indian quid-pro-quo, China's policy sees a strong, capable Pakistan as an asset to China in its own right. Of course China would like to see Islamabad exercising greater caution and predictability in its dealings with India. It wants Pakistan to do a more convincing job of combating Uighur militancy. It would prefer Pakistan to run a better-functioning economy. But none of these concerns obviate the essential fact that an India that is forced to look nervously over its shoulder at its western neighbour is easier for Beijing to manage.

The early chapters of this book look at these India-centric foundations for the China-Pakistan relationship. The first chapter deals with three crucial wars. The Sino-Indian war of 1962 made the value of strategic cooperation fully apparent to the Chinese and the Pakistanis and brought a rapid resolution to their own outstanding border dispute. The Indo-Pakistani war of 1965, in which there was a real prospect of Chinese intervention on Pakistan's behalf, formed the basis of China's status as the "all-weather friend" in the Pakistani public imagination. The 1971 Indo-Pakistani war—in which Beijing failed to come to Islamabad's aid—ostensibly showed the limits of the relationship. Yet in many ways it set in motion security cooperation of an even more significant nature. China and Pakistan have never been treaty allies and their armies come from such radically different traditions that the two sides have often talked past each other on matters of strategy. But after Pakistan's devastating defeat, China helped the country to develop a set of military capabilities to ensure that it would never face the same fate again. Central to this was China's backing for Pakistan's nuclear ambitions, the subject of the book's second chapter. Close collaboration on an area of such high sensitivity has built a level of trust between the two militaries that a more conventional security partnership might never have delivered. And although it ensured, as the third chapter shows, that during subsequent crises on the subcontinent China was far more likely to try to defuse the risk of war than to swing in behind the Pakistanis in a confrontation with New Delhi, the fundamental nature of China's support has been unwavering. Even as the Sino-Indian relationship has improved, India's rise as a potential competitor to Beijing has further reinforced the original rationale for its partnership with Pakistan.

While the relationship between China and Pakistan could once be seen almost exclusively through a South Asian security framework—as a subset of the China-India and India-Pakistan rivalries—there are now a host of factors that transcend it. India still provides the strategic glue that binds the two sides together, but the dilemmas Beijing is wrestling with in Pakistan and Afghanistan are at the crux of a far larger set of issues.

The fourth chapter looks at Xinjiang—the restive, Muslim-majority region in China's north-west—and the role that China's struggles with terrorism have played in the Sino-Pakistani relationship. While Pakistan was once the main religious and economic outlet for the Uighurs, Xinjiang's indigenous Muslim inhabitants, it has now become their principal connection to the world of extremism. The linkages between security threats in China and the rise of extremist forces in south-west and central Asia have become the greatest sore point in Sino-Pakistani ties, and even raised anxieties in Beijing about whether Pakistan's "Islamization" puts the underlying basis of the relationship in doubt. Militancy in Pakistan has also threatened to derail the two sides' plans to add a serious economic dimension to a partnership that has been almost entirely about security. Chinese investments and Chinese workers in Pakistan have become targets for militants trying to stoke tension between Islamabad and Beijing, turning the country into the most dangerous place to be an overseas Chinese worker. Yet as the fifth chapter argues, when there has been a serious enough strategic imperative for China, the two sides' grand economic projects have been able to overcome seemingly insuperable obstacles. From the Karakoram Highway to Gwadar port, political and military factors have continued to provide momentum even when the commercial rationale is absent.

The sixth chapter focuses on Afghanistan, where China has struggled to decide whether militancy or the presence of a geostrategic rival poses the greater threat. The period since 9/11 has seen China sit on the sidelines of a war that it wanted neither the Taliban nor the United States to win. Yet as the US withdrawal has loomed ever closer and the terrorist threat from Xinjiang has grown, the balance in the Chinese debate has tipped in favor of the view that stabilizing China's western periphery is the more pressing task—even if it involves cooperating with Washington. Pakistan is the country where China's concerns about the spillover of instability in Afghanistan are greatest, and it is to Pakistan that China looks for a long-term political solution there. The final chapter traces China's evolution from free-rider to potential regional stabilizer, and the Obama's administration's often-frustrating efforts to find common cause with Beijing. Where China's assertiveness in East Asia has resulted in intensifying strategic rivalry with the United States and the discomfort of its neighbours, this is a region where Chinese assertiveness—including leaning on its Pakistani friends—is exactly what Washington has been seeking.

For Xi Jinping's new government in Beijing, sitting on the sidelines no longer looks like the most prudent approach. As the epilogue sets out, China hopes to use its financial and economic weight to change the balance of incentives in its western neighbourhood, launching a set of vastly ambitious trade and infrastructure initiatives that could be transformative in their impact. Pakistan is set to be the greatest beneficiary. With the West's strategic footprint diminishing as the war in Afghanistan winds down, China is stepping in with tens of billions of dollars of investments in projects that were once thought to be little more than pipe-dreams. While this is partly driven by a sense of strategic and economic opportunity on Beijing's part, it is also motivated by fear. Pakistan's troubles, and the threat of looming chaos in the region, have reinforced to China how much its interests will be harmed if its only reliable friend is left fragile and faltering.

In-depth studies on the China-Pakistan relationship are few and far between, with virtually no full-length treatments appearing since the early 1970s. This is partly because the subject is something of an intellectual orphan, falling between a variety of regions and disciplines, and partly because the obstacles facing analysts in their efforts to find reliable sources and establish basic facts make it that much more tempting to neglect. The Sino-Pakistani relationship encompasses some of the most sensitive areas of the two sides' national security policies. Officials in China and Pakistan are naturally circumspect when discussing it. And this is not just true for foreign researchers—even the limited number of Chinese and Pakistani analysts who study the relationship are liable to run into roadblocks. One Chinese academic complained that virtually every time he requested a declassified document from the foreign ministry archives they treated his interest as reason enough to classify it again.

As a result, much of the contemporary analysis of the China-Pakistan relationship is mediated through a series of distorting prisms. In India, the circulation of leaks and rumours about nefarious Sino-Pakistani activities is virtually a cottage industry. In Pakistan, political leaders have often been eager to dress up tentative plans between the two sides as firm agreements, and to portray Chinese backing for their position as far stronger than exists in reality. In China, articles on topics such as the nuclear relationship are designed to mislead, not to enlighten. At times it seems that almost any questionable claim can quickly gain traction, be recycled, and take on the status of accepted truth. China's supposed plans for military bases in FATA,[3] Pakistan's supposed intentions to lease China a tenth of its territory,[4] and the purported presence of 11,000 Chinese troops in Pakistan's north[5] are only a few of the most recent on a long list.

The mysteries and distorted claims about Sino-Pakistani ties have sometimes made it difficult for outside observers to reach accurate assessments. It would be one thing if every wild story turned out to be a myth, but some of the most outlandish-seeming claims have proved to be entirely accurate. As one nuclear expert writes: "China's deal with Pakistan was so dramatic that there was little consensus among U.S. government officials over what ultimate agenda it served".[6] Anyone tempted to downplay all the rumours that emanate from this unusual relationship risks missing developments of transformative importance.

This book is the culmination of six years of traveling between the different countries that are its main focus—China, Pakistan, Afghanistan, India, and the United States—confirming and disconfirming claims, testing out hypotheses, and assessing the reliability of various sources against real-world events. While it doesn't seek to provide a comprehensive history or anatomy of the relationship, I hope it will help to provide a starting point for thinking through the most important issues at stake. Over the period of research, the relationship has also started to open up. The reflexive protectiveness that had long characterised discussion of the subject, particularly in China, is beginning to ease. A few years back, many of the officials I met with were suspicious of why a foreigner was so interested in talking to them about the relationship. By the time I was finishing my research, almost everything was on the table, from debates in Beijing about whether to launch nuclear strikes on India if Islamabad came under threat, to China's complaints about the Pakistani intelligence services' ties with Uighur militants. Yet in the study of both Chinese and Pakistani foreign policy, it remains an unusual case. The pathologies of China and Pakistan's most difficult relationships have been exhaustively explored, and do much to shape our understanding of the two countries—but a very different perspective is opened up when we look at how they deal with their friends.

1

A FRIENDSHIP FORGED BY WAR

"We have been let down by the Americans" Ayub said, "but they are frightened of Chinese involvement". "And that, Mr President, is now the only card in your hands", said the Information Secretary. Ayub sat up and, putting the book down on the table, said: "Then let us use that card".

September 1965[1]

Nixon: Could you tell the Chinese it would be very helpful if they could move some forces or threaten to move some forces?

Kissinger: Absolutely.

Nixon: They've got to threaten or they've got to move, one of the two.

…Nixon: This should have been done long ago. The Chinese have not warned the Indians.

Kissinger: Oh, yeah.

Nixon: All they've got to do is move something. Move a division. You know, move some trucks. Fly some planes. You know, some symbolic act. We're not doing a god-damn thing, Henry, you know that.

December 1971[2]

1971

In Zulfiqar Ali Bhutto's suite at the Pierre Hotel on Fifth Avenue, the mood was bleak. "One could see at a glance that it was all up for

9

Pakistan this time," noted one of the Pakistani officials in attendance.[3] Bhutto, recently reappointed as foreign minister and deputy prime minister, had arrived in New York ready for the diplomatic fight of his nation's life. He knew that the situation in East Pakistan was grim. The Pakistani army had been decimated, would soon run out of fuel in the west, and Indian troops were advancing on Dhaka from all sides. There were fears that India could push on to enforce its territorial claims in Kashmir, leaving only a rump state behind.[4] International sympathy for Islamabad's position was limited. Hundreds of thousands of Bengalis had been killed in the Pakistani military's futile campaign to prevent Bangladesh from gaining its independence, drawing global outrage. And time was running out. On 9 December 1971, the UN Secretary General received a telegram from Dhaka conveying a message from General Farman Ali, who led the Pakistani forces in East Pakistan: the command was ready to give up and wanted the UN to arrange the withdrawal.[5] Bhutto, who was barely off the plane, scrambled to get hold of Pakistan's president, Yahya Khan, to find out whether this was the government's position or just freelancing by the general.[6] It was clear that his room for manoeuvre was rapidly disappearing.

Bhutto at least hoped to receive support from two powerful backers: the United States and China. Pakistan was still basking in the glow of appreciation for facilitating the rapprochement between Washington and Beijing. Islamabad's role was notable not only for its success in ensuring the secrecy of communications between the two sides, when any leak could have derailed the whole venture, but its willingness to devote serious attention to the delicate process at the highest levels of government during a time of national crisis. The legendary secret operation that brought Henry Kissinger to China on a PIA jet plane, while the world believed him to be recuperating from a stomach ache at a Pakistani hill station, had been orchestrated that July. Nixon's own breakthrough visit to China was supposed to take place in a few months' time. Neither man wanted their treatment of Pakistan to damage Chinese perceptions of US reliability. As Kissinger put it: "We cannot turn on Pakistan and I think it would have disastrous consequences with China that after they gave us an airport we massacre them."[7] Even more importantly, with India supporting the Bengali rebels, and the Soviet Union backing India, Beijing and Washington needed to ensure that Pakistan was not fatally weakened by such a constellation of forces.

What they were actually willing to do about it was another matter. Despite President Nixon's avowed policy of "tilting" towards Pakistan, there was fierce resistance within the US government to putting any such measures into practice to support a country that many believed was responsible for a near-genocidal level of slaughter.[8] Pakistan's attempt to invoke the 1959 bilateral security agreement between the two countries received short shrift. Bhutto had breakfast with Kissinger at the Waldorf Astoria on 11 December. "Chinese wallpaper and discreet waiters made one nearly forget that eight thousand miles away, the future of my guest's country hung by a thread," he recalled in his memoirs.[9] Kissinger advised Bhutto that "Pakistan would not be saved by mock-tough rhetoric," a speciality of his breakfast companion. "It is not that we do not want to help you; it is that we want to preserve you. It is all very well to proclaim principles but finally we have to assure your survival." He urged him to work out a common position with the Chinese. Bhutto replied that the Chinese "were confused by the evident schism" in the US government: "What should they believe?"[10]

For the United States, the possibility of Beijing intervening militarily was real. Nixon and Kissinger had been talking up the prospect for months as a means of deterring New Delhi's involvement, Nixon closing his angry meeting in November with the Indian Prime Minister, Indira Gandhi, by issuing the warning that "it would be impossible to calculate with precision the steps which other great powers might take if India were to initiate hostilities".[11] Kissinger directed the White House and State Department staffs to "leave India to its fate" if China provoked border incidents.[12] But the Chinese were keeping their counsel. Since 23 November, China's ambassador to the UN, Huang Hua, had been conducting secret meetings with Kissinger in CIA safe-houses in New York, the principal channel of communications between the two countries at the time. At the initial meeting, Kissinger and Alexander Haig, his military aide, gave a military briefing that suggested, with a wink, that India had left its northern border with China exposed. As the situation for Pakistan worsened, that wink became a set of explicit messages. Nixon told Kissinger that he "strongly" wanted to encourage Chinese action: "But damnit, I am convinced that if the Chinese start moving the Indians will be petrified".[13] On 8 December, he gave his assent for Kissinger to convey a note to Zhou Enlai stating: "If you are ever going to move, this is the time."[14] Two days later, another meeting took place in the New York safe-house. Kissinger told the Chinese officials that the United States would be moving ships into the vicinity and allowing Jordan, Iran, Saudi Arabia and Turkey to send American arms to the Pakistanis. But the purpose of the session was laid out starkly: "When I asked for this meeting, I did so to suggest Chinese military help to Pakistan, to be quite honest."[15]

When Ambassador Huang sent word on 12 December that he needed to see Kissinger again urgently, which was the first time the Chinese had solicited a meeting, it seemed a fateful moment: "We assumed that only a matter of gravity could induce them into such a departure. We guessed that they were coming to the military assistance of Pakistan."[16] "They're going to move," he told Nixon, "No question, they're going to move".[17] The two men discussed the possibility of a Soviet response to any Chinese action, and Nixon took the dramatic decision that in those circumstances the United States would provide China with military backing. He had already ordered an aircraft carrier task-force to head as far as the Straits of Malacca. Now it was sent into the Bay of Bengal "to give effect to our strategy and to reinforce the message to Moscow",[18] which duly responded by sending a nuclear-armed submarine to tail the task-force. Nixon's move was a signal to China too, one that brought with it the risk of an all-out superpower war. Nixon made his first use of the Hot Line to Moscow in a message that concluded: "I cannot emphasize too strongly that time is of the essence to avoid consequences neither of us want."[19] Kissinger helpfully noted that if the Soviet Union decided to "wipe out China" then the president's upcoming visit there would be pointless.[20]

The Pakistanis were also, at least ostensibly, trying to discern Beijing's intentions. Following the bleak news about the situation in Dhaka, the Chinese deputy foreign minister had called on Bhutto at Pakistan's mission to the UN, where he "urged very strongly" that Pakistani forces hold out for another week, claiming that "there could be great benefits".[21] Iqbal Akhund, a senior Pakistani diplomat, relates:

In a delegation meeting in the minister's hotel room next morning, the question on everyone's mind was "Will the Chinese? Won't the Chinese?" Bhutto's chaperon, the Colonel, said that a massive Chinese intervention was needed without a moment's notice. Bhutto asked opinions about what, if anything, China was likely to do. He must have known the answer quite well and was probably testing the diplomatic acumen of the delegates. Each delegate answered the question in his lights and hopes.[22]

In fact, he knew the answer perfectly well. Bhutto had been sent to Beijing in November to request Chinese support. There were plenty of signs that something was amiss. China allowed a rare public demonstration during the visit, and he was taken to see the underground shelters the Chinese had built for protection from Soviet attack, as if to signal its own security fears.[23] The trip itself was only taking place following China's decision to decline Yahya Khan's request for a "morale-boosting" visit from a senior Chinese leader to Pakistan.[24] Bhutto's mission was the second of its sort that year—a delegation headed by Foreign Secretary Sultan Khan and Lt-Gen. Gul Hassan Khan had visited in April. Both drew blanks. "China never, during these or subsequent talks, held out any possibility of coming to Pakistan's aid with her armed forces," Sultan Khan later noted.[25] In the November talks "there was never any question of active Chinese military involvement and such an eventuality was not even discussed."[26] This was not the message that Bhutto conveyed to the Pakistani public. On returning to Pakistan, he claimed that his visit had been "a complete success" and that the results were "tangible" and "concrete".[27] After meeting Bhutto, Yahya Khan announced that in the event of an Indian attack the Chinese would intervene and help Pakistan as much as they could.[28] Yahya Khan had made similar statements even before the Bhutto trip.[29] It was bluff. And the Indians were not falling for it.

India had been aware of the Chinese position throughout. In January, Indian intelligence had assessed that Beijing was unlikely to fight for Pakistan but would "adopt a threatening posture on the Sino-Indian border and even stage some border incidents and clashes".[30] But by June, they had obtained a detailed read-out of the Pakistanis' April visit to Beijing.[31] More importantly, they concluded that China had not undertaken the necessary build-up of forces and supplies for a military intervention.[32] India demonstrated its confidence with the decision to move three of the six divisions assigned to the Chinese border in the eastern and western Himalayas to the East Pakistani front.[33] India's position was reinforced by the August agreement with the Soviet Union, the Indo-Soviet Friendship Treaty, which implied the strong threat of a response from Moscow to any Chinese military action. Privately, the Soviets had pledged that they would open diversionary action if China tried to involve itself.[34] The possibility of China's intervention still informed the timing of the war—prosecuting it in winter would make it harder for

Chinese troops to cross the snow-covered passes on the border.[35] But by the time India was drawing up its contingency plans, it had already concluded that Beijing would be unwilling and unready to act. Although it is omitted from Kissinger's own dramatic recounting of the events, US intelligence assessments had reached the same conclusion.[36]

In New York, Bhutto responded angrily to General Farman Ali's surrender message. In a telegram to Yahya Khan, he insisted that "we must fight to the bitter end…otherwise we will suffer final disgrace, be rendered friendless and ultimately finished. The Chinese must intervene physically and immediately."[37] The next day, Yahya Khan would ask China to do exactly this, telling the Chinese ambassador that "he would rather the Chinese than the Russians took over East Pakistan".[38] On 12 December, the answer came back from Beijing, reinforcing what both Yahya Khan and Bhutto must already have known: China would "continue to support Pakistan morally, economically, and politically, but its capability to intervene was limited and 'please do not pin much hope on it'."[39] This did not stop General Headquarters in Rawalpindi from sending one last, desperate message to officers in the East on 13 December, telling them to hold out because support was on its way: "Yellow from the north and white from the south".[40] It was soon clear to the temporarily heartened troops that neither the Chinese nor the Americans were in fact riding to the rescue, though at one point they believed that a contingent of Indian commandos was the Chinese coming to save them.[41] Pakistan's final surrender would come four days later.

If there had been any thought to step in on China's part, the timing could not have been worse. The Chinese military was in state of turmoil. Mao had removed virtually the entire high command following Lin Biao's fatal flight in September: China's military chief and Mao's chosen successor had died in highly suspicious circumstances, his plane crashing over the Mongolian desert as he fled the country after what Mao claimed was a "coup attempt".[42] Over a thousand senior Chinese military officials were purged, the air force was grounded, the PLA itself was in disgrace, and Beijing was gripped by a sense of political crisis. In the meantime, China still had to sustain its military support to the North Vietnamese, and was seriously concerned about the risks of a major clash with the Soviet Union.[43] Following the Sino-Soviet border altercations in 1969—in which a series of low level conflicts over disputed territory threatened the prospect of full-scale war—the Soviets had moved 45 divisions to China's northern border.[44] Bhutto himself was a witness to a massive Chinese civil defence programme put in place to prepare for the possibility of nuclear strikes.[45] But it was not military disarray or fear of war with the Russians that was decisive. Nor was it simply the snowy passes—if they had wanted to, the Chinese could have made the necessary preparations at least to make threatening gestures on the Sikkim and Kashmir fronts, as they belatedly hinted they might do in December 1971.[46] Rather, it was a political judgement that would foreshadow many other crucial episodes in the relationship between the two countries over the decades to come: China would not pull Pakistan out of the holes it insisted on digging for itself.

It was clear to virtually every Pakistani visitor who passed through Beijing how uncomfortable China was with the crackdown in East Pakistan. Zhou Enlai, in his meetings with the Pakistani delegation in April, made several pointed "suggestions" about the handling of the situation; advice that came "after great deliberation and consultations with Chairman Mao".[47] "Participation by the army is only the first step, and the major problem of winning the hearts of the people through economic and political measures should be tackled quickly," he advised.[48] He would later state in public that China did not "provide arms [to a country] to be used against its own people".[49] The fact that pro-Chinese political factions were a target didn't help either. Of even greater concern was the fact that Beijing saw a Pakistani strategy that was heading for defeat on all fronts: voiding public support in East Pakistan, shredding international sympathy, and creating a pretext for Indian intervention.[50] Zhou stressed the need for "a speedy solution that would take into account the wishes of the majority of the people in East Pakistan", but he didn't see one coming.[51] Neither did China see a viable military solution once India was engaged. The Chinese military attaché, on a visit to the Pakistani army's General Headquarters in Rawalpindi, saw the map showing Pakistani and Indian positions in the first week, and remarked that the fighting on the western front was more or less over.[52] By the time Zhou Enlai delivered his strident speech against India after the fall of Dhaka, Indian diplomats were comfortable enough to dismiss it as "impotent rage".[53]

Chinese support to Pakistan did have its value. While at times Beijing moved slowly with some of Islamabad's emergency requests, it maintained its economic and military aid throughout the year.[54] This included a large shipment of arms to the Pakistani army in East Pakistan, the training and equipping of two additional divisions, and a further $100 million of assistance. It scrapped at the UN Security Council on Pakistan's behalf and, in the aftermath of the war, vetoed Bangladesh's application for UN membership until the withdrawal of Indian troops had been confirmed and Pakistani POWs had been returned, despite the reputational costs. China's public expressions of support were valued at a time when these were thin on the ground, and provided some cover for Pakistani leaders to pretend that private reassurances went further.[55] But it fell well short of what many in Pakistan had hoped for and, in some cases, even expected. As the end of the war grew ever nearer, a Chinese intervention looked more and more like Pakistan's only possible escape route from self-inflicted disaster. But ultimately Pakistan would lose half its population, a fifth of its territory, and see ninety-three thousand of its soldiers become prisoners of war without even a token skirmish on the Sino-Indian border.

China's role in the 1971 war captures much about the relationship: the oscillation between hope, self-deception, public exaggeration, and resigned realism on Pakistan's part, and on China's, a blend of tempered support, gentle scolding and steely pragmatism. The Washington-Beijing liaisons have since become a feature of almost every Pakistani crisis. It is not difficult to trace a line straight through to Sino-Pakistani-US relations around the Kargil crisis or the aftermath of the Bin Laden killing: Bhutto's disappointing visit to China in November 1971 would be mirrored by Nawaz Sharif in June 1999 and Yousuf Gilani in May 2011, episodes that will be dealt with in later chapters. Over the decades to come, China would become Pakistan's only reliable diplomatic, economic and military backer. But would it be there for Pakistan in its hour of need? The answer in 1971, and ever since, has been: only up to a point. As a *Dawn* editorial in February 1972 put it:

Had we…not presumed that we would get unlimited Chinese support, regardless of our objectives and conduct, the country might have been saved from humiliation and defeat. The People's Republic of China has been a great friend of Pakistan. Let us honour this friendship by being rational and realistic and by not imposing unnecessary burdens and strains on the friendship. Objective reality must be measured by its own size and not by the length of its shadow.[56]

A FRIENDSHIP FORGED BY WAR

1965

The seeds of the Pakistanis' misplaced hopes had been sown six years earlier. The Indo-Pakistani war in September 1965 did not involve a great deal more Chinese military activity than in 1971, and the war itself was a disaster for Pakistan, from the first failed attempts by Pakistani troops to precipitate an insurgency in Kashmir to the appearance of Indian artillery within range of Lahore International Airport. But the effect of China's stance during the conflict on public opinion in Pakistan was profound.

As one strong account of China's role puts it:

> Of all of Pakistan's supporters, China spoke the loudest. She gave Pakistan unqualified moral support and, at the same time, threatened India with 'grave consequences'...By linking the Sino-Indian and the Indo-Pakistan conflicts, the Chinese fostered a sense of urgency among the powers about terminating the Indo-Pakistan war...it inhibited some of the great powers from siding openly with India and from putting as much pressure upon Pakistan as they might otherwise have been inclined to do; [and] it contributed to bringing about ceasefire on terms acceptable to Pakistan.[57]

When Liu Shaoqi, the Chinese Prime Minister, arrived on a visit to Lahore in February 1966, he was carried in the arms of cheering crowds, prompting the US Consul General to lament that "Pakistan is lost".[58]

China's crushing victory in its own war with India in 1962 was itself one of the sources of Pakistan's overconfidence, leading Rawalpindi to underestimate the capabilities of the Indian armed forces when it launched its ill-conceived venture in Kashmir.[59] The prospect of Chinese involvement was also part of Bhutto's pro-war case to Ayub Khan: Indian troops in Assam would be forced "to fight on two fronts" if, as Bhutto also mistakenly believed, India moved against East Pakistan and China entered the war.[60] Aziz Ahmed, Ayub Khan's foreign policy adviser, also argued that "the most powerful factor in Pakistan's favour was its growing friendship with China which would stop India from invading Pakistan even if it was driven out of Kashmir."[61]

In practice, most of the great powers did not believe that Beijing was willing to embark on an all-out war with India again in 1965, but it gave serious signals that a military intervention might be in the offing. China had the requisite manpower positioned, and CIA analysts believed that its deployments were "adequate for small-scale frontier clashes", which "would cause the Indians great consternation and divert

Indian effort and supplies away from fighting with the Pakistanis".[62] China's Foreign Minister, Chen Yi, flew in to Karachi in the first days of the war and announced that Beijing backed Pakistan's "just action".[63] The Chinese government and media kept up a drumbeat of denunciations of India's "naked aggression", and steadily escalated its claims of Indian "intrusions" into its own territory.[64] This culminated in a threat that if the Indian government did not dismantle "all its military works for aggression on the Chinese side of the China-Sikkim boundary or on the boundary itself" within three days, it would be responsible for "all the grave consequences of its inaction".[65] The statement prompted the Indian diplomat in Beijing who had received the note to ask the perhaps superfluous question, "Is this an ultimatum?" (the answer: "Yes").[66] It was published in full in the *People's Daily*, the Chinese Communist Party's official newspaper, on 17 September. Although China had resisted Pakistan's requests to make military preparations earlier in 1965, not believing that war with India was likely, it finally stepped up its mobilization on the Sikkim-Tibet border and in Ladakh, the two locations that Mao had decided should be readied for possible intervention.[67] Liu Shaoqi sent a letter to Ayub Khan assuring Pakistan that it would respond to an Indian attack. China also reached a set of agreements with Indonesia and Pakistan about the joint supply of military equipment, much of which was to be airlifted from Hotan. Detailed planning meetings were undertaken with the Pakistani army and air force over their needs for tanks, recoilless guns, shells, and aircraft.[68]

But cooperation on logistics was more straightforward than on strategy. On 19 September, during the crucial period after the Chinese ultimatum, Ayub Khan embarked on a secret mission to Beijing with Bhutto (which nearly proved fatal—an Indian air attack struck the airfield just as they were about to take off).[69] Ayub Khan was seeking support, equipment, and clarity on what a Chinese response would actually amount to. He was thrown by the answer he received. China would maintain pressure on India "for as long as necessary", he was told, but he was encouraged by Zhou Enlai and Chen Yi to mount guerrilla attacks on India "even if one or two major cities were lost". "You must keep fighting," they insisted, "even if you have to withdraw to the hills." A stunned Ayub Khan replied, "Mr. Prime Minister, I think you are being rash." He returned from Beijing "tired and depressed" and "decided to put the China card back in the deck".[70] The Pakistani leadership had no intention of prolonging the conflict in those circumstances and soon signed a ceasefire agreement. As one Pakistani diplomat described it: "Pakistan fought in the British tradition—short-duration wars that come to a head, then a ceasefire. The Chinese experience of warfare was very different—extended conflict over the length and breadth of the country. Even if they had 'stood by us', there were two very different conceptions of what that meant."[71] Mao had decided that China would intervene under two conditions—that India attacked East Pakistan, and that Pakistan requested Chinese intervention.[72] In the end, neither of them obtained.

Despite the disagreements, China's support left a significant impression on the Pakistani public, especially by comparison with the United States, which responded to the war by cutting off aid and military supplies. While Pakistan's president only gave measured thanks to China in his public statements, students in Karachi paraded with banners of Zhou and Chen and called on the Chinese ambassador to convey their appreciation.[73] A "huge crowd" burned down the US Information Library.[74] "Bitterness toward the U.S. is deep-seated", noted a State Department research memorandum.[75] The 1965 war had a catalytic effect on the Sino-Pakistani relationship. From that point on, with US military aid suspended, China became Pakistan's primary arms supplier, a position it has relinquished only for brief periods ever since. China also established itself as the populist cause, a true friend of Pakistan's by contrast to the untrustworthy Americans—whatever the actual level of material support either side was providing. It was also the year that Pakistani officials claim to have started negotiations with China for the technology and materials necessary to build a nuclear bomb, barely a year after China's own first test.[76] Although Pakistan's efforts to improve relations with Moscow and Washington in the aftermath of the war would lead to a temporary cooling in political ties with Beijing, the tone and pattern of cooperation between the two sides was now set.

1962

The path to the "all-weather friendship" had been a tortuous one. Although Pakistan has the distinction of being one of the first states to recognize the People's Republic of China—and the first Muslim one—it would be more than a decade before the relationship began in earnest.

When the first Pakistani ambassador, Major General Nawabzada Agha Mohammad Raza, presented his credentials to Mao in 1951, he was coolly received—"I have great pleasure in receiving the letter of credentials of the King of Great Britain, Ireland and the British Dominions beyond the seas, presented by you."[77] "There was no mention of the fact that the Ambassador was representing Pakistan," a successor of his Indian counterpart noted gleefully in a speech to the US Congress.[78] At the time, there was little doubt that Beijing tilted in India's direction. Pakistan was a country run by feudal landlords, industrialists and the military. It would formally ally itself with the United States by joining the region's two Western treaty organizations, SEATO in 1954 and CENTO in 1955, and signing a bilateral cooperation agreement with Washington in 1959, resulting in substantial American aid and military supplies. SEATO in particular was conceived with the clear intent of containing China, and Pakistan quickly agreed to the establishment of an NSA listening post at Badaber, near Peshawar, to spy on Chinese and Soviet communications.[79]

Beijing's bedfellow in the early 1950s was India, its anti-colonial, non-aligned neighbour across the Himalayas that had inherited most of the socialists during Partition, among the other spoils, and would ultimately end up in close security cooperation with the Soviet Union. The Sino-Soviet split was one of several factors that eventually prised the relationship apart, but the 1950s—at least for a few years—represented the high point of "*Hindi-Chini bhai bhai*", the Hindi phrase used at the time meaning "Indians and Chinese are brothers". It was India, not Pakistan, that consistently supported Beijing's assumption of the Chinese seat at the United Nations in Taipei's place. While India played a key role in helping to squash Tibetan appeals at the UN after Chinese troops invaded in 1950,[80] Pakistan was providing transit facilities for US aircraft to supply the Tibetan rebels.[81] The "five principles of peaceful coexistence" mentioned in the preamble to the agreement reached by China and India in 1954 formed the basis of the Non-Aligned Movement's own principles in subsequent years, and would assume a central role in Chinese foreign policy over the decades to come.[82] China's dealings with India would, however, prove to be one of the cases to which the five principles—"Mutual respect for each other's territorial integrity and sovereignty", "Mutual non-aggression", "Mutual non-interference in each other's internal affairs", "Equality and mutual benefit" and "Peaceful co-existence"—least applied.

While the border dispute between India and China ultimately brought them to war in 1962, in the 1950s it was Pakistan that had territorial issues with China. Beijing laid claim to 3,400 square miles of Pakistani territory in Kashmir, encompassing tracts of the old principality of Hunza, whose rulers, the Mirs had traditionally recognized Chinese suzerainty.[83] When the British seized control of the kingdom in 1891, the Mir fled to China.[84] During Partition, the Kuomintang, China's ruling party at the time, conducted secret negotiations over restoring Hunza's status as an independent state under Chinese fealty, before the Mir finally decided to accede to Pakistan. Sporadic Chinese border violations around Hunza were being reported from 1953, and in 1959 Ayub Khan announced that "any Chinese intrusions into Pakistani territory would be repelled by Pakistan with all the force at her command."[85] In September 1959, the Pakistani government received a Chinese map showing a line of territorial claims running from the Mintaka pass down to Shimshal pass and eastward. In October, following Sino-Indian clashes, Ayub proposed a "joint defence union" with India, stating that "I can see quite clearly the inexorable push of the north in the direction of the warm waters of the Indian Ocean."[86] Both Pakistan and China had mostly been careful, however, not to antagonize each other. China refrained from denouncing Pakistan's membership of the Western treaty organizations, saving its verbal firepower for the United States, and when the countries' two prime ministers met on the sidelines of the Asian-African Bandung conference, Muhammad Ali Bogra assured Zhou Enlai that the military agreements did not reflect any Pakistani hostility towards China: India, he explained, was still the focus.[87] Even Ayub Khan's "joint defence union" proposal—which was summarily rejected by New Delhi—prompted little more than a raised eyebrow from Beijing, a letter faux-innocently asking against whom the joint defence was proposed.[88] 1959 instead proved to be one of the pivotal years in the unravelling of the Sino-Indian relationship.

In many ways, the road to the Sino-Pakistani all-weather friendship runs through Lhasa. The 1959 uprising there, the Chinese military's subsequent crackdown, and the Dalai Lama's fifteen-day journey on foot across the Himalayas to find asylum in India redounded significantly to Pakistan's benefit. Nehru's attempts to tread the line between accepting Chinese sovereignty and supporting Tibetan autonomy no longer cut any ice in Beijing, which was paranoid about India's supposed designs to establish Tibet as a "buffer".[89] China's perception that India had supported the uprising and cooperated with the CIA to arm the rebellion eventually led Mao to believe that "forceful blows" needed to be struck.[90] It was the intersection of the Tibet issue with the two sides' border dispute that resulted in outright war. Two years earlier, as part of its campaign to establish full control over Tibet, China had completed the 750-mile Aksai Chin section of the Western Military Road that linked Xinjiang with Lhasa. The road crossed a flat plateau and was serviceable in winter, whereas direct routes from the centre of China into Tibet suffered from hazardous terrain and climatic conditions, as well as insurgent attacks from Tibetan tribes.[91] India belatedly discovered the road in 1958 and claimed that 112 miles ran through Indian territory. Border talks accelerated in the aftermath, culminating in Zhou Enlai's proposal for a comprehensive settlement in April 1960: an east-west territorial swap, in which Chinese control over Aksai Chin and Indian control over the southern slope of the eastern Himalayas would be acknowledged. Nehru rejected the proposal.[92] His "forward policy", adopted in November 1961, instead saw a steady increase in altercations and tension, as the two sides' troops went nose-to-nose. Mao concluded that negotiations, restraint, or a period of "armed coexistence" would not stop India from its policy of using military force to challenge Chinese control of disputed territory. He authorized the PLA chief of staff to conduct a "fierce and painful" attack on the far weaker Indian forces.[93] In a multi-stage series of offensives in October and November 1962, China overran Indian positions and routed its defences in the east, before calling a unilateral ceasefire and withdrawing troops. It was a devastating defeat for India and for Nehru himself, who was physically and mentally broken by the experience. His daughter, Indira Gandhi, personally blamed Zhou Enlai for having hastened his death.[94]

The 1962 war hangs over most of the subsequent developments in the region. The ambivalent Soviet stance over the Sino-Indian border dispute—it professed a position of neutrality, and only deviated from that stance briefly because of its need to keep the Chinese on board during the Cuban Missile Crisis—was one of the last straws in the Sino-Soviet split.[95] Within a few years, Pakistan's good offices would help bring about the Sino-American rapprochement and a virtual alliance against Moscow for the remaining years of the Cold War. India's comprehensive defeat in 1962 shifted the consensus in the country towards the acquisition of nuclear weapons, and led to Pakistan's subsequent decision to follow suit—with China's help.[96] 1962 also helped to plant the idea of the "two front war" in the minds of policymakers in the three capitals. At one juncture, the Pakistani government suggested to the US Embassy in Karachi that Pakistan's neutrality "could be ensured" by Indian concessions in Kashmir, implying the possibility of a military intervention if they were not forthcoming.[97] "The nightmare of a combined attack by Pakistan and China, with the possibility of defeat, collapse, and even anarchy in India was much on my mind,"[98] noted J.K. Galbraith, then US ambassador in New Delhi, who worried about Pakistan "forming some kind of Axis with Peking".[99] It was on Ayub Khan's mind too, however briefly. Qudrat Ullah Shahab, a writer and senior Pakistani official, was approached by a Chinese student who suggested that he should persuade Ayub Khan to exploit the situation by moving the Pakistani army forward in Kashmir. Shahab, unsure if this might be some message from Beijing, woke the president at 3am to tell him. Ayub Khan told Shahab to "go home and go to bed".[100] Ayub had also been asked by the United States if Pakistan might make a "gesture of assurance" to Nehru, thereby enabling India to move troops towards the eastern front with China.[101] He would do no such thing, and as US military assistance to India grew, he became increasingly disquieted by Washington's "redefining the purpose of their regional pacts".[102] If the United States was going to arm non-allied India then the value of the alliance was inevitably frayed and the grounds for holding back from Beijing's offers of friendship looked tenuous. Indeed, the lack of coordination with China in the circumstances was an active problem for Pakistan—not only had the war brought about an increase in Western backing for the Indians, but with India facing crushing defeat, Beijing had pulled back rather than taking advantage of the situation to press for a border settlement that could have included Kashmir. Pakistan's president lamented, "I wish the Chinese had consulted us before they ordered the cease-fire and in future, too, I hope that before they take any precipitate steps they will consult us, as we may be able to give them sound advice."[103] Ayub Khan moved carefully but decisively. As his biographer notes: "The Americans and the British knew that by temperament, tradition and discipline, Ayub would not go too far with the Chinese, but he might go far enough to upset the balance of power in the region."[104]

The man who became the head of the "China camp" in Pakistan's internal debates was Zulfiqar Ali Bhutto. Then in his early days as

Pakistan's youngest cabinet minister, he saw the simmering Sino-Indian conflict as an opportunity. The dispute was a chance to strengthen Pakistan's own hand on Kashmir, and Bhutto urged Ayub Khan to take back his inopportune statement that the Sino-Indian territorial dispute was simply "India's problem" and instead send a signal to Beijing by "questioning the very basis" of India's stand.[105] He sent a signal of his own in 1960 when he used his discretionary powers as head of Pakistan's delegation to the UN to abstain on Beijing's membership of the body rather than voting against it.[106] Following US complaints, Bhutto's discretion was revoked by a foreign minister still keen to adhere closely to Washington, but the tide was turning in favour of those who favoured a new tilt in Pakistani foreign policy. China's path to war with India did indeed provide a significant opening for Pakistan, with the negotiations on the Sino-Pakistani border dispute dovetailing uncannily closely with the conflict. China had initially resisted Pakistan's offer of talks but then moved with tremendous speed, starting ten days before the outbreak of war and concluding shortly afterwards.[107] China's reply to the Pakistani offer, which stated its willingness to sign a provisional boundary agreement, came two days before its first demarche to India over its "forward policy" in February 1962.[108]

The agreement had been negotiated on the Pakistani side by Bhutto's predecessor as Foreign Minister, Manzur Qadir, under the close supervision of Ayub Khan, but it was Bhutto who arrived in Beijing in March 1963 to sign the agreement with his Chinese counterpart, Chen Yi, and win much of the acclaim.[109] The settlement announced was on terms clearly favourable to Pakistan. China would transfer 1,942 square kilometres that it controlled to Pakistan.[110] Although its nominal concessions were substantial, Pakistan transferred none of the territory under its control, and the final demarcation—which included six of seven contested passes—accorded closely with the line of actual control that it advocated. Pakistan was not the only beneficiary of Chinese efforts at the time—Afghanistan also saw a relatively generous agreement put in motion that same year—but the China-Pakistan accord was of genuine strategic importance.[111] It infuriated India, which still claimed much of the territory in question, several thousand square kilometres of which had now been assigned to China. Notionally it was still a provisional agreement that could be reopened in the event of a broader set of talks on Kashmir. In reality, it would entrench Chinese and Pakistani control over northern Kashmir, providing the basis for a mammoth set of infrastructure projects between the two sides which continue to this day.

The three wars that frame this chapter were the last ones in which Galbraith's "nightmare" of an attack on India from two fronts was realistically contemplated. The nuclearization of the subcontinent fundamentally changed China's handling of subsequent Indo-Pakistani confrontations, and Zulfiqar Ali Bhutto's successors were to receive an even cooler reception when they flew to Beijing during periods of conflict to solicit Chinese support. China's leaders no longer counselled their Pakistani counterparts to prepare to wage guerrilla warfare from the hills. Instead, after 1971 the most serious military cooperation took place away from the spotlight of war. In reality, China's greatest contribution to Pakistan's security has never really been the prospect of an intervention on its behalf. Beijing gave Pakistan something far more important than that: the ultimate means of self-defence.

2

NUCLEAR FUSION

[China does] not advocate nuclear proliferation at all, but we even more strongly oppose nuclear monopolies.

Deng Xiaoping, 1975[1]

As long as they need the bomb, they will lick your balls. As soon as you have delivered the bomb, they will kick your balls.

Li Jue, China's nuclear weapons chief, speaking to Abdul Qadeer Khan, head of Pakistan's nuclear enrichment programme, about the Pakistani army[2]

Non-existent is the issue of China's nuclear and missile proliferation to Pakistan.

Zhou Gang, Chinese ambassador to India[3]

In January 2004, a strange handover ceremony took place in Tripoli. In a meeting room at Libya's National Board for Scientific Research, the country's nuclear chief, Matuq Mohammed Matuq, presented two white plastic bags to Donald Mahley and David Landsman, the American and British heads of the disarmament effort in Libya. Emblazoned on the bags in red letters was the name of an Islamabad tailor, Good Looks Fabrics and Tailors. The contents were so sensitive that most of the senior members of the International Atomic Energy Agency (IAEA) did not even have the security clearance to look at them. The task of examining the documents was left to Jacques Baute, a French IAEA official, who confirmed their veracity and sent them on a plane straight to Washington, where they were taken from Dulles Airport by armed couriers to a high security vault at the Department of Energy. One of the bags contained drawings and blueprints. The other contained detailed technical instructions. Between them, they provided step-by-step instructions for assembling a nuclear bomb.[4]

It was not hard to work out where they had originated. While the primary text was in English, a number of the papers were in Chinese. There was also a collection of handwritten notes based on a set of lectures given by Chinese weapons experts in the early 1980s, whose names, and the dates the seminars spanned, were included in the documents.[5] The design in the documents was for a Chinese nuclear warhead, 453kg in mass, and less than a metre in diameter.[6] It was notably similar to a weapon known to have been tested by China in the 1960s, the CHIC-4. While too large for Libyan Scud missiles, it could have been easily airdropped or fitted on a more sophisticated system, such as the North Korean Nodong missile or Iran's Shahab-3 missile.[7] In principle, the simple device could also have been used by terrorist groups: one nuclear expert noted that "you could drive it away in a pickup truck".[8] The documents were missing a few of the crucial designs required for implosion, but all in all there was about 95 per cent of the information needed to make a bomb[9]—crude by the standards of modern weapons but smaller and more sophisticated than those dropped on Hiroshima and Nagasaki.[10]

The deal that Colonel Gaddafi cut with the United States and the United Kingdom—the dismantling of Libya's Weapons of Mass Destruction programme in return for its emergence from pariah status—was the beginning of the end for the A.Q. Khan proliferation network.[11] A.Q. Khan's nuclear black-marketeering had played a crucial role in bringing the bomb to Pakistan before those same nuclear secrets were sold to an assortment of rogue states. After years of denying US intelligence reports that had become increasingly incontrovertible, the haul of material in Libya finally forced the Pakistani government to act against the man who was then still a national hero, known as the "father" of the nuclear programme that had enabled Pakistan to go toe-to-toe with India.[12] The haul even included centrifuge components that were still in their "Khan Research Lab" cargo boxes.[13] Within days of the handover, Abdul Qadeer Khan was removed from his official position by Pakistan's National Command Authority, which controls the country's nuclear programme, and placed under house arrest. In the aftermath, the story of his theft of centrifuge designs from URENCO, the European nuclear power consortium, and the eager customers from Tehran to Pyongyang has been widely retold.[14] Over two decades, A.Q. Khan and his associates had proliferated nuclear technology, material and designs in a black market that spanned four continents. But the documents, and A.Q. Khan's subsequent efforts to clear his name, also cast fresh light on the murky question of Beijing's involvement in the Pakistani nuclear weapons programme, a vital precursor for his proliferation activities. While the basic facts of the two sides' collaboration have been clear to Western intelligence agencies for a long time, some of the important details were elusive—and remain so. "The specific nature of its nuclear agreements with China" is, notes one Pakistani nuclear expert, "one of the most closely guarded secrets in Pakistan".[15]

If the military relationship lies at the heart of China-Pakistan ties, nuclear weapons lie at the heart of the military relationship. Economic relations between the two sides have traditionally been weak, a problem to fix rather than a source of strength. Cultural ties have always been thin. Beyond the subcontinent, Pakistan looks to the West or to the Islamic world for intellectual and cultural influence, never to the Middle Kingdom. The underpinning of the relationship is widely understood to be a common strategic concern—about India—and the military ties that stem from it. Yet there are enduring questions about what this actually amounts to.

China has never committed soldiers on Pakistan's behalf, even when the country was being dismembered in 1971. It has been an essential military equipment supplier, all the more so given its willingness to prop up crucial parts of Pakistan's military-industrial infrastructure and to keep the tanks, guns and ammunition flowing when virtually all other options were cut off. This is not to be underrated. As one expert on the Pakistani army put it: "The prevailing view in the armed services appears to be that there is only one country that can be trusted to maintain military supplies irrespective of Pakistan's internal developments."[16] But the high-end American kit—the F-16s, the Harpoon anti-ship missiles, the P-3 Orion anti-submarine aircraft—has always been more prized by Pakistan's armed forces, and doubts about the quality of Chinese equipment persist to this day.[17] A shared strategic opponent has not entailed that China and

Pakistan are joined up in their views on tactics, calculations of acceptable risk, or the legitimacy and advisability of specific military actions. And although the relationship is at times referred to as an "alliance", it is no such thing. There have been no defence treaties, security guarantees, or serious preparations for joint military responses to different contingencies.[18] When Bhutto, in 1974, suggested to Zhou Enlai that the two sides enter a defence pact, "the Chinese premier politely declined the suggestion".[19] It has stayed that way ever since. A treaty signed in 2005 gives some legal justification for one side to come to the other's aid but no obligation.[20] For a long time even the military cultures of the two countries seemed incompatible. Anecdotes from the visit of a Pakistani military delegation to Beijing in 1966, as they attempt to replace the equipment that had been lost in the 1965 war, are illustrative:

When our officers met their Chinese counterparts, who wore neither smart uniforms nor any badges of rank, they found this somewhat disconcerting and confusing. In fact, a Pakistani General at the time of the Delegation's departure asked one of the very modest-looking individuals, who was dressed in unpressed trousers and jacket, to fetch his suitcase. The man actually moved to comply. I was horrified and stopped him, and apologized for my countryman's blunder— he was a Lieutenant General in the People's Liberation Army and a veteran of the Long March.[21]

Zhou Enlai, after enquiring why the Pakistanis only required fourteen days of ammunition from China—"How can a war be fought in that short time?"[22]—went on to probe the generals:

"I would be interested to know if you have prepared the people of Pakistan to operate in the rear of the enemy...I am talking about a People's Militia being based in every village and town. Since Pakistan lacks an industrial base to replenish supplies, this kind of defence is obviously well-suited to its needs."

There was a stunned silence among the Generals. The concept of putting arms into the hands of the common man was totally alien to them; in fact, it was deemed a threat to law and order in Pakistan. The notion of a prolonged conflict involving the citizenry of Pakistan was not part of the defence strategy planned by these professional soldiers...When the generals met at my home for dinner that night they appeared to be upset, and one of them said: 'War is a serious business and should be left to the professionals. Imagine a People's Militia!...What does Zhou Enlai know about soldiering and military affairs anyway?'... I reminded him that Zhou Enlai had fought in more battles than one could count. For several years he was a Divisional Commander and then Chief of the General Staff of the People's Liberation Army.[23]

A Pakistani military elite that emerged through Sandhurst and the British imperial army, and a Chinese leadership that had come to power through the Long March, guerrilla warfare, and Leninist re-education campaigns in Yan'an, hardly seemed destined to be "all-weather friends". Yet in parallel to these talks about small arms, an act of procurement on a far more spectacular scale was already being contemplated, which was worth the risk of foregoing any number of American jet fighters. The area where the value of the Sino-Pakistani military relationship has been greatest has been the one about which they can say the least.

Before Zulfiqar Ali Bhutto was hanged in 1979, he wrote a last testament by hand in his prison cell. While much of the document focused on responding to the charges levelled against him by General Zia, who had seized power from Bhutto in a coup two years earlier, there were also a couple of references that would initially be mysterious to the text's readers:

> In the light of recent developments which have taken place, my single most important achievement, which I believe will dominate the portrait of my public life, is an agreement which I arrived at after an assiduous and tenacious endeavour spanning over eleven years of negotiations. In the present context, the agreement of mine, concluded in June 1976, will perhaps be my greatest achievement and contribution to the survival of our people and our nation.[24]

They were not mysterious for long. It was already clear by the early 1980s that this achievement was securing Chinese support for the development of a Pakistani bomb. The final, decisive meeting is immortalized in a photograph that shows Bhutto and a frail Mao Zedong shaking hands, the last shot taken of a meeting between Mao and any foreign leader.[25] Then terminally ill, he would die a few months later, but the agreement stuck. Discussions between the two sides had been underway since that defining year. "1965 was critical for us," recalled Aga Shahi, one of the architects of the policy, in a later interview. "We made a pact with Beijing that ushered in decades of assistance we could not have got elsewhere."[26] Pakistan's decision to move ahead with a nuclear programme in the first place was itself closely intertwined with the decision to throw its chips in with China. The "pro-bomb camp", led by Bhutto and others in the foreign ministry, and the "anti-bomb camp", led by Finance Minister Muhammad Shoaib and a number of close economic advisers to Ayub Khan, were also at odds over the development of relations with Beijing.[27] The latter group wanted to tread cautiously, minimizing the risks to the US-Pakistan relationship and Pakistan's standing in the international community. The former believed that the US-Pakistan alliance was doomed to disappoint, and with the Non-Proliferation Treaty and other restrictions on nuclear trade in the offing, the window of opportunity to compete with India was closing. Bhutto's famous pronouncement in 1965, that "If … India builds the atom bomb…. Pakistan will eat grass or leaves, even go hungry, but we will get one of our own", would hence bind Pakistan's fate up with the strategic calculations of its eastern neighbour for decades to come.[28] The final impetus for the deal, though, was provided by India's nuclear test in 1974. "Smiling Buddha", as the first detonation of an Indian bomb was codenamed, threatened to tip the South Asian military balance decisively in favour of New Delhi, and bracket India with nuclear-armed China instead. But as in so many other areas, Chinese assistance to Pakistan helped to ensure that India would instead be re-hyphenated with its other neighbour. During the Pakistani foreign minister's visit to Beijing after the nuclear test, China gave its consent to help Pakistan develop a "nuclear blast" capacity.[29]

Reinforcing Pakistan's balancing role was not the only motivation for Beijing: at least in theory, nuclear cooperation was a two-way street. Not so long before, China too had been stuck on the outside of the nuclear club. The threat of US atomic weapons being used on the Chinese mainland loomed large during the Korean War and the Taiwan Strait crisis of 1955, prompting Beijing's decision to acquire nuclear capabilities of its own.[30] Yet crucial Soviet assistance to China's strategic weapons programme had been abruptly curtailed as ideological tensions between Mao and Khrushchev grew. At one point, China's bomb designers made daily trips to Beijing railway station in the hope of picking up a Soviet prototype that was promised but never arrived.[31] Moscow also reneged on its agreement to provide the uranium hexaflouride (UF6)—the gaseous uranium compound required for enrichment—that China needed for its first bomb. UF6 became the "weakest link in the chain"[32] of China's nuclear industrial production. A few final clues for implosion were gleaned from the reassembled scraps of some shredded documents the Soviet weapons specialists left behind in China before their abrupt departure.[33] After that the Chinese scientists were on their own.

Within a few years China would become the fifth country in the world to test a nuclear bomb, and Beijing moved quickly to acquire all the accoutrements of a strategic weapons programme. However, the sudden cut-off of scientific cooperation with the Soviet Union, and the absence of contact with the Western nuclear powers, left the Chinese scientists well aware that their nuclear programme was still lagging far behind those of the countries against which they had established it to defend themselves.[34] Weaknesses in their uranium enrichment capacities would be one of the main drivers for China's decision to join the IAEA in 1984, which promised access to superior enrichment technology.[35] Vulnerabilities in the Chinese weapons programme would also provide part of the impetus for agreeing to intelligence and military cooperation with the United States in 1979.[36] Beijing even asked Iran to pass on copies of its nuclear contracts with the West, in the hope that they might furnish some clues. But Pakistan promised something different—full spectrum collaboration: "One critical factor the two nations had in common was denial of certain Western technologies. Thus, their relationship was mutually beneficial—every piece of technology Pakistan managed to acquire would be available to the Chinese for reverse engineering."[37]

In September 1976, A.Q. Khan joined the Pakistani delegation at Mao's funeral, where he and his colleagues met three leading Chinese nuclear officials, Li Jue, Liu Wei and Jiang Shengjie. Jiang Shengjie was the nuclear fuel bureau chief, and one of China's top nuclear scientists.[38] Liu Wei managed the development of China's nuclear plants and had been in charge of the "Bureau of Architectural Technology", one of the two organs that originally launched China's nuclear weapons programme, overseeing the experimental nuclear reactor and cyclotron supplied by the Soviets. The most senior figure was Li Jue, who was in charge of research and development for China's nuclear weapons programme. He had run the Ninth Bureau—the "most secret organisation in the entire nuclear program"—during the critical phase of its development, overseeing uranium enrichment, nuclear testing, and the weapons research facility, China's own Los Alamos.[39]

This was one of A.Q. Khan's first overseas trips as a representative of the Pakistani government. He had only made his permanent return to Pakistan at the end of the previous year, bringing with him the designs for virtually every centrifuge he could lay his hands on at URENCO's facilities in the Netherlands. By July he had established his own research laboratory reporting directly to the Pakistani prime minister, and by September he had settled on the Punjabi town of Kahuta, about 20 miles south-east of Islamabad, as the location for his secret plant.[40]

While Pakistan's needs were certainly on the table in the meetings, so too were China's. He briefed them on how European-designed centrifuges could help China's enrichment programme. "Chinese experts started coming regularly to learn the whole technology" from Pakistan, A.Q. Khan states in his account.[41] Pakistani experts were sent to Hanzhong, near the ancient Chinese capital of Xian, where they helped "put up a centrifuge plant". "We sent 135 C-130 plane loads of machines, inverters, valves, flow meters, pressure gauges," he wrote. "Our teams stayed there for weeks to help and their teams stayed here for weeks at a time."[42] But what Pakistan got in return was far greater.

In 1982, a C-130 Hercules transport aircraft belonging to the Pakistani military left Urumqi, capital of the north-western Chinese province of Xinjiang, headed for Islamabad carrying five lead-lined, stainless steel boxes, inside each of which were 10 single-kilogram ingots of highly enriched uranium (HEU), enough for two atomic bombs.[43] It is likely that this was the only time a nuclear weapon state transferred HEU to a non-nuclear country for military use. China had already sent 15 tons of uranium hexaflouride to Pakistan—somewhat more than a bomb's worth—to ensure that the nuclear project continued on schedule: "China's gas was most likely used in Pakistan's first round of enrichment while the Pakistan Atomic Energy Commission was still struggling with UF6 production," according to one Pakistani nuclear expert's account.[44] Their scientists had also been closely involved in technical cooperation, as a regular visitor to Khan Research Laboratories explains: "The Chinese were working on triggering mechanisms, the centrifuges, vacuum systems. They brought rocket propellant and super-hard metals like maraging steel…. They brought in fissile material and Khan gave them the data on enrichment and metallurgy. They helped Pakistan import and experiment with high explosives and Khan gave them his work on the centrifuge rotors."[45] Chinese officials stayed at Khan's guesthouse at Kahuta, which was done up in the style of a Chinese hall.[46]

But by 1982, General Zia was nervous about the slow pace of Pakistan's progress. The Israeli strike on Osirak, destroying Iraq's latent nuclear programme, drew fears that India could do the same thing—or even the Israelis themselves.[47] Five days before the operation, the Israeli ambassador to the UN had warned that "there is abundant evidence indicating that [Pakistan] is producing nuclear weapons".[48] Israel had made plans for a pre-emptive attack. As had India.[49] Even Moscow was now a potential threat—Pakistan had already embarked on its programme of support for the *mujahideen*'s anti-Soviet campaign in Afghanistan, with the obvious risk of retaliation. Zia sent his military aide, Lieutenant-General Syed Ali Zamin Naqvi, to request weapons-grade fissile material and the bomb design from China, in an effort to speed Pakistan's efforts along.[50] Deng Xiaoping agreed. In each area where the Soviets had pulled the plug on Beijing, the Chinese would prove to be far more obliging to the Pakistanis.

The scope of this cooperation was ascertained relatively quickly by Western intelligence agencies. The papers that eventually turned up in Tripoli in plastic carrier bags had even been in the hands of US agents before. Until he was told to stop by Zia, A.Q. Khan had the habit of carrying weapons designs in his briefcase.[51] During one trip abroad in the early 1980s, US intelligence officers gained access to his luggage in a hotel room and found drawings of a bomb and the instructions to make it, the very documents that would later be sold to Libya and possibly other customers too.[52] Their Chinese provenance was as clear then as it would be three decades later. In fact, so thoroughly had US intelligence penetrated Pakistan's nuclear programme that American weapons experts were even able to create a detailed model of the bomb, which they showed to Pakistan's foreign minister in 1987 as a demonstration of just how much they knew.[53] The drawings themselves were shown to Zia by Vernon Walters, former deputy director of the CIA, as early as 1982.[54] In spite of this, the political pressure on Pakistan and China from the United States could at best be described as modest. The three sides had been working as a virtual alliance against the Soviet Union in Afghanistan since the 1979 invasion, and proliferation issues were of lower salience than the opportunity to deal the Soviets a fatal blow. The US National Security Advisor, Zbigniew Brzezinski, articulated the stance most pithily in his argument to President Carter, "Our security policy cannot be dictated by our nonproliferation policy."[55] The Chinese were informed of this stance in the course of bilateral meetings in 1980:

Secretary Brown: "Our big problem with Pakistan was their attempts to get a nuclear program. Although we still object to their doing so, we will now set that aside for the time being and concentrate on strengthening Pakistan against potential Soviet action."

Deng Xiaoping: "That is a very good approach…We applaud this decision."[56]

The Reagan administration thought much the same thing. Evidence of Pakistan's covert nuclear programme was certainly an irritant, not least since it threatened to torpedo Congressional support for the upgrading of the US-Pakistan security relationship, but it was not the first-order concern. In 1981, an agreement was reached to sell Pakistan the F-16 fighter jets that it would later adapt to become part of its nuclear strike force. At the time, the only other recipients of the state-of-the-art aircraft were NATO allies and Japan.[57] A Congressional amendment to the arms sales package specified that aid would be cut off if Pakistan tested a nuclear weapon. But the administration understood clearly that the nuclear programme would continue to move ahead, even if it stopped short of an actual detonation. The Chinese had not taken US proliferation concerns especially seriously even before the Soviet invasion. Kissinger had joked with Chinese leaders that the best way to contain India's ambitions was to arm Pakistan and Bangladesh with nuclear weapons.[58] The Chinese expected that any US objections could be weathered—and they were right.

When it came to Pakistani transfers of Western technology to China's nuclear programme, the United States was ambivalent—and some in the US government were even tacitly supportive. In 1973, Kissinger had assigned a small group to assess Soviet threats to China and how the United States could help to address them.[59] The conclusion: China's nuclear arsenal was vulnerable, the PLA's technology, logistics and industrial capacity were poor, the air force was mostly obsolete, and the navy was in an even worse state.

If the United States was willing to support a "hardening" of China's defensive capacities, there would be several advantages. It could help tie down Soviet forces on its eastern frontier, reduce the temptation for Moscow to coerce China or launch surprise strikes, reinforce China's anti-Soviet resolve, and minimize the prospects of a nuclear crisis between the two powers.[60] Any transfer of US military technology or arms sales to China would be a matter of high sensitivity, of course, and some of it would have to be undertaken through friends and allies who faced fewer restrictions. While the bulk of the heavy-lifting would end up being undertaken by the Europeans and the Israelis,[61] Pakistan—so recently the bridge between Washington and Beijing—was another obvious place to turn. The man spearheading early efforts to launch the programme of US-China military collaboration, Michael Pillsbury, told Pakistani officials that "logically, it would need Pakistan's cooperation".[62]

For a number of years, there was hesitation on the US and Chinese sides about proceeding. A further study in 1975 by James Lilley, the National Intelligence Officer for East Asia, which suggested that US military ties with Beijing could strengthen those Chinese leaders who favoured closer links with the West, was taken up by Kissinger on his next visit to China.[63] Mao was cool to the American offer, stating, "As for military aspects we should not discuss that now. Such matters should wait until the war breaks out before we consider them," to which Kissinger responded, "Yes, but you should know that we would be prepared then to consider them."[64] They were indeed. Six weeks later, during President Ford's trip to Beijing, authorization was given by Washington for a sale by the British company, Rolls Royce, of 50 Spey jet engines that would be used to power PLA Air Force fighters, the first military-related technology sold to China by the West.[65] Ford also agreed to the sale of two high-powered US computers that could be used by China for nuclear warhead and ballistic missile development.[66] But it was only after the Soviet invasion of Afghanistan that the Sino-US security relationship began in earnest. China would end up receiving everything from arms sales and technology transfers to the US field manual for the "Air-Land Battle" doctrine that underpinned the US defence of Europe against Soviet invasion. But at the heart of US concerns was China's nuclear arsenal. Its vulnerability to Soviet attack derived from its small size, its lack of sophistication, its weak command and control infrastructure, and the lengthy and complex preparations required before the weapons could be launched.[67] The top US priority was to improve Chinese early-warning capacities,[68] reducing the state of readiness in which China needed to keep its liquid-fuelled missiles and thereby the incentives for either China or the Soviet Union to launch first strikes.[69]

The United States chose to address the problem directly. In 1979, the secretive Sino-US "Chestnut" programme was put into motion.[70] Between August and December, the CIA airlifted equipment to China for a pair of monitoring stations that were established in the Tian Shan mountains, at Korla and Qitai,[71] close to Urumqi and the Sino-Soviet border, with operations beginning in late 1980.[72] Chinese technicians from the PLA 2nd Department were trained at a SIGINT training centre near San Francisco.[73] As well as monitoring military communications and radar signals from Soviet air defences, their antennae could detect any change in the alert status of Soviet nuclear forces. The listening posts meant that China was able to increase its warning time for nuclear attacks and Washington was able to replace the capacities it was losing with the fall of the Shah. The "Tacksman" listening stations in the mountains of northern Iran performed a similar function for the United States but had to be closed or destroyed following the 1979 revolution.[74] The final details of the agreement were sealed during a secret trip by the head of the CIA, Stansfield Turner, who visited Beijing, in a disguise replete with moustache, in December 1980, his last as Director of Central Intelligence.[75] "It was clear that the Chinese leadership, Deng especially, regarded this cooperation as a major strategic decision for them," noted his aide, future Defense Secretary Robert Gates. "It was for us, too, as we sat down with people with whom we in intelligence had been at war since 1949."[76]

But there was a more ambitious goal too. As one US army journal in 1979 argued: "The flow of Western technology made possible by the shift in U.S.-Chinese relations may strengthen [Chinese] military capabilities to the point where the Soviet Union is increasingly forced to pursue a conservative, defensive, and détente oriented strategy"—especially China's strategic forces, which, although "relatively primitive", could be "expected to improve strikingly as a result of China's new emphasis on orderly technological development, and the flow of commercial and military technology."[77]

Pakistan was certainly one of the early sources of this "flow". The debate over whether Pakistan should receive an advanced radar system as part of the F-16 sales illustrated the balance of considerations. The CIA warned in 1982 that "the sale of the AN/ALR-69 Radar Warning Receiver to Pakistan entails a significant risk of the equipment being exploited by China…China has obtained French weapons—and possibly U.S. air-to-air missiles—from Pakistan and has negotiated agreements on joint weapons developments based on Western arms technologies acquired by Pakistan".[78] The radar would give China "the potential of a significant improvement in radar warning capability" and China "would benefit from access to Western avionics fabrication technology gaining several years in the development of a modern radar warning system".[79] The transfer to Pakistan went ahead regardless.

However, it is far from clear that the transfers of Western technology did a great deal to help China's nuclear programme. A.Q. Khan's P1 centrifuges—the stolen Dutch centrifuge technology—did not operate well and there is no reason to believe that China had more luck with them than Pakistan did. Chinese weapons-grade uranium throughout the period came from its gaseous diffusion plants—where it had achieved a genuine breakthrough in the enrichment performance in the early 1980s—and not from gas centrifuges.[80] China's centrifuge programme was still in development by the 1990s, and when it finally did establish large-scale centrifuge plants at Hanzhong, the very location where A.Q. Khan claimed to have helped to assemble a facility, China simply purchased them wholesale from a familiar source: Russia.[81] China's nuclear programme did benefit from another set of Western technologies, but these came directly from the source. A 1984 Defense Intelligence Agency estimate suggested:

There is evidence that the Chinese have been successful in assimilating into their nuclear weapons program United States technology in areas such as high explosive, radiochemistry, metallurgy, welding, super computers, numerical modeling, high speed photonics, and underground drilling…Increased access to this technology and continued Chinese efforts will in the 1980s and early 1990s show up as qualitative warhead improvements.[82]

The thanks for this, however, were owed to "overt contact with U.S. scientists and technology and covert acquisition of U.S. technology,"[83] not to the Pakistanis. By this time US-China military exchanges and arms sales had become increasingly normalized, US defence and high-technology hardware sales reaching $5 billion in 1985.[84] Whatever deal Bhutto struck with Mao, it is clear who got the better end of it.

This was even more obviously true of Pakistan's missile programme. While there is a view that "if you subtract China's help, there wouldn't be a Pakistani [nuclear] program",[85] there is also a good case that Chinese aid was largely a "supplemental contribution": Pakistan's acquisition of the bomb certainly relied on its own scientific and technical prowess too.[86] As one Pakistani nuclear scientist puts it: "It is quite likely that the development of nuclear weapons by Pakistan would have succeeded but without Chinese assistance this would have taken longer."[87] It is harder to make the same claims about delivery mechanisms for those weapons. Pakistan's missile programmes had a far weaker technical base than its nuclear programme. Until the United States choked off its F-16 sales in 1990, it was still these planes rather than ballistic missiles that were seen as the primary delivery vehicle for its nuclear arsenal. But India's tests of its first short-range ballistic missile in 1988 and an intermediate-range ballistic missile in 1989 prompted an attempt by Pakistan to demonstrate that it had its own matching capabilities. In February 1989, Pakistan proudly announced that it had tested its own Hatf missiles, named after the Prophet Muhammad's sword. Foreign observers were unimpressed by the hurriedly developed series, which suffered from limited range and accuracy. The Hatf-1 was dismissed by US experts as an "inaccurate battlefield rocket that can travel 80km"; the Hatf-2 as "two Hatf-1s put together".[88] But even before these missile tests, Pakistan had again turned to its old friend for help. The Chinese surpassed themselves. They had already assisted in Pakistan's crash effort to demonstrate an indigenous missile capability. But now, not only would they transfer to Pakistan some of their very latest models—the M-11 and the M-9 missiles had only recently been inducted by the PLA itself—but they ensured that Pakistan could develop its own rockets in the future.[89] The M-11s, developed by the Sanjiang Space Group in Hubei Province, gave Pakistan the 300km range missile that Islamabad had pretended the Hatf-2 provided.[90] The M-9s, the domestic version of which Beijing would use in an "exercise" during the 1995–96 Taiwan Strait crisis to intimidate Taipei, gave Pakistan the capacity to strike New Delhi.[91]

The outright handover of the M-11 missiles did not go unnoticed. In late 1992, US intelligence spotted a shipment of the missile parts passing through the port of Karachi.[92] They were destined for the air force base at Sargodha, in western Punjab, which soon became the focus of international attention, just as the nuclear facilities at Kahuta had been before it.[93] Thirty of the missiles were stored in crates there, and satellite photos revealed shelters for the crates, mobile launchers, and missile maintenance areas.[94]

After the unhelpful publicity the missiles attracted, China began supplying both M-11s and M-9s in unassembled form, which required the development of a dedicated missile assembly facility near Rawalpindi.[95] Chinese experts showed up in Sargodha and other locations to train Pakistani technicians to become self-reliant for future production.[96] Virtually every time a new missile was added to Pakistan's arsenal, it could be traced to a Chinese prototype. The Shaheen-I, rolled out in 1999, bears a striking resemblance to the M-9. The 2000km-range Shaheen-II, displayed at the Pakistan Day parade in 2000, is believed to be based on China's M-18 missile or an adapted M-9.[97] Pakistan's first cruise missile, the Babur, put into production in 2005, appeared to be based on China's DH-10s (though both are ultimately reverse-engineered US cruise missiles). Its current missile defence system uses Chinese HQ-9 surface-to-air missiles. Even Pakistan's rocket launcher for battlefield nuclear weapons was based on a Chinese design.[98] The only notable exceptions were the long-range Ghauri missiles—the first missiles that gave Pakistan the capacity to strike any city in India—and they came from North Korea, in one of the most controversial A.Q. Khan deals. Pyongyang provided Pakistan with Nodong missiles, in return for which it not only received cash but may also have got its hands on crucial documents and components to support its clandestine uranium enrichment programme.[99]

Unlike in the early 1980s, during the crucial phase of Sino-Pakistani nuclear cooperation, which proceeded with little serious challenge, Chinese missile transfers generally took place in the teeth of international opposition. The transfers began when China was at the low ebb of its post-Tiananmen isolation, and when the collapse of the Soviet Union meant that the United States no longer had the same need to maintain its Cold War quasi-alliance with either China or Pakistan. The sale of the M-11 launchers resulted in US sanctions in 1991—a black-listing of the companies involved—which were eventually followed by a two-year freeze of high-technology sales to China.[100] On each occasion, China would make a new promise or sign a new agreement with the United States in order to have the sanctions suspended, only to continue its transfers exactly as they had agreed with the Pakistanis. At every point where they were challenged, the Chinese would counter with complaints about the US sales of F-16 warplanes to Taiwan, which had started shortly before the M-11 missile transfers.[101] Beijing also remained on hand to support the Pakistani nuclear programme itself, exporting five thousand ring magnets in 1994, which, it was reported, enabled Pakistan to double its production of highly-enriched uranium.[102] There are even suspicions that China tested a warhead on Pakistan's behalf in 1990 at its facility in Lop Nur, Xinjiang, well in advance of the 1998 explosion in the Chagai hills in Balochistan that formally announced Pakistan's membership of the nuclear club.[103] Neither did that Pakistani test bring a halt to Chinese proliferation: China increased its shipments of specialty steel and guidance systems following the Indian and Pakistani tests.[104] Over the course of the next decade, China would continue to provide technology and support for the expanded production of Pakistan's ballistic missiles.

And there is one more act of Sino-Pakistani proliferation that may yet take place, though disentangling truth from fiction in the many stories surrounding it is a challenging task. Nuclear cooperation between China and Pakistan has long had an interested third party. The question is whether and how that country might decide to cash in its chits.

The establishment of Sino-Saudi relations had a "Kissinger moment" of its own. Much as Pakistan acted as the middleman for the Sino-US rapprochement, so too were Saudi Arabia and China brought together with Islamabad as the conduit. In Kissinger's place was Prince Bandar Bin Sultan, the *éminence grise* of Saudi foreign policy, and like the US opening it caught everyone completely off-guard.

In 1985, Saudi Arabia was seeking intermediate-range ballistic missiles but Saudi officials were making no headway in Washington. The Pakistanis suggested that the Saudis consider another option, which they were willing to help facilitate.[105] Bandar, then ambassador to the United States, duly floated the prospect of a purchase to his Chinese counterpart.[106] He received his answer in Pakistan. During Bandar's visit, on the pretext of talks about the two sides' petrochemical industries, he met with Chinese officials in the garden of their embassy in Islamabad. The message they delivered was clear: "Yes"; and "Come to Beijing to discuss the details".[107] Saudi Arabia had no diplomatic relations with China at the time and Bandar and his half-brother, General Khaled Bin Sultan, made a series of secret trips to Beijing and to Chinese missile bases elsewhere in the country, across the course of which an agreement was thrashed out.[108] The missiles in question were East Wind (Dong Feng) CSS-2 missiles, which were distinguished by the fact that they were highly inaccurate, serving little military use with conventional warheads, designed instead for the purpose of carrying nuclear ones. Fifty of these intermediate-range missiles and nine launchers were sent to Saudi Arabia amid elaborate concealment.

The incident, when finally discovered by the United States, would bring about one of most serious crises in the history of its relations with Saudi Arabia, and a near-conflict with Israel—but, for the Saudis, it was worth it. Riyadh was deeply concerned about the Iranian threat, which was vividly manifested at the time by the Iran-Iraq war, into which the Saudis risked being drawn. The justification given by Khaled Bin Sultan is that they were seeking "a weapon which would make an enemy think twice about attacking us", "not intended to be used, except as a last resort" and seeking it from "a country able to supply such a weapon at speed and without constraining conditions".[109] The Chinese and the Saudis both provided assurances to the United States that they would not be armed with nuclear warheads, but the missiles' presence on Saudi soil has posed a standing question ever since. A number of accounts suggest that Riyadh, which provided substantial financing to the Pakistan's nuclear programme,[110] has reached an agreement that would see Pakistani warheads transferred into the Saudis' possession if they decide that the security situation in their neighbourhood requires it.[111] The speculation has been fanned by the Saudis themselves. In May 1999 Prince Sultan, the Saudi Defence Minister, visited the nuclear enrichment facility at Kahuta and the missile factory at Ghauri,[112] the first foreign visitor who had been allowed there apart from the Chinese (even Benazir Bhutto was denied the opportunity to visit Kahuta while she was prime minister).[113] On the same visit he met A.Q. Khan, who made a return trip to Riyadh later that year. Despite the obvious issues over their provenance, when Saudi defectors and Israeli intelligence officers fed out stories about a Saudi-Pakistani nuclear deal in the intervening years, they had an undoubted verisimilitude.[114]

But it has been the advances in the Iranian nuclear programme—and in the West's negotiations with Tehran—that have elicited claims from US and Saudi officials that seem to carry greater weight. King Abdullah himself warned visiting US envoy Dennis Ross in 2009 that if Iran crosses the nuclear threshold "we will get nuclear weapons", and there was a flurry of stories citing intelligence reports about warheads "waiting and ready" in November 2013 when the Iran intermediate deal was on the eve of completion.[115] Even President Obama's former non-proliferation chief, Gary Samore, stated at the time, "I do think that the Saudis believe that they have some understanding with Pakistan that, in extremis, they would have claim to acquire nuclear weapons from Pakistan."[116] It is a leap to imagine an outright transfer of Pakistani warheads to Saudi control, as opposed to an arrangement that simply places Pakistani-controlled missiles on Saudi soil. But if it ever happened, the original Saudi missiles—or even the updated models that it is believed the Chinese may have provided—were designed to carry precisely the same nuclear warhead design that China transferred to A.Q. Khan.[117] The Pakistanis have since adapted that design for their own arsenal but that is a far from difficult gap to bridge.[118] It remains possible that this is all an elaborate bluff to exert pressure on Western efforts to deal with Iran. But there is a prevalent suspicion that, as David Ottaway puts it, "Pakistan has become the kingdom's nuclear protector, with China's help".[119]

Collaboration between China and Pakistan on an area of such significance and sensitivity as the two sides' nuclear ties has built an unusual level of mutual trust between them. At the same time, it provides one of the relationship's enduring sources of imbalance: Pakistan is in China's debt, and knows it. Not that China's support was an act of generosity—Beijing continues to extract strategic benefit from the decision—but the collaboration remains considerably less vital to Chinese interests than it is to Pakistan's, whose autonomy and even survival as a state have been preserved by its nuclear capacity.

Pakistan has repaid the favour when it can, though as much by chance as by design. Stray, unexploded US tomahawk missiles launched at Afghanistan in response to Al Qaeda's attacks on US embassies in Africa in 1998 found their way from Balochistan into the hands of the Pakistani military, and then into the possession of the Chinese.[120] A reverse-engineered cruise missile based on these advanced US models showed up in both countries' weapons arsenals a couple of years later. The US stealth helicopter that crashed in Abbottabad during the raid on Bin Laden in 2011 was another treasure trove for China to which the Pakistanis were happy to provide them access before it was shipped back to the United States.[121] But none of these chance gifts compare to the thirty-year process of Chinese support for the Pakistani nuclear programme.

Over time, nuclear weapons have only become more central to Pakistani military strategy. This is a partly a function of the growing conventional military capabilities gap with India. For many years India had its pick of some of the best Soviet equipment, and now it sits in the enviable position of being able to choose between Russian, European, Israeli and American suppliers, as well as having a far greater resource base with which to make the purchases, and a far more substantial territorial capacity to absorb a nuclear attack. Weapons sales from the United States have ensured that Pakistan can at least stay within touching distance. But they don't do much more than that. As one US diplomatic cable put it, they "essentially buy time to delay Pakistan considering the nuclear option in a conflict with India. Given India's overwhelming military superiority, this would only be a few days, but these days would allow critical time to mediate and prevent nuclear conflict."[122] It is only the nuclear weapons themselves that provide any meaning to the notion of strategic balance.

But for Pakistan—unlike China—the bomb has always been seen as an enabling factor rather than just a means of ensuring others' restraint. The 1965 war was interpreted by some as Pakistan's last push for Kashmir before the looming prospect of Indian nuclearization made it impossible.[123] As their nuclear programme grew in the early 1980s, Pakistani army officers actively debated what new opportunities having strategic weapons of their own would open up in Kashmir—some believing that "a bold Pakistani strike to liberate Kashmir might go unchallenged if Indian leadership was indecisive".[124] The Kargil war was partly an answer: the first time Pakistan had the opportunity to conduct a military operation in Kashmir under a nuclear umbrella came barely a year after the 1998 test. Since then, a series of terrorist attacks on major targets in India have occurred, without retaliation, albeit with the deniability afforded by state-backed militant groups rather than regular troops. For some Pakistani strategists, it has been a vindication of the notion that nuclear weapons now provide the level of deterrence required to make asymmetric attacks a credible—and relatively cost-free—strategic option.[125] "For 15 years this country is bleeding from attack after attack, and there is nothing we can do," said Raja Mohan of the Observer Research Foundation, a New Delhi think tank. "The attacks correlate directly to Pakistan's acquisition of nuclear weapons. From the moment they got nukes, they saw it as an opportunity they could exploit. And India has no instruments to punish Pakistan or change its behavior."[126]

Pakistan has now started to move beyond the principle of minimum deterrence through a significant expansion of its nuclear capabilities.[127] This is often justified with reference to India's Cold Start doctrine, an operational plan devised by the Indian Army in 2004 for a rapid penetration into Pakistani territory that would enable India to enact swift retribution for a Pakistani attack. Described in one US diplomatic cable as "a mixture of myth and reality", it may never be put to use on the battlefield by India.[128] Yet alongside fears about American designs on Pakistan's nuclear weapons, it has been used as a rationale not only for the development of what is a growing nuclear arsenal, which may already exceed India's, but also for the addition of a new generation of tactical weapons.[129] Lieutenant General Khalid Kidwai, who supervised Pakistan's nuclear assets for nearly fourteen years, has referred to the intent of these short-range weapons being to "pour cold water on Cold Start".[130] As a result, the dangers inherent in another nuclear crisis in South Asia are now considerably greater than they were a few years ago.[131] Pakistan now has the means to strike many more Indian targets. It has a growing number of missiles that are vulnerable to misuse—smaller, mated with warheads, and more likely to result in miscalculation, rapid escalation, or even loss of control of individual weapons.[132] When coupled with the ambiguity about whether jihadi attacks in India are acts of the Pakistani state itself, rogue actors in the state apparatus, or simply ISI-trained militants operating without state sanction, there is now an acute risk that another Mumbai-style attack could result in war on the subcontinent or an environment in which the security of Pakistan's nuclear arsenal is imperilled. China is uncomfortable with these implications. That has not stopped it from supporting the Pakistani nuclear programme, but it has prompted Beijing to play a growing role in helping to defuse crises on the subcontinent and pushing Pakistan towards lasting ways to stabilize its relationship with India. Beijing may still be a vital enabler for Pakistan but nowadays it is also determined to limit the potential risks.

3

RE-HYPHENATING INDIA

So long as the Indian government oppresses the Kashmiri people, China will not cease to support the Kashmiri people in their struggle for self-determination. So long as the Government of India persists in its unbridled aggression towards Pakistan, China will not cease supporting Pakistan in her just struggle against aggression. This stand of ours will never change, however many helpers you may have such as the U.S., the Modern Revisionists and the U.S.-controlled United Nations.

Chinese note to India, 1965[1]

China and the South Asian countries have a great deal of common ground and converging interests just as all neighbours do. However, as neighbours, it is difficult not to have some differences or disputes from time to time. We stand for seeking common ground on major issues while reserving differences on minor ones. We should look at the differences or disputes from a long perspective, seeking a just and reasonable settlement through consultations and negotiations while bearing in mind the larger picture. If certain issues cannot be resolved for the time being, they may be shelved temporarily so that they will not affect the normal state-to-state relations.

Jiang Zemin, "Carrying Forward Generations of Friendly and Good-Neighbourly Relations and Endeavouring Towards a Better Tomorrow for All", 1996[2]

No country can choose its neighbours, and a distant relative may not be as helpful as a near neighbour. China and India should not seek cooperation from afar with a ready partner at hand.

Li Keqiang, "Seize the new opportunities in India-China Cooperation", 2013[3]

In December 1996, Jiang Zemin was due to make a state visit to Pakistan. It was a rare event in Sino-Pakistani relations. Although Chinese heads of state had made the trip before, neither of the men who wielded ultimate power in China, Mao Zedong and Deng Xiaoping, had ever taken the six-hour flight across the Karakoram mountain range. With Deng, now in the last few months of his life, having fully handed over the reins to Jiang, this would be an unusual opportunity for Pakistan to play host to a Chinese president who could actually call the shots. It would be another decade before they would have the chance again. Jiang had even spent several months living in Pakistan, in 1976, as an engineering consultant at the Heavy Machinery Complex and Heavy Forge and Foundry in Taxila.[4] Yet the Pakistanis were viewing the visit with trepidation. Jiang's arrival in Islamabad looked set to be completely overshadowed by the first leg of the journey: he would be flying in from New Delhi, where he would make the first ever visit to India by a Chinese head of state. This would draw further public attention to a development that was making Pakistan increasingly uncomfortable. Chinese policy in South Asia was steadily taking on what Beijing described as a more "balanced" quality.[5]

The Sino-Indian relationship had been undergoing a gradual process of normalization, and entered a new phase after Prime Minister Rajiv Gandhi's breakthrough visit to Beijing in 1988.[6] The Soviet Union's collapse accelerated the transition in Chinese foreign policy away from Cold War rivalries towards a focus on economic goals, whether through outright trade diplomacy, or through the stabilization of China's regional security environment in order to concentrate on economic development. India no longer occupied the status in Beijing's eyes of Soviet quasi-ally, and, in addition to its prospects as a trade partner, might even become an asset in China's growing struggle with the United States. In the year preceding Jiang's visit, the Taiwan Strait crisis had seen the staging of the greatest display of US military might in East Asia since the Vietnam War, as Washington deployed two carrier battle groups in response to China's intimidatory missile tests in the vicinity of Taiwan.[7] With US-China relations already fundamentally altered by the Tiananmen Square massacre, this was the closest the two sides had come to confrontation since the early 1960s. For China, concepts such as "anti-hegemonism" and "multipolarity" were the order of the day, and major developing world powers such as India were potential supporters.[8]

An old friend like Pakistan wouldn't be forgotten, but the relative value of the relationship seemed to be diminishing.

The Pakistanis watched Jiang's visit to India closely. There was already one worrying sign for them. A Chinese foreign ministry spokesman declared on Indian soil that "it is not in the interests of China to sell advanced weapons to its immediate neighbours".[9] This was a promise that Islamabad could probably afford to discount, though: Beijing had regularly made and broken them before, and would indeed do so again. But China had saved the real blow for a speech that Jiang would deliver in Pakistan itself, at the national assembly. The language sounded bland but the message was well understood by the parliamentarians in attendance. The Chinese president failed to mention Kashmir explicitly—a point of sensitivity for the Pakistanis in its own right—but his references to "seeking a just and reasonable settlement through consultations and negotiations" and "shelving" disputes were clear and pointed.[10] It undercut Pakistan's position that Kashmir should be resolved through international mediation, not bilateral negotiations, at precisely the time when Islamabad was on a renewed push to internationalize the dispute.[11] Worse, it seemed to reflect a willingness on China's part to shift its stance on an issue of deep significance to Pakistan for the sake of better relations with India. The passage of the speech was received in "pindrop silence" according to the US ambassador, Thomas Simons.[12] It is still cited today by Pakistanis as a warning sign for what might happen if the attractions of warmer ties with the old enemy grow too great for Beijing to resist.[13]

Nearly twelve years later, on 5 September 2008, US officials were desperately trying to get an answer out of Jiang's successor, Hu Jintao. The centre of the action was Vienna, where the Nuclear Suppliers Group (NSG) was meeting to reach a decision about whether an exemption should be granted to India. The NSG had been founded after India's nuclear test in 1974, in which material and technology supplied by the United States and Canada under bilateral agreements committing India to their peaceful use had instead been diverted to its bomb programme. As a result, the United States and six other governments concluded that the Non Proliferation Treaty (NPT) alone would be insufficient to halt the spread of nuclear weapons, and established a informal "nuclear cartel" to coordinate and control exports of nuclear material, equipment and technology.[14] India's undeclared nuclear activities outside the NPT left it barred from most international nuclear commerce for decades. But now the United States was leading the effort to persuade the members of the NSG to grant India a waiver and allow it to engage in the civil nuclear trade. It was the final hurdle to clear in a process that had started when the Bush administration sought a symbolic centrepiece in its plans for a fundamental transformation of the US-India relationship. Instead of being a source of contention and division between the world's largest democracy and its most powerful, as it had been only a few years before, the civil-nuclear agreement would make the United States the principal country responsible for bringing India into the international nuclear order—on India's terms.[15] New Delhi would not place all its nuclear facilities under safeguards, would not be a member of the NPT, and would not sign the Comprehensive Test Ban Treaty.[16]

Getting to Vienna had been a long and gruelling task. Domestic opposition in both India and the United States needed to be overcome, an India-IAEA agreement needed to be reached, and an array of countries needed to be persuaded that this was a means of strengthening the non-proliferation order rather than undermining it—or at least to swallow their reservations. NSG meetings are generally low-key affairs, attended by mid-level officials who are able to convene without attracting even a hint of press attention. Not this one. The final push to gain the unanimous agreement required for the waiver involved a diplomatic marathon at the highest levels of the governments involved in what was by now a 45-nation body. From the president down, every top US official was deployed to cajole and persuade the hold-outs. Opponents to the exemption were gradually peeled off, with the Japanese, the Norwegians, the Dutch, and the New Zealanders all folding. In the closing stages, it appeared that there were two countries blocking the deal—Ireland and Austria.[17] Ireland's consent was finally secured in a phone-call between George W. Bush and Taoiseach Brian Cowen.[18] Austria was in the middle of an election campaign and its government feared that the India exemption could be exploited by the opposition Green Party. The Austrian Foreign Minister, Ursula Plassnik, was at a European Council meeting in Brussels, and proving to be elusive. Condoleezza Rice had to break from her landmark visit to Libya to place a call to the German Foreign Minister, Frank-Walter Steinmeier, who managed to track Plassnik down. She finally instructed her negotiator to agree.[19] It seemed there was now a green light.

Yet at a late stage in the negotiations, the behaviour of the Chinese delegates took an unexpected turn. China had been among the countries to express their reservations about the deal, but had given assurances in Vienna and through separate bilateral communications with the Indians and the Americans that it "won't be an obstacle".[20] Beijing had provided discreet support to the principal opponents of the deal, who were starting to cast around for additional ballast in their attempts to resist US pressure, but China largely hid behind them, quietly supporting their amendments but otherwise keeping its head down. Signs that something was afoot were first evident when the Chinese negotiators started putting forward proposals of their own.[21] These included language that could have opened the door for Pakistan to seek a similar waiver, which attracted near-complete opposition from the other NSG members and curiosity about whether Beijing was genuinely testing the water or just finding ways to bring about procedural delays.[22] At this stage, Chinese officials still had cover from the European opponents of the deal, but it became increasingly evident that Beijing had been counting on the Europeans to hold out and that its negotiators were not actually authorized to give their nod to the exemption. The result was a minor panic. Chinese officials proposed an adjournment, to no avail. Then, at midnight, China's two senior negotiators, including Cheng Jingye, the head of the Chinese delegation, walked out.[23] With the diplomacy in Vienna in danger of unravelling, the focus switched back to the channel between Washington and Beijing. Hu Jintao and Wen Jiabao had been avoiding calls from the Indian prime minister,[24] but were now on the spot. They blinked. Rice reached Yang Jiechi, the Chinese Foreign Minister, to urge China not to block the deal.[25] With a few hours to go until the meeting was scheduled to break up, the junior official that the Chinese had left in the room conveyed China's evidently very reluctant assent. To rub salt into India's wound, Chinese diplomats—including Yang, on the eve of a visit to New Delhi—attempted in the immediate aftermath to pretend to their Indian counterparts that they had been supportive all along.[26]

China had been hoping and expecting that the US-India civil nuclear deal would fall at one of the many hurdles in its way—the US Congress, the Indian parliament, the non-proliferation hard-liners—but all of them had been cleared. It paved the way for what many in Beijing saw as a potential "anti-China" containment effort and a soft alliance being hatched between Washington and New Delhi, a refreshed version of the

Indo-Soviet relationship: friends, if not actually allies.[27] Observers in Beijing were hardly reassured by the alternative explanation furnished by US and Indian advocates of the deal.[28] In this account, "containment" or even "counterbalancing" was a crudely reductive way of thinking about what was going on—India had no interest in being dragged into a US containment effort, and the United States had no interest in mounting one anyway.[29] But instead, they portrayed an even grander scheme that would disrupt China's rise to pre-eminent status in the coming century: a baton-passing across the Anglosphere from the United States to India, as from the UK to the United States over the early decades of the 20th century. India was not merely the short-term ally, it was the like-minded successor, which the United States would "help become a major world power in the twenty-first century."[30] China had tended to be dismissive of India's prospects for surpassing its own rise, seeing the country as ten years behind it economically and showing little sign of catching up. But India was on an economic roll now, and with access to US arms and technology, the picture looked altogether different.[31] China no longer felt confident that it had the luxury to be disdainful: what Shyam Saran, the former Indian Foreign Secretary, described as the "Chinese predilection to dismiss India's role in international affairs as that of a pretender too big for its boots, while China's super power status is, of course, regarded as manifest destiny".[32]

But China had a tried and tested solution to hand. If the United States was going to smooth the path for India's ascent, Pakistan would be the means for China to hold it down.

Nominally, India is the principal point of continuity in the China-Pakistan relationship, yet in some ways it is anything but. The Sino-Indian and Indo-Pakistani rivalries today are vastly removed from those that laid the foundations for the Sino-Pakistani relationship in the 1960s. While their border dispute certainly hasn't gone away, India and China are now two globally capable powers that clear $74 billion in trade,[33] and collaborate closely on climate talks[34] and WTO negotiations,[35] even as their corporate giants square up over ports and pipelines around South Asia and the Middle East. And the India-Pakistan rivalry now takes place between one state with a $225 billion economy and the means to pursue a strategy of asymmetric conflict under a nuclear umbrella, and another with an economy closer to $2 trillion and an acute sense that even a limited war could be devastating to its position as a centre of global commerce.

Yet in recent years, it is striking how far the original rationale for the "all-weather-friendship" is reasserting itself. Nehru said in 1962, "It is a little naïve to think that the trouble with China was essentially due to a dispute over some territories. It had deeper reasons. Two of the largest countries in Asia confronted each other over a vast border. They differed in many ways. And the test was whether any one of them would have a more dominating position than the other on the border and in Asia itself".[36] While the US-India deal had a significant impact on Chinese perceptions, India's rising power in the region and beyond was already a fact that China had to address, and the pattern of relations with many of Beijing's other neighbours since 2008 suggests that the rivalry would have intensified even without US involvement.

The difference between the spirit of the Jiang speech in 1996 and the spirit of a Chinese blogosphere that invented the term "South Tibet"[37] to refer to disputed territories in the Indian state of Arunachal Pradesh can be seen very directly among generations of South Asia specialists in the Chinese foreign policy community.[38] The older generation are almost exclusively India experts, and still stress the need for "balance" in China's relationships with the two South Asian powers. The younger generation is seeing the emergence of a growing number of Pakistan hands who generally believe that China should accept its rivalry with India and embrace the strategic relationship with Islamabad, for all of Pakistan's internal challenges. The spirit of the 1990s has certainly not evaporated: the older generation is, of course, the more senior in level, and Chinese sensitivities over issues such as Gwadar's potential use by the Chinese navy continue to reflect their influence. But the younger generation is more closely attuned to the broader trends in Chinese foreign policy. Those younger specialists see China in an environment of growing strategic competition, and are more inclined to believe that a forceful stance on territorial and other bilateral disputes is a natural reflection of the realities of China's new power position. After decades of dismissing alliance politics as a product of "Cold War thinking", they are also more comfortable with the prospect of Beijing developing closer friendships and alliances of its own to facilitate its strategic goals.[39]

If the US approach to India over the last decade has been one of de-hyphenation from Pakistan, China's has been one of re-hyphenation. [40]

The balancing role that Pakistan plays in Beijing's India policy goes well beyond forcing India to keep a large number of its troops and military assets focused on its western frontier, though that undoubtedly helps. It also ensures that India is kept off balance, distracted, absorbing diplomatic, political and strategic energies that could otherwise be directed towards China. It puts a constant question mark over India's aspirations to transcend its own neighbourhood. Every time a US Secretary of State declares support for New Delhi's policy to "Look East" towards the Pacific, China sees another reason to keep India on edge in its own backyard.[41] But while the spectrum of support that Beijing provides is a crucial enabling factor for many dimensions of Pakistan's policies towards India, there are important limits to what China is willing to tolerate. In the past, where conflict between the two sides could be more readily controlled and limited, China could back Pakistan without paying too high a price. In a context where conflicts may take on a nuclear dimension, and where the role of terrorists and non-conventional forces blurs the lines of responsibility, that is no longer true.

China would like to see the India-Pakistan relationship exist in a state of managed mistrust, where tensions can be navigated bilaterally, economic ties can flourish despite political antagonism, and the risks of full-scale war are very distant. In other words, a version of China's own relationship with India. An example of everything that China does not want to see came within a year of the two sides' becoming declared nuclear weapon states—and as a result, Beijing hung Pakistan out to dry.

Eighteen months after Jiang Zemin's 1996 visit to South Asia, India went ahead with five underground nuclear tests in Rajasthan, and Pakistan responded with six of its own in Balochistan, fundamentally changing the strategic situation in the region. In the lead up to May 1998, the relationship between New Delhi and Beijing had seemed to continue on its upswing. The Chinese chief of the general staff was on his first visit to India and plans were underway for further demarcation of the Line of Actual Control in Kashmir.[42] Even verbal attacks on China by the Indian Defence Minister—calling it "potentially threat number one"—were offset through private reassurances to Beijing.[43] In the end, China appeared to be riled less by the nuclear tests themselves than by the justifications given by the Indian Prime Minister, Atal Bihari Vajpayee. In the immediate aftermath, China's reaction was relatively restrained.[44] Then a letter sent by Vajpayee to President Clinton was leaked to the press, stating that the threat from China—and its assistance to Pakistan—had motivated them:

We have an overt nuclear weapon state on our borders, a state which committed armed aggression against India in 1962. Although our relations with that country have improved in the last decade or so, an atmosphere of distrust persists mainly due to the unresolved border problem. To add to the distrust that country has materially helped another neighbour of ours to become a covert nuclear weapons state.[45]

China moved from statements that it was "seriously concerned"[46] to declarations that India's tests showed "outrageous contempt for the common will of the international community", and expressions of "deep shock and condemnation".[47] Qian Qichen, China's Vice-Premier, angrily stated that "This gratuitous accusation by India against China is solely for [the] purpose of finding excuses for the development of its nuclear weapons."[48] The *People's Daily* claimed that it "wrecked in a single day the results of improving relations between these two countries over the past 10 years and more."[49] But China was not willing to sustain this performance for long. Beijing understood the rationale for India's weapons programme perfectly well and had no intention of letting the testing derail the relationship. In the short term it even appeared to create additional diplomatic space to exploit—Beijing saw a chance to use the rift opened between Washington and New Delhi to improve ties with both sides.[50] This calculation proved to be wrong. The mutual diplomatic energy invested between the United States and India following the tests, and President Clinton's visit barely two years later, helped to lay the groundwork for a far more dramatic breakthrough in relations under President George W. Bush. It was New Delhi's calculation that proved more accurate—its period of isolation would be brief, and the acquisition of nuclear weapons would not only serve its immediate strategic objectives, but also catalyze a shift in perceptions of its status into that of a first-rank power.

While the US, Chinese and Indian manoeuvring would continue over the next few years, Beijing faced the immediate issue of how to respond to Pakistan. First there was the ritual of a visit to Beijing from a visiting Pakistani delegation and the associated international speculation. The Pakistani Foreign Minister, Shamshad Ahmed, arrived on 19 May amid articles in the press claiming that he was seeking a "nuclear guarantee" from China in order to stop Pakistan pressing ahead with its own test.[51] One foreign ambassador in Beijing was quoted saying: "The Chinese can offer what no other country can offer, which is a public guarantee that they will reduce India to ashes if India dares to attack Pakistan. If they make this offer, which we should know fairly soon, there will be no need for Pakistan to test its own nuclear weapons."[52] This wholly implausible suggestion was neatly dismissed with the line from a Chinese researcher, "China is not a country that provides nuclear umbrellas to other countries".[53] In fact, other than a reassurance that China would not actually sanction Pakistan, Islamabad received very little. There was no encouragement given to Pakistan's testing and Jiang Zemin went as far as sending a letter to the Pakistani government, at Bill Clinton's urging, discouraging it from doing so.[54] Even diplomatic support was thin. China expressed its "deep regret" over the test in its swiftly issued statement, a clear contrast with its denunciations of India but very far from a tacit endorsement.[55] The Chinese permanent representative to the UN initially refused to support a Security Council resolution "strongly deploring"[56] Pakistan's action—lacking "clearance to support the statement from his superiors in Beijing"—but did so the next day.[57] In a nationally televised speech after the tests, Pakistan's Prime Minister Nawaz Sharif described "the manner in which China has supported us on this occasion" as "praiseworthy" and stated that "we are proud of our great neighbour".[58] It would have been churlish not to acknowledge the backing of the country that had done so much to give Pakistan its nuclear capabilities in the first place, but however understanding of Islamabad's position Beijing was in private, the manner of China's public support was distinctly lukewarm.

The nuclearization of South Asia had a profound effect on how China handled conflicts and near-conflicts in the region. While Beijing continued to provide backing to Pakistan outside the context of crises—ensuring, above all, that it had the military capabilities and technologies that it required—the Jiang-Clinton double act in 1998, which resulted in the "U.S.-China Joint Statement On South Asia" that June, would set the future pattern.[59] Washington and Beijing may not have seen eye to eye on the region but both sides at least agreed on the need to prevent all-out war. Given the stakes that were now involved—hundreds of millions of people threatened by the possibility of nuclear exchange, potentially even the entire population of Pakistan—Islamabad could not expect to count on China's support, especially if it brought the crises about itself. It would learn that lesson decisively within barely a year of its nuclear test.

In the spring of 1999, Pakistan infiltrated 1,000 troops from its para-military force, the Northern Light Infantry, across the Line of Control in Kashmir. The location was the inhospitable mountainous territory along the Himalayan borderlands above Kargil, where high-altitude warfare has been conducted by the two sides over the decades. Each year, the Indian and Pakistani forces retreated to their winter positions to reduce the strain of the extreme conditions on their respective forces. But this year, Pakistan put in motion a bold plan to seize the Indian positions and interdict the strategically important road running between Srinagar and Leh that functioned as the principal supply route for the Siachen Glacier.[60] It was intended that the troops, posing as Kashmiri militants, would go undetected until they had time to harden their positions, forcing India to accept the occupation of the disputed territory and redraw the LoC in Pakistan's favour. The incursion was intended to "right the wrong" of India's seizure of Siachen in 1984 and preempt any future land-grab on India's part. Like Operation Gibraltar and Operation Grand Slam in 1965, another set of audacious operations in Kashmir, it would involve only a handful of planners on the Pakistani side.[61] Like those 1965 operations, it would go horribly wrong. Unlike 1965, the ensuing war would take place between two nuclear-armed states, the only conflict in the world to do so since the Sino-Soviet skirmishes in 1969. And unlike in 1965, China would provide no backing whatsoever for Pakistan's position, working quietly with the United States to cut the political ground from under its feet.

General Musharraf, the lead instigator of the Kargil operation, was on a pre-arranged visit to Beijing at the end of May. At this stage, although the crisis had already started to escalate—India had detected the incursion unexpectedly quickly—the situation on the ground seemed to be holding in Pakistan's favour. The Indian army was suffering major losses and failed to displace the Pakistani force. Air combat operations had just started, but disastrously for India, which had already lost two planes.[62] Crucially, despite the discovery of a Pakistani soldier by the Indians, with his documentation and identity papers, Pakistan was still able to maintain the fiction that this was being conducted by *"mujahideen"* rather than conventional military forces.[63] Even then, it appeared that China was discouraging Pakistan from a confrontation that risked turning into all-out war.[64] But the Pakistanis hoped that a negotiated settlement with the Indians would serve to consolidate its gains and so— while disappointed at the lack of support—were not overly concerned by Chinese expressions of concern and hopes of de-escalation. However, Musharraf's Beijing visit was notable for quite another reason. While he was in Beijing, Indian intelligence intercepted a telephone call that he received from his chief of staff.[65] When the Pakistani Foreign Minister, Sartaj Aziz, met his Indian counterpart, Jaswant Singh, the next month, hoping to reach agreement on the retention of the newly acquired territory, Aziz was instead confronted with the tapes, which revealed the degree of the Pakistani army's complicity in the Kargil operation.[66] India—which subsequently released the transcripts of Musharraf's conversation to the media—took a firm position, demanding the withdrawal of Pakistani forces and a restoration of the status quo.[67] At the same time the situation on the ground was shifting against Pakistan, as the Indian army started recapturing positions.[68] The risk that the situation would actually escalate to nuclear exchanges was limited. There is some evidence that the two sides readied their warheads for possible use, though this is strongly denied by both Pakistan and India.[69] The possibility of nuclear war was, however, at the top of the list of concerns for the two powers that would be dealing with the denouement of the crisis—the United States, first and foremost, and China.

As the situation in Kargil started to run away from Pakistan's control, the securing of international support started to become Islamabad's only option, other than a serious escalation of the conflict or outright defeat. Pakistan hoped that it might at least be possible to use the crisis to place the Kashmir issue back on the international agenda, and draw in third party involvement.[70] With Chinese backing for its stance and American pressure on India, there was still the prospect of retrieving something from what was rapidly turning into another debacle. But the United States and China were speaking with remarkably similar-sounding voices. Musharraf informed a meeting of military chiefs at the beginning of June that the Chinese leadership had counselled Pakistan to withdraw troops.[71] The Pakistani foreign minister flew to Beijing to meet with Li Peng, China's second-ranked leader, who told him that Pakistan "should exercise self control and solve conflicts through peaceful means and avoid worsening the situation".[72] Tang Jiaxuan, the Chinese Foreign Minister, reiterated that "China had always supported Pakistan's principled stance on the issue of Kashmir, but at this time, it is of utmost importance to defuse tensions and find a way out of the prevailing situation."[73] Washington was conveying the same consistent message, at first in private to the Pakistani ambassador, then to Nawaz Sharif and General Musharraf, and then in public when it appeared that the private messages were not eliciting the necessary response.[74]

But the final crucial diplomacy took place when Nawaz Sharif made two last trips to Beijing and Washington. Sharif arrived in China on 28 June and the message delivered up and down the line by Jiang Zemin, Premier Zhu Rongji and Li Peng was absolutely clear—China would continue to provide support for Pakistan's long-term security and economic interests but Islamabad needed to de-escalate the situation and pull back its troops.[75] Chinese officials were in regular contact with their US counterparts as the visit progressed to make sure that there was no daylight between the two sides' positions.[76] Nawaz Sharif cut his trip short. When he made his next and last roll of the dice, an unscheduled visit to Washington, the Americans had already been well briefed on the content of the meetings in Beijing.[77] For good measure, on 1 July the Chinese foreign ministry made a public call for India and Pakistan to "respect the line of control in Kashmir and resume negotiations at an early date in accordance with the spirit of the Lahore declaration", a blow to Pakistan's position.[78] The Lahore declaration was an agreement that had been reached by India and Pakistan at a historic summit of the two prime ministers only a few months before Kargil, but its appearance in a Chinese foreign ministry statement was also a signal to Pakistan of the degree to which the United States and China were coordinating their lines. Nawaz Sharif arrived for his summit with Bill Clinton at Blair House with Pakistan almost completely isolated. The choice in the end was to fight a war with India bereft of support or to withdraw troops to the Line of Control. Pakistan chose the latter.

Unlike its stance during so many past crises, China's stance during Kargil could not be spun by Pakistan as "standing by in its hour of need". There were plenty of things that Beijing was willing to indulge but outright military adventurism was not one of them. It was a lesson to Pakistan that although nuclear weapons brought many benefits, one of the costs was that in circumstances of crisis the balance of China's calculus had now moved further towards the goal of preventing war rather than taking Pakistan's side in one. The crisis also set a pattern that would be repeated during the "Twin Peaks Crisis" of 2001/2 and after the Mumbai attacks in 2008—close Chinese coordination and cooperation with the United States.

The period after the militants' attack on the Indian parliament in December 2001, the first "peak", was the closest that South Asia has come to nuclear war, and has been described as "South Asia's Cuban Missile Crisis".[79] If the December attack had been successful, it would have killed much of India's elected leadership.[80] The prospect of war, which brought a million troops to the borders of the two countries, was sufficiently acute for US and British diplomats to be evacuated for fear of nuclear attack.[81] China's role was more limited than during Kargil, given that diplomatic efforts were not so uniformly directed at placing pressure on Pakistan, which wanted to de-escalate the situation too. The United States was trying to choreograph a series of high-level visits to the region in the hope that no attacks would take place while they were in town, and China was one of the countries that played along, sending the likes of Zhu Rongji, the Prime Minister, to India in the middle of the crisis.[82] As significant, however, was what it didn't do; as one US official argues: "The 'dog that did not bark' in all this was China—all we had to do was keep the Chinese informed…we had good relations with the Chinese and, for that matter, the Russians…. They did not stick their noses into it except to counsel moderation… This was a good example of the US working with Russia, after its unique relationship with India for so many years, and China. They let the US and EU lead [on this]."[83]

After the Mumbai attacks, in which 166 people were killed by Pakistani gunmen, China undertook something that resembled shuttle diplomacy—though both China and India were careful to stress that it was no such thing, and India made sure that the Chinese diplomat in question would have to split his trips to Pakistan and India with an interval in Beijing. Nothing would appeal to India less than Chinese "mediation". But He Yafei, the Vice Foreign Minister, was sent to the two countries with the explicit goal of reducing tension and the status of a special envoy.[84] Again, coordination was close between China and the United States in Beijing and New Delhi over the handling of the aftermath of the crisis. Also important was the issue of Chinese vetoes in the UN Security Council. At Pakistan's request, Beijing had been routinely blocking any attempt to impose sanctions on Jamaat-ud-Dawa,[85] the Lashkar-e-Taiba front organization, but in the aftermath of the attacks China made it clear to the Pakistanis that such blanket protection would no longer be provided.[86] The question was not whether LeT was responsible—the gunman who was captured quickly spilled the beans, and calls from LeT handlers in Karachi were intercepted as the attacks were going on—but what level of involvement the Pakistani army might have had.[87] Pakistan's permanent representative to the UN duly stated that he would accept the JuD sanctions decision when it came.[88] China made sure, however, that it prevented the addition of Hamid Gul, the former ISI chief, to the list of names that were approved by the UN Sanctions Committee.[89] Sanctioning LeT leaders was one thing, targeting their ISI backers was quite another.

Some analysts have given alternative readings of these crises. There are attempts to suggest that, in the circumstances, China's persisting with weapons sales—as it undoubtedly did—or making boilerplate statements about Sino-Pakistani cooperation amounted to warnings directed at India.[90] This is certainly not how it was interpreted in Washington, Beijing, or, most importantly, Islamabad. Pakistan is well aware that while it can sometimes expect understanding and a level of protection from whatever China views as excessive external pressure, its leash is a short one. The problem, as the crises have accumulated, is that while unprovoked Indian adventurism may elicit a different Chinese response, China—like everyone else—is now instinctively inclined to see some level of Pakistani culpability. As one Chinese expert explains:

If India invades Pakistan, we would be willing to respond. If India launches air strikes on Pakistan, we would be willing to respond. If India threatens Pakistan with nuclear weapons we may even be willing to extend our nuclear umbrella to Pakistan, though we wouldn't be the first ones to use the 'n-word'. But when it's Pakistan that causes the problem, we can't back them. What could we say after Mumbai? They obviously had military training. We couldn't defend that.[91]

As with its enduring assistance to Pakistan's nuclear programme, the most significant backing that China provides does not come in the midst of the latest crisis, but from the steady, long-term commitment to ensure that Pakistan has the capabilities it needs to play the role that China wants it to. The US-India deal changed China's sense of what that amounted to, how unabashed its pro-Pakistani tilt should be, and the degree to which it was willing to bend the rules in the process. No case illustrates this more obviously than China's direct response to the nuclear deal itself.

When the India exemption was put to the NSG, China was one of the club's most recent members.[92] Its application was received in January 2004, at the very same time as the Libyan government was handing over the Chinese bomb designs to the IAEA in A.Q. Khan's tailor's bags. Naturally, the question of China's nuclear cooperation with Pakistan was one of the chief subjects of discussion with existing members, and a source of uneasiness.[93] Like India, Pakistan was a non-signatory of the NPT, so the NSG rules would require China to refrain from supplying it with nuclear technology and fuel. The NSG had a provision, however, that allowed the fulfilment of existing contracts, even if they were with non-signatories. These agreements, the parameters of which needed to be spelled out to the other members, were then said to be "grandfathered" in.[94] In China's case, this grandfathering applied to the nuclear power plants that it had built, and was committed to build, at the Chashma complex in Punjab. In 2004, this amounted to the existing 300-MW reactor, Chashma-I, and the yet-to-be-built Chashma-II, another 300-MW reactor. NSG members were told that the construction of and the fuel supplies for the second reactor would be the end of China's nuclear exports to Pakistan.[95] But as the parameters of the US-India civil nuclear deal were announced in July 2005, Pakistan decided it wanted a counter-play. Musharraf's tactic was not to oppose the agreement but to push for a like-for-like deal.

The problem was that Pakistan's shocking proliferation record meant that the prospects for the United States offering one—it was put on the table for discussion by US officials a few years later before being very quickly taken off—or the NSG granting a similar exemption for Pakistan were virtually non-existent.[96] Pakistan's best option was the familiar one: China. During a state visit to China in February 2006, Musharraf requested Beijing's assistance with two more nuclear power plants, Chashma-III and IV.[97] China gave approving signals but by the time of Hu Jintao's state visit in November, when the Pakistanis had hoped to make a more formal announcement, it was evident that the Chinese were not willing to make any practical arrangements until the fate of the India deal was clear. Any attempts that Beijing made to raise the prospect with Washington were rebuffed. The United States stated that any further nuclear power plants would be in violation of the terms of China's commitments when it joined the NSG.[98]

In 2010, observers were surprised to discover that China National Nuclear Corporation had signed agreements to provide two new 300-MW reactors at Chashma, with Shanghai Nuclear Engineering Research and Design Institute providing the reactor design.[99] Initially there was scepticism among foreign officials and informed observers—Pakistan appeared to have been over-selling the prospects of a Chashma deal, and this may well have been more of the same.[100] But the agreements were real.[101] Attention quickly moved to the NSG and how China would approach the process of securing international consent. Its approach was simply to brazen it out. When China was asked for clarification at the NSG plenary in Christchurch, New Zealand, in June 2010 it responded a few months later with the position it has maintained ever since: that these reactors had been grandfathered in China's original 2004 agreement.[102] None of the other NSG members accepted this position. But there was little consensus about how to respond. While the violation was blatant, there was no real appetite for a serious fight with China over a couple of power plants under IAEA safeguards, and for many of those who had opposed the US-India deal in the first place there was a dose of "We told you so".[103] Some officials closely involved in the NSG process suggested that there was a tacit agreement that, even if China's justification was not really accepted, a blind eye would be turned if Chashma III and IV were really the end of the process.[104] Why a tacit agreement should hold when a formal agreement had been so readily disregarded was not entirely clear. And in March 2013, reports of a new Sino-Pakistani agreement to build another 1000-MW power plant, and potentially many more beyond that, emerged. A Chinese foreign ministry spokesperson clarified that it was—of course—grandfathered.[105]

What the United States had achieved with India in 2008 through a major diplomatic effort, and a series of commitments on India's part to bring it closer in line with the global nuclear order, China achieved for Pakistan by fiat, with no new commitments on Pakistan's part. Among Chinese experts and officials in private, there was virtually no attempt to suggest that it was anything other than a tit-for-tat.[106] The different situation—nuclear trade with India is open to all, whereas nuclear trade with Pakistan is essentially China's preserve—does China no harm, and was the most that Pakistan could have hoped for in the circumstances.

It was, nonetheless, a forceful display of China's willingness to provide backing to Pakistan in the face of uniform, albeit weak, opposition— and a demonstration to India that the United States would not care enough to make any serious efforts to stop it, or even to extract a price. In the early stages of the debate in the US government various options for responding to the Chashma nuclear deal were discussed, but it was concluded that there were bigger fish to fry in the US-China relationship, and, beyond *pro forma* objections, China was given a pass.[107] The military implications of the Chashma deal were minimal—civilian nuclear cooperation does provide a cover for cooperation with military applications, but this was not the point. It was less about balance of power than about balance of prestige. As one former Chinese foreign ministry official put it, "After the India deal, Pakistan needed this".[108]

For all the bilateral problems that exist between Beijing and New Delhi, many senior Indian officials continue to point to China's backing to Pakistan as their greatest source of concern.[109] Through its "all-weather" support, Beijing is perceived to play an enabling role for many of the most egregious elements of Pakistani behaviour. Beijing has undoubtedly been pressing Pakistan to stabilize its relationship with India and has encouraged it to improve trade ties with that goal in mind. The limits of China's backing for Pakistan are also clear. But so are the fundamentals of its encouragement for Pakistan's role in "containing" India. Even ostensibly consistent elements in Sino-Pakistan military-to-military relations have a heightened strategic importance for India nowadays. In the 1970s and 1980s, China's weapons supplies to Pakistan were significant largely because of Pakistan's lack of alternatives but, as Deng Xiaoping himself noted, they were "rather poor in quality".[110] While Chinese technology still lags behind some of the most advanced Western militaries in certain important respects, the gap has closed, and Pakistan benefits from some of the most up-to-date PLA equipment. Just as India was caught off guard when Pakistan tested the Ghauri missile in 1998, temporarily giving it greater reach than anything in India's own arsenal, New Delhi now needs to be constantly attuned not only to developments in Pakistan's indigenous capabilities, but also to ways in which it might benefit from developments in China's own military advances, from nuclear submarines to UAVs.[111]

As the Chashma deal demonstrated, recent years have also seen a renewed impetus to press ahead with sensitive projects that in the time of Jiang Zemin, or in the early years of Hu Jintao, might have prompted pause on Beijing's part. Now, from dam building in Kashmir to assuming operational control of Gwadar port, China is willing to act despite the reaction it will elicit in India. And while Sino-Pakistani military cooperation naturally provides the focal point for India's concerns, many of the supposedly economic projects are also seen through a strategic lens. In some cases, such as the claims about an influx of PLA troops to work on infrastructure-building in Gilgit-Baltistan, these anxieties are wildly overblown.[112] In others, as the fifth chapter of this book explains, the strategic nature of the supposedly economic initiatives is not only beyond doubt, it is almost the only reason they are going ahead.

In recent years, the slowdown in Indian economic growth and complications in US-India relations have undoubtedly eased Chinese concerns about India's take-off as a credible rival. The epilogue of the book details some of the Xi Jinping government's refreshed efforts to improve relations between the two sides, which have expanded even further since Narendra Modi's election victory. But this cannot obviate the fact that for Beijing, whatever the ebbs and flows in its bilateral ties with New Delhi, Pakistan's utility as a balancer, potential spoiler, and standing counterpoint to India's ambitions has never gone away.

If interactions between the United States, China, India and Pakistan were shaped entirely by geopolitical and economic considerations, the basic framework would be fairly clear: a group of countries pursuing hedged policies towards each other, using their rivals' opponents to gain leverage, trying to maintain sufficient levels of cooperation to continue to extract economic benefits even as strategic competition persists. But an additional cross-cutting element complicates matters, ensuring that instead, leaders on all sides have to lower their sights from the world of high strategy to the world of IEDs, Kalashnikovs, and jihadi propaganda videos: the militant factor. In this respect, for all the years of Sino-Pakistani friendship, China shares many of the same concerns as the United States and India. Yet as the next chapter lays out, Beijing's history with Pakistan and its militants is a complicated one: China was integrally involved in the thinking and practice of Pakistan's sponsorship of extremist networks in the first place, and has derived some strategic advantages from it ever since.

4

THE CHINESE WAR ON TERROR

China has a good understanding of almost everything in Pakistan, political, security or economic, that might affect the bilateral relationship, but there is one piece they just don't get: Islam.

Pakistani Sinologist, Islamabad 2011[1]

China is taking a risk by stoking up Uygur resentment while brushing aside Isa Alpetkin's model of peaceful Uygur national development. An old Turkish proverb has it that 'you can hit a Turk ten times, and he'll do nothing. The eleventh time, he'll kill you'.

Hugh Pope, in *Sons of the Conquerors: The Rise of the Turkic World*[2]

In April 2010, the International Department of the Chinese Communist Party (IDCPC) played host to an intriguing set of guests. A delegation from Pakistan's Jamiat Ulema-i-Islam (JUI) was making a rare visit to the IDCPC's gleaming modern headquarters off Fuxing Road in Beijing.[3] The JUI is part of the Sunni fundamentalist Deobandi movement, and most of its international relationships are flavoured accordingly. It was in JUI *madrassa*s that many of the Taliban leadership received their education,[4] JUI intermediaries helped facilitate the Taliban's military and financial relationships in the Gulf,[5] and JUI-linked militant groups helped provide logistical support to Osama Bin Laden while he was in Pakistan.[6] When its "in-depth consultations" with the CPC's polished vice-minister Liu Jieyi were publicly announced, along with the news that "both sides had agreed to promote party-to-party cooperation", it naturally raised a few eyebrows.[7] Certainly the JUI-F, whose leader, Maulana Fazal-ur-Rehman, headed the delegation, was a political party, but this was also a movement that acted as a barely concealed front for jihadi groups.[8] And their trip to Beijing was by no means a unique occurrence.

The previous year, a group of visitors from Pakistan's Jamaat-e-Islami (JI), led by Amir Qazi Hussain Ahmad, had made the same journey to west Beijing, and went a step further: signing a formal memorandum of understanding with the CPC.[9] The JI's friends are a shade less colourful than those of its sometime-rival, sometime-ally the JUI, but the agreement to cooperate on "security issues" with the Chinese Communist Party was eye-catching nonetheless. On returning to Pakistan, Hussain publicly defended the MOU on the grounds that it was a means "to invite atheists towards Islam".[10] From China's perspective, though, he was largely on-message. Officials noted with quiet satisfaction his statement that the JI "backed its stance on Taiwan, Tibet and Xinjiang" and his disavowal of "separatist Muslim movements".[11] Those with long memories knew that this was not the first time that Beijing had turned its attention to Pakistani religious parties. In the late 1990s, the likes of JI had been approached as part of a Chinese campaign to ensure that Uighur militant groups operating in Pakistan and Afghanistan were starved of support.[12] The new spate of invitations to China could only mean one thing: Beijing had a problem, and didn't believe its existing channels in Pakistan were doing enough to solve it.

A few weeks later, the nature of that problem was vividly illustrated. On 29 June 2010, Dubai's State Security Court found two ethnic Uighurs guilty of a terrorist plot. 35-year-old Mayma Ytiming Shalmo and 31-year-old Wimiyar Ging Kimili were each sentenced to ten years in prison after being caught in the early stages of a plan to attack the Dragon Mart, an enormous shopping mall on the outskirts of Dubai known as the largest Chinese trading hub outside mainland China.[13] It was the first recorded occasion that the group known as the "Turkistan Islamic Party" or "East Turkistan Islamic Movement" had attempted an operation outside its usual turf in China and Central Asia. The trial provided a rare insight into the workings of an organization whose continued existence people had doubted until a series of jihadi propaganda videos announced its return in the lead-up to the 2008 Beijing Olympics.

According to the court documents, Shalmo, the main plotter, had been recruited by the East Turkistan Islamic Movement (ETIM) during a pilgrimage to Mecca in 2006.[14] There he met a fellow pilgrim from China who spoke to him about "jihad against their country's government".[15] He travelled with the recruiter from Saudi Arabia to Pakistan, where he spent a year in an ETIM camp in Waziristan receiving weapons and explosives training, as well as instructions on making detonators from the group's electronics expert.[16] After being assigned to attack the Dragon Mart by ETIM's deputy commander, Shalmo flew from Islamabad to Dubai where he conducted scouting missions at the mall. He also secured the support of his English-speaking co-conspirator, Kimili, who accompanied him on shopping expeditions to purchase the bomb-making materials. They were paid for with $10,000 worth of funds, which had been sent from Turkey through a *hawala* network. Local authorities in Dubai appear to have been alerted by a suspicious wire transfer that the men made between the UAE, China, and Saudi Arabia, and by the Chinese embassy, which had been monitoring the two men as a result of their Uighur ethnicity.[17] When they were captured, police who raided Shalmo's home in Al Ain found a large collection of chemicals acquired from chemists and paint supply stores, including potassium permanganate, concentrated sulphuric acid, nitrol, acetone, and nitric acid. Chemical experts at the trial said that the device, if detonated, would have had an 80-metre blast radius. Their goal was to "draw the world's attention towards the Turkestani Muslims' cause in China".[18] But they claimed they had not planned to kill anyone.[19] The target was instead a symbolic one: a huge statue, standing outside the mall, of a Chinese dragon coiled around the globe.

Xinjiang is China's only Muslim-majority province and by some way its largest, encompassing more than a sixth of Chinese territory. Its land boundaries span Kyrgyzstan, Tajikistan, Kazakhstan, Russia, Mongolia, Afghanistan, India, and the entirety of China's 520km border with Pakistan. The region holds China's most substantial deposits of oil, coal and natural gas, as well as sensitive military installations such as the Lop Nur nuclear weapons testing facility. Since the 1990s, it has also been the source of the principal terrorist threat facing China, though the real scale and nature of that threat continue to be a matter of controversy. Xinjiang has long been wracked with tension between the Chinese state, the swelling ranks of Han Chinese migrants, and the native Uighur population. Aspirations towards greater autonomy or outright independence have never been far from the surface of political life in the province, and the consolidation of stable Chinese government authority has been a project under continuous challenge. One estimate suggests that central Chinese state control in Xinjiang has been effective for only 425 years over the course of two millennia,[20] and the province experienced stretches of independent rule as recently as the 1930s and 1940s.[21] In contrast to Tibet, the government in Beijing did not need to mount a full-scale military conquest when they incorporated it into the newly forged Chinese state between 1949 and 1950.[22] As in Tibet, though, grievances over economic opportunities, population control policies, and land rights have readily escalated, taking on a more potent ethnic, nationalist and religious character. This has been reinforced by periods of outright repression of linguistic, religious and cultural rights, and the routine designation of large numbers of young Uighur men as "separatists" or "terrorists", fair game for arrest, detention, or worse. Although these phases—such as the Cultural Revolution or the Strike Hard campaigns of the 1990s—have alternated with stretches of comparative liberality, the Uighurs' sense of themselves as an oppressed minority whose way of life is under attack by the Chinese state is pervasive, and political resistance has been the result.[23] For decades, this resistance was largely secular and pan-Turkic in inspiration,[24] but by the 1990s, the impact of the religious revival across the region[25] and the proliferation of transnational Islamist groups had started to give it a more explicitly Islamic character.[26]

Pakistan was at the heart of this shift. While the closest ethnic and cultural links and the simplest land-borders to cross for the Uighurs were in Central Asia, the Soviet presence there acted as a barrier to trade, travel, and—through its stymying of religious activity—Islamic influence, leaving China's south-western neighbour to become the main conduit instead. Until the 1980s, cross-border movement between China and Pakistan was limited by logistical constraints and political restrictions, but in the course of Deng Xiaoping's economic reforms the Uighurs were given newfound freedom to expand trade with neighbouring countries.[27] Pakistan was the obvious place to turn. The Karakoram

Highway had been completed in 1979 and was gradually opened up in the years that followed. A network of relationships between Pakistani and Uighur traders existed even before the new trade route was completed: many of the Uighurs who fled to Pakistan in the 1930s and late 1940s, fearing persecution from the Chinese Communist Party, had set themselves up in Gilgit, the Pakistani city midway between Kashgar and Islamabad. A modest two-way flow of products saw Uighur traders buy wool and leather goods, clothing, and cutlery and sell tea, hides, electrical equipment, and silk to the Pakistanis.[28] Even more important than the small-scale trade links, Deng's reform and opening process extended to religion. During the 1980s, China allowed Uighurs to travel through Pakistan to perform the Hajj or to receive religious education. Many of those who were studying in Pakistani universities and *madrassas* stayed on, and the transit points that were put in place for Uighurs on the way to Mecca, particularly in Rawalpindi, where they stopped while their Saudi visas were secured, became established centres of the Uighur community.[29] The total number of Uighurs in Pakistan was never large by comparison with Central Asia, but their presence and activities would become increasingly sensitive as Chinese concerns over extremist influence there grew.

The 1980s were a relatively peaceful time for Xinjiang, when Beijing saw economic and religious opportunities for the Uighurs as the best means to stabilize the province, but in the 1990s, that changed. Unrest in Xinjiang was already brewing by 1988, when small-scale protests in Urumqi erupted over the publication of a book that many Uighurs believed contained racial slurs.[30] Tensions over growing Han migration and economic inequality had started to increase, and, following the fall of the Soviet Union, China had reason to view the disturbances in the province as a serious strategic threat: as the Tajiks, Turkmens, Kazakhs and Uzbeks all established their own independent Central Asian homelands, Beijing feared that separatist sentiment in Xinjiang would strengthen.[31] The expansion of new transit and trade routes across the former Soviet republics made it far easier to move across the long-closed borders, giving easier access to overseas Uighur communities and other new pockets of support and influence.[32] One of the most problematic cases was Tajikistan. The country was convulsed by civil war almost immediately after achieving its independence in 1991, drawing in Central Asian militants who would later give vital backing to their

Xinjiang counterparts. The near-collapse of state authority made it a major corridor for weapons, drugs, and militants, running all the way through from Afghanistan to China's western borders.[33]

Beijing's concerns went beyond the practical support that might be extended to separatist groups—they were also worried about an Islamic revival in Xinjiang. Islam had become a rallying point for Uighur protests, which officials increasingly pinned on the influence of "illegal religious activities".[34] The result was a cycle of unrest, violence and repression. Thousands are estimated to have fled from the often brutal campaigns of arrests, raids, executions and extra-judicial killings that took place.[35] The "Strike Hard, Maximum Pressure" campaign is described by one Xinjiang expert as having "condemned hundreds of men and women to death by shooting, used torture to obtain confessions, jailed thousands, and stripped many others of the right to work or to practice Islam—all in the name of quelling 'splittism', religious extremism, and terrorism".[36] Many found shelter in neighbouring Kazakhstan or Kyrgyzstan, or went further afield. Some were caught up in the war in Tajikistan.[37] Others made their way to a Pakistan that was now awash with the men, money, machine-guns and sense of mission left over after the *mujahideen*'s battles against the Soviets. Inside and outside Xinjiang, the cocktail of political tension and violence threatened to have a convulsive impact. A leaked Chinese government document in 1998 listed Uighur independence movements as the main threat to the stability of the Chinese state.[38]

Many of the Uighurs who became embroiled in the world of militancy across this period appear to have had little intention of doing so. In some cases, extremist groups controlled the crucial transit routes they used through Central Asia. In other instances, young men heading to Pakistani *madrassas* to seek religious education, or simply a new life away from the Chinese government's crackdowns, arrived at what were essentially way-stations for jihadi recruitment. The stories of two Uighurs from Kashgar who were captured together in Afghanistan in 1999 and sent to a POW camp in the Panjshir valley are representative. Nur Ahmed went to Pakistan to study in a *madrassa* in Rawalpindi, which provided him with free board and lodging.[39] After six months of Quranic memorization—Ahmed spoke no Urdu or Arabic and so could understand neither the text nor his teachers—his principal encouraged him to go to fight in Afghanistan. A Taliban representative in Peshawar paid for his travel by car to Kabul where Ahmed received twenty days of light weapons training before being sent to the front. He was soon captured. With him was Abdul Jalil, who made his way to Pakistan via Karachi and ended up in Kashgarabad, a large building and guesthouse in Rawalpindi that was run and financed by fellow Uighurs. He was told that a *madrassa* in Kabul would give him free tuition, board and lodging and duly headed there with three other Uighurs. After two months he was instructed to go and fight with the Taliban. He received only five days of weapons training before being sent to the front, where he too was quickly captured. Both Jalil and Ahmed were told that they would be fighting against Americans and Russians in Afghanistan. They were instead being sent into the middle of a civil war.[40] Similar stories of naive-sounding young men stumbling into trouble crop up again and again in the Guantánamo Bay case files. Of all the nationals who were detained in the first US military campaign in Afghanistan in 2001–2, Chinese Uighurs were seen to pose the least threat of resuming their involvement in militant activities, and US courts ordered every single one of them—twenty-two in all—released.[41]

China's credibility problem when it comes to Uighur "terrorists" goes well beyond the fact that so few of them seemed to be a credible threat. Beijing's tendency to attribute almost any act of violence in Xinjiang to "separatists", to claim malevolent intent behind even the most peaceful of protests, and to criminalize political groups such as the World Uighur Congress and the East Turkistan Information Centre leaves the line between the terrorist, the activist and the aggrieved citizen permanently blurred.[42] However, this well-founded scepticism about Beijing's approach should not obscure the fact that there is, and has long been, organized militant opposition to Chinese rule in Xinjiang.

The first major clandestine opposition group had pan-Turkic and Marxist affiliations, rather than Islamic ones. Formed in 1967, the Eastern Turkistan People's Revolutionary Party was composed of young Uighurs and former officials from the short-lived East Turkistan republic. It was backed by the KGB, which provided weapons, funds and radio transmitters,[43] and advocated an "independent, secular, and communist East Turkistan oriented towards the Soviet Union".[44] The main instigator of insurrectionary activities through the late 1960s and the 1970s, deemed at one point to be the most serious "counter-revolutionary separatist conspiracy"[45] since the founding of the PRC, it would eventually fade from the scene following the arrests of its leaders and the withdrawal of Soviet support.[46] Taking over its mantle was the forerunner of the East Turkistan Islamic Movement: the East Turkistan Islamic Party (ETIP). Like its Marxist predecessor, ETIP also tapped into pan-Turkic currents and sought an independent homeland, but it was closely associated with the Islamist revival in Xinjiang. It first came to prominence during an uprising at Baren, near Kashgar, in April 1990. Like many of the descriptions of militant activity in Xinjiang throughout the decade, accounts of the Baren incident are contradictory, and seem to reflect competing political objectives over how the scale of the violence, the motives behind it, and the response from the Chinese government should be seen.[47] The local ETIP leader was a man named Zäydin Yusuf, who had recruited members of the party at mosques in Southern Xinjiang,[48] which were used to "disseminate a call to arms".[49] Hundreds of men marched on government offices in Baren, protesting against everything from the Chinese government's policies of forced abortions for Uighur women to the exploitation of Xinjiang's resources, chanting the *shahada* and in some instances jihadi slogans.[50] The Chinese government sent in troops but in the resulting riots the Uighur fighters captured rifles and ammunition. In the end, large-scale military deployments and even the PLA Air Force were required to crush the mini-insurrection.[51] ETIP appear to have suffered from the subsequent clampdown, with many of its activists arrested or killed.[52]

The Chinese government held other Islamist groups responsible for the attacks that plagued Xinjiang in the intervening years. A bus attack at Chinese New Year in 1992, for instance, was attributed to the "Shock Brigade of the Islamic Reformist Party".[53] The "East Turkistan Democratic Islamic Party" was credited with bomb attacks that killed four victims in 1993.[54] A series of bus bombings in Urumqi on the day of Deng Xiaoping's funeral in February 1997—the last major attack in Xinjiang for a decade—was pinned on the "East Turkistan National Unity Alliance".[55] But it was ETIP that was the reference point for future generations of militants, who would hark back to Zäydin Yusuf and the Baren rebellion in their propaganda videos. When the organization was reconstituted, it was in a new base: Afghanistan.

Uighurs had been involved in the *mujahideen*'s campaign in Afghanistan in the 1980s but only in small numbers, and not in separate fighting units. One visitor to the training camps they attended in Khost and Paktia described them as "lost in the huge crowd of foreign militants. They didn't have a very visible presence."[56] It did nonetheless mean that a cadre of Uighurs were radicalized and integrated into a network of relationships with other militants. These relationships would prove useful for ETIP's new leader, Hasan Mahsum, who is believed to have taken over the leadership of the party in 1997. Mahsum was born in Shule County, in the far west of Xinjiang, and studied at an Islamic school established by one of ETIP's founders.[57] He was imprisoned for several months as a result of his role in the Baren uprising, and following a subsequent arrest in October 1993 on terrorism charges, he was sentenced to three years of re-education through labour.[58] After another arrest during the first Strike Hard campaign in 1996, he finally left Xinjiang. His travels took him to Saudi Arabia, Turkey and Pakistan, where he sought funding and support from sympathizers for the ETIP's activities, without a great deal of success.[59] Taliban-led Afghanistan proved more fertile territory. The Taliban granted Mahsum an Afghan passport[60] and allowed him to set up training camps, as well as running the operations of the group out of Kabul, which in 1998 became the headquarters of the group now known as the East Turkistan Islamic Movement (ETIM).[61] China claims that ETIM sent "scores of terrorists" into China, establishing bases in Xinjiang and setting up training stations and workshops to produce weapons, ammunition and explosives.[62] The group's capacity to operate effectively in Xinjiang remains a point of debate, but the scale of its Afghan base was in less doubt: ETIM itself claims to have trained its members in camps in Khost, Bagram, Herat, and Kabul.[63]

It was not only ETIM activities in Afghanistan that were a problem for China. It was also the Central Asian militants who worked with them, whose backing would later prove essential to the group's survival. The most important of these was the Islamic Movement of Uzbekistan (IMU). The organization was founded by Tohir Yuldashev, an Islamic leader from the Ferghana Valley, and Juma Namangani, a former Soviet paratrooper who had fought as a conscript in Afghanistan in the Soviet forces.[64] The two men were initially based in Uzbekistan, but they spent much of the 1990s operating from outside the country. Namangani, who ran the IMU's military operations, was heavily engaged in the civil war in Tajikistan, where he led a group that included Chechens, Arabs, Afghans,

Tajiks—and Uighurs—in opposition to the Dushanbe government.[65] Yuldashev spent the same period in Peshawar, where he built relations with the Iranian, Pakistani, Saudi, Turkish and Russian intelligence agencies, transnational terrorist groups, and Pakistani militants and financiers, including the JUI.[66] Yuldashev and Namangani formally established the IMU in 1998, and moved their operational base to Afghanistan. They continued to launch forays into Uzbekistan, Kyrgyzstan and Tajikistan from bases in the north of the country, as well as fighting on the Taliban's behalf.[67] From China's perspective, however, the greatest problem they posed was their capacity to provide a network and support base for an array of other Central Asian militants. The IMU would ultimately become ETIM's hosts, first in Afghanistan and later in Pakistan, where the two groups ended up becoming virtually intertwined.[68]

China's response to the Uighur militants' growing connections to extremists across the region was to internationalize its Strike Hard campaign. Governments in Central Asia were pressed by Beijing to clamp down on the "three evils": terrorism, separatism, and religious extremism.[69] The founding in 1996 of the Shanghai Five, which later evolved into the Shanghai Cooperation Organization, was in large part a product of Beijing's concerns about Uighur militants and their Central Asian backers.[70] For much of the 1990s, Kazakhstan, Tajikistan, and Kyrgyzstan—the original members, with Russia and China—were the principal focus, and China provided aid and military support to facilitate their efforts.[71] In the late 1990s, as ETIM established its base in Afghanistan, China's campaign stepped up in south-west Asia too. The task in Afghanistan and Pakistan, however, was a more complex one for the Chinese than that of bolstering the tough, secular-minded Central Asian states in their crackdowns on religious militants (and other opponents that were tarred with the same brush). For Pakistan, these militants were a vital asset of its intelligence services, and in Afghanistan, they comprised its government.

China has been intimately involved in Pakistan's history of using irregular forces as an instrument of its military strategy. For all the early disagreements between Zhou Enlai and Ayub Khan about the utility of guerrilla warfare, it proved to be one of the two sides' closest areas of tactical cooperation. In the early 1960s, the Pakistani army launched a series of studies of the concept of low intensity conflict.[72] While Mao and Zhou had urged Pakistan to do so in the context of a defensive strategy in a war with India, the Pakistanis' greatest interest in Maoist military doctrine was from the offensive side: a people's war in Kashmir. Pakistan had already used non-state actors in Kashmir—largely Pashtun tribal militias—in the first Indo-Pakistani war in 1947, but the 1965 and 1971 wars involved more systematic attempts to put the approach into practice.[73] In 1965, companies of irregulars were infiltrated across the Line of Control in the (mistaken) belief that local forces would rise up in support.[74] And in 1971, irregular forces were raised in East Pakistan, some of which were believed to be responsible for among the war's worst atrocities.[75]

China and Pakistan even collaborated directly. For much of the 1960s and 1970s, Beijing armed and trained insurgencies in India's northeast, such as those among the Nagas and the Mizo.[76] The Manipuri rebels, who received training in Tibet, named their militia force the "People's Liberation Army" in tribute to their instructors.[77] China even dallied with the idea of aiding the Naxalites, India's Maoist movement, a group of whom met with Mao Zedong and intelligence chief Kang Sheng in 1967.[78] Pakistan's support, mostly run out of East Pakistan, went back even further, and it was the Pakistani military that would make some of China's early connections. In 1962, when one of the Naga militants stopped over in Karachi en route to meet with the exiled leader of his group in London, his Pakistani hosts introduced him to a "Chinese friend", who promised aid and military assistance.[79] Five years later, China came through on its promise: Beijing went on to train groups of Naga fighters in western Yunnan, who made their way there through the jungles of northern Burma[80] and returned to India equipped with assault rifles, machines guns, and rocket launchers.[81] In May 1969, China and Pakistan established a coordination bureau "to oversee the supply of arms, training and funding" to the various insurgent groups.[82] While formal state assistance to the north-eastern insurgencies was cut off under Deng Xiaoping, the Chinese military has never backed away entirely, with arms continuing to flow from China too freely to be dismissed as the work of a few rogue salesmen. The seizure of a mammoth haul of illicit Chinese weapons in Bangladesh in 2004, destined for Naga and Assam groups, was the biggest in Bangladeshi history.[83]

On an even larger scale, however, and of deeper lasting consequence, was the joint effort to help the *mujahideen* in the 1980s against the Soviet Union. Beijing supplied a large share of the guns and ammunition that would arm the *mujahideen*'s efforts, paid for by the United States and Saudi Arabia, and managed by Pakistan, whose intelligence services ran the campaign, trained the fighters, and mostly controlled who received the weapons.[84] For the United States and China the primary focus was the Soviet Union, but Pakistan had a longer-term agenda, one even more central to its national goals. Not only could the Pakistani military systematically test out the use of irregular forces in Afghanistan, a country where it was keen to acquire "strategic depth", but the influx of weapons, men and money could be readily redeployed eastward.[85]

Kashmir had been in General Zia's mind from the very inception of the war. In early 1980, Zia met Maulana Abdul Bari, a JI leader who had been involved in the 1965 operations.[86] He told Bari that the Afghanistan campaign was a means to "prepare the ground" for a larger conflict in Kashmir, and that ammunition and financing from it would be diverted to the Kashmiri cause.[87] When asked who in the Afghan campaign would receive the biggest share of arms and financial assistance, he replied: "Whoever trains the boys from Kashmir".[88] JI and Jammu and Kashmir Liberation Front volunteers would indeed receive training at ISI camps in the 1980s.[89] When the opportunity came to redirect resources in Afghanistan more decisively towards Kashmir after the Soviet withdrawal, it was the camps in Afghanistan under the control of Gulbuddin Hekmatyar's Hizb-e-Islami, Pakistan's favoured faction among the *mujahideen*, that provided the initial flow of fighters. The training facilities in Paktia brought together the Arab, Afghan and Kashmiri guerrillas who would later show up in Indian territory with the very same Chinese-made weapons that had been supplied to arm the anti-Soviet campaign.[90] The United States was sufficiently concerned about the redirection of arms that it warned the Indians about the risk to politicians and government officials visiting Kashmir, who they feared might be targeted by the long-range sniper rifles that had been sent to Pakistan to kill Soviet military officers.[91]

The cross-pollination of personnel, financing, training, weapons, and ideology between these different militant organizations—Afghan, Kashmiri, sectarian, and global terror groups such as Al Qaeda—would eventually metastasize beyond the control of the Pakistani government, but for much of the 1990s they worked hand in glove. The legacy of the 1980s was not simply the rise of well-trained, well-armed militant groups, but the rise of the state apparatus to manage them. Across the period, the ISI would emerge as the force it is today, changing from a backwater institution to a financially flush and autonomous powerhouse in Pakistan, which established and consolidated control over the Kashmiri militant groups and many of the forces involved in the Afghan campaign.[92] This was not a one-way process. Over time, the line between the objectives of the Pakistani state and those of the Islamic militants blurred. Some individuals in the security services started to demonstrate as much affinity with the extremists, all the more so when they became "former" agents who maintained close liaison relationships with both the militants and their previous employer.[93] As Hamid Gul, one of the leading examples of this phenomenon, stated when asked about his plans to maintain training camps for the *mujahideen* after the Soviet withdrawal: "We are fighting a jihad, and this is the first Islamic international brigade in the modern era. The Communists have their international brigades, the West has NATO, why can't the Muslims unite and form a common front?"[94] At the time he was still the chief of the ISI.

This creeping reverse influence took place in concert with Zia ul Haq's broader Islamization agenda. One of his first moves as army chief was to change the army's motto from Jinnah's "Unity, Faith, and Discipline" to "Faith, Piety, and Struggle in the Path of Allah".[95] Zia allowed members of the fundamentalist organization Tablighi Jamaat to preach at the Pakistani Military Academy, encouraged commanders to join their troops in congregational prayers, and instituted assessments of troops' religiosity.[96] He changed the recruitment patterns for the military, drawing in larger numbers of lower-middle class recruits—who were seen as more vulnerable for targeting by JI and other religious organizations—rather than relying on the traditional military families.[97] The lines were perhaps at their fuzziest in the case of the Taliban. In one sense the Taliban were the ultimate ISI asset, financed and militarily supported by literally hundreds of Pakistani advisers in their campaign to consolidate control in Afghanistan.[98] In many other respects, though, they exacerbated precisely the problems they were supposed to solve—fostering Pashtun nationalism rather than calming it, bolstering militants in Pakistan rather than redirecting their attention, and ideologically influencing elements in the Pakistani army rather than operating under their control.[99] One retired ISI officer said that the ISI's operatives in Afghanistan "became more Taliban than the Taliban".[100] Beijing would ultimately come to view these developments—the rise of Pakistani-supported militant groups, the changing nature of the Pakistani army, and the "Talibanization" of Pakistan—with greater and greater unease, but that was a long way off. In the 1990s, while China treated growing extremism in the region as a matter of concern, it still seemed that the nexus between the militants and the Pakistani military could be used to its advantage.

Despite their religious bonds, the situation of the Uighurs has hardly been a *cause célèbre* in Pakistan or the wider Muslim world. Located at the far fringes of Islam's heartlands, "East Turkestan" does not even feature on many purported maps of the Caliphate. What concern there is for the Uighurs' situation has tended to come mostly from Turkic compatriots in Central Asia, Germany, and Turkey itself, rather than from South Asia or the Middle East. In Pakistan, Xinjiang's low status in the hierarchy of popular causes is compounded by the fact that relations with China are seen as simply too important to allow a few disaffected Uighurs to get in the way. Even Pakistani religious groups have been willing to minimize their significance for the sake of ties with Beijing— as Hussain Haqqani notes: "Magazines and newspapers associated with the Jamaat-e-Islami amplified the theme that Muslims around the world had an obligation to free their coreligionists from Soviet communist occupation. Muslims in Eastern Turkistan—China's Xinjiang province—were also initially identified for liberation, but the development of close ties between China and Pakistan made their liberation a lesser priority."[101] Mosque closures, destruction of religious texts, restrictions on Islamic education, bans on fasting during Ramadan, and other measures meted out to the Uighurs by the Chinese state over the years have never mobilized angry street protests in Pakistan in the way they would if a Western power were responsible.[102] There have been attempts to reconcile this uncomfortable trade-off between religious solidarity and geopolitical necessity. Pakistani criticism of the Uighurs' irreligiousness or fondness for drink (for which Uighurs criticize Pakistanis too) casts aspersions on their standing as Muslims.[103] Conspiracy theorists claim that Turkistan separatists are supported by the United States or India in order to drive a wedge between China and Pakistan.[104] Either way, when it comes to dealing with the Uighurs, Islamabad has always been willing to act at Beijing's behest.

At times the Pakistani government has addressed the issue very directly, whether cracking down on Uighurs whose terrorist credentials were at best thin, or working to restrict the flows of people, propaganda and arms across the border to China. In the late 1990s, the community centres in Rawalpindi, Kashgarabad and Hotanabad were closed down, leaving hundreds of Uighurs homeless.[105] Uighur students, whom China claimed were responsible for a series of bombings in 1997, were deported,[106] and there are claims that the Pakistani military executed a number of Uighurs at a training camp.[107] The ecosystem of Islamic militancy in the region that Pakistan fostered was more open to their Uighur co-religionists, however. Extremist groups in Pakistan and Afghanistan may not always have been willing to support terrorist operations in China itself, or to take up the "East Turkistan" cause in a serious way, but they have been happy to welcome the additional recruits to the jihadi movement. The Pakistani government sought to manage this, translating its relationships with militants into a channel that could be utilized on Beijing's behalf. The ISI used its influence to dissuade the groups that it sponsored from directing any of their energies towards China. It also facilitated meetings for Chinese officials and intelligence agents to strike deals with whomever they needed to in order to isolate the Uighur militants from potential supporters among extremist organizations in Pakistan and Afghanistan.[108]

As a result of its own concerns with domestic terrorism, China has often been portrayed as if it is naturally aligned with states facing similar threats. In many respects, however, its security has been parasitic on the fact that these groups consider the United States, India and other countries to be higher priority targets. Beijing's preference has been to make offers, not enemies. Its pitch to Islamic militants in the region generally took the same form: don't bother us and we won't bother you. Depending on who China was talking to, money or the offer of small arms supplies might be put on the table too.[109] In return, Beijing expected that not only would the groups themselves refrain from targeting China, they would also refuse any support to Uighur organizations that did.[110] China's efforts were wide-ranging. At one end of the spectrum were the Pakistani religious parties who trooped to Beijing in 2000 to declare their support and friendship; their *madrassas* and training camps had been used by Uighurs,[111] and China wanted that stopped.[112] With the Taliban, whose relationship with Beijing is explained in greater depth in Chapter 6, China reached an understanding: Afghanistan would not be used as a base for ETIM attacks, and Beijing would gradually move towards the normalization of relations with the largely isolated Taliban government, including vital economic support.[113] Chinese intelligence agents are even believed to have met Al Qaeda to sound out its intentions.[114] In the 1990s those intentions were certainly not hostile. Osama Bin Laden went as far as to refer to China in his public statements, claiming in 1997: "The United States wants to incite conflict between China and the Muslims. The Muslims of Xinjiang are being blamed for the bomb blasts in Beijing. But I think these explosions were sponsored by the American CIA. If Afghanistan, Pakistan, Iran and China get united, the United States and India will become ineffective." He went on to say, "I often hear about Chinese Muslims, but since we have no direct connection with people in China and no member of our organisation comes from China, I don't have any detailed knowledge about them."[115] For Al Qaeda, as for other jihadi groups, the default position was that it was better to avoid taking Beijing on. Not only did they have quite enough enemies already, but as Bin Laden's remarks suggest, there was also the sense that China and the jihadis had a couple of adversaries in common.

At the turn of the millennium, developments seemed to be moving in China's favour. Beijing had reached a *modus vivendi* with the Taliban, ensuring that ETIM was largely forced to embed itself with the IMU rather than running its own autonomous camps.[116] Governments across the region had supported China's crackdown on even peaceful Uighur political activities. Rather than taking up the Uighur cause, militants across the region seemed willing to give China a pass. The large-scale attacks in Xinjiang that had taken place virtually every year in the preceding decade had stopped in 1999.[117] Not only did Beijing's brutal pacification campaign appear to have worked, it did so without resulting in any serious blowback in the wider Islamic world. The 9/11 attacks did not derail these developments—instead, they just presented a golden opportunity to work the other side. After years of fruitless lobbying by the United States and other sceptical foreign governments to designate ETIM as a terrorist group, the credibility threshold shifted. In January 2002 the Information Office of the State Council, the equivalent of China's cabinet, released a dossier entitled "East Turkistan Terrorist Forces Cannot Get Away with Impunity" that still provides the basis for many of the claims circulated about them today.[118] The document lists bombings, assassinations, industrial sabotage and other attacks resulting in 162 deaths over the prior decade. Many experts on Xinjiang question the veracity of its claims, but in August 2002, US Deputy Secretary of State Richard Armitage announced that the United States considered ETIM a terrorist organization and would freeze any assets it held in the United States.[119] In September, the UN followed suit.[120] The group was now on the run anyway, as the US invasion of Afghanistan destroyed its base of operations. ETIM's basic camp at Tora Bora—described in one report as "a primitive hamlet with only one Kalashnikov rifle"—where some Uighurs received simple training, was rolled up and a number of its residents ended up in Guantánamo Bay.[121] The IMU itself was also significantly depleted, with many members killed in Northern Afghanistan, including the group's leader, Juma Namangani.[122] Others, including most of those at Tora Bora, fled across the border to the Federally Administered Tribal Areas of Pakistan, which would become ETIM's home for the next decade.[123]

The forced escape across the Hindu Kush was a mixed blessing for China. In theory, it meant that the Chinese could now go through the Pakistanis directly when they wanted a problem dealt with, rather than through a more complex set of interactions with the Taliban. 2003 saw an early success that seemed to confirm this view—ETIM's leader, Hasan Mahsum, was killed by the Pakistani army during a raid in South Waziristan.[124] The more restricted geographical focus—Uighur militants were almost entirely based in a single FATA agency—made it easier for China to establish its own intelligence networks to inform on them.[125] But the location posed other problems. The Pakistani security forces were very reluctant to conduct operations there on a significant scale, lest it upset the delicate balance of its relationships with various tribes and militant groups in the region. The dense network of terrorist organizations in FATA also provided a base from which ETIM could professionalize and project itself more effectively. For all the Chinese government's claims about the threat it posed, its track record at the time was extremely thin. The very point at which ETIM was designated a terrorist organization in 2002 was the point at which many experts asked whether it existed at all.[126] Some Chinese counter-terrorism experts started to raise more concerns about Hizb-ut-Tahrir—a transnational organization that was expanding its influence in Xinjiang[127]—than ETIM, which seemed to have been virtually wiped off the map. It would be six years before it proved otherwise.[128]

In 2008 a group called the Turkistan Islamic Party (TIP) hit the airwaves. In a series of videos, a masked man, believed to be either ETIM's "overall" leader, Abdul Haq al-Turkestani, or its military commander, Emeti Yakuf, appeared making threats to the Olympic Games that were due to be held in Beijing later that year.[129] They featured burning Olympics logos and hooded men in military fatigues, who warned visitors ("particularly the Muslims") not to attend the Games.[130] The propaganda material and videos were notable for being coordinated by Al Fajr, the jihadist media forum run by Al Qaeda, giving them a reach—including Arabic translations—that had previously eluded the group.[131] That same year, China would also experience the first successful terrorist attacks in Xinjiang in a decade.

There were a couple of false starts. In January 2008, Chinese authorities claimed to have raided a bomb-making facility and arms cache in Urumqi.[132] Then, in March, a flight from Urumqi to Beijing had to make an emergency landing in Lanzhou after a 19-year-old Uighur woman was caught leaving two soft-drink cans filled with petrol in a toilet cubicle, attracting the attention of a flight attendant who noticed the smell and the woman's "suspiciously emotional state".[133] Reports citing Chinese sources claim that the woman and her Central Asian travelling companion were carrying Pakistani passports, and that a third member of the group, who escaped, was a Pakistani national.[134] "This was a well prepared, meticulously planned, tightly coordinated, terror attack activity," asserted the *Global Times* newspaper, stating that as a frequent traveller through Urumqi airport, the woman had "lulled the security guards into complaisance".[135] Subsequent accounts suggest that the woman, Guazlinur Turdi, had "spent a significant amount of time in Pakistan" and that the third suspect, a Pakistani man who was detained a week later, had "masterminded" and "instigated" the attack.[136]

Pakistan, which was already coordinating closely with China on security for the Olympics, made an additional public show of assistance. General Musharraf, who was due to visit China shortly afterwards, included a stopover in Urumqi at Beijing's request, a visible demonstration of support for Chinese policy in Xinjiang.[137] Pakistani officials claimed to have blocked "all the key border crossings" between Pakistan and the restive province in order to "prevent militants coming into the country".[138]

Veteran China watchers remained suspicious: the low-tech plane incident sounded as if it might have been inflated by the Chinese government to justify heavy-handed security measures around the Olympics or another crackdown in Xinjiang. Yet, low-tech methods of this sort were in fact the hallmark of a new wave of attacks.

On 4 August 2008, four days before the opening ceremony of the Games, two men armed with knives and explosives drove a truck into a squad of border patrol police officers in Kashgar, killing sixteen of them.[139] The driver attempted to throw a home-made explosive device at the group, but it blew up in his hand. Another attacker hurled primitive explosives at the gates of the police station. Two more incidents in Western Xinjiang—a stabbing of security officers and a bomb attack on government offices—took place within the next ten days.[140] The last effective attack in Xinjiang had been in 1999; the subsequent five years saw a series of incidents involving knives, axes, and primitive bombs directed at government installations and ordinary Han Chinese in Kashgar, Hotan and Turfan.[141] Now, after a long hiatus it seemed that terrorist violence had returned to Xinjiang. "We find these tactics much more difficult to deal with," noted a Chinese Public Security Bureau official working on counter-terrorist strategy in the province. "We have been able to stop the larger plots in the past but these attacks are harder to predict."[142]

What was far less clear was whether the Turkistan Islamic Party was actually involved. The primitive nature of the attacks was effective, and may have required some level of coordination and planning, but certainly didn't require weapons training in Waziristan. In their pre-Olympics propaganda videos, the TIP had claimed responsibility for various small-scale explosions in cities such as Shanghai, Kunming and Guangzhou, but even the Chinese government, often so eager to pin blame on nefarious East Turkistan separatists, drew the line at allowing the group to take credit for bus fires that it had nothing to do with.[143] The TIP made no comment on the 2008 attacks, and the presumption was that they were indigenous in nature rather than imports from Pakistan. Two years later, however, after a set of attacks in Kashgar, the eagerness to blame—and to take credit—was far more pronounced.

On 30 July 2011, two knife-wielding men hijacked a truck and drove it into groups of people at a busy Kashgar night-market before jumping out and stabbing pedestrians. At least eight people were killed before the crowd managed to overpower the attackers, one of whom they beat to death.[144] The following day, a group of twelve Uighur men attacked a restaurant in "Gourmet Food Street", a Han Chinese area, throwing explosives into the crowded eatery and then attacking the fleeing patrons with knives.[145] At least six people were killed before police arrived at the scene. The finger-pointing began almost immediately. The Kashgar city government quickly claimed that an initial probe had showed that one of the men involved had confessed to receiving explosives and firearms training in ETIM camps in Pakistan.[146] This was unusual—while the Chinese government was more than happy to attribute attacks to ETIM, the fact that the group's training facilities were on Pakistani territory was a fact that was normally politely glossed over. It was sufficiently serious for the ISI chief, Ahmed Shuja Pasha, to fly to China to discuss the situation in the immediate aftermath of the attacks.[147] Five Uighurs were subsequently arrested in Pakistan and deported to China.[148] The TIP claimed responsibility for the attacks in a video released a couple of months later, which appeared to show one of the perpetrators at a Waziristan training camp.[149]

The story was not as clear-cut as it appeared: Chinese counter-terrorism experts in Beijing didn't believe that ETIM/TIP had a great deal to do with the events in Kashgar. Their assessment was that this was a convenient piece of blame deflection from a local government that was seeking to shirk responsibility for the deteriorating security situation in Xinjiang.[150] One Uighur scholar who visited Kashgar and Hotan in the aftermath stated that the perpetrators had "grievances but no training", remarking that: "I doubt that the attackers were trained in Pakistan… They were all locals, from Hotan and Kashgar, and only armed with knives, and had no weapons."[151] That view was ultimately reflected in a statement from the Chinese foreign ministry in October, which stated the attackers had been trained and armed locally, not in Pakistan.[152] The sense that this had become a political football was reinforced when Xinjiang's top government official, Nur Bekri, claimed to the press during a major gathering of Chinese provincial and national leaders in 2012 that there were "countless links" between "East Turkestan activists and terrorists from our neighbouring country".[153] Again, it appeared to be an embarrassment for Pakistan but, again, the statements were coming not from the central government but from Xinjiang, where officials were under significant political pressure: the province was being roiled by tensions that went far beyond the capacity of a small number of militants holed up in North Waziristan.

On 5 July 2009, Urumqi had experienced the worst communal violence to take place in China in several decades. A protest over the killing of two Uighurs in Guangdong blew the lid off years of accumulated grievances and resentments between Han Chinese and Uighurs. The protest escalated into rioting, which saw "marauding gangs" of Uighur men slashing, stabbing and beating Han Chinese in a bloody rampage.[154] It echoed the Lhasa riots the previous year, in which Tibetan rioters burned and looted Han shops, but this was far deadlier—official Chinese estimates put the death toll at 197 and others place it much higher. By the time Han vigilante groups had mobilized, a heavy security presence had locked down much of the city, though not enough to prevent reprisal killings.[155] Officials quickly blamed the events on the World Uighur Congress and its "close links with terrorist organizations", while Uighur political groups blamed heavy-handed behaviour by the Chinese government.[156] Both accounts underplayed the disturbing level of inter-communal tension that the explosion of violence exhibited.

The 5 July events left deep wounds in Xinjiang and placed Chinese policies in the province under the closest scrutiny they had faced since the 1990s. The Xinjiang police chief and Urumqi party secretary were both sacked,[157] and the longstanding party secretary of the province, Wang Lequan, seen as the architect of the Chinese government's hardline approach over nearly two decades, was removed from his position.[158] The pressures were not just internal but international. Hu Jintao was forced to leave the l'Aquila G8 summit early to go back to China and manage the problem.[159] The Turkish prime minister denounced the events as "a kind of genocide".[160] Beijing went into a diplomatic frenzy trying to shut down a motion at the Organization of the Islamic Conference (OIC) condemning China's response to the violence and its treatment of Muslims, and to prevent the secretary general of the OIC from visiting Xinjiang (unsuccessfully in the latter case).[161] The Uighur issue also appeared to be firmly on the radar of the transnational terror groups who had previously tended to ignore it. Al Qaeda issued its first threats directed at China, with propaganda chief Abu Yahya Al Libi, from Pakistani soil, calling on "our Muslim brothers in Turkistan" to "seriously prepare for jihad".[162] Its offshoot, Al Qaeda in the Islamic Maghreb, promised retaliatory attacks.[163] And in March 2012, the Pakistani Taliban for the first time linked the killing of a Chinese national to "revenge for the Chinese government killing our Muslim brothers in the Xinjiang province".[164] Beijing's efforts at deflecting attention from Xinjiang and keeping the issue low in the pecking order for transnational terrorist groups had once been remarkably effective. After 5 July, it looked as if this was going to be a great deal harder.

Heightened tensions in Xinjiang, concerns over ETIM safe havens, anxieties over whether militant groups in the region might turn on China: this was a scenario that smacked of the 1990s. Beijing instinctively turned to its old playbook: pushing Pakistan to crack down on Uighur groups; using the ISI's reach into the world of militancy to dissuade them from attacks; and approaching militants through other intermediaries in Pakistan. The problem was that none of these levers worked the same way that they did ten years before.

Few people illuminate China's problem more clearly than the man Beijing invited to the Chinese Communist Party's International Department in April 2010. Maulana Fazal-ur Rehman, whose photo with Wang Yang, now one of China's four vice-premiers, is cheerfully displayed on the IDCPC's website, would have seemed a natural person to approach.[165] For the last two decades, Fazal-ur-Rehman had managed to straddle the worlds of militancy and mainstream Pakistani politics. In the 1990s, he was chair of the national assembly's Standing Committee on Foreign Affairs, where he spent much of his time lobbying and deal-making for the Taliban.[166] In 2006, he was the man Musharraf turned to when he needed support for the Pakistani government's efforts to strike peace deals with the militant groups that would go on to form the TTP.[167] In 2007, it was the Chinese themselves who were desperately seeking his support to help secure the release of the Red Mosque hostages. But in the aftermath of the Lal Masjid operation, as the divide between the Pakistani government and the new wave of Pakistani militants widened, keeping a foot in both camps became a great deal harder. In April of that year, a mysterious rocket attack was launched on his home in Dera Ismail Khan.[168] A few months later, Pakistani intelligence discovered Fazal-ur Rehman's name on a Taliban hit list.[169] In April 2011, he was the target of two attacks in two days.[170] On the first occasion, a suicide bomber killed twelve and injured more than twenty members of a group waiting to welcome him in Swabi, barely minutes before he arrived. The next day, twelve more people were killed as another suicide bomber struck a police van providing security for Fazal-ur Rehman's convoy in Charsadda. A few weeks later, Pakistani security officials confirmed that he was now "top of the new hit list prepared by the Taliban leadership".[171] By the time China had got round to cultivating him as a broker who could help navigate its own complex relationships with Islamic extremists, it was already too late.

The same was true of the Pakistani government and intelligence services. Relations with the Kashmiri groups that operated under the ISI's direct patronage were still intact, along with a spectrum of groups in the Afghan insurgency, but in the aftermath of the Red Mosque siege they had entered a state of open warfare with other militant groups. Even formerly trusted ISI intermediaries such as Colonel Imam, a founder of the Taliban, or Khalid Khawaja, another intelligence liaison between the military and the militants, were not safe—both men were killed in North Waziristan by the TTP, despite the direct pleas from Mullah Omar and Sirajuddin Haqqani that Baitullah Mehsud, the TTP leader, spare Colonel Imam's life.[172] Inevitably, as the Pakistani state's relationship with various militant organizations has fractured, its capacity to persuade them to steer clear of the Uighurs' cause has diminished. As the next chapter explains, these groups have been willing to make a specific target of China—especially its economic activities in Pakistan—if it helps to exert pressure on the Pakistani government. They have certainly not been deterred from affording protection to Uighur militants.

Few of the Uighurs in Pakistan have any connection to militancy. The bulk of the Uighur community, numbering a couple of thousand, is in Rawalpindi, and operates under the close watch of the Chinese government. Particularly since 9/11, the Chinese embassy in Islamabad has maintained a strong interest in them, extending benefits such as funding for scholarships and school fees, collecting precise information about the numbers and locations of Uighurs in Pakistan, and establishing an "ex-Chinese association"[173] to manage its contacts.[174] But while this community has its own political divisions over relations with the Chinese government, they are carefully monitored, and are largely naturalized in Pakistan anyway. The real concern is with the tiny group of people in Waziristan seeking to launch attacks in China.

Uighur militants in Pakistan may only number in the tens—Chinese officials in Pakistan have talked about estimates of between forty and eighty people.[175] Unlike the Afghan Taliban, whose roots and relationships in the tribal areas of Pakistan were extensive, when ETIM militants fled after the US invasion of Afghanistan they were in a position of near-complete dependency. ETIM members are virtually wholly reliant on the IMU for their shelter and supplies, and the IMU in turn needs local militant commanders to provide their blessing and protection. Initially this was in the Wana region of South Waziristan, but after tensions with one of the Waziri tribal leaders, Maulvi Nazir, they were expelled in 2007[176] and forced to set up in North Waziristan instead, under the protection of the Pakistani Taliban leader, Beitullah Mehsud.[177] Doubts about their capacity to launch attacks, and their autonomy to decide to do so even if they were able to, are pervasive among terrorism experts in Pakistan and China. "A single spark can start a prairie fire" was the justification given by one Chinese expert—quoting Mao—of the relentless focus on such a small, depleted band.[178] But there was little suggestion that they are currently an active threat.

Beijing has nonetheless leaned hard on Pakistan to deal with the handful that remain. A retired Pakistani general described the 2008–09 period as "the most difficult period in the [Sino-Pakistani] relationship that I can remember" owing to China's constant pressure on the Uighur issue, first in the run-up to the Olympics and then over a perceived threat to China's National Day celebrations.[179] The issue for China goes beyond the capacity of the militants themselves. ETIM's very weakness poses the standing question: why can't or won't the Pakistani army just wipe them out?

The issue has become perhaps the greatest sore point in the China-Pakistan relationship. Some on the Chinese side are understanding of the Pakistani government's explanation—that operations in North Waziristan are too difficult to undertake but that they are genuinely doing all they can apart from a full-scale military intervention in the tribal areas. Others are simply cynical, suggesting that if the army dealt with the threat too comprehensively it would make Pakistan less useful to China, giving the Pakistani government reason to allow a manageable, small-scale ETIM presence to persist.[180] But a more disturbing explanation is also advanced: that religious sympathies may be superseding Islamabad's commitment to the bilateral relationship, and even endangering the secular-strategic rationale that underpins it. "We see it in their eyes when we're sitting in the meetings. They're not comfortable with what we're asking," claimed a Chinese expert who is close to the PLA.[181] "When we provide them with intelligence on ETIM locations they give warnings before launching their attacks," noted another, in a complaint that would be familiar to

Western officials.[182] China has even received evidence of ISI agents visiting ETIM training camps.[183] "We certainly think there's a strong chance that they have contacts and relationships with ETIM and the Uzbeks," said another Chinese analyst.[184] Accusations of Pakistani support for militants in Xinjiang go back a long way too. In 1990, when the Chinese arrested two Pakistani nationals in Xinjiang for inciting unrest, they were infuriated to learn that the two men were ISI operatives—"former operatives", they were quickly assured.[185]

Fairly or not, Pakistan's approach to the Uighur issue has become the totemic example for those on the Chinese side who have started to raise broader concerns about the creeping "Islamisation" of the Pakistani army. It is one thing for China to provide comprehensive military assistance to an avowedly India-centric army, but quite another if elements in that army have goals that extend beyond the logic of balancing and deterrence towards the demands of *jihad*. "We're not worried about the generals, we're worried about the brigadiers," argued one Chinese expert. "The generals were already old enough for their habits to be set by the time Zia came in. They drink. They send their children to study in the United States or Great Britain. The younger ones are sending their children to study in the Gulf."

For China it risks becoming a losing proposition either way. A Pakistani military that grows ever more closely enmeshed with an Islamist and militant agenda undermines China's basic strategic goals in South Asia. A Pakistani military that can no longer keep China off the terrorist target list, that has even become a target in its own right, undermines China's security at home and the safety of its projects and personnel abroad. And it is the latter threat that has posed the biggest problems for the weakest pillar of the China-Pakistan relationship—the economy.

5

THE TRADE ACROSS THE ROOF OF THE WORLD

It was well past midnight when suddenly Prime Minister Chou En-Lai walked into the guesthouse without any protocol, saying he had come for a private talk with an old friend. During the meeting I asked him what was his thinking about the Middle East, especially the Chinese trade with these countries...I pointed out that most of China's trade was through the port of Shanghai which was far off from these countries. The nearest outlet for China's trade with the Gulf was Karachi, not Shanghai, if you see the map. I explained to him that there was an ancient trade route but lost to modern times, not only for trade but for strategic purposes as well.

Ghulam Faruque, Pakistani Commerce Minister[1]

No matter how hard they try to turn Gwadar into Dubai, it won't work. There will be resistance. The future pipelines going to China will not be safe. The pipelines will have to cross our Baluch territory, and if our rights are violated, nothing will be secure.

Nisar Baluch, General Secretary, Baluch Welfare Society[2]

Investors are like pigeons, when a government frightens them with poor decisions they all fly off together.

Zhu Rongji to General Musharraf, 2001[3]

At the peak of the Cultural Revolution, in August 1968, the Pakistani Foreign Minister, Mian Arshad Hussain, arrived in Beijing bearing a gift for Mao Zedong—a basket containing Pakistan's national fruit, roughly four dozen mangoes. Mao himself was not fond of mangoes, but he had another purpose in mind for them. The fruits were divided up by his head of security, Wang Dongxing, and presented to the Capital Worker-Peasant Mao Zedong Thought Propaganda Teams.[4] Mao had directed military chief Lin Biao to establish these army-led units in order to suppress the activities of the Red Guards, but discerning which of the competing centres of power Mao favoured at the time was not always straightforward. The propaganda team sent into Qinghua University had seen five of their number killed and hundreds wounded in their first foray against the bottle-and-grenade-wielding students, who didn't yet know that they had lost Mao's support.[5] The delivery of the Pakistani mangoes on 5 August was therefore a portentous moment. It is claimed by the *People's Daily* that the workers responded rhapsodically: "These are not simple mangoes, they are the rain and dew; they are the sunshine."[6] With the fruit came definitive evidence of Mao's personal blessing for their efforts to subdue the warring student factions. It signalled the end of the Red Guards' violent and chaotic role in the Cultural Revolution. Over the next year the PLA fully took over the process of winding down the excesses of the student vanguard's activities, and millions of youths, including a 17-year-old Xi Jinping, were sent down to the countryside for "re-education". China as a whole was swept up in "mango fever". Replicas of the fruit were made in the name of the Beijing Municipal Revolutionary Committee and sent around the country.[7] Badges and posters were created displaying workers bearing the mango platter. A factory in Henan started producing a line of "Golden Mango" brand cigarettes, which continues to this day.[8] Attempts to preserve the original fruits were made, not altogether successfully. The arrival of replicas in Chengdu was greeted by half a million people.[9]

When Pakistan next found itself at the centre of a Chinese mango fever, it would be in the belly of one of modern capitalism's most powerful forces: Walmart. A sample of Pakistani mangoes shipped in July 2012 had earned "overwhelming success" in the Chinese stores of the behemoth from Bentonville.[10] The first 40-ton container delivery arrived from Karachi the following month, with a similar amount due to follow every week for the duration of the season. "Pakistan's mangoes have become a centre of attraction in the largest retail chain of China…where the king of fruit is being offered for sale," announced Durrani Associates, a major Pakistani fruit exporter, "China can be the biggest market of Pakistani mangoes and within three years exports can be doubled."[11] One article in the Pakistani press breathlessly related that this would add "millions" to Pakistan's balance of payments, after "years of struggle" to break into the Chinese market.[12] There was a hitch, though. Elsewhere in Asia, a rising low-cost competitor was hitting Pakistan's superior but pricey fruit exports. "We have lost the Asian markets slowly and gradually due to the strong hold of Chinese mangoes," lamented the CEO of one of Pakistan's other leading fruit exporters, Harvest Tradings. "Every year we find new markets theoretically but practically, due to the lack of required infrastructure and strict conditions of other nations on exports of the fruit, we haven't been able to tap those markets."[13]

Like so many economic interactions between China and Pakistan, this one was destined to end in disappointment. A few months after the Walmart story appeared, Pakistan announced that it had missed its mango export target for the year, owing partly to competition from China, its all-weather friend.[14] The story was the same the previous year and it would be the same again in 2013. The shipments to China itself never picked up, either. Logistical problems and phytosanitary requirements were the ostensible factors conspiring to deny Chinese consumers the larger, sweeter Pakistani mangoes.[15] But the inability of the two sides to achieve a breakthrough on the export of Pakistan's national fruit was symbolic of a deeper set of problems.

China's transformation from an autarkic communist backwater into the world's second largest economy should have been a tremendous opportunity for Pakistan. At the time of Mao's mangoes, Pakistan's GDP per capita was ahead of China's, and the country was dubbed a "model developing country" by Harvard's Development Advisory Service, while China under the Cultural Revolution was in economic reverse.[16] But by 2012 the average Chinese earned five times as much as the average Pakistani, and China's economy was 35 times the size of Pakistan's. Close political and security ties alone were never going to be a guarantee of close commercial ones, but in certain aspects they might have been expected to smooth the way, whether it came to market access or tapping the vast new streams of Chinese financing and investment. Yet for a long time the story of the economic relationship between the two sides has been one of excitable headlines touting large numbers, ports, pipelines, and energy transit routes followed by frustration, disappointment, stalled projects, and much smaller figures buried away in statistical reports. Commercial ties are expanding—bilateral trade reached $12 billion in 2012—but continue to fall well short of expectations, and look even worse in comparative context. Sino-Indian trade, at $66 billion in 2012, is more than five times larger than China's trade with Pakistan, and the total volume of trade between China and Pakistan from 1995 to 2007, at $20 billion, was barely half of the Sino-Indian annual trade volume in 2007 alone.[17] If this can partly be explained away by India's sheer scale, telling comparisons can be made with a couple of China's smaller neighbours. The Philippines, which is roughly the same economic size as Pakistan, trades at three times its level with China. Vietnam, an economy half the size of Pakistan's, has four times the amount of bilateral trade with the Chinese.[18] Moreover, 75% of Sino-Pakistani trade is composed of Pakistani imports of Chinese goods, with only a few billion dollars' worth heading in the opposite direction. It was only in 2011 that China even broke into the top five destinations for Pakistani exports, at a level still substantially below the EU and the United States.[19]

The story for investment has been as disappointing as for trade. While grand announcements are made virtually every week about another new influx of Chinese money, the hard numbers have rarely borne them out. Even in the good years for Pakistan, the period between 2000 and 2005 when overall FDI increased by 600%, the investment flow from China only crept up in tiny increments. It amounted to barely $400,000 in 2004/5.[20] A surge in 2006/7, the single period in the last decade when China made the official list of the top three investors in Pakistan, was followed by outflows of Chinese investment in subsequent years.[21] While these figures from Pakistan's state bank almost certainly don't capture everything, in 2013, informal estimates by Pakistani experts for total Chinese investment in the country still run only between $5 billion and $7 billion.[22] And when it comes to handing out hard cash, Pakistan has received short shrift. Islamabad's requests for direct grants from Beijing, of the sort that the United States provides, have elicited the response that this was "unbecoming" for relations among friends.[23] In an interview with Pakistani reporters, Zhou Enlai had criticized US economic aid to Pakistan as a form of neo-colonialism.[24]

When the Zardari government looked to China to provide it with a multi-billion dollar soft loan to help it through the financial crisis in

2008, it was rebuffed.[25] The gap between the enormous figures publicized during bilateral visits and the support that is actually delivered is stark: a RAND study puts the total level of financial assistance pledged from China to Pakistan between 2001 and 2011 at $66 billion, but finds that only 6% of it ever came through.[26] One leading Chinese expert pithily summarizes the economic section of his essay on Sino-Pakistani relations with the heading: "China-Pakistan Economic Ties: Tiny and Weak".[27]

In the context of the broader Sino-Pakistani relationship, the weakness of economic ties has long been seen as a problem by both sides. As Ye Hailin puts it: "The objective has not been to strengthen the two countries' welfare interests but to strengthen them against common threats. It should be described as a shield to protect their traditional security interests rather than a bridge to lead to common prosperity and wealth."[28] The relationship is often described as a stool with two legs, and there have been fears that the absence of a solid economic foundation risks destabilizing the whole edifice. Even before Deng Xiaoping's reforms took off in the 1980s, there were attempts to remedy the imbalance. 13% of China's overseas assistance before 1979 went to Pakistan, with the bulk of it tied to purchases from Chinese companies.[29] But it was in the 1990s that the risk really started to look acute. China, focused on sustaining its rapid growth rates, started improving ties with India, which had embarked on a dramatic economic reform process of its own after 1991. The attractions of the booming Indian economy for China have since become a standing admonition and threat to Pakistanis: while the serious business is being transacted with their larger neighbour, Pakistan could end up being written off by Beijing as too plagued with violence, and too willing to put security obsessions over economic needs, to play a mature role in China's long-term regional plans. If this is partly a geopolitical anxiety, the more basic fear is that Pakistan might simply fail to take advantage of a once-in-a-generation chance to use China's economic take-off to fuel its own.[30]

A combination of economic structure, cultural preference, and the vicissitudes of geography used to be enough to explain the weak commercial relationship between China and Pakistan. The two economies lacked complementarity. China was actually a competitor for Pakistani exports, most significantly its dominant textile sector, undercutting it in third countries and eroding the country's comparative advantage.

Pakistani exporters had a "mental fixation with the western markets", as one expert put it.[31] And while China's east-Asian neighbours benefited from exposure to its booming coastal cities, the Shenzhens and Shanghais, Pakistan bordered on China's poorest provinces. But this was all supposed to change. After China's push to rebalance the coastal and interior economies, Xinjiang enjoyed a sustained boom, becoming one of China's fastest growing provinces.[32] A combination of political will, easy finance, and the China-Pakistan free-trade agreement that took effect in 2007 should have been able to overcome ingrained biases towards Europe, the United States and the Gulf.[33] While China may still be partly a commercial competitor, at the very least Pakistan would be well placed to benefit from the same major infrastructure investments, financed by huge sums from Chinese state banks, that were transforming economic life across much of the developing world.[34] Pakistan was certainly ready to give the Chinese privileged access to projects, and China extended a similar set of courtesies—as one former Pakistani diplomat put it: "There was a willingness to do things for the sake of political relations—giving loans, we don't have to stand in line; expeditious processing, approvals, facilitation and so on. We could take advantage of the political relationship but then the commercial side has to work."[35]

The problem for Pakistan is that its chits over the last decade have mostly been placed on a series of "mega-projects" that are premised on the value of the country's strategic economic geography. During Musharraf's presidency, a series of plans were dusted off that imagined Pakistan as the heart of a network of trade and energy corridors connecting China's west to the Indian Ocean and from there to the Middle East. Yet most of these projects were set in motion during a period when the security situation appeared to be under control. And while some of the investments—such as the Thar coal project—had the flavour of being political favours on China's part, the ambitions that underpinned Musharraf's plans seemed plausible for a country that was establishing a profile for itself as a leading emerging market. Pakistan was even included as one of Goldman Sachs' "Next 11" group, the proto-BRICS, in 2005,[36] its GDP growth that year clocking in at almost 9%.[37] In subsequent years, not only have growth rates plummeted and violence reached crisis levels, but Chinese workers in Pakistan have become targets to a degree that was unimaginable when the grand initiatives were first launched.[38] Instead of being known as China's gateway to the Gulf,

Pakistan has developed a reputation as the most dangerous country to be an overseas Chinese, with kidnappings and killings taking place with disturbing regularity. Insecurity has not only put paid to plans for some of China's largest investments, but even posed a risk to the economic relationship as a whole: at certain points the Chinese have threatened to pull every one of their workers out of the country.[39] The question has switched from whether the political and security relationship between the two sides will help to give Chinese investors privileged access to a booming new market, to whether these close ties are sufficient to keep the major economic projects alive.

The Karakoram Highway is the most potent symbol of China-Pakistan relations, the close-to-literal realization of the claim that their friendship is "higher than the highest mountain". Stand at the Khunjerab pass, 15,397 feet high, and you can see a memorial to the "pioneers" who built the "eighth wonder of the world".[40] More than a thousand Chinese and Pakistanis died in the construction process, a stunning feat of engineering that took 27 years to complete. What you see little of is trucks. For anyone familiar with bustling Chinese border posts by Kazakhstan or even North Korea, the relative calm is striking. One reason for the lack of commercial activity can be found 100 miles south of Khunjerab at Attabad, where a huge lake, 14 miles long and more than 100 metres deep, has submerged the road since a landslide in January 2010. In 2006, plans had been launched for trebling the width of the KKH and adding an all-weather surface that could accommodate heavy vehicles.[41] Much of the early work on this task would end up under water. While the engineers have pushed ahead with resurfacing limited stretches of the road, the more serious effort instead had to been channelled into the "Attabad realignment project", a vast tunnelling job through the moun-tains to reconnect the two sections of the highway.[42] In the meantime, small boats—the largest of which can barely fit an SUV on board—shuttle a small volume of goods back and forth across the lake. The China Road and Bridge Corporation, the state-owned infrastructure giant responsible for the work, estimated that it will be completed by mid-2014, but delays continued to set it back.[43] Either way, a period of at least four and a half years will have passed with virtually no overland trade between the two countries. Some of the commercial activity that used to take place by road was diverted to planes flying between Kashgar and Gilgit. Other goods joined the larger bulk of seaborne trade that passes through Karachi. But the truth is that even before the landslides, cross-border movement on the Karakoram Highway was very limited, with the route distinguished for its scenery more than its traffic. In the preceding years the road bore no more than 7–8% of total Sino-Pakistani trade, at best a few hundred million dollars' worth a year.[44] The bulk of Pakistan's commerce is with Guangdong and Zhejiang provinces, on the south and east coasts, not across the border with Xinjiang. This remains the principal reason that, for years, talk of building a railway across a similar route elicited almost equal levels of eye-rolling in Islamabad and Beijing: "There is no economic rationale for it whatsoever".[45]

Not so long ago, the Karakoram Highway had been billed as the final leg of a more recent and even grander project—the establishment of a trade and energy corridor running all the way down to Gwadar, the Baloch port at the mouth of the Persian Gulf. Yet at the opposite end of the corridor, the story was the same. In February 2013, Chinese companies took over the running of a port that had not had a single ship dock in the previous four months, and at best operated at 15% of its capacity.[46] Water shortages had seen as many as 20,000 people leave the city over the previous year.[47] Infrastructure links with the rest of Pakistan were seriously underdeveloped. Most economic activity was at a standstill. Gwadar was about as far away from the promises of a "Dubai miracle"[48] on the Makran coast as it was possible to imagine, and the transport and energy corridor appeared to be little more than a "pipe dream", as one Pakistani official dismissed it.[49]

The building of Gwadar port had been launched with great hopes for its transformative economic impact. Gwadar was a small fishing village located in a deepwater natural harbour, which Pakistan had purchased from Oman for $3 million in 1958 with a view to developing it as a port site. The opportunity to do so was once offered to the United States by Zulfiqar Bhutto in the 1970s.[50] The Americans didn't bite. A formal plan to build Gwadar into a major commercial centre was proposed in 1993,[51] with the task handed to a British consortium a couple of years later, but the initiative was stalled by political and financing problems.[52] Then in 2001, on the fiftieth anniversary of China-Pakistan relations, Chinese Prime Minister Zhu Rongji announced that China would underwrite the project.[53] China agreed to provide $198 million of the $248 million required,[54] and China Harbour Engineering Company—

the sister company of China Road and Bridge Corporation, which was rebuilding the KKH—took responsibility for its first phase.[55] That involved the construction of three multipurpose ship berths and a service berth, and dredging of a deep-water channel, as well as erection of roads, port buildings and facilities.[56] At the same time, a $200 million road link to Karachi,[57] the Makran Coastal Highway, was given the go-ahead, and built by the Frontier Works Organisation,[58] the Pakistani military entity that had been established to construct the KKH in the first place. Gwadar's first phase was finished in 2006 and the port was opened to great fanfare at a ceremony in January 2007.[59]

Given that the port was developed partly in order to reduce the bottleneck at Karachi, the Makran Coastal Highway was of limited use—the real value would only come when Gwadar was connected up to the rest of Pakistan. That was expected to come during the second phase of the port's development. The contract to run and manage the facility itself was given to the Port of Singapore Authority (PSA). It would involve the construction of four container berths, a bulk cargo terminal, two oil terminals, a roll on/roll off terminal, and a grain terminal.[60] An oil refinery—to be built separately by China—was planned,[61] along with the crucial high-quality road links to the Balochistan capital, Quetta, and Ratodero in northern Sindh.[62] Phase 2, at a cost estimated to run between $600 million and $1 billion, would take Gwadar from an over-developed fishing village to a genuine commercial hub.[63]

Yet very little of "Phase 2" was ever undertaken. The oil refinery was never built.[64] The PSA made derisory progress on developing the port. And after General Musharraf's departure in 2008, resources due to have been spent on infrastructure connections were diverted from his "pet project".[65] Gwadar stood virtually isolated. Mutual recriminations over the situation went on for years. The PSA and some sections of the Pakistani government blamed the navy, which had refused to hand over 584 acres of land that were earmarked for the port's operational activities.[66] Other sections of the Pakistani government blamed the PSA for failing to fulfil its commitments.[67] Following protracted court battles, the Singaporeans pulled out of the contract, which was taken over in February 2013 by China Overseas Port Holdings Company.[68] But the difficulties in building the roads, the PSA's reluctance to develop the port, and the slow-motion legal process that finally saw Chinese companies stepping back in were not just the result of foot-dragging.

The port and associated developments have been a major target for Baloch nationalist groups. While the potential economic benefits of the project are undeniable, even political moderates in Balochistan believe that most of them will be diverted elsewhere in Pakistan, and that the project will be used by the Pakistani military to consolidate its presence in the region.[69] Some described their opposition to the port as a "last stand" for the Baloch cause.[70] Its success would bring about a huge population influx, with Gwadar expected to become a 2-million-person city, and the Baloch "fear that they will become a minority in their own land".[71] It is the less moderate who have had the most telling impact, though. On 3 May 2004, the Baloch Liberation Army killed three Chinese engineers and injured nine more working on the project, when a remote-controlled car bomb blew up the bus carrying them to the port.[72] Subsequent rocket attacks struck Gwadar airport,[73] a hotel where Chinese engineers were staying,[74] and a Chinese construction company.[75] Chinese workers narrowly escaped another bus bombing in 2007, though the Pakistani police protecting them were less fortunate.[76] Many other attacks on roads, pipelines and other infrastructure in the province have simply gone unreported.

When it became increasingly clear by 2011 that Chinese companies would be taking over the running of Gwadar port from the Port of Singapore Authority, it raised the question of why they would risk assuming responsibility for a facility that was little more than a white elephant with an enormous target sign painted on it.[77] Certainly they had been reassured that the Pakistani navy would be more forthcoming on the land rights issue than it had been with the Singaporeans, and there was the promise of money set aside for the necessary road building work. But the suspicion endured that non-economic motives must also be involved. Like the Karakoram Highway, Gwadar has never entirely convinced as a commercial proposition. The "transport and energy corridor" is not vulnerable only to security threats in Balochistan and to landslides and floods in Gilgit-Baltistan, but also to the cold logic of the market: for all the talk of how a pipeline would cut thousands of miles off the journey of a barrel of oil from the Middle East to China's interior, the cost of sending it overland via Gwadar and Xinjiang would run at between four and five times that of the sea route through Shanghai.[78] There are certainly scenarios in which such a route might be used, though they are rather bleak, featuring either naval blockades or worse, as an article on Chinese strategy in the Indian Ocean suggests: "The wartime experience of the [Republic of China] showed that, if China's "backdoors" could be kept open, a regime based deep inside the country could be kept alive—even if an enemy had managed to occupy China's coastal ports."[79] They also stretch credulity, given how straightforward it would be to prevent the functioning of the corridor. One US naval expert observes that "it would be easier for the United States to prevent the unloading of oil at Gwadar than to blockade the Strait of Malacca".[80] But the standing point of curiosity has been whether the port might have utility even if it never became the commercial and energy transit hub that was once intended: instead becoming a permanent Chinese naval facility.

The Pakistani government has flip-flopped on the issue, alternating between touting the port as a potential expansion of its naval capabilities—even publicly claiming that China had agreed to help it establish a base there[81]—and playing down this possibility as Indian scaremongering.[82] The rationale for using Gwadar for this purpose is fairly clear: Karachi, the principal operating base for the Pakistani navy, was subjected to an Indian blockade in 1971[83] and there was the serious prospect of a repeat in 1999.[84] Blockading Gwadar, 645 kilometres further along the coast—"away from Pakistan's traditional confrontation sea zone", as a report from the Balochistan government put it—would be a more difficult proposition.[85] In 2005, the Pakistani Chief of Naval Staff said that Gwadar would be "the country's third naval base", and would "improve the country's defence in deep sea waters".[86] The port is sufficiently deep to accommodate submarines and aircraft carriers. And from China's perspective, its proximity to the Persian Gulf may provide a potential location for oil transhipment, but it would also offer something unusual for the Chinese navy: a permanent, reliable facility for ships needing support points close to the Middle East, North Africa or East Africa. This seemed a long way off back in 2001. In my discussions with Chinese experts and officials over the last decade, scepticism about the military value of Gwadar and an emphasis on the economic rationale that underpinned the project was consistent—talk of its being developed as a naval base was dismissed as a myth.[87] But in the last few years, a couple of things changed. The security situation in Pakistan deteriorated markedly, making the economic corridor plans look less and less plausible. And the Chinese navy embarked on an increasingly far-flung set of activities.

Since 2008, the PLA Navy has conducted the most extensive set of long-distance operations in its history. While its anti-piracy deployments in the Gulf of Aden provided the most significant ongoing test of the navy's needs for overseas support locations, they were even more clearly in evidence during the huge evacuation of 35,000 Chinese workers from Libya in 2011.[88] It was the first time that the PLA Navy had been deployed to conduct a NEO—non-combatant evacuation operation—to protect its citizens on the other side of the world, and with turmoil in the region continuing, it seemed to Chinese strategists as if it wouldn't be the last time. While the exercise was a success, a great deal of chaos bubbled below the surface as the numbers of Chinese evacuees proved far greater than expected, requiring boats and planes to be chartered on an emergency basis at great expense.[89] It raised the issue of which staging points in the region China could reliably expect to use in a crisis. China's Sudanese friends allowed it to use Khartoum as the logistics point for air transport,[90] but the refuelling location for the frigate, *Xuzhou*, which was sent to support and protect the evacuation, was the Omani port of Salalah.[91] Chinese experts have argued that ports such as Salalah, Aden or Djibouti can be relied on for routine refuelling but that Pakistan is the likeliest country to agree to long-term arrangements for "more comprehensive supplying, replenishment, and large-scale repairs of shipboard weapons".[92] Trust between the two militaries makes it arguably the only plausible candidate for such a facility. The Libya incident also highlighted the value of forward deployed military assets—the only reason the *Xuzhou* could be used was because she was already operating in the Gulf of Aden as part of an anti-piracy mission. One of the definitive pieces of analysis on the evacuation contends that "from this point forward, there is a strong likelihood that the PLAN will seek to assume a more sustained presence in the Indian Ocean region, perhaps extending toward the Persian Gulf as well".[93]

It was after the Libya deployment that the same Chinese experts and officials I had been interviewing started to change their tune. I increasingly heard the argument that even if the economic utility of Gwadar was fundamentally in doubt until the situation in Pakistan changed, its potential as a naval facility might change China's calculations about the port's value. When the Pakistani Defence Minister, Chaudhry Ahmed Mukhtar, made his statement about China agreeing to develop a naval base at Gwadar, the Chinese foreign ministry issued an official denial, but as one expert familiar with the discussions put it: "It wouldn't be a naval base. It would just be a facility to which we had access when we needed it. And we didn't even agree to that during the visit, so he shouldn't have made his statement. But that's exactly what we're considering."[94] The former Chinese ambassador to India, Pei Yuanying, has directly stated in an interview with the *People's Daily* that "Gwadar port will become a logistics support base for supplies and maintenance along the route of large fleet when the Chinese naval fleet goes to the Suez Canal, the Mediterranean, and the Gulf of Aden" [*sic*].[95] Existing plans for the development of the port are purely economic, and some Chinese and Pakistanis continue to see the finger-pointing at Gwadar as a distraction—whatever happens in Balochistan, the Chinese navy, if it wishes, can use Karachi, which is already its main repair facility in the Indian Ocean. "For us, Karachi is fine," said one Chinese official. "It's for Pakistan that Gwadar is really useful. They want us to upgrade it to a naval base that can be used by both Pakistani and Chinese ships. The main reason? India."[96] There is little surprise that the stories about Gwadar refuse to disappear, and it is now Chinese naval strategists rather than Indian ones who are talking up the port's long-term prospects, however dire the short-term economic and security situation there appears. "The Singapore company put more value in the commercial benefits in operating the port, but for China, its strategic value is greater than the commercial significance," said one Chinese expert. "I do believe China will build the port at the astonishing 'Chinese speed' to materialize the port's strategic values."[97]

The history of the Karakoram Highway's construction is itself a demonstration that in China-Pakistan relations, strategic intent can—eventually—trump an array of physical, cultural, economic and security obstacles. The story is littered with disasters, almost as many man-made as natural. As Muhammad Mumtaz Khalid, the principal historian of the road, remarks: "Thoughtless urgency would become a peculiar feature of this mega-project, and perhaps for all future ones. Any presidential order, or for that matter any higher command dictates, would rarely be questioned by the Corps' top brass regardless of the serious technical, financial and administrative problems, time constraints or frictions of terrain and weather."[98] Arbitrary deadlines and very poor preparation from the Pakistani side, especially for the extreme altitude, dogged the early phases of a venture that was launched with extraordinarily minimal surveying or planning. The raising and dispatch of Pakistan's Khunjerab force in 1966, which was supposed to begin the process of building the road down from the border, is described by one military officer as "the worst [operation] ever done by anyone".[99] Many of the first contingent needed to be rescued. In two years, the poorly prepared force had achieved only a 13km pilot cut, prompting an offer from the Chinese to take over the task. China had completed its portion of the road before the Pakistanis had even started theirs.[100] The assumption of greater and greater Chinese responsibility for realizing the ambitious project became so pronounced that the Pakistani government, during the worst of its financial difficulties, even considered handing over the whole task to the Chinese and disbanding the newly established Frontier Works Organisation, the paramilitary body that had been leading the task on the Pakistani side.[101] The road did enjoy its first "opening ceremony" in February 1971, but it was closed again almost immediately by floods and landslides, and while a desperate attempt to clear a route for the first Chinese trade delegation in July was successful,[102] the 1971 war and its aftermath stalled most of the subsequent construction efforts.[103] It would prove to be many years before the road was upgraded to a level that could be meaningfully considered functional. Even the second opening ceremony, which took place in June 1978 at Thakot bridge with Zia ul Haq and China's Vice-Premier Geng Biao in attendance, was a false start.[104] There was still over a year of additional work required, and the last Chinese workers only left Pakistan on 19 November 1979, "after a hot cup of tea at the chilly Khunjerab pass", thirteen years after Ayub Khan had first given the project the green light.[105]

Like many other joint Sino-Pakistani projects, the KKH would have been killed off quickly if its economic value had been the only thing it had going for it: the highway was conceived as a political and territorial project, not as the most logical trade route between the two sides. Its direct military utility is questionable, given that it would be easy to interdict in the event of war, and no logistical planner could expect to count on a reliably landslide-free supply route. But it "altered the balance of geographical politics on the subcontinent", expanding the reach of the Pakistani government into previously inaccessible frontier regions, and consolidating Sino-Pakistani control over territory that India claims as its own.[106] As the roadbuilding initiative was launched, Ayub Khan "was pleased to remark that in order of priority the first urgency was strategic and one of the immediate significance". The "economic and commercial importance of the highway" was only "the second objective" for Pakistan.[107] The same was true for China. The principal construction phase for the road closely paralleled the Cultural Revolution, a period that was distinguished by very little normal economic planning. The largest centrally directed Chinese economic project at the time was the vast "Third Front" programme to develop an industrial base in the west of the country that could act as a strategic reserve in the event of war with the United States or the Soviet Union.[108] The route, especially the development of the border-crossing at Khunjerab rather than the more obvious Mintaka Pass, was carefully devised to keep it further from the Soviet border.[109] China's sense of encirclement, vulnerability and isolation was acute, and Pakistan in the mid-1960s was one of the few countries that mitigated it. The Sino-Pakistani air agreement of 1963, China's first with a non-Communist country, breached the Western ban on commercial air services to China, and ensured that it was no longer "air-locked".[110] The Karakoram Highway itself provided a "'welcome out' sign at their backdoor".[111]

Military and political considerations underpin many of the other principal joint economic projects too. China's investments in Pakistan's civil nuclear power sector, addressed in more detail in the second chapter and in the epilogue, do have commercial utility—they give China's nuclear industry the opportunity to showcase power plants outside its home market. But they have also been inextricably bound up with the long-standing programme of Sino-Pakistani nuclear weapons cooperation and, in more recent years, the response by Islamabad and Beijing to the US-India nuclear deal. It is even more obvious in the defence sector, the one area of commercial relations that can genuinely be said to be booming. Exports to Pakistan, which comprise 55% of Chinese arms sales, propelled China to become the world's fifth largest arms exporter in 2012.[112] The major defence-industrial relationships between China and Pakistan are the successors of the procurement agreements of the 1960s and 1970s, when China swung in to assist Pakistan during and after its wars with India. Companies such as the China Precision Machinery Import-Export Corporation, the Chinese missile exporter, and the principal Chinese defence-production companies, Poly Technologies and

Norinco, have longstanding relationships with Pakistan dating back to their days as arms of the Chinese state. When Norinco and Heavy Industries Taxila (HIT) announced in 2012 their plans to jointly sell the tanks and other security vehicles they produce together to new markets, it was the culmination of decades of cooperation.[113] Norinco is the successor of China's fifth ministry of machine building, which oversaw tank, artillery and small arms production.[114] HIT is the huge military-industrial complex in the Punjab that was originally established with Beijing's assistance to maintain and rebuild the Pakistani army's fleet of Chinese T59 tanks after the 1965 war.[115] There is now a lengthening list of such joint ventures, including the JF-17 fighter aircraft, developed for Pakistan's air force by China's Chengdu Aircraft Industrial Corporation and Pakistan Aeronautical Complex;[116] and the F-22P frigates[117] and the PNS Azmat fast attack vehicles, built by Karachi Shipyard and Engineering Works, the China Shipbuilding and Trading Company and other Chinese firms.[118] The value of defence-industrial ties for Pakistan goes well beyond their economic or military value. Not only do they grease the wheels of the China-Pakistan relationship, they ensure buy-in from some of China's highest-ranking party and military families, who have controlled companies like Poly Industries since their inception.[119]

While nuclear plants and armaments production are in secure locations, other Chinese companies operating in Pakistan are less fortunate. Telecoms, power, and mining have promised some of the most significant new infusions of Chinese manpower and resources, but have faced some of the most acute security risks. Huawei, the world's largest telecoms equipment company, has become Pakistan's dominant telecoms infrastructure operator, and ZTE, Huawei's state-owned counterpart, spent several years as its largest telecoms vendor. China Mobile, the mammoth Chinese mobile telecoms company, made Pakistan the destination for its first overseas acquisition, purchasing Paktel, the fifth largest Pakistani mobile operator, for $284 million in January 2007.[120] "If we cannot succeed in Pakistan, we'd better not go anywhere else," the company's Chairman Wang Jianzhou declared after the acquisition.[121] The hydropower sector in Pakistan features a roll-call of Chinese megafirms working on a range of current or prospective projects: Sinohydro,[122] China Three Gorges Corporation,[123] and Gezhouba Group.[124] And the mining sector has seen Chinese companies such as China Metallurgical Group Corporation[125] and China Kingho Group drawn in by the opportunities to tap natural resources in Balochistan and Sindh.[126] Some of the companies and projects have struggled—China Mobile did poorly with its revenue and customer base, its new brand "Zong" ending up in last place among the operators in Pakistan;[127] the hydro projects have hit an assortment of financing hurdles.[128] But for a list of companies that reads like a "Who's Who" of the major Chinese investors in the developing world, the challenges of unfamiliar markets, corruption, and politicized deal-making are par for the course. Since 2004, though, they had to navigate security threats of a novel sort.

The violence that convulsed Gwadar port was at one level predictable. When it came to security, Balochistan was understood to be a special case—an on-off insurgency had been running there virtually throughout Pakistan's history, and accusations of external involvement ran back for decades.[129] Soviet help to Baloch agitation was raised by the Chinese as a subject of concern as long ago as the 1970s, and the involvement of the Americans, the British, and (especially) the Indians in backing the Baloch nationalists has been a source of finger-pointing for many years.[130] In that sense, China knew what it was signing up for when it agreed to develop a port in the restive province. In the rest of the country, however, it believed that—as Pakistan's close friend—it was safe from the sort of political targeting that Gwadar attracted. Events in South Waziristan would therefore come as something of a shock.

The Gomal Zam dam project, about 13km west of Tank, the winter headquarters of the FATA agency, had a long prehistory: a feasibility report on the dam's construction was first commissioned by the British Royal Corps of Engineers in 1898.[131] An abortive effort to build the dam was finally made in 1963 but it was not until August 2001, when a Chinese consortium was brought in to lead the construction, that it looked as if it would finally be realized.[132] The South Waziristan region had a fearsome reputation but the project provided demonstrable local economic benefits, including irrigation and electricity, and it was hoped that the dam-building could proceed in peace. But by the time construction was underway, the tribal agency had become the principal location for foreign fighters fleeing Afghanistan. As a result, there was growing US pressure on the Pakistani government to launch military action against the Al Qaeda-linked militants who had set themselves up there.[133] In January 2004, the army launched its first operation in South Waziristan. In October that year, two Chinese engineers working for

Sino Hydro went missing. The two men, Wang Teng and Wang Ende, had been heading to work at the dam early in the morning when they were seized, their abandoned vehicle being found nearby.[134] The initial hope for the Pakistanis and the Chinese was that the kidnappers were simply bandits seeking ransom, which was not uncommon in the area and could have been dealt with quickly and quietly. There were also rumours that some of the kidnappers were foreigners—specifically Uzbeks, which would have linked them to Uighur terrorist groups.[135] But the identity of the real protagonists was far more troubling: Pakistanis with a political agenda.

The operation had been ordered by a one-legged militant commander who had once been held at Guantánamo Bay, Abdullah Mehsud, who was a member of the region's largest tribe. In an interview with a Pakistani journalist, he argued his case: "We have no enmity with the Chinese people, and I am sad that we had to kidnap the Chinese engineers," he said. "But desperate people do desperate things and the only way we thought we could compel the Pakistan government to stop its military operations in South Waziristan was to kidnap engineers belonging to Pakistan's best friend, China."[136] The national and local reaction was swift. General Musharraf publicly stated that he would personally shoot Abdullah Mehsud dead if he had the chance.[137] Abdullah Mehsud was summoned before local *jirgas* led by Mehsud elders in an attempt to persuade him to release the hostages.[138] The government sent four of his cousins—including his brother-in-law—to engage in negotiations. The Pakistani government had been so concerned about the engineers' safety that it was even willing to consider his immediate demand to give the kidnappers and their hostages safe passage to nearby Spinkai Raghzai, in territory under the control of Mehsud and his men. Initially it seemed as if there might be an amicable resolution. Abdullah Mehsud allowed messages in Chinese to be passed to the Chinese embassy and to Sino Hydro. But ultimately the army decided to move. Pakistani commandos dressed as members of local tribes launched an attack on the mud hut in Chagmalai where the kidnappers and their hostages were holed up. The two kidnapped men had been wired with explosives, and Wang Teng, the younger of the two engineers, who also spoke some English, had urged the Pakistani government not to conduct a military operation given the danger it would place them in. His young wife was waiting for him at the Sino Hydro office in Dera Esmail Khan. The kidnappers were killed in the raid, but so was Wang, who was hit by bullets as he tried to duck behind one of Mehsud's men.[139]

The tragic incident derailed the dam project. The Chinese companies pulled out for three years, only resuming in 2007 when the Frontier Works Organisation had taken charge and a far more robust level of security protection was provided.[140] At the time there was reason to hope that the kidnapping might be a one-off. Even Haji Mohammad Omar, who was one of the principal leaders of the Pakistani militants operating in FATA, denounced the whole operation: "Abdullah Mahsud committed a blunder. He shouldn't have kidnapped the Chinese engineers. And after the botched kidnapping attempt, he should have agreed to the government's offer of safe passage for the five kidnappers in return for the release of the two Chinese hostages. I am still unable to understand why he so carelessly sacrificed five young and loyal militants who organised the kidnapping and obeyed his every order," said Omar.[141] The Chinese were not, for the most part, seen as a legitimate target, and even Abdullah Mehsud had been apologetic about his political tactics. The Pakistani government's relationship with the militants was not yet at breaking point. And from China's perspective, Pakistan—and General Musharraf—had acted quickly and forcefully. But in fact, the kidnapping was only the start.

The Lal Masjid siege in 2007, detailed in the prologue, knocked out all grounds for believing that the Gomal Zam kidnappings might be an aberration. The Pakistani government's relationship with the Mehsud tribe, and others that went on to form a mainstay of the Pakistani Taliban, moved from a period of half-hearted military forays, negotiations, and peace deals into outright warfare. And the Chinese were turned into legitimate targets for groups that had previously left them alone. In the aftermath of the revenge killings of three Chinese engineers in Peshawar that followed Lal Masjid, it was clear that there had to be a dramatic shift in the level of protection provided.[142] As a result, Pakistan and China put in place an extensive battery of security and emergency response mechanisms. A joint liaison committee for the safety of Chinese workers was established, consisting of officials from the National Crisis Management Cell and the Chinese embassy.[143] A 24-hour hotline connected the Chinese diplomats with the interior ministry and all Pakistani provinces, alongside an early warning system for Chinese associations, company heads, and student groups. There was a scramble to register everyone. Estimates of the total number of Chinese nationals in Pakistan have run between 10,000 and 13,000, among whom a 2009 embassy estimate suggested 5,000 were labourers, 3,500 engineers and 1,000 business people.[144] Thousands of additional Pakistani security personnel were deployed to protect Chinese projects. Workers in some of the most dangerous locations travelled in armed convoys or armoured personnel carriers, or even commuted to work by helicopter. In supposedly safe locations, Chinese businesspeople took additional precautions, with drivers being assigned at short notice, and information about their destinations and routes withheld until the start of the journey.[145] The Chinese embassy itself responded to the heightened security risk by buying in a 20-day stockpile of food, water and diesel oil, and was reported to have started a vegetable plot "as a reserve food source".[146] Chinese officials now described security concerns in Pakistan as their "top priority".[147] Musharraf's successor would find out that they weren't bluffing.

In October 2008, Asif Zardari was on his first visit to China as Pakistan's head of state. This was an issue in its own right—the Chinese had not been at all happy that he had failed to follow tradition and make China his first overseas destination.[148] Claims that trips to Dubai, London and New York were not official visits didn't cut much ice, and his subsequent attempt to over-compensate by turning up every six months was an even greater hassle for over-worked Chinese officials.[149] The Chinese government was already suspicious of him. The PPP, Zardari's party, was the creation of Zulfiqar Ali Bhutto, who had taken on a leading role in the early days of upgrading Sino-Pakistani relations, but the Chinese tended to see his daughter Benazir Bhutto, whose assassination catapulted Zardari into the presidency, as inclined in a more pro-American direction.[150] None of this made for an auspicious set of circumstances for a visit in which Zardari would be asking for several billion dollars to help cover Pakistan's balance of payments crisis.[151] China, which had been lobbied by the United States not to give Pakistan the money,[152] didn't need that much persuading—Beijing also thought it would be more helpful if Pakistan were forced to go through an IMF programme, and China had no history of financing Pakistan on that sort of scale. Zardari got a frosty reception from Hu Jintao, who was reported to have reacted with incredulity to his requests for such lavish assistance.[153] Overshadowing the trip, however, was the fact that another two Chinese engineers had been kidnapped.

On 29 August, Long Xiao Wei and Zhang Guo, two engineers who worked for ZTE, had been repairing a telecommunications tower in Lower Dir, a district in Swat Valley, and were on their way home when they were abducted along with their driver and security guard.[154] The Pakistani Taliban soon claimed responsibility: "Our aim is to hit the government's interests wherever they are. We kidnap everyone irrespective of whether he's Pakistani or Chinese and we'll continue to do this until they stop killing our people," said the spokesman, Muslim Khan.[155] He went on to say that the military operation against the Red Mosque was launched under pressure from the Chinese and indicated that the Taliban would take revenge for the martyred students. Yet again, China had found itself caught in the middle of a confrontation between the Pakistani government and the militants, this time in a part of the country that was once a tourist haven known as the "Switzerland of Pakistan".[156] Violence in the region had been on the increase for several years. Maulana Fazlullah, the "Radio Mullah" who ran Taliban operations in Swat and would later become the leader of the Pakistani Taliban, had set up illegal FM radio stations in which he demanded the imposition of *sharia* law.[157] Following the Lal Masjid operation, Fazlullah urged his supporters to launch a *jihad* against the Pakistani government, and formed an alliance with militants operating in FATA.[158] Swat saw an alternating sequence of talks, truces and battles between the Pakistani army and the Taliban. In the early months of Zardari's coalition government, which took power after the February 2008 elections, talks with the militants broke down. Zardari assumed the office of the presidency days after the kidnappings had taken place.

The South Waziristan incident in 2004 had been dealt with in less than a week. By the time Zardari arrived in Beijing, the Chinese engineers in Swat had been in captivity for one and a half months. In some respects, the Pakistanis were operating under more constraints on this occasion: Beijing made it clear that it did not want to see any of the hostages killed, reducing the scope for a repeat of the commando raid four years earlier, and the Pakistani army had poor intelligence anyway on the location where they were being held.[159] China was not, however, convinced by Pakistan's response, comparing it unfavourably with Musharraf's, and even raising the prospect of curtailing all of its other economic projects if the situation was not effectively addressed.[160] The men were not freed after a military operation. The two hostages escaped shortly after Zardari's return from Beijing, though one of them—who slipped and broke his leg in the escape—was recaptured.[161] After extended negotiations with tribal elders, contacts with the Chinese embassy brokered by former ISI chief Hamid Gul, and Chinese offers to the Pakistani Taliban to pay a ransom, he would finally be released as a "goodwill gesture" on the eve of Zardari's next visit to China. Muslim Khan, the Taliban's spokesman, claimed that this was as a result of the Pakistani government's agreement to support the imposition of *sharia* law in parts of Swat.[162] In practice, the deal involved money—paid for by the ISI—and the release of twenty militants, which had been bargained down from the original demands for over 130.[163]

Zardari was not the only one to feel the heat. The army chief Ashfaq Kayani had been in Beijing in September 2008, his own first overseas trip since taking the position.[164] Although the new president received much of the stick, Beijing knew perfectly well that the responsibility for the slow response to the hostage crisis didn't lie with the civilian government but with Pakistan's security services. The man in the firing line was the Director General of the ISI, Nadeem Taj. Under Taj, the ISI had been directly tied to the bombing of the Indian embassy in Kabul and was believed to be either complicit in practices such as ISI warnings being provided to militants before drone attacks, or unwilling to stop them. Pressure from Washington to remove him had been intense, and Kayani was keen to replace Musharraf's appointee with his own man anyway.[165] Chinese unhappiness at the intelligence services' slow response to the kidnappings, conveyed during his visit, provided additional reinforcement.[166] Days after Kayani returned from Beijing, Taj was kicked upstairs to take over a more senior but less powerful position as commander of the Gujranwala Corps, and replaced by Shuja Pasha.[167]

Zardari's difficult first year of relations with China cast a long shadow over economic ties between the two sides during his time in office. The kidnappings, alongside ETIM's seeming return to the scene (detailed in the previous chapter), certainly deepened Beijing's security concerns. But the slow response to the kidnappings was also a broader symbol of the new government's diminished capacity to exercise power, and of China's own trouble working out what levers it needed to pull to get things done after Musharraf's fall.[168] Virtually all the major economic initiatives between the two sides had been set in motion under Musharraf's tenure and very few of them made significant progress after he had gone. The "mega-projects"—Gwadar, the KKH expansion, and the enormous new hydro-electric dams among them—appeared to go into a state of suspended animation. As one former Chinese diplomat put it, if projects "are threatened by insecurity, it's easy: we stall them".[169] Security problems alone are not responsible for the weakness of the economic relationship, which long predates the rise of the TTP, the Red Mosque crisis, and the PPP government. Neither are they solely responsible for the broader difficulties that face the Pakistani economy overall, which—in addition to being hit by the global economic crisis—has struggled with problems ranging from energy shortages and infrastructure problems to corruption and the central government's painfully small tax revenue base. Moreover, the protection mechanisms that were put in place for Chinese workers in the aftermath of the Swat Valley kidnapping proved relatively successful. There were a couple of near-misses: a group of Chinese engineers narrowly escaped the Mehran naval base attack,[170] though they were not the target, and there are suspicions that a bombing in Karachi was directed at the Chinese consulate.[171] But during the remainder of the PPP's term in office, the only confirmed attack took place against a Chinese woman, Hua Jiang, who was shot by the Taliban in Peshawar's bazaar in February 2012 with her interpreter.[172] Variously described as a "student" or a "tourist", and inevitably suspected to be an intelligence operative, she was travelling without the battery of protection that had become common for Chinese moving around the country.[173]

But after the events of 2007 and 2008, it took a long time for Beijing to recover enough confidence to make big economic bets on Pakistan again. Arms sales and heavily protected nuclear plants were one thing, infrastructure projects and normal commercial investments quite another. In 2011, China's largest private-sector miner, Kingho Group, pulled out of a $19 billion deal that would have been the country's largest, citing security concerns for its personnel following bombings in Pakistan's major cities.[174] Chinese officials routinely noted that the viability of the proposed transport and energy corridor to connect Xinjiang through to the Arabian Sea[175] is contingent not just on the stability of Balochistan, or the safety of specific contingents of Chinese workers, but on security in much of the rest of Pakistan too.[176] While China strenuously insisted that Pakistan should not be bracketed with its war-torn neighbour, in reality they were also looking with growing nervousness at developments across its western border, and the ripple effects of the militant resurgence there for Pakistan itself. And a new term entered the vernacular among Chinese policymakers, and started to be used with ever-greater frequency: "Talibanization".

6

TEA WITH THE TALIBAN

Now, we're all talking about Syria. [By the] second half of next year, the most important topic will be Afghanistan.

Wang Yi, Chinese Foreign Minister, 2013[1]

I think we all desperately hoped that British soldiers were dying for something more noble than helping Karzai's drug dealing cousin to sell gas from northern Afghanistan to the Chinese.

Former senior diplomat to Kabul, speaking to *The Telegraph*[2]

The start of China's latest round of adventures in Afghanistan was marked the same way the last couple ended—with a plane crash. Twenty minutes after its take-off on 24 February 2003, a clear sunny morning, a Cessna 402B twin-propellor aircraft plunged into the Arabian Sea 35 kilometres from Karachi, killing everyone on board.[3] The nine passengers included Joma Mohammad Mohamadi, Afghanistan's Minister of Mines and Industry, and Sun Changsheng, chief executive officer of China Metallurgical Group Corporation Resources Development, the giant Chinese company's Pakistani subsidiary. Mohamadi had taken up his position in Afghanistan's interim government the previous summer after a long career as an engineer at the World Bank, and a previous stint running the ministry of water and power in the 1970s. He was the third federal minister to be killed in the first year of Hamid Karzai's new administration.[4] Inevitably for a suspicious plane crash in Pakistani territory, the rumours started up almost immediately. Mohamadi's daughter suggested that it was her father's unwillingness to extend the benefits of a new gas pipeline to the right people that resulted in his untimely death—"All I know is that my father and his top advisers were in Pakistan signing the final agreements for a $2.5 billion gas pipeline to be built across Afghanistan, a lucrative project that many people wanted a piece of. But my father wouldn't sell out, and my brother once cautioned him, 'You'll be lucky if they give you a warning.' But he wouldn't listen."[5] A lawsuit brought by the young Chinese executive's family described the accident as "of such a nature which in the ordinary course of things does not happen".[6]

MCC, a Chinese state-owned engineering and construction conglomerate, had chartered the plane to fly the minister and a group of his officials out to see their new Pakistani venture, the Saindak gold and copper mine in the far west of Balochistan. Saindak was rumoured to be a location used by Chinese agents to maintain covert contacts with the Afghan Taliban after they fled the US invasion.[7] That February morning, though, it was supposed to act as a showcase that would help MCC secure an even greater prize: the biggest mining contract in Afghanistan's history. Aynak, in Logar province, is estimated by geologists to hold the world's second largest copper deposit, worth as much as $88 billion.[8] Afghanistan's mineral riches had been uncovered by repeated geological surveys conducted by the Russians and the British over the preceding century, and Aynak, which had been used for copper-working since ancient times, was identified as one of the country's two truly world-class deposits.[9] The Soviet Union had made the most concerted attempt to get a mine on the site into operation, but its efforts were derailed by the *mujahideen*'s campaign.[10] During the Taliban years, it was used as an Al Qaeda training camp, infamous for its elite training course whose alumni included one of the USS *Cole* attackers and four of the 9/11 hijackers.[11] There would be a gap of nearly two decades before another effort was made to tap the rich seam of copper that lay beneath.

The Chinese embassy in Kabul resumed its functions in February 2002, almost exactly nine years after rocket attacks on the compound forced the withdrawal of all of its diplomatic staff.[12] Afghanistan's interim government was seeking sources of revenue that were independent of the Western aid that constituted the bulk of its financing, and the newly arrived Chinese officials had learned that it was considering making Aynak one of its first tenders.[13] They tipped off their colleagues at MCC.[14] A Korean conglomerate was already making a pitch for the mine and MCC would need to move quickly with its own proposal.[15] From the perspective of Chinese resource needs, the appeal was obvious: twenty-five years of production at the mine would be equal to a third of China's entire copper reserves.[16] Like many state-owned companies, though, MCC was motivated by commercial considerations as much as any national goals. It was in the process of diversifying away from its traditional field of domestic steel mill construction, and planned to make the more lucrative avenue of natural resource development its new focus.[17] The Afghan mining minister's trip to Pakistan was part of a seven-year wooing campaign to make Aynak one of the jewels of MCC's burgeoning corporate empire that ran from Australia to Argentina. The company's ambitions in South-West Asia were being driven by the man who died with him in the plane, Sun Changsheng, but the crash derailed MCC for barely a few months.

MCC and its partner, Jiangxi Copper, prepared a mammoth bid for the mine that included plans to construct an on-site power plant, an associated coal mine to fuel it, a cement mill, and—at the request of the Afghan government—a railway line connecting the mine to the Uzbek and Pakistani borders. 10,000 jobs were promised.[18] The companies worked hard to persuade the new Mining Minister, Mohammad Ibrahim Adel, and his superiors that their bid should be looked on favourably. Adel certainly did that, advocating for MCC throughout the tendering process, and China's proposal showed distinct signs of benefiting from inside information from the ministry of mines.[19] Allegations persist—"with a high degree of certainty", according to a US official cited by the *Washington Post*—that a $30 million bribe paid in Dubai heightened the minister's desire to smooth things along.[20] Nevertheless, for the Afghan government the numbers looked good anyway: three $808 million payments, royalties at 19.5% (one of the highest in the world), and investments that could end up totalling as much as $10 billion.[21] It surpassed the other bidders on virtually every count. Aynak was more than just a good deal for the Afghan state, it was potentially a big step towards providing it with an autonomous financial underpinning: estimates suggested that it could generate $390 million of tax revenue a year, nearly a 50% increase in the government's income.[22] The initial investment alone would represent more than 70% of all the investments in the country from 2002 to 2007 and 35% of all the international assistance provided across the same period.[23] A commitment from a major Chinese company was attractive for another reason too. Afghan leaders hoped that China's relationship with Pakistan might help to protect the mine, the revenue stream, and possibly even the future security of the country.[24] Would the ISI really allow their assets to attack Chinese facilities? The Afghan government hoped not. Any insurgent advance on Kabul would now worry Beijing too, with the mine barely 20 miles south-east of the capital. On 20 November 2007, the ministry of mines made the formal announcement that everyone had been expecting. The Chinese consortium had won the contract, opening a new chapter in China's relations with Afghanistan.[25]

What MCC could not have anticipated, however, was Aynak's elevation to a symbolic status that supposedly made the copper mine deal representative of virtually everything about Beijing's approach to the country and the long war that was intensifying there. Rarely has so much been written about a mine from which so little was actually extracted. The drumbeat began almost immediately after the announcement. "While America is sacrificing its blood and treasure, the Chinese will reap the benefits," argued Robert Kaplan, claiming that China was "free-riding on the public good we offer".[26] "We do the heavy lifting and [China] picks the fruit," echoed S. Frederick Starr.[27] With China contributing nothing to the military campaign and very little by way of aid, the case that it somehow hadn't "earned" the juicy contract wasn't hard to make. There were even claims that American soldiers had taken on the responsibility for physically protecting the mine from Taliban attacks.[28] While that was untrue in a narrow sense, the notion that China was unfairly taking advantage of the Western security presence in Afghanistan proved difficult to shake off.

From Beijing's perspective, the argument was more than a little odd. Certainly the Aynak site needed an immediate level of protection, like other such projects in an insecure neighbourhood, but if there was one thing China did not want to see, it was a rival power setting up a long-term military presence in its backyard. Beijing had been deeply concerned about US bases in Afghanistan and the wider region since the very first days after 9/11. Afghan officials routinely described their

Chinese counterparts pulling out maps of the country, stabbing their fingers anxiously at the various locations, and pressing them about Washington's grand designs.[29] What's more, however ambivalent China was about the prospect of the Taliban taking control of the country again, it had dealt—and continued to deal—amicably enough with them when it needed to. Beijing's approach in Afghanistan relied on a carefully hedged policy that avoided picking sides or making unnecessary enemies. Any perception that the Chinese were only able to extract resources under the condition of armed American protection against the insurgency would be entirely antithetical to China's goals not only in the region but in the wider Islamic world.

In the end, free-riding was to be the least of the US or the Afghan government's concerns. Six years later, with production at the facility still to begin, the conditions of the contract being renegotiated, and an emergency trip by Hamid Karzai to China to determine whether the whole deal might be abrogated, the real question was whether the Chinese companies would risk taking a ride at all.[30] If Aynak symbolized anything it was that for China, Afghanistan remains largely a land of threats, real, potential, and imagined, rather than one of opportunities. The moment at which Beijing finally realized it had to take some responsibility for influencing the political and security situation there had little to do with its multi-billion dollar investments and a lot to do with its fears that chaos in Afghanistan might end up destabilizing two places it cares about a great deal more: Pakistan and Xinjiang.[31]

Technically, Afghanistan is China's neighbour, but only just. They share a tiny sliver of a border at the Wakhjir pass, 47 miles long, which has been closed to through-traffic since the founding of the PRC. On the Chinese side, the Karakoram Highway runs close by, winding its way towards the nearby Khunjerab pass and on into Pakistan. China's frontier patrols have use of a recently built road that turns off by the border,[32] but this new construction is not the result of any undeclared plans to open the route up: it is to make it easier for the security services to keep the border sealed. On the Afghan side is the Wakhan corridor, a narrow, mountainous, sparsely populated salient that forms part of Badakhshan province. The infrastructure there is even less developed—a rough road finishes 100km away from the Chinese border.[33]

The two countries have not actually been neighbours for that long. The only reason a China-Afghanistan border exists at all is because of the 1895 agreement between London and St Petersburg to keep their two empires geographically separated, with Wakhan as a buffer.[34] The deal involved neither the Chinese nor the Afghans, and elicited complaints at the time from the emir of Afghanistan about being stuck with "the Kirghiz bandits in the Wakhan".[35] Tajikistan and Pakistan are now the states kept apart by the thin strip of land. The border area is underdeveloped for good reason. For decades, Afghanistan has represented a security threat to China because of either the military presence of a strategic rival or the risk of Islamic militancy spilling over into Xinjiang, and more recently both at the same time. While the Afghan government has approached Beijing about the possibility of putting a direct transit route in place, China's reluctance to contemplate doing so has deep roots.[36] The closed border has proved a reliable means of containment.

For the first decades of the relationship, Afghanistan was largely peripheral to China's interests. Kabul recognized the new Chinese government relatively quickly, on 12 January 1950, but Beijing moved slowly to respond, with diplomatic relations only being formally established in 1955.[37] In contrast to its policies in many other countries in the region, China gave little support to communist parties in Afghanistan, its non-aligned status for a time sparing it the Cold War machinations in which China felt prompted to involve itself elsewhere. The two sides reached a border agreement in the flurry of Chinese diplomatic activity that took place after the war with India in 1962, but although subsequent years saw an exchange of state visits, a treaty of non-aggression, and agreements reached on trade, aid and economic cooperation, it remained a thin relationship that rarely drew attention in Beijing.[38] That started to change in the 1970s, as a series of convulsions in Afghan politics appeared to draw the country closer and closer to the Soviet Union. Each time there was a changeover of government in Kabul—the 1973 coup, the 1978 Saur revolution, and Hafizullah Amin's seizure of power in 1979—China had doubts over whether to extend recognition to the new regime, and feared that if Moscow's hand was not actually behind the coups, it was only a matter of time before Afghanistan became a full Soviet ally.[39] The outright invasion in December 1979 at least provided greater clarity on that count.

As it would a quarter of a century later, Afghanistan moved from being a country that China felt it could safely ignore to being geostrategically central. As one Chinese media outlet put it at the time: "It is precisely because Afghanistan is of vital importance to the Soviet global strategy that the Soviet Union has taken the risk of seizing it."[40] Some of the language that Chinese officials used openly at the time in their assessment of Moscow's intentions and the impact of its military occupation on China's interests would be used again privately after 9/11 to refer to the United States. While Afghanistan's geostrategic location was believed to have provided the general rationale for the Soviets' actions, its particular effect on China was "encirclement", especially when combined with Moscow's presence in Asia.[41] The building of long-term bases was seen as proof of the Soviet Union's intentions for a permanent presence, which would help it gain "a strategic edge over China and Pakistan".[42] Unlike the United States though, the Red Army occupied the Wakhan corridor, building an air base in Badakhshan, and creating anxieties about another front across which Soviet attacks on Chinese territory could ultimately be launched.[43] Beijing also feared that Moscow would push on from landlocked Afghanistan towards the Indian Ocean. As Geng Biao, the Chinese Vice-Premier, put it: "If the Soviets' barbarous aggression goes unchecked, the next target is Pakistan."[44] The solution was resistance. China would give massive support to the Afghan rebels, who would "explode the myth of the invincibility of Soviet hegemonism," Xinhua declared in 1980.[45]

China was already starting to agitate against the Soviet presence even before the invasion, and as early as April 1979 the United States had learned from Afghan sources of Beijing's willingness to supply weapons to the *mujahideen*.[46] In the 1980s that would be substantially ramped up, and Afghanistan became a central front for China. In what has been described as one of the most important clandestine operations in the PRC's history, Beijing became the arms-supplier-in-chief for the guerrilla war against the Soviet Union.[47] In the early years of the campaign in particular, when the United States was trying to downplay the scale of its involvement, Washington not only wanted to avoid having US weapons turning up on the battlefield, but also sought to source them from other Communist countries, providing deniability of US involvement.[48] This necessitated purchases from states like China that were able to provide Soviet-designed weapons. The range provided by Beijing was extensive, from AK-47s and RPG-7s to 107mm rockets and 60mm mortars. At Pakistan's request, the Chinese even brought back into production a single-barrelled rocket launcher that the PLA itself had discontinued.[49] Easily handled by one man, it would play a vital role in the *mujahideen*'s attacks on Kabul. Until 1984, China provided the bulk of all the arms and ammunition supplied,[50] and continued to supply them on such a scale that large unused caches were being found in Afghanistan more than a decade after the Soviet withdrawal.[51] The coalition of countries involved in the operation was broad, with weapons coming from Egypt and Israel, among others, but China was in the central group. Along with the CIA, the ISI, and the Saudi General Directorate, "There were four intelligence services that met every week in Islamabad", according to Afghanistan scholar Barnett Rubin.[52] China's activities in Afghanistan even had the imprimatur of the CPC red aristocracy: the man who acted as an assistant military attaché in Islamabad in the early 1980s, facilitating liaisons with the ISI during the *mujahideen*'s campaign, was Mao Zedong's grandson, Kong Jining.[53] While strategic considerations were important—Deng Xiaoping expressed his desire to turn Afghanistan into a "quagmire" for the Soviet Union—China also profited handsomely from the weapons sales.[54] The money came from the United States and Saudi Arabia, and is estimated at $100 million a year for the Chinese military in the first few years of the campaign alone,[55] "huge profit margins", as Steve Coll describes them, during a period when it was desperate for cash.[56] Arms purchases were agreed with the CIA station in Beijing, and although a small proportion of them, typically 10–15%,[57] were provided as "aid", the American officials negotiating the deals found that Beijing drove a hard bargain.[58]

Nominally, China's direct involvement was limited. Most of the weapons were sent by sea to the port at Karachi, at which point the ISI took over.[59] The only exceptions were a few air-freight deliveries and the supply of Chinese mules, which were sent down the Karakoram Highway before being used as a means of transport for weapons and supplies across the mountains into Afghanistan.[60] Pakistan was determined to control the flow of arms to its preferred groups, as well as the strategic direction of the war, and some Pakistani officials insist to this day that China's direct relationships with the *mujahideen* were restricted to the small Maoist faction, Shola e Jawed or "Eternal Flame".[61] One notable member of that group, Rangin Spanta, went on to become Afghanistan's foreign minister and national security adviser under President Karzai,[62] but most of them were killed by Pakistan's closest allies among the *mujahideen*, Gulbuddin Hekmatyar's Hezb-e-Islami, in the bloody infighting in Peshawar that followed the war.[63] China's interest however went well beyond the Maoists, who ultimately received little serious support. Beijing is believed to have infiltrated ethnic Tajik military officers into Afghanistan in order to circumvent Pakistan's restrictions and establish direct links with groups that would go on to form the Northern Alliance.[64] Ahmed Shah Masoud, one of the leading commanders, was known to be among the direct recipients of Chinese military aid.[65]

China was also involved in one of the decisions that would be seen as a turning point in the war. In January 1986, Senator Orrin Hatch visited Beijing, accompanied by a phalanx of US officials from the CIA, the NSC, and the Defense and State Departments who were managing the covert programme in Afghanistan, on a mission to secure Chinese support for the escalation of the *mujahideen*'s campaign.[66] A group of administration officials, and their supporters on Capitol Hill, were concerned that the *mujahideen* were losing the war and needed to be armed with more sophisticated weaponry in order to turn the tide. In particular, they wanted to see them provided with Stingers—a portable, shoulder-fired weapon that could launch heat-seeking missiles at Soviet helicopters and transport planes.[67] This was a controversial proposal in the United States, where cautious officials were concerned about the Soviet reaction to the introduction of highly visible US weapons, and the possibility that the missiles, if diverted outside Afghanistan, could be used against NATO forces in Europe or even to shoot down passenger aircraft.[68] The road to consensus in Washington ran through Islamabad, and the road to Islamabad ran through Beijing. General Zia had not actually asked for the missiles, which was a telling argument used against the hawks:[69] Pakistan, after all, was the country most immediately at risk of Soviet retaliation, and Zia himself was afraid that the missiles might be used by terrorists against his own plane.[70] China's support, it was believed, might prove persuasive. Hatch met the head of Chinese intelligence to urge his backing for the increase in the provision of US assistance to the *mujahideen*, particularly a new wave of operations that involved ISI officers accompanying the Afghan rebels on their guerrilla strikes. Hatch then asked if the Chinese would agree to support the Stinger supplies and "if he would communicate his support directly to Pakistani President Gen. Mohammed Zia ul-Haq as part of a coordinated lobbying effort".[71] In Hatch's lively account, "His eyes lit up. His face hardened. 'We acquiesce' he barked out."[72] It took "months of secret negotiations"[73] with the Chinese and with Zia before everyone was satisfied that the risk was worth taking, but China's willingness to persuade Pakistan to request the Stingers "cleared the way" for their introduction.[74] The ISI's Afghanistan Bureau Chief described it as the "single most important unresolved matter in defeating the Soviets on the battlefield,"[75] and the decision to give the the green light would prove to "tip the balance on the battlefield" in the *mujahideen*'s favour.[76]

As with the United States, China's agenda in Afghanistan at the time was purely geopolitical, and once the Soviet Union embarked on the withdrawal of men and matériel in June 1988, leaving only the rusting hulks of tanks and MiG 21s behind, China's involvement rapidly wound down. Two months later came the infamous plane crash that killed the US Ambassador, Arnold Raphel, and Pakistan's President, Zia ul Haq. And on 15 February 1989, Boris Gromov, commander of the 40th army, became the last Soviet soldier to walk across the Friendship Bridge and out of Afghanistan.[77] While China's formal diplomatic representation survived the early years of the Najibullah government, it quickly washed its hands of the matter as Afghanistan slid into civil war.

For most of the 1990s, China was officially absent from Kabul. The only remnants of its presence were three Afghan employees who still received payment twice a year from Beijing to tend to the old embassy, which had been the unfortunate victim of stray rockets as a result of its backing onto the presidential palace.[78] Even the Chinese dogs there had been shot, one by the *mujahideen*, one by the Taliban.[79] Towards the end of the decade, however, Beijing embarked on a process that might have seen its diplomats setting up again at their old address in Wazir Akbar Khan under contentious circumstances. Had it not been for 9/11, there was a good chance that China would have ended up being the first non-Muslim country to recognize Taliban-ruled Afghanistan.

Despite the Pakistani army's deep involvement in backing the movement, Chinese officials had never been enthusiastic about the Taliban's rise. The ideological and security threat that the fundamentalist militia could pose to Xinjiang and the wider region was clear well before they took power, and when the Taliban made their decisive breakthrough in the civil war, the Islamabad connection was not enough to line Beijing up behind the new regime. While the fall of the northern city of Mazar-e-Sharif in May 1997 provided sufficient excuse for Pakistan to extend diplomatic recognition to the "Islamic Emirate of Afghanistan" and prod Saudi Arabia and the UAE into doing the same, Beijing demurred. [80] There seemed little reason to push back against the near-global consensus that had been arrayed against the Taliban since their first days after sweeping into Kabul in 1996 were marked by the imposition of its peculiarly brutal version of *sharia* law, and the execution and mutilation of former president Najibullah, who was seized from the UN's compound.[81] Following the Al Qaeda bombings of the US embassies in Nairobi and Dar es Salaam, as pressure mounted on the Taliban over their provision of sanctuary to the terror group, China happily backed the UN Security Council's decision to establish a comprehensive set of sanctions against them.[82] It had its own, more direct concerns than Osama Bin Laden. After the Taliban takeover, Afghanistan had become a base for ETIM and other Central Asian militants affiliated to them, such as the IMU, and the training camps that the Uighur group established were in locations—including places in and around Kabul—that left no ambiguity about the fact that they operated with the consent of the country's new masters.[83]

Pakistan had been assuring China that this problem was amenable to negotiation. If Beijing was willing to open channels to the increasingly embattled regime, a deal of sorts might be reached. The Taliban were in desperate need of money and international legitimacy. The United States had curtailed the early diplomatic and commercial flirtations that had once given the Taliban hope that their impeccable anti-Iranian credentials, along with the promise of a pipeline deal, might provide them with a path to respectability in Washington.[84] Even Saudi Arabia had pulled out its diplomatic representative from Afghanistan as a result of Mullah Omar's recalcitrance over Osama Bin Laden.[85] For China, the depth of its isolation could be turned into an opportunity. "We urged China and the Taliban to establish formal contacts so that their mutual mistrust can be eliminated," said one Pakistani diplomat cited by Ahmed Rashid, "the Taliban pose a threat to nobody and want the best of relations with China".[86]

The value of a discreetly expanded relationship was already in evidence in the aftermath of the 1998 US cruise missile attacks on terrorist training camps in Afghanistan. Pakistan gave China access to a stray missile that landed on its territory, but Chinese agents also found willing salesmen on the other side of the border as they sought to recover what-ever they could from the Tomahawks.[87] These contacts took more open form in early February 1999, when a group of five Chinese diplomats flew into Kabul for a preliminary set of meetings with Taliban officials. Afterwards, China announced the opening of formal trade ties, flights between Kabul and Urumqi, and the provision of food aid.[88] At the end of the year, there were rumours that the PLA had agreed to provide low-level military support to the Taliban, via Pakistan, in return for the cut-off of training assistance for Uighurs.[89] But China proceeded cautiously. Tang Jiaxuan, the Chinese Foreign Minister, turned down a chance to meet his Taliban counterpart when he was on a visit to Pakistan in 2000.[90] Instead a much lower-level diplomat who was accompanying him, Sun Guoxiang, the Deputy Director of the Foreign Ministry's Asia Department, met the Taliban's ambassador in Islamabad, Sayyed Mohammad Haqqani.[91] Haqqani assured Sun that they would not allow anyone to use Afghan territory against Beijing: "Some foreign enemies of the people of Afghanistan and vested interests are bent upon creating misunderstanding and differences between the two friendly countries by leveling false and baseless allegations."[92] But the decisive assurances that Beijing sought could only come from the very top: Mullah Omar himself.

The preparations for a meeting with the Taliban's reclusive leader were made in Islamabad. Following the first round of UN sanctions, the Taliban's embassy there had become their principal diplomatic outlet to the world. The Chinese ambassador to Pakistan, Lu Shulin, an Urdu speaker who had studied at Karachi University in the 1960s, conveyed an official request for a meeting through his Afghan counterpart, Abdul Salam Zaeef. In his autobiography, Zaeef would describe the Chinese ambassador as "the only one to maintain a good relationship with the embassy and with [Taliban-run] Afghanistan".[93] Additional groundwork was laid in an "unofficial" visit to Kandahar in November 2000 by a delegation from the think-tank attached to China's ministry of state security, the Chinese Institute of Contemporary International Relations (CICIR).[94] The following month, the intelligence agents and academics were followed by Lu Shulin himself, who visited Afghanistan as part of a three-man team. In Kabul, he met a powerful group of Taliban leaders, including the Vice-president of the Council of Ministers, Mullah Muhammad Hassan Akhund, who oversaw the defence, intelligence and security apparatus, and the Interior Minister, Mullah Abdul Razzaq Akhundzada.[95] The two men would later become members of the Quetta Shura, the Taliban's ruling body in exile. After his visit to Kabul, Lu took an Ariana flight down to Kandahar, the birthplace of the movement and the country's *de facto* capital, where he became the first senior representative of a non-Muslim country to meet the Taliban's amir, and one of only a tiny handful of non-Muslims that Omar ever dealt with. This fact became vividly clear to the Chinese diplomats when they presented him with a gift, in the shape of a small camel figurine, to which he reacted as if they had handed him "a piece of red hot coal", believing the representation of a living being to be idolatrous.[96]

In their discussions, Lu raised China's concerns about "rumours that the Islamic Emirate of Afghanistan was allegedly assisting the Muslims in Xinjiang".[97] Mullah Omar assured the Chinese ambassador that "Afghanistan never had any interest or wish to interfere in China's domestic issues and affairs, nor would Afghanistan allow any group to use its territory to conduct any such operations or support one to that end."[98] Both sides emerged from the meeting only partially satisfied. The Taliban's leadership had hoped that China might be helpful in fending off a new set of UN sanctions, which included the imposition of an arms embargo, travel bans, a prohibition of flights from Afghanistan, and the mandatory closure of the Taliban's overseas offices. Beijing did not veto the resolution, but, instead of supporting it, as it had the unanimously approved sanctions of 1999, made a point of abstaining, expressing concern "that the Afghan people would suffer from the measures proposed in the resolution".[99] Even more importantly, China gave the go-ahead for a set of commercial interactions that would help mitigate the sanctions' impact. Huawei and ZTE were believed to have agreed to provide a limited phone service in Afghanistan, ZTE signing a contract to install 5,000 phone lines in Kabul, and Huawei to install 12,000 lines in Kandahar.[100] Chinese companies, such as Dongfeng Agricultural Machinery Company, began repairs to Afghanistan's power grid, fixing dams in Kandahar, Helmand and Nangarhar. For their part, the Taliban "ordered the East Turkistan group to cease their attacks against China".[101] While in practice this only seemed to result in their having to join IMU camps instead of operating their own independent camps, the distinction was not without consequence—the Uighurs were not expelled from Afghanistan, but they were effectively subsumed into the activities of the Central Asian groups rather than being given the freedom to pursue a China-centric agenda.[102]

The prize that the Taliban and their Pakistani sponsors really craved from Beijing was diplomatic recognition, and, despite Afghanistan's increasingly pariah-like status, the possibility of granting it was at least under consideration. China's formal stance was that it would not make a decision until the UN's position had been determined, but its growing diplomatic and economic engagement in Afghanistan was taking things in a clear direction. Relations experienced a setback, however, with the destruction of the large 8th century Buddha statues in Bamiyan. China, along with Japan and Sri Lanka, was later described by Taliban officials as being one of the most active states in lobbying against the spectacular act of cultural vandalism once the plans were made public.[103] When a Taliban commercial delegation arrived in China a couple of months after the dynamiting of the statues, they found that all of their official meetings with the Chinese government had been refused.[104] Although the threads between the two sides were picked up again, many of the plans were destined never to come to fruition. A Chinese delegation visited Kabul later that year to ink an MOU spelling out plans to upgrade economic and technical cooperation, which was signed by Mullah Mohammad Issa Akhund, the Taliban's Minister of Mines and Industries. The announcement of the deal came on 11 September 2001.[105]

Jiang Zemin, the Chinese president, watched the 9/11 attacks on Phoenix TV, a Hong Kong network—CCTV, the state broadcaster, was not running the news story. He called other Chinese officials and told them to turn their televisions on. Within two hours, he had placed a call to President George W. Bush to express condolences and pledge China's support.[106] This was not just rhetoric. China offered intelligence support and even a form of military assistance, in the form of minesweepers, as the United States prepared to invade Afghanistan.[107] The FBI was allowed to set up an office in Beijing.[108] Terrorist financing intelligence was shared.[109] The Chinese embassy in Washington also informed the Pentagon that it could call on the services of the man who "knew the location of every arms cache in Northern Afghanistan and a lot else besides": Chen Xiaogong, who had run Chinese intelligence operations in Afghanistan in the 1980s, and was now serving as military attaché.[110] Chen's advice and the minesweepers were both rebuffed by the Secretary of Defense, Donald Rumsfeld, who was barely minded to involve traditional US allies in the invasion, let alone the Chinese military.[111]

Whether or not the United States took up the offers didn't much matter to China. The pledges of assistance served the dual purpose of securing US acquiescence to its stance on domestic terrorism issues, and shoring up ties with Washington at precisely the moment when many in Beijing believed strategic competition between the two sides was about to escalate.[112] In this respect, 9/11 was a relief to a Chinese government that now saw the United States training its sights on the greater Middle East rather than the Asia-Pacific. Nonetheless, China was concerned by the escalating US military presence in its neighbourhood. All of a sudden, an arc of countries near China's western border that had been seen as peripheral to US interests became the locations of new military bases and supply routes. And nowhere was this shift more concerning, and more sudden, than in Pakistan.

Within two days of the 9/11 attacks, the United States had delivered to Pakistan not only a "with us or against us" ultimatum, but a specific list of demands, which ranged from a break in relations with the Taliban to an extensive package of military and intelligence cooperation.[113] The decision on whether to accept the bulk of Washington's requests needed to be reached quickly by Musharraf, and it was. While restricting the scope of certain elements—such as overflight rights—and questioning others, the answer from Islamabad was a slightly qualified "yes". China had to play catch-up on what exactly was going on. As a Pakistani observer of the relationship noted: "There was no consultation with China. Usually there would be a mechanism for consultation with China on issues of such significance but Musharraf took the decision in a very short space of time."[114] As a result, within barely a week of the 9/11 attacks, Jiang Zemin dispatched Wang Yi to Islamabad as a special envoy to gauge the scope of Pakistan's security cooperation with the United States and to gain some assurances.[115]

Wang was China's youngest deputy minister, a former visiting scholar at Georgetown University and a career Asia specialist who would go on to handle some of the country's trickiest portfolios—Japan and Taiwan—before being appointed as China's foreign minister. This was an equally delicate assignment. The visit has been portrayed in some accounts as China "shoring up Pakistan's support for the US effort."[116] While in one sense this is true—Beijing certainly did not think that

Pakistan should get itself "bombed back to the Stone Age" by the United States, as Deputy Secretary of State Richard Armitage was supposed to have threatened[117]—China also wanted to ensure that its interests in the region were not harmed, and was not entirely comfortable with what was envisaged in the new terms of the US-Pakistan relationship. Intelligence cooperation in dealing with Al Qaeda was one thing, US bases in Pakistan, overflight rights, and land supply routes were quite another. Wang made sure that he had "clarified the Pakistani position that under no circumstances would Pakistan allow its cooperation with the U.S. to undermine Chinese strategic interests".[118] He raised the suggestion that Pakistan could put forward a timeframe for the United States to leave Afghanistan. He also began what would be a longer-running conversation, in which Beijing asked that Pakistan give China the same opportunities to establish intelligence-gathering capabilities in the country as the Americans, whether it came to signals or human intelligence.[119] On 2 October the Chinese government released details of a phone call between Jiang and Musharraf, quoting Jiang as stressing that "the fight against terrorism should have concrete evidence and specific objectives. It should also abide by the purposes and principles of the UN Charter and the recognized norms of the international law."[120] It reflected China's apprehension and ambivalence over US activities in the region that would recede only a decade later when it believed that the United States was finally on its way out.

In Afghanistan itself, during the early, relatively peaceful years after the invasion, China picked up where it had left off on September 11, 2001. The Pakistani ambassador to China at the time later described a "sense of relief" in Beijing at the Taliban's ousting.[121] ZTE and Huawei were back to set up digital telephone services, providing 200,000 subscriber lines to the country.[122] ZTE later won a major contract to construct a national fibre-optic cable network.[123] Chinese construction companies such as China Railway Shisiju Group got to work on the rebuilding of the Kabul-Jalalabad road[124] and sections of the ring road in Faryab province.[125] Chinese companies took on the repair of hospitals in Kabul[126] and Kandahar,[127] the latter of which the Chinese had built in the 1970s, and returned to the Parwan irrigation project that they had first established in the 1960s.[128] Two Chinese lions were sent to Kabul zoo in 2002[129] to replace what had once been its main attraction, Marjan the lion, who had survived coups, the Soviet invasion, the civil war and the Taliban.[130] A less wholesome trade also sprang up in Kabul—large numbers of Chinese "restaurants", most of which were barely-concealed brothels.[131] The overall scale of China's economic presence was still modest but it was diverse and growing, and by the time the enormous Aynak copper mine project had been announced, China was on track to become Afghanistan's largest investor. On diplomatic and security matters it kept its head down—but few noticed or expected much more of it. After all, Afghanistan was not supposed to be a conflict zone any more.

By 2006, the Taliban had comprehensively regrouped. During the US invasion, thousands of fighters slipped across the border with Pakistan and melted back into the parts of the country that had once been their homes in the 1980s and 1990s—Balochistan, the North-West Frontier Province and FATA.[132] Mullah Omar himself had left Afghanistan for Quetta in 2002, where he stayed at guest-houses run by the JUI, which ran the provincial coalition government.[133] The Balochi city became the Taliban's unofficial capital. A leadership group in exile was formed and the process of rearming, reorganizing, recruiting and fundraising was quickly underway, with the support of the ISI.[134] By 2003, the Taliban were launching guerrilla attacks in Afghanistan again.[135] By 2004, the greater parts of several southern provinces were already considered to be under Taliban control.[136] And by 2006, the take-off of suicide bombings, IED usage, outright Taliban military offensives, and escalating numbers of civilian and coalition casualties marked a country that had unambiguously been plunged back into war again.[137]

China's reaction to these developments was a mix of caution, ambivalence, and hedging. On the one hand, it did not want to see a return to the late 1990s, with parts of Afghanistan turning into a safe haven for ETIM again. On the other hand, it didn't want to see a US victory in the country either, with the risk of a long-term military presence on China's borders and a staunchly pro-Western government in Kabul. Its preferred outcome—a politically independent, autonomous and stable Afghanistan that was not run by religious extremists—was not on the table. In 2005, China had made the closest thing to a public demand for an end to the US military presence in the region as a whole when it joined a statement from the Shanghai Cooperation Organisation (SCO) calling for a timetable for the closure of US bases in Central Asia.[138] The US facilities at Karshi-Khanabad in Uzbekistan and Manas in

Kyrgyzstan had become the subject of controversy after the "Tulip Revolution" toppled the Akayev regime in the latter country. When the United States supported the extradition of refugees who had fled the Andijon massacre in Uzbekistan, the furious Uzbek president, Islam Karimov, fearing that he might be next, shut down the K2 base and pushed the SCO to issue its statement.[139] From China's perspective, the growing Western presence in the region started to look like an arm of the democracy-promotion agenda that it feared, the so-called "colour revolutions", which had now crept towards China's borders. In Afghanistan, Beijing watched like a hawk to see whether the US bases being built in the country foreshadowed a permanent presence, and took particular note of any military activities in Badakhshan or Nuristan province that might be too close to its territory for comfort.[140]

Outright backing for the Taliban was out of the question for China, but so was outright backing for the Americans. This was a war in which Beijing wanted neither side to win, and neither side to blame Beijing for supporting its opponents. The solution was to hedge. China had not broken its contacts with the Taliban since the war, and meetings between the two sides continued, including a visit to Beijing in 2002 from the brother of one of the most powerful Taliban commanders, Jalaluddin Haqqani.[141] Even in exile, the pre-9/11 deal that the two sides had reached was useful to both sides, and former Chinese officials claimed in interviews that a mutual understanding was reached that its basic elements should be maintained.[142] The Taliban would keep their distance from Uighur militant groups, and China would treat the Taliban as a legitimate political grouping rather than a terrorist outfit, quietly maintaining relations and judiciously separating the language it used when referring to them from the language it used of groups such as Al Qaeda.[143] It even supplied them with arms, which prompted diplomatic protests from the United States and the UK after a few too many of them showed up in attacks on their troops.[144] The weapons China supplied included HN-5 anti-aircraft missiles, landmines, rocket-propelled grenades, components for roadside bombs, and armour-piercing ammunition.[145] Some Chinese arms had been kicking around since the 1980s. Some had found their way to the insurgents via Iran. Others, however, went directly to the Taliban from China, through Pakistan.[146] Beijing provided support to Hamid Karzai's government in Kabul too, but well short of the level that would make the insurgents think that China was backing it too fulsomely. China ranked 23rd on a donor list published in 2009,[147] and some of its activities smacked of tokenism: its training of anti-narcotics police was described by one participant as "being taken on a visit to Xinjiang and lectured about China's reform and opening policy."[148]

However, China's delicate dance with the different political forces operating in Afghanistan faced its most exacting test with the various economic projects that it had set in motion. Some of them attracted controversy for their own reasons. The Chinese work on the highway system—which was publicly criticized by the Afghan finance minister for its slow progress[149]—was widely seen as poor, and the roads required resurfacing after the companies in question had left.[150] At one point there was a rumour that China had been using prison labour to construct the Kabul-Jalalabad road, though it appears that this was just the result of shock among local Afghans about the basic conditions in which the Chinese workers lived.[151] In the most egregious instance, a Chinese hospital in Kabul was opened, closed the following day, and never used by a single patient owing to the sheer scale of its construction defects and the lack of resources to run it.[152] Even the Chinese brothels were mostly shut down in 2006.[153] But the scope of China's early economic activities was limited, and by the time the insurgency was in full flow, most of them had been wound up. An investment such as the Aynak copper mine, on the other hand, was on a qualitatively different scale; its success or failure would have strategic implications for the government in Kabul, the ISAF stabilization effort, and the broader future of the country. The Taliban's decision on how to treat these projects had ramifications that went well beyond their relationship with Beijing.

Trying to answer the ostensibly simple question of whether the Taliban were targeting Chinese investments in Afghanistan or laying off them is fraught with complication. In the early years of the insurgency, it appeared that the best way to reach a conclusion was to look at China's roadbuilding projects, some of which were taking place in parts of the country where the Taliban's presence was growing. China's work in the east of the country seemed to proceed remarkably untroubled by militant activity, and gave the Afghan government reason to believe that it might be operating under Taliban—or Pakistani—protection.[154] But one incident in 2004 in the northeast of Afghanistan served to illustrate just how muddy that picture was. On 10 June, in the early hours of the morning, a group of twenty assailants gunned down Chinese workers as they slept in their tents, using assault rifles, rocket-propelled grenades and hand grenades.[155] The construction workers, who were mostly from Shandong, and in many cases had arrived barely two days before the attack, were employed by China Railway Shisiju Group on a World Bank-funded highway project near Kunduz. Eleven of them were killed. It was the deadliest attack on foreigners in the country to date and was initially assumed to be a deliberate Taliban effort to sabotage the government's reconstruction efforts. Kunduz, although located in a part of the country that was believed to be safe at the time, was rare among northern provinces in having a half-Pashtun population, and various Taliban-affiliated armed groups maintained their reach there even after the invasion.[156] It had been the last Taliban holdout in the country after the US invasion, a former IMU stronghold, and the location for the so-called "Airlift of Evil" in November 2001, when the Pakistani air force evacuated hundreds of Taliban commanders, ISI agents, and Al Qaeda and IMU fighters before they could be captured by US forces.[157] Yet the Taliban, who had been happy to claim responsibility for the murder of a group of aid workers from Médecins Sans Frontières barely a few days before, rushed to disavow responsibility—"We deny the accusation of killing the Chinese workers in Kunduz province of Afghanistan," Abdul Latif Hakimi, a spokesman, told the press in a telephone call. The deaths, he said, "should not have happened."[158] The Taliban even organized a demonstration in Takhar, near Kunduz, "to show their support for the Chinese".[159] The Kunduz military commander said that hundreds more people held a demonstration in Kunduz city to "condemn the killing and call on the Chinese company to continue its work repairing the key highway from Kabul to the Tajik border".[160]

The evidence instead pointed to militants affiliated with Gulbuddin Hekmatyar's organization, Hezb-e-Islami. Hekmatyar had once been Pakistan's favourite son among the *mujahideen*, but his inability to build a national following in the 1990s saw him thrown overboard by his sponsors in favour of the Taliban, who were seen as better able to consolidate power in Afghanistan.[161] Hekmatyar fled to Iran for several years, was expelled in 2002, and returned to Pakistan in an effort to work himself into a position of power in the new insurgency.[162] Whatever his motives, being tied to the killing of Chinese workers would not be helpful to him as he sought to get himself into the ISI's good graces again. Hezb-e-Islami had even established direct contact with the Chinese soon after Hekmatyar's return from Iran—during which time he "made concerted efforts to placate China, as well as to urge the Muslim leaders in Xinjiang to stop their separatist agitation".[163] In an interview conducted with him a couple of months after the killings, he denied involvement in the incident. The journalist, however, would not let him off the hook:

Question: Are you behind the recent killing of the Chinese?

[Hekmatyar:] I have no idea about it. The Taliban have split now. The other faction is led by Mullah Soban. It could be his brainchild. I have expelled some miscreants from my party. It could be their handiwork. I really have no idea.

Question: But the Afghan government strongly suspects that you have masterminded it. They have good reasons to believe this. In fact, you have admitted it off-the-record while talking to some journalists…

[Hekmatyar:] It is not true. I cannot accept the responsibility if some miscreants have masterminded it at the U.S.' behest. I believe it is the handiwork of the Americans. They have used some greedy mujahideens for this inhuman act to defame the true mujahideens. I suspect that the Americans have also masterminded the killing of Chinese in Gwador, Baluchistan. The U.S. agenda is to malign jehad and jehadis.[164]

The lesson for China was that even with all of its political ducks seemingly in a row, its projects would still be exposed to serious security threats. Whether as a result of individual grievances, divisions within militant organizations, or simply commanders with their own agenda, investment in an all-out war zone carried high risks. Ultimately, Beijing's relations with the Quetta Shura and the ISI could not provide a definitive guarantee against attacks. And nowhere would this be clearer than in China's biggest investment.

Following the Aynak deal's grand announcement in 2007, the most striking fact about the copper mine project was how little then happened. It started slowly as both sides appeared to make painful progress even with basic paperwork.[165] As the project crawled forward and the scheduled date for the copper's extraction moved further and further back, the question of the reasons for the delay grew more and more acute. Some members of the Afghan government raised the prospect of throwing the Chinese companies off the project and reopening the bids.[166] Other accounts suggested that Chinese money was helping to ensure that officials in the ministry of mines didn't complain too much.[167] But the Chinese companies involved had a long list of grievances of their own. In public, there were a couple of excuses they could point to that were less sensitive. Ostensibly the discovery of a major archaeological site—Mes Aynak—was the main cause of the hold-up.[168] But this was not sufficient reason for the lack of progress on other infrastructure that was nowhere near the dig. "We're just useful idiots for the MCC," said one French archaeologist working on the project.[169] Security problems were another reason cited. Yet while Logar was certainly insurgent territory, the group operating in the province was the Haqqani network, the militants tied most closely to the Pakistani government— once described by the top US military officer, Admiral Mullen, as a "veritable arm of the ISI".[170] If they had wanted to stage a major attack on the facility, they could have done so. They had been responsible for some of the most spectacular militant operations in Afghanistan in recent years,[171] and it is unlikely that the ANA's protection force at the mine and a few decommissioned Chinese People's Armed Police who were based inside the facility would have been enough to stop them.[172] Instead, whether they did so of their own volition or with Pakistan's guidance, the Haqqanis kept well away from targeting the mine.

There were still security issues in the environment of the mine but, at least initially, the handful of stray rockets didn't seem to go beyond the risks that MCC could reasonably have anticipated for an investment in such a location. Researchers from organizations such as Integrity Watch Afghanistan conducting interviews around the mine had a strong sense that they were not centrally directed insurgent attacks, but rather stemmed from local grievances that the national and regional government had still not addressed.[173] Land claims from the surrounding villages remained unresolved, despite the Afghan government's pledge to do so. Other issues piled up too—the lack of skilled workers, corruption among Afghan officials, and the unfeasibly high costs of the proposed railway project.[174] And a vicious cycle was developing—the number of attacks in the vicinity of the mine was rising, MCC was growing increasingly nervous about its investment and withdrawing workers from the project, and the local people were growing less and less happy about the slow progress of an investment that was supposed to yield significant economic benefits for them.[175]

Political motives were also read into the delay—some officials in Kabul suggested that, while the Chinese company had the foothold it needed, it lacked any rationale for moving expeditiously with the project.[176] The main beneficiaries of royalty payments would be the current Afghan government, which might not survive, and the NATO coalition, which wanted economic projects like this one to succeed quickly. The fact that US officials were urging China to move forward with the investment was an *a priori* reason for a major state-owned company not to do so. At the very least, there was a strong case for waiting to see how the political and security situation in the country developed.

MCC was going through its own difficulties too: the company reported a loss of over a billion US dollars in 2012, with cost overruns, delays and the plummeting cost of iron ore hitting the company.[177] By the end of the year, only a skeleton crew was left at the mine, and the Afghan government was struggling to persuade MCC to move ahead with operations. "We had meetings with them (the Chinese investors) and assured them these rocket attacks happen anywhere and they are not the direct targets. We had repeatedly meetings with them but could not make them confident," said Sardar Mohammad Sultani, the Deputy Interior Minister. "The timing of those workers returning to Afghanistan will depend on conditions," said an MCC spokesman.[178]

Even in a supposedly less complicated part of the country, China still found itself running into problems. For several years after the Aynak deal, there was virtually no Chinese economic activity in Afghanistan, as if China Inc. was collectively reserving judgement over the future of the country. Then, in December 2011, came the announcement that China National Petroleum Corporation, the largest Chinese oil and gas producer, had won the bidding process for Afghanistan's first major oil contract.[179] It did so with a local partner that seemed to have every political base covered, and a commercial relationship with China that went back a surprisingly long way. Watan Group had achieved a level of notoriety after being blacklisted by the US government following its controversial handling of a security contract for the Kandahar-Kabul road, a vital logistics route for coalition convoys.[180] A US Congressional report exposing Watan's payments to Taliban commanders followed press reports that as much as 10% of the $360 million contract may have been handed out as protection money to the insurgency.[181] The episode cast a spotlight on the two men who ran Watan, Rashid Popal and his brother Ahmed Rateb Popal.

Rateb Popal had last been in the public eye immediately before the invasion of Afghanistan, during the final, chaotic press conference held by the Taliban's ambassador in Pakistan. Interpreting for the ambassador was a distinctive figure—a six-foot tall man with a black turban, big beard, eye-patch, damaged hand and prosthetic arm, who spoke with a New York accent.[182] Born into a prominent Pashtun family, Popal had studied at Queens College, Flushing (New York), and had picked up his injuries while still a schoolboy in Kabul during the Soviet invasion. The bomb that blew up in his hands had been intended for the Russian embassy.[183] After spending ten years in prison in the United States on heroin-smuggling charges, he returned to Taliban-run Afghanistan in 1998 seeking business opportunities. One of his first ventures was a steel factory, which he established with help from an outside source—China.[184] Over the next few years, he would live between Pakistan and Afghanistan, acting as a broker for business deals between the Taliban and the Chinese, who provided one of the few commercial avenues available at the time.[185] After the US invasion, however, his importance to China's interests in Afghanistan grew considerably: Popal was a cousin of the new Afghan president, Hamid Karzai, and members of the Karzai family were believed to be major shareholders in Popal's company.[186] He was known to receive a lavishly generous level of hospitality in Beijing.[187] Watan Group went into business with a couple of Chinese partners, working with Huawei to install digital networking equipment in government ministries and establishing Sino-Afghan Steel, the realization of Popal's original joint venture of the late 1990s.[188] But the CNPC deal was on a more serious scale.

In comparative terms, the investment itself was relatively small—there are believed to be only 87 million barrels at the Amu Darya field—and the terms, as with Aynak, were generous for the Afghan government: 15% royalties and 50–70% of the profits, as well as a promise to build the country's first refinery.[189] In theory though, it positioned CNPC well to win larger future tenders, and to connect its Afghanistan oilfields with the company's growing energy infrastructure in Central Asia.[190] Yet again, however, the project would be dogged with problems. The three oil blocks were in the northern province of Sar-e-Pol, up towards Afghanistan's Central Asian borders, far from any serious insurgent threat, in territory controlled by the Uzbek warlord Rashid Dostum. Dostum was not happy about his cut. He had played a crucial role in Karzai's presidential re-election campaign—returning to the country to help swing a major voting block behind him[191]—and had long treated this part of the country as a personal fiefdom. Just as Karzai was due to visit China for the SCO summit in June 2012, press stories appeared about men loyal to Dostum intimidating Chinese engineers and demanding a share in the proceeds.[192] Posters of Dostum were hung around villages and towns near the Sar-e-Pol site. The Afghan national security council accused him of "undermining the national interest" and threatened to arrest him.[193] Dostum retorted that "China is a trustworthy friend of Afghanistan. It has made the largest investment in the mineral resources of the country. I do not have any problem in that regard. However, I rightfully demand for the rights of the people of the Sar e Pul and Jawzjan, who have to be considered as a top priority as far as the selection of the workforce is concerned."[194] It was a poor omen. The problem was fixed, and the field started pumping oil within a few months, but in the eyes of Chinese diplomats it was the second occasion on which the Afghan government had failed to get the local politics squared. And a year later the project had stalled again, with drilling halted and most of the Chinese workers sent home, this time supposedly owing to a dispute over transit arrangements with Uzbekistan.[195] In practice though, the more serious disagreement was between CNPC and Popal's Watan Group over lucrative subcontracts.[196]

The stuttering progress of the oil project yet again cast a pall over the willingness of investors, Chinese or otherwise, to take a risk on Afghanistan. This was supposed to be the simple, successful project in a peaceful part of the country that should have been more akin to a venture in Central Asia than in the insurgency-racked regions in the East and South. When the Afghan government launched another oil tender in September 2013, it found "no important takers".[197] Aynak itself appeared to be close to unravelling completely. In 2013, MCC's proposed renegotiation of the terms of the contract would absolve it of almost all the major infrastructure commitments that had made the deal so attractive to the Afghan government in the first place, and push back the proposed start date for mining to 2019.[198] The ripple effects were significant. The other major investment in Afghanistan, the Hajigak iron ore mine, which was run by an Indian company, had been premised on the delivery of much of that same infrastructure—without it, that company too wanted a renegotiation of terms.[199] Hamid Karzai flew to Beijing in September 2013 seeking a deal. The Afghan government had been split. One side proposed simply throwing the Chinese off the project altogether. The case against doing so was not commercial, it was political: "Others for strategic reasons want [renegotiation of the contract] to happen … so China remains committed to helping Afghanistan when the money dries up in this country."[200]

This was not just a hopeful punt on the part of the Afghan officials. Even as China's economic engagement with Afghanistan was stalling, its diplomatic engagement was increasing exponentially. For years, Chinese diplomats were known for turning up to the array of international jamborees on Afghanistan's future, reading out their talking points, and then playing virtually no role at all in the remainder of the proceedings.[201] Bilateral relations were amicable but distant—Afghanistan's top leadership would troop off to China from time to time but there were no reciprocal visits of any comparable seniority. Then, in 2011, everything started to change. Not only did Chinese officials suddenly appear to care about the agreements that were being reached in major international gatherings[202] in Istanbul and Bonn, they were willing to disagree openly with Pakistan—the Holy Grail, from Afghanistan's perspective, given China's influence over its friend.[203] The shift in behaviour was stark: "Before, you would attend meetings on Afghanistan and the neighbours would be silent, and here you have them taking a lead," said one of the diplomats in attendance at the Istanbul summit, in an interview with Reuters. "The Chinese for the first time were very comprehensive and constructive, you could really see an elevated role of China in the region and more outspoken than ever before."[204] Another official states, "They were very vocal and raised several issues during the drafting. We weren't even allowed to begin the final version until the Chinese delegation had arrived."[205] China was also convening a flurry of meetings of its own, with bilateral and trilateral get-togethers with Pakistan, Afghanistan, Russia and whatever other configuration looked like it might be useful,[206] even conspicuously including India.[207] Its meetings with the Taliban intensified, taking place in Pakistan and even in China itself, and the contents of these exchanges started being relayed to other countries rather than being kept closely held between Beijing and Islamabad.[208] Afghanistan also received the first visitor from the Chinese politburo standing committee in several decades, Zhou Yongkang, the security chief.[209] For observers who were used to a Chinese political approach in Afghanistan that prioritized avoiding attention, there was suddenly a lot that stood in need of explanation. Some analysis of

Zhou's visit, for instance, pointed to his former role at CNPC and his reputation as chief of China's oil lobby to suggest that resources were the motivation for his surprise trip. It was nothing of the sort. "We don't really have economic interests in Afghanistan right now," argued one Chinese analyst. "None of the projects are moving. There's only one concern there: security."[210]

China was paying serious attention to it again, and the catalyst for the surprising acceleration in Chinese activity was an increasingly ominous date: 2014.[211] The Americans were leaving.

7

LORD, MAKE THEM LEAVE—BUT NOT YET

Personally, I must have said on no less than ten occasions to my American friends that the United States should aid Pakistan.

Deng Xiaoping, 1979[1]

Our friend is in trouble and we need to provide as much help as possible.

Yang Jiechi to Richard Holbrooke, 2009[2]

When President Obama spoke to President Xi he said 'We are not Afghanistan's neighbours, you are neighbours. You should be ready'. Now we are ready.

Chinese official, 2014[3]

On Friday 24 August 2012, two US Hellfire missiles struck a militant training camp in the Shawal valley, near the border of North and South Waziristan. The target of the drone strikes was Abdul Shakoor Turkistani, the chief of Al Qaeda's forces in FATA, who was killed along with three of his commanders. Turkistani had been appointed as Al Qaeda's leader in the tribal areas in April 2011, a few weeks before Osama Bin Laden's death. A jihadi newsletter claimed that he was "supervising training camps", as well as preparing militants for attacks in Europe and the United States.[4] He was known to be a member of Al Qaeda's executive council, the *majlis shura*. His position on the US targeting list, therefore, was hardly controversial. But he had another identity too. Abdul Shakoor—or Emeti Yakuf, one of his other commonly used pseudonyms—was the head of the Turkistan Islamic Party, the Uighur militant group still known to Beijing as the East Turkistan Islamic Movement.[5] Yakuf was one of those believed to have been responsible for the propaganda videos threatening attacks on the Beijing Olympics in 2008.[6] One of the European attacks he appeared to have been plotting was an attack on the Chinese embassy in Norway.[7] When China had issued an eight-man "most wanted" list of terrorists in 2008, he was the second person named, and on 15 February 2010 he took over the job of the man who occupied the number one slot.[8]

His predecessor had suffered exactly the same fate. In May 2010, Abdul Haq al Turkistani, ETIM's previous leader, was also killed in a US Predator air strike, on a compound in the village of Zor Babar Aidak, near Mir Ali in North Waziristan.[9] Abdul Haq had been the figure most closely involved in ETIM's deepening relationships with other militant groups in the border region, and was an influential enough leader to represent Al Qaeda in its dealings with insurgent forces in both Pakistan and Afghanistan. A few months earlier, he had been seen at a meeting with Baitullah Mehsud, the Pakistani Taliban chief, and several senior commanders of the Afghan Taliban.[10] The deaths of these two leading figures—and two others on the eight-man list who also lost their lives—would be a serious blow for ETIM and a major victory for the Chinese government. And US drone strikes were not just decimating ETIM's leadership, they were also responsible for the deaths of some of its most important supporters. In July 2012, six Uzbeks belonging to an IMU splinter organization that was close to ETIM were killed in a strike.[11] In June 2012, the top Al Qaeda ideologue who had called for a jihad against China—Abu Yahya al-Libi— was the victim of four missiles fired at another North Waziristan compound.[12] Thirteen Uighurs and two Turks, all of them confirmed by ETIM as its members, were killed in Afghanistan's Baghdis province in another Predator strike a few weeks before Abdul Haq, a major loss for a group that may only number in the tens.[13]

While ETIM and its supporters were supposed to constitute China's main terrorist threat, there was no question that it was the United States that was proving to be their most lethal opponent. Yet this was a role that should have been occupied by Pakistan: all the names on China's "most wanted" list were believed to be living on Pakistani soil. In 2003, Pakistan's army had been able to claim the credit for taking out the previous ETIM leader, Hahsan Mahsum, in an operation in South Waziristan.[14] But since then, it had not been delivering results. The eight-man target list that China issued in 2008 was made public partly as a dig, published as it was on the eve of President Zardari's visit to Beijing, and partly as a gesture of despair. The Pakistanis had been sitting on the names for years and nothing seemed to have been happening. Pakistan handed over nine Uighur militants to the Chinese in 2009, but as long as members of ETIM's top leadership were operating in territory controlled by groups that Pakistan considered to be the "good Taliban," they appeared to be safe.[15] Then the US drone campaign began in earnest. ETIM's leaders were both killed in locations that Pakistan had been unwilling to touch—a region in North Waziristan under the authority of a Taliban commander, Hafiz Gul Bahadar,[16] who was linked to the ISI-sponsored Haqqani network[17] and periodically engaged in peace deals with the Pakistani army.[18] US officials roundly denied that Washington was doing any of this for Beijing's benefit. But it was hard to escape the fact that the United States had done more to support the elimination of "anti-Chinese elements" in Pakistan in two years than the Pakistani government had in ten. Pakistani officials were sheepish: "It may have taken a U.S. missile to kill one of China's most wanted Muslim separatists. But still, the Chinese probably see this as a good development," as one Pakistani security official put it.[19] The Chinese wondered, nonetheless, why they were relying on their strategic rival to accomplish the task rather than the country that was supposed to be their closest friend.

Since 9/11, the mantra that the United States and China have common objectives in the region is one that Beijing has been happy enough to recite without really believing it to be true. Both sides could agree that "stability" was good and "terrorism" was bad, but at any level of specificity, the picture quickly became clouded. Beijing's counter-terrorism strategy has been essentially parasitic on the United States being a more important target for transnational militant groups than China. With the exception of ETIM and its supporters, Beijing's interest was not to embroil itself in a battle with extremists in the region, it was to ensure that it didn't get on the wrong side of them. That meant steering well clear of whichever side the United States was on. "Stability" in Afghanistan was not especially appealing to the Chinese either, if it just meant a stable environment for the United States to entrench its military presence.[20] China was far happier to see the US army embroiled in a series of debilitating wars across the Middle East and South-West Asia than either of the alternatives—a successful consolidation of US power in the region, or a heightened US focus on East Asia. Yet in the period since President Obama took office, there is no doubt that the two sides have moved much closer together in both their dealings and their views on the region. From a starting point where China seemed determined not to involve itself in Afghanistan, was unwilling to engage in meaningful exchanges about Pakistan, and refused any bilateral cooperation with the United States in either country, it has reversed its position on all counts. The basic reasons for this are clear enough: the United States is withdrawing from Afghanistan, and the aftermath looks worrying. Without the geopolitical threat of "encirclement" by US bases that had such a hold on China's strategic imagination, Beijing has started to view the future of the region through a very different prism. But it has been the security developments in Pakistan that have had the most potent impact. China's doubts over Pakistan's handling of militancy within its borders, whether ETIM, the TTP, or the longer-term threat posed by the creeping advance of extremism in Pakistani society, have led it discreetly to find common cause with Washington on a growing array of issues there. One former senior US diplomat stated: "There used to be a group of countries that China wasn't willing to talk to us about properly. Pakistan is the only one that's left."[21] Within a few more years, that may no longer be true.

For veterans of the US-China relationship, any talk of Pakistan conjures up an almost nostalgic sense of the two periods during which the country was at the heart of bilateral relations, and those relations themselves were in their warmest phase. First, when Islamabad was playing its discreet and vital role as matchmaker, in the secret diplomacy of the 1970s, to bring Washington and Beijing together, and second, in the 1980s when the triumvirate were in their quasi-alliance against the Soviet Union. Across nearly two decades, China and the United States shared an interest in Pakistan's fate and believed that some degree of synchronization of messages and support might be helpful. After the anxious efforts at coordination during the 1971 war, detailed in the first chapter, Chinese officials consistently urged their US counterparts to give Pakistan more aid and better weapons than China could provide itself, and even weighed in on Pakistani politics. American and Chinese leaders compared notes on the messages the two sides were sending to Zia ul-Haq about the situation of Zulfiqar Ali Bhutto, whom neither side wanted to see executed, and even whether China might offer him asylum (Deng: "If he wants to come, then we will be prepared to receive him". Brzezinski: "He could use the same villa as Sihanouk did!" Deng: "I think he has a better place.").[22] But in subsequent decades, the China-Pakistan relationship would disappear into a secretive space from which it has still not fully emerged.

Following the end of the Afghanistan campaign, the fall of the Soviet Union, and the Tiananmen Square protests, both Sino-US relations and US-Pakistan relations took a sharply negative turn. After more than a decade of turning a blind eye to Pakistan's nuclear programme, there was no longer a strong enough political imperative for Washington to continue to do so. And China was no longer a Cold War friend but a country that suddenly looked like it was on the wrong side of history, and potentially an economic and military rival over the long term to boot. China and Pakistan had enjoyed relatively healthy military-military ties with the United States, but suddenly saw arms supplies cut off and sanctions imposed. Pakistan was the third largest recipient of US aid behind Egypt and Israel, most of it being military aid; in 1990 it was abruptly stopped.[23] The Pressler Amendment required American assistance to be cut off if the administration failed to certify that Pakistan was not in possession of a nuclear device, a position that became virtually impossible to maintain. US military sales to China were suspended the day after the world watched the PLA's tanks and machine guns trained on unarmed students.[24]

In the 1990s, when Pakistan featured in US-China exchanges it was largely for one reason—nuclear proliferation. From the M-11 missiles to the 5,000 ring magnets destined for the nuclear weapons facilities at Kahuta, Chinese assistance to Pakistan's nuclear and missile programmes was a constant source of US criticism and sanction.[25] For a Chinese military that was starting to see the United States taking the place of the Soviet Union as its primary threat, arms sales and security cooperation with Pakistan now required protection from US pressure and scrutiny, rather than being part of the continuum of the three sides' cooperation.

This was a relationship that was moving even more firmly under the control of the Chinese military, the defence companies linked to it, and China's security services. Their mentality was highly defensive. The notorious line about Pakistan being "China's Israel"—part explanation, part sarcastic jibe—was delivered by its military intelligence chief after one too many meetings with US counterparts on the subject.[26] There was also a sense in Washington that Chinese missile sales to Pakistan were carefully timed to take the form of retaliation for moves on the US side, such as the F-16 sales to Taiwan in 1992.[27]

For Beijing and Washington, the 1998 nuclear tests and the Kargil crisis of 1999 did bring about a certain shift in South Asia's status: the threat of war in the region was treated as a joint US-Chinese security concern for the first time since the 1970s, and China's special relationship with Pakistan was seen to provide a helpful source of leverage rather than just a proliferation problem. But 9/11 had a far more significant impact. While China was uneasy about the scale of the US military and intelligence footprint in Pakistan, it also meant that Washington was resuming the role that Beijing wanted to see it play: providing the arms and aid to Pakistan that would bolster its capabilities against India, and bringing the country out of the near-pariah status that it had flirted with at points in the 1990s. Despite its initial reservations, for much of the George W. Bush administration the arrangement suited China quite well. The United States shifted strategic focus from Afghanistan to Iraq relatively quickly, moderating Chinese fears about its presence in the region, but was still delivering huge packages of military assistance to Pakistan. Despite the United States' best efforts, China almost certainly got a look at some of the US kit too.[28] And with Pakistan now being granted the status of "major non-NATO ally" by the US government, the China-Pakistan relationship, which had been perceived in a largely nefarious light for the previous decade, was now treated in more neutral terms. Beijing still faced continued US pressure over its dealings with the likes of Iran—but no longer with Pakistan, whose rogue state days were over, at least for a while.

Sino-American consultations did take place during times of crisis. Beijing was asked by Washington to play a role in reducing tensions during the so-called "Twin Peaks" crisis of 2001/2, when India and Pakistan were on the verge of war, and in the aftermath of the 2008 Mumbai attacks.[29] When Pakistan faced a financial crisis that same year, the United States also encouraged China to steer Pakistan towards an IMF programme rather than bailing it out, and Beijing was more than happy to oblige.[30] A regular South Asia dialogue was established at assistant secretary level as part of the array of US-China bilateral talks that were put in place covering different regions of the world under the auspices of the "strategic dialogue".[31] For most of the officials who had been involved in the exchanges with the Chinese, though, the view was pretty uniform: outside the context of acute peril for Pakistan, China wouldn't talk about the country and its problems seriously, particularly when it came to the question of its support to militant groups. At best it was willing to play a "water carrier" role, passing on messages about US concern but not reinforcing them with matching expressions of its own.[32]

Until the very final period of Musharraf's tenure, this didn't seem to matter much: South and South-West Asia were a long way down the list of issues featuring on the US-China bilateral agenda, and Beijing's unwillingness to be helpful was a matter of at most, minor regret. But by the time the Obama administration came to office, Pakistan and Afghanistan were gripped by a near-constant sense of crisis. The insurgency in Afghanistan was drawing the United States back into full war-fighting mode. The insurgency in Pakistan itself was spreading from the tribal areas, and convulsing its major cities with terrorist violence.[33] And the political and economic situation was unravelling. Musharraf's last, chaotic year in office saw popular mass protest movements, the imposition of martial law, the assassination of Benazir Bhutto, and the beginnings of a full-blown financial meltdown.[34] By 2009, any pretence that the US problem in the region was just a few foreign fighters hiding out in the tribal areas had also evaporated. Instead, it was now the entire ecosystem of militancy, from the Southern Punjab to the ISI's extremist-sponsoring S Wing, and the political environment that sustained them that were in the US crosshairs.[35] The very nature of Pakistani society, education, politics, and the military seemed to be treated as a legitimate matter of concern by US policymakers as they contemplated the world's only fragile nuclear-armed state. And however quiet they were about it, Pakistan's stability was becoming a subject of anxiety for policymakers in China too.

At the start of 2009, Chinese officials were preparing for Afghanistan and Pakistan to take a serious place in the US-China conversation again.

The 2008 presidential election, with its talk of the "right war"[36] and the "war of necessity", seemed to have staked Afghanistan out as a subject of heightened focus for the incoming president.[37] Chinese officials knew that they had assets in both countries, not least their position of special influence in Pakistan, and were anticipating—and somewhat fearing— that they would be asked to deploy them.[38] Officials from the new Obama administration were not expecting a dramatic change in China's approach, but it was hoped that the scale of the crisis in Pakistan, the reframing of US Afghanistan policy to place it in a more regional context,[39] and the simple fact that "Af-Pak" was being accorded an elevated status in US foreign policy might make Beijing more willing to be cooperative.[40] Chinese officials were somewhat surprised by the first request they received, to open up Chinese territory for non-lethal supplies to support the coalition effort in Afghanistan.[41] For some US officials, this would be a symbolic measure—to demonstrate the fact that the two sides could now be military partners, and overcome the deep, residual Chinese suspicion that the American presence in the region had some ulterior, China-directed motive in mind.[42] But many on the Chinese side remained suspicious.[43] It didn't seem that China could be particularly useful, given the absence of a direct transport route to Afghanistan— supplies would still have to make their way through Central Asia—and the risks of being visibly associated with the NATO war effort were substantial. Yet for logisticians on the US side, the China route had practical advantages, and for the strategists it reduced the risk of relying on Russia for the Northern Distribution Network. Discussions went all the way down to the question of whether Ford Ranger pickup trucks, made in Thailand and destined for the Afghan police, were a "non-lethal" supply[44] but eventually petered out, especially after the July 2009 riots in Xinjiang elevated Chinese fears about the reaction across the Muslim world, and even from its own population.[45] The US arms sales package to Taiwan in January 2010 definitively ended the discussion.

But the more pressing matter during the first year of the new administration was Pakistan. By April 2009, the Pakistani Taliban had taken control of Swat Valley, and moved within 100km of Islamabad.[46] The new US Secretary of State, Hillary Clinton, stated that the Taliban advance posed "an existential threat", and urged Pakistanis to "speak out forcefully against a policy that is ceding more and more territory to the insurgents".[47] It was hoped that China, if it truly appreciated the scale of the crisis, could lean on its old friends and make them see sense: that it was high time the Pakistani military struck back, diverting the necessary troops from its eastern frontier. Chinese officials listened—but were dismissive. They were happy to talk about Pakistan but suggested that the threat was hyped.[48] What the Chinese heard from the Pakistani military was more reassuring, and while they were happy to provide any additional equipment or supplies if the Pakistanis asked for them, and continue their bilateral assistance, they saw no reason to interfere. When the State Department gave a proposal to its counterparts in the Chinese foreign ministry for cooperation on stabilizing Afghanistan and Pakistan, US officials were told that the Pakistan part of it would not even be considered.[49] If anything, Washington's worries were themselves a source of Chinese concern. While the Taliban advance might be a problem, the possibility of the United States deciding that Pakistan could no longer be trusted with its nuclear weapons was in some ways a greater one. Every statement coming out of Washington fretting about the security of Pakistani nuclear facilities or a "failing" Pakistani state rang alarm bells in Beijing, in a way that even the possible diversion of nuclear materials did not.[50] As one Chinese official put it: "If terrorists did get hold of nuclear weapons, we're certainly not going to be their first target."[51] Nonetheless, despite their outwardly sanguine stance in bilateral meetings with the Americans, the Chinese had been thinking about the subject ever more seriously.

The Chinese military's planning for major crises in neighbouring states is a subject as sensitive as it is secretive.[52] North Korean and Pakistani generals have operated for years under the supposition that US defence planners are poised to seize the right opportunity to swoop in and grab their nuclear assets. American officials make little attempt to conceal their concerns about the implications of state fragility or failure in either country. But China is a great deal less comfortable spooking its friends and allies with that kind of speculation, and Washington's efforts to draw Beijing into discreet discussions about contingency planning have been routinely rebuffed.[53] However, for crisis planners in the Chinese military, their friends are one of the main sources of concern.

The risks in China's north-east and south-west are longstanding, whether it be large flows of North Korean refugees[54] or the spillover from the Burmese government's conflicts with the ethnic groups that straddle the Chinese border.[55] In recent years, though, concerns about the state that lies across the mountain passes to China's north-west have assumed growing importance. Official Chinese expressions of anxiety have appeared in coded form, studiously avoiding the name of the country in question. In 2009, a set of instructions was issued by the Chinese government for methods to deal with nuclear emergencies, allusively mentioning the "rising numbers of nuclear facilities in neighbouring countries and threats of attacks" and the fact that "the threat of global terrorism is a reality".[56] In private exchanges, representatives of Chinese military intelligence were less veiled. Pakistan had started to appear high on a list of countries of concern in its neighbourhood, perhaps second only to North Korea, and China was preparing for a number of scenarios, from the familiar—war with India—to the novel—the further weakening of the Pakistani state and the diversion of nuclear materials into the hands of terrorists.[57] The events that had prompted the scenario-planning just kept accumulating. The Mumbai attacks in December 2008 saw the sub-continent again pushed to the brink of war, this time by Lashkar-e-Taiba, an ISI-backed militant group which China's own diplomats had protected from sanctions at the UN Security Council on Pakistan's behalf.[58] There was speculation that terrorists might be seeking to get the Pakistanis to deploy their nuclear weapons—by putting the country on a war-footing with India—precisely so that they could seize them.[59] The aftermath of the Mumbai attack saw less military brinkmanship than during the last crisis on the subcontinent in 2001, but Chinese officials wondered whether India would show the same restraint if Mumbai were to happen again.[60] The nature of the attacks in Pakistan itself was also becoming more worrisome. In 2009, uniformed militants infiltrated the army's General Headquarters in Rawalpindi,[61] and in 2011 militants managed to stage a major attack at the Mehran naval base in Karachi, the assailants clearly benefiting from insider assistance both times.[62] On the latter occasion Beijing had a close view: China's own engineers and technicians were nearly killed in Karachi, the vehicle in which they escaped being fired at by militants from point blank range.[63] Pakistani security forces took fifteen hours to regain full control of the base. In August 2012, Chinese engineers again needed to be shifted to a "high profile secure location" as Kamra air force base, where China and Pakistan were jointly assembling the JF-17 fighter jet, came under attack in a five-hour gun battle.[64] Although

Pakistani officials denied it, there were rumours that nuclear weapons were stored at or very close to the base.[65]

"One conclusion we reached was that there is very little that we can do unilaterally if there's a crisis in Pakistan," said one Chinese expert who had worked on the scenario planning, "Any action would have to be coordinated."[66] A 2011 article based on briefings by senior US officials went as far as to claim that "China has, in secret talks with the US, reached an understanding that, should America decide to send forces into Pakistan to secure its nuclear weapons, China would raise no objections."[67] People familiar with the exchanges described that as "an over-interpretation", but the fact that issues of this nature were being discussed between the two sides was not fiction: Pakistan's internal stability has been addressed at length in talks between some of the most senior figures in US and Chinese policymaking.[68] As one Chinese expert with whom I discussed the subject put it:

"Would we accept a U.S. intervention to seize Pakistan's nuclear weapons? No. Are we as worried as [the United States] about the security of Pakistan's nuclear weapons? No. Nuclear weapons are all they have, it's the single thing we're sure they'll protect. But China is willing to help Pakistan defend a Pakistani bomb. We won't help them protect an Islamic bomb. If it's under the control of a mullah, then everything changes. It's not unconditional."[69]

An illustration of what has been a quietly growing Sino-US comity in policy towards Pakistan came during a period of exceptional tension in US-Pakistan relations. It followed the most notable occasion on which the United States did indeed send forces, undetected, deep into the country.

For a select group of Chinese soldiers watching television footage of the aftermath of the Navy SEALs raid on Osama Bin Laden's compound in Abbottabad on 2 May 2011, much of what they were seeing would have been familiar. In December 2006, Abbottabad, where the compound was located, had been the location of an extensive set of joint Sino-Pakistani counterterrorism exercises.[70] The hills that loomed behind Bin Laden's house were used for "large-scale intelligence gathering", "ambushes" and "search and destroy missions".[71] Cadets from the Pakistani military academy witnessed a Chinese martial arts and Pakistani unarmed combat show, featuring "special tactics against terrorists".[72] The world's most wanted terrorist is believed to have set up home barely a few streets away from the military academy in the previous year.[73]

The aftermath of the May operation saw US-Pakistan relations plunge to one of the lowest points in their history. They were already under strain that year following the Raymond Davis incident, in which the CIA contractor, a former US special forces operative, shot and killed two Pakistanis in downtown Lahore.[74] The sheer accumulation of frustration among American officials over Pakistan's double-dealing with militant groups was also at its peak, perhaps epitomized by the devastating December 2009 attack on a CIA border camp in Afghanistan, Forward Operating Base Chapman, in which seven agents were killed by a bomber affiliated to a Taliban group closely linked to the Pakistani intelligence services.[75] It was the worst attack the CIA had suffered in decades. The Abbottabad raid confirmed the worst fears of both sides. Pakistan's military demonstrated either incredible negligence, or a profoundly disturbing willingness to afford protection even to the leader of Al Qaeda, in a garrison town barely 75 miles from Islamabad. The United States demonstrated that it was prepared to conduct unilateral operations in the very heart of Pakistan, a performance that it might repeat if another major security threat—such as an incident involving Pakistan's nuclear arsenal—occurred. The Pakistani military was humiliated by the raid, of which it was unaware until the US special forces had left the country. It faced serious tensions both internally, as seething junior officers criticized the leadership over its relationship with the United States, and externally, as the big question—"Who knew he was there?"—echoed around the world's capitals. With its back against the wall, Pakistan turned to an old friend.[76]

Prime Minister Yousuf Gilani was due to go to Beijing within two weeks of Bin Laden's death, and the trip now took on a completely difference resonance, drawing febrile speculation about Chinese support to an embattled Pakistan in the face of US pressure. The world's media ran front-page stories on China's promise to expedite delivery of JF-17 fighter jets,[77] and claims from the Pakistani defence minister that China had agreed to build a naval base at Gwadar.[78] New meaning was read into old phrases about China being "our best and most trusted friend".[79] Extended analysis in serious newspapers looked at the building of a "China-Pakistan alliance".[80] Beijing, it appeared, was ready to provide the backing that Pakistan needed if relations with Washington continued to plummet.

The country that was least worried about this, though, was the United States. Before and after Gilani's visit, China went to unusual lengths to ensure that US diplomats in Islamabad and Beijing were carefully briefed on exactly what had and had not been offered to the Pakistanis.[81] For China, the deteriorating US-Pakistan relationship was not an opportunity to poke a stick at the Americans or to further deepen Sino-Pakistani ties, which were already quite as deep as they needed to be. It was a serious source of concern. China was already worried enough about the situation in Pakistan without the additional threat of a shutdown of US aid and military support, or even an outright confrontation between the two sides. Bin Laden's location in Abbottabad reinforced fears among Chinese officials about extremist sympathies in the Pakistani military.[82] Not only would Beijing resist any attempt to take advantage of the situation, it would try to help resolve the problem. The Pakistanis were told that while they could continue to count on China's regular economic and military support, Beijing was not going to backfill for the Americans, and Islamabad urgently needed to patch up its relationship with Washington.[83] Pakistani proposals for a defence agreement between the two sides were rebuffed.[84] "We're willing to give them everything they ask for in terms of defence cooperation but not actually to sign a defence pact," said one Chinese expert.[85] And while they were happy to speed up the delivery of the already-promised fighter jets, Chinese officials explicitly denied that a deal had been agreed for a naval base at Gwadar.[86] Privately, the Chinese gave reassurances that they would protect Pakistan if there was any attempt to impose sanctions on the country or on specific individuals for their links to Bin Laden.[87] They were happy to have a chance for a look at the downed US stealth helicopter.[88] But they maintained their basic line to the Pakistanis—fix your relationship with the United States—in what would prove to be a difficult period ahead for US-Pakistan ties. As on so many occasions in the past, Beijing made the limits of its support to Pakistan crystal clear. And as has happened with increasing frequency it made sure that US officials knew this.

The story of Sino-US cooperation in Afghanistan followed a similar path, from deep scepticism to growing alignment. In late 2009, the State Department submitted a "Joint Action Plan" with a very modest set of proposals for areas in which the two sides could work together: vocational training for Afghans, scholarships to US and Chinese universities, equipment provision to hospitals, agriculture projects and so on.[89] It elicited a resounding silence. Hillary Clinton ultimately had to raise the fate of the document in one of her meetings with the Chinese foreign minister, so hard was it to get a response.[90] All that came back was more obfuscation. The story was the same on the ground. The US ambassador in Kabul at the time was Karl Eikenberry, a Mandarin speaker and Sinologist, who had dealt extensively with Chinese officials in a career that included two tours as attaché in Beijing.[91] But despite his being on good terms with his Chinese counterpart, even the smallest suggestions for joint activities drew blanks. At one point he proposed that the two of them take a trip together to Logar province. After he was told that it would require a two-month long security clearance process, the real reasons were privately made clear: Beijing didn't want the US and Chinese ambassadors even being seen in public together on a bilateral basis.[92] By the summer of 2010, about the only example of bilateral cooperation on Afghanistan was the US embassy's provision of security advice to the Chinese delegation in advance of its visit for the July 2010 Kabul conference.[93]

China's involvement in the multilateral processes around Afghanistan and Pakistan was equally desultory. At a succession of different conferences, from London to The Hague, Chinese officials turned up, made *pro forma* statements, and then engaged in virtually none of the substance of the subsequent discussions.[94] It was even worse at the donor group meetings for Pakistan, the freshly established "Friends of Democratic Pakistan", where China only sent junior officials and stressed that it would only provide assistance bilaterally. At least the Chinese Foreign Minister, Yang Jiechi, was the man sent to say very little during the Afghanistan discussions.[95] If China wasn't going to engage multilaterally or through any form of cooperation with the United States, American officials suggested that there were a couple of things that it might helpfully do that were purely bilateral in nature. In Afghanistan, simply moving ahead with its copper mine investment at Aynak would provide significant support to the Afghan economy.[96] And financial aid to Pakistan would be even more helpful than any comparable escalation of assistance to Afghanistan, given how difficult it was to get assistance packages there through the US Congress.[97]

Beijing continued to demur. For a host of reasons, detailed in the previous chapter, Aynak was going nowhere fast.[98] China certainly had little intention of putting together anything that even faintly resembled the Kerry-Lugar bill, the most significant US effort in many years to step up civil rather than military aid to Pakistan.[99] This was not a civilian government that Beijing felt much like rewarding. Any of the more ambitious US hopes that Beijing might use its influence with Pakistan to steer it away from its assistance to insurgent groups operating in Afghanistan were even further away from realization. Expectations of China in Washington had never been high, when it came to Afghanistan and Pakistan, but its behaviour for the first two years of the Obama administration fell short of even the most modest of them. At one level this didn't matter too much. China had been a relatively marginal actor in Afghanistan over most of the last decade, and a continued position on the sidelines wouldn't greatly affect matters either way. But the sense persisted that a major source of economic capacity and diplomatic influence remained untapped.

The sharpest debate underway in Beijing was not just over what its response to US requests should be, but over what US policy in Afghanistan actually amounted to.[100] For much of 2009, Chinese officials watched the painfully drawn out policy review process in Washington in a state of some confusion.[101] Above all, it was unclear whether a Chinese contribution would help the United States consolidate a sustained military presence or speed its way to an exit. President Obama's speech at the end of the year, in which a troop surge was announced alongside a withdrawal date, did not help to clarify matters.[102] Different Chinese agencies reported different answers over the course of 2010. The Chinese military watched the build-up of US bases in Afghanistan, listened to what they were being told by their American counterparts, and believed they were seeing plans put in place for the long haul. The foreign ministry detected something different—a political dynamic in Washington that would override the US military's preferences and make the 2014 withdrawal date a far more important part of the Obama speech than the surge.[103] By 2011, it was clear who was right.

On 10 May, a full line-up of China's diplomatic, military and economic leadership was in Washington for the US-China strategic and economic dialogue (S&ED), the Obama administration's annual jamboree that involved as many as twenty government agencies on the two sides. Despite China's ambivalence, US officials had kept plugging away with the exchanges on Afghanistan, and this would be an important set-piece occasion on which to signal that the Chinese position was changing. Luo Zhaohui, who had returned to Beijing from Pakistan to take over as head of the Asia department at the ministry of foreign affairs, informed US diplomats that China had identified three areas that might be amenable to bilateral cooperation.[104] Sections of the long-forgotten "action plan" were going to be put into motion.[105] The content—agricultural and health projects, and the joint training of Afghan diplomats—was less important than the form: China wanted the cooperation announced as part of the outcomes of the meeting in Washington.[106] A modest programme of bilateral cooperation would now get underway.[107] Chinese officials were already using different language to talk about the prospect of the withdrawal of US troops: instead of asking when it would happen, they started expressing concern that the United States should not leave too hastily.[108] Beijing had finally come to believe that the prospect of withdrawal was real, and wanted to be in a position to influence what happened next.[109] The change in China's stance was publicly on show in the two multilateral conferences on Afghanistan that took place later that year in Istanbul and Bonn. At the first, US officials were struck by the fact that Chinese diplomats were not only finally speaking up,[110] but also willing to split openly with the Pakistanis on certain issues.[111] The continued closeness between China and Pakistan was clear in Bonn—Pakistan refused to turn up to the meeting at all, following the border incident at Salala at which 24 of its soldiers were killed by NATO forces,[112] but China represented its position in the relevant meetings.[113] This was a responsibility that Beijing would have been unwilling even to contemplate a year before.

If these developments were too small in scope to suggest that Beijing was really intending to play a more significant role in dealing with Afghanistan post-2014, an array of developments in 2012 left less doubt. In June, Afghanistan was formally admitted as an observer to the SCO, the regional organization that China had formed and in which it still plays a leading role.[114] A bilateral "partnership agreement" was signed during Karzai's visit to Beijing for the SCO summit.[115] And in September, China sent the first politburo-level visitor to Afghanistan in forty years, Zhou Yongkang, the security chief.[116] The same year, its level of involvement in regional diplomacy intensified—China started convening an increasingly regular sequence of trilateral and bilateral meetings: China-Pakistan-Afghanistan; China-Pakistan on Afghanistan; China-Russia-India on Afghanistan;[117] and China-India on Afghanistan, to name only a few.[118] In its meetings with the United States, Beijing even started to suggest that it might play a role on the vexed issue of political reconciliation in Afghanistan through talks with the Taliban, with whom China had been conducting meetings of its own.[119] After many years in which its exchanges with the Taliban had essentially been kept covert, the fact that China was, as one former Chinese official claimed, "the only country other than Pakistan that has maintained a continuous relationship with the very top leadership of the Taliban" was a potential asset now that the United States was seeking a political solution rather than a military one.[120] Beijing's own meetings with the Taliban, which took place with Pakistan's encouragement, were more about allaying Chinese concerns about whether they would allow Afghanistan to become a base for Uighur separatists, and sounding them out about their intentions.[121] "I would describe them as 'contacts' rather than serious meetings," argued one Chinese expert.[122] But the Taliban representatives also expressed their support for a Chinese role in facilitating a political reconciliation process in which they were looking for any leverage they could gain over what they saw an overbearing Pakistan presence.[123]

For Pakistan, the shift in China's position from bystander to activist could be portrayed in a positive light. This was in evidence in April 2011 when Pakistan's Prime Minister, Yousuf Gilani, and the ISI chief Shuja Pasha sat down for a meeting with Hamid Karzai in Kabul. Gilani told Karzai that the US had "failed" both their countries, and that Pakistan's economic problems meant it could not be expected to support long-term development projects in the region.[124] China, he suggested, would be a better partner, and was ready to take on a greater role.[125] The press reporting on the meeting, based on leaks from the Afghans in attendance, was met with a raft of denials from the Pakistanis, whose foreign ministry spokesperson described it as "the most ridiculous report we have come across".[126] But it reflected the reason why Pakistan had been so keen for the new trilateral conclaves with the Chinese and the Afghans to go ahead—the Kabul government's uniformly hostile view of its future relations with Islamabad might be reframed if Pakistan's capacity to act as spoiler of Afghanistan's security was sweetened with the promise of Chinese money.

In other respects, though, Beijing's decision to involve itself to a greater degree in Afghan affairs as the 2014 transition approached made Pakistan uncomfortable. In the past, Islamabad had virtually been given a free hand there. For two decades, its aid to the Taliban barely elicited a bat of the eyelid from its closest security partner, and much of Beijing's Afghanistan policy was effectively run through Pakistan. But now, China was starting to express preferences of its own, which were different enough from those of the Pakistanis to act as a constraint.[127] China cared more about stability in Afghanistan than Pakistan did, and was considerably less hung up on India's role in the country, which many on the Chinese side saw as potentially helpful if it took the form of investment and support for political stability. For Beijing, the overriding priority was simply to steer the different forces in the country towards a political settlement that would help fend off the worst-case scenarios that it feared: civil war, a buoyant insurgency that could destabilize Pakistan too, proxy wars taking off between New Delhi and Islamabad, and an environment in which terrorist groups hostile to China might flourish.[128] The Afghans, who had already planted seeds of doubt about how reliably the Pakistanis were addressing Chinese counter-terrorism concerns, saw a little room to create daylight between Islamabad and Beijing, and plenty of political and economic benefits that might accrue from an expanded Chinese role in the country.[129] "Pakistan's interests are still central to our Afghanistan policy but we don't see things the same way", noted one Chinese official, "They're more optimistic about the Taliban than we are, and more optimistic about controlling them. We're not so sure…We're talking to the first generation Taliban, the Quetta Shura, but the second generation is different. We can deal with the Pashtunwali version but not the Wahhabi version."[130] These concerns on China's part—and the prospect that they might nudge it towards the role of regional stabilizer—would also have important implications for its relations with the United States.

Afghanistan has been at the nub of a broader shift in US policy, officially dubbed the "rebalance" to Asia but still more often referred to by its original, catchier title: the pivot.[131] The drawing down of the US presence and paring back of strategic focus in South-West Asia was supposed to facilitate the scaling up in East Asia. As Hillary Clinton's article that gave birth to the term put it:

As the war in Iraq winds down and America begins to withdraw its forces from Afghanistan, the United States stands at a pivot point. Over the last 10 years, we have allocated immense resources to those two theaters…. One of the most important tasks of American statecraft over the next decade will…be to lock in a substantially increased investment—diplomatic, economic, strategic, and otherwise—in the Asia-Pacific region.[132]

While this is still framed in diplomatically broad terms about addressing the "opportunities and challenges" presented by the world's most dynamic region, much of the focus is on dealing with one challenge above the others: a rising, and increasingly assertive China. The Asia pivot was portrayed as bringing an end to what the Assistant Secretary of State for East Asian and Pacific Affairs, Kurt Campbell, described as a "a little bit of a Middle East detour over the course of the last ten years".[133] It was a detour that Beijing believed left it with a crucial period of license while Washington was bogged down in Iraq and Afghanistan. For the United States to turn to China for help in this part of the world while pursuing what Beijing inevitably dubbed a "containment" policy in the Asia-Pacific region smelled to some Chinese like a trap.[134] It looked distinctly like the Americans leaving behind a mess in the region for China to clean up, dragging it into the looming chaos in its western periphery just as the US-China competition in East Asia was heating up.[135] Others in China, however, see a chance not only to enter a political and economic space that the United States is vacating, but to do so in a way that is consonant with both US and Chinese objectives and potentially a way of stabilizing the relationship itself.

The argument was formulated most forcefully by Wang Jisi, one of China's leading foreign policy intellectuals, who advanced the case for China "marching West" as the US pivots to the East.[136] He contended that Beijing's internal efforts to rebalance between coastal and interior regions need an international strategy to underpin them, drawing on China's traditional historical, economic and political focus on the interior rather than the maritime realm. On the economic front, the "westward" economy, running down the old Silk Road, now has the highest growth rate and the highest growth potential. On the security front, he argues that the separatist, terrorist and extremist threat is best negated through a strategy to stabilize not only China's western periphery but also the countries surrounding it. And above all else, that unlike in East Asia, which was increasingly taking on the qualities of a zero-sum game with the United States, China's western periphery sees "significant scope for cooperation" in investment, energy, counter-terrorism, non-proliferation and regional stability, with an "almost non-existent risk of military confrontation" between the two sides.[137]

Wang's position as one of the country's most influential advisers on US-China relations has in many ways been eclipsed by the ascendance of more hawkish voices who believe that Washington and Beijing are destined for strategic rivalry. The "march West" argument itself was viewed unsympathetically by those in the PLA who viewed the military (and naval) buildup that China was undertaking in its east as the essential security task over the years to come.[138] For others, it was simply counterintuitive—looking west from China, the obvious images that come to mind are fragile states, rising forces of Islamic militancy, major narcotics flows, and the world's fastest growing nuclear arsenals. It is to the east that the more obvious opportunities for economic development and the demonstration of military prowess lie.[139] But when the new leadership in Beijing took office in November 2012, it soon demonstrated that it bought important elements of the underlying case that Wang Jisi had been making. At the very least, it appeared to believe that a rising power of China's stature should be able to advance east and west, walk and chew gum at the same time. And the country that would do most to determine whether a march west would end in triumph or disaster was Pakistan, which had a new leadership of its own.

EPILOGUE

THE DRAGON MEETS THE LION

Our leaderships have been enthusiastic advocates of comprehensive, meaningful ties, and to this end, have also visited China, often more times than warranted. They have also loved to sign agreements, seeing them as photo ops, but then failed to execute them or occasionally, to even honour the commitments made. Resultantly, the Chinese are disappointed but too polite to say that we lack both the focus and capacity, to the required degree, to bring these projects to fruition. But more than anything, it has been China's deep misgivings about our less than categorical commitment to confronting the menace of extremism and militancy that continues to raise doubts and misgivings in Beijing.

Tariq Fatemi, 2013[1]

Nawaz Sharif wasn't going to make the same mistake as his predecessor. Asif Ali Zardari's decision in 2008 to jet off to Dubai, London and New York before belatedly making China his first "official" overseas trip was never entirely forgiven in Beijing.[2] Sharif's maiden visit, by contrast, was being planned before he had even been sworn into office.[3] He had serious business to do there. On 11 May 2013, his party had won an unexpectedly comprehensive victory in the parliamentary elections, the first in Pakistan's history to take place after a civilian government had completed a full five-year term. Zardari's Pakistan People's Party (PPP), the long-standing rival party to Sharif's Pakistan Muslim League (PML-N), had been routed, holding on to only a handful of seats outside its traditional base in Sindh.[4] There would be no need for the anticipated period of

165

concessions and coalition-building—Sharif's comeback from military coup, prison, and forced exile in Saudi Arabia was already complete.[5] After years of stagnant growth, his mandate from the Pakistani people was clear: "The economy, the economy, the economy", as he proclaimed at the PML-N's victory party.[6] Sharif's election campaign had been a blizzard of plans to get it functioning again—new motorways, industrial zones, bullet trains and, above all, fixing Pakistan's chronic energy problems.[7] For all these ambitions, there was an obvious place to turn for financing, knowhow and sheer industrial muscle. Yet after years in which the major economic initiatives with China had languished, convincing Beijing that Pakistan was a better investment bet now that the conservative Punjabi industrialists were back in charge would be no easy task.

Sharif and the Chinese had dealt with each other plenty of times before. This was, after all, the third stint as Prime Minister for the man dubbed "the Lion of the Punjab" by his supporters, and Beijing maintained extensive ties with his brother, Shahbaz Sharif, during his years as Chief Minister of their home province. But during the two sides' previous interactions in office, Nawaz Sharif was an altogether weaker figure. His last official visit to China as premier was a desperate shuttle during the 1999 Kargil fiasco in a fruitless bid for Chinese support, while he fended off acute challenges to his position at home. Those were the final days of a cycle that had seen Sharif and Benazir Bhutto alternately holding power and conniving with the army to depose each other. Beijing knew who was really running the show, and when General Musharraf seized power a few months later, Chinese officials carried on as if nothing had really changed. Not only did China not mind governments run by the army, it generally preferred them. For much of Zardari's term, Chinese officials would mutter that they missed dealing with Musharraf and military rulers who could "get things done".[8] Their half-hope was that the elections of 2008 might just be another temporary aberration before normal service was resumed. But for the last few years, the PML-N had operated as the Loyal Opposition, ensuring that Zardari's government, however fragile or unpopular, would not be forced from office. Sharif wanted to return to power with civilian rule in Pakistan as a normal fact of political life, not as a gift from the army that could easily be taken away.[9]

For China, the newfound resilience of Pakistani democracy was not the only unfamiliar element in the emerging political landscape. The polls also confirmed the rise of new electoral forces in Pakistan as a fact rather than a flash in the pan. Imran Khan's Pakistan Tehreek-e-Insaf (PTI) won the second highest number of votes nationwide and swept to power in the sensitive province of Khyber-Pakhtunkwa, which sits between Islamabad and the tribal belt.[10] A year before the elections, Imran Khan had visited Beijing at the invitation of the Chinese Communist Party's International Department, and Chinese officials had conveyed an unequivocal message about their security concerns: "There wasn't any discussion on Xinjiang," Imran Khan said to the press on his return, "they were more worried about stability in Pakistan."[11] War-weary Khyber-Pakhtunkwa had been roiled by a Taliban insurgency in recent years, and the PTI had a conciliatory—or indulgent—policy towards them. "We have no enmity with the Taliban," said the incoming chief minister. "We appeal to the Taliban that we are not at war with you, this province is yours".[12] This province had an additional interest to Beijing: long stretches of the Karakoram Highway snake through it on the way south from Gilgit-Baltistan. Even more important to Chinese economic ambitions in Pakistan, however, was Balochistan, where Gwadar port sits, and here too the elections brought the prospect of change. Despite the majority won there by the PML-N and its allies, Nawaz Sharif had appointed a moderate Baloch nationalist politician as chief minister, the first to come from its middle classes rather than the *sardar*s, the traditional tribal leaders.[13] It was a conciliatory message. Abdul Malik would accompany Sharif to China on his inaugural trip, a symbol of the new government's efforts to pacify the province whose nationalist insurgency continued to threaten the viability of China's projects there.

None of these political shifts meant that the Pakistani army had relinquished control over its traditional national security prerogatives, least of all in Balochistan. But China was now contemplating a country where power appeared more diffuse than in the days when it could transact virtually all of its essential business with the military leadership. In recent years, it had watched Pakistan's vibrant media sector take off.[14] It had seen a Supreme Court taking on an unusually assertive role under Chief Justice Ifitkhar Chaudhry.[15] Now it had politicians with popular mandates to deal with too. One Chinese Pakistan hand, who had been wearily claiming before the elections that they were far more interested in who the next Chief of Army Staff would be after General Kayani's retirement, was afterwards enthusiastically enumerating Beijing's efforts to deal with the widening spectrum of parties who had their hands on political office: "JI is running ministries in K-P [Khyber-Pakhtunkwa]. Some of the provincial governments will virtually be conducting their own foreign policy!"[16]

Sharif would be dealing with a changed cast on the Chinese side too. The Communist Party had just gone through its own once-a-decade changeover, with the seven members of the new Politburo Standing Committee taking the stage at the Great Hall of the People in Beijing in November 2012. The political colour of the new politburo would have been familiar to Pakistan's prime minister. After ten years in which many of the highest offices had been occupied by members of the CCP's left-leaning Communist Youth League faction, the blue-blooded "princelings" were now firmly back in control.[17] Six members of the new leadership group—the privileged children of high-ranking officials, whose careers had advanced through positions of power in the wealthy coastal provinces—were from the elite faction, including the new general secretary Xi Jinping himself. Its ageing head, believed at one point to be close to death but still wielding influence over personnel decisions from the shadows, was Jiang Zemin, the party chief and president when Nawaz Sharif last held office.[18]

There were echoes of the late 1990s in the economic field too. Then and now, China was facing a potentially serious growth slowdown and simultaneously contemplating a major programme of reform. In the 1990s, it was the Asian financial crisis that was the drag on growth, and the prospect of WTO membership that was the prize for reformers. This time, Beijing's reform plans were motivated by concerns that the entire Chinese growth model could no longer be sustained.[19] From Pakistan's perspective, however, there was at least one crucial difference between 2013 and 1998: China's western provinces were now drivers of China's economy rather than charity cases. In 2012, Yunnan and Xinjiang clocked in at the double-digit GDP growth rates that had once been the norm in coastal Zhejiang and Guangdong, neither of which even hit the magic 8% growth number once believed to be the minimum required to stave off large-scale social unrest.[20] While rising labour costs and a saturation of infrastructure investment in the east and south meant that it was getting harder and harder to pull off the same trick that had propelled China's thirty-year boom, there was still considerable scope to do so in the poorer interior. But maintaining high growth rates in these provinces, and thereby providing an alternative engine for a Chinese economy that was heading into a difficult phase, would require the transformation of the underdeveloped road, rail and energy infrastructure serving China's west.

The Central Asian piece of the puzzle was well advanced, with gas pipelines running from Turkmenistan,[21] and oil pipelines running from the shores of the Caspian Sea in Kazakhstan.[22] A "Eurasian corridor" was already being utilized by companies which wanted to take advantage of the land route between China and Europe that shaved weeks off the time it took to ship the goods by sea.[23] Xi Jinping would sell an even grander vision of a "Silk Road Economic Belt" during his extended tour of the region later in the year.[24] But the South Asian infrastructure, which promised to connect China's interior to the ports of the Indian Ocean rather than to faraway Shanghai and Shenzhen, was still lagging far behind.[25] Two of these transport corridors would be at the top of the agenda of the new Chinese Prime Minister, Li Keqiang, when he made his first overseas visit in May 2013. The destination of the man with the burden of steering the Chinese economy through these turbulent waters would not be East Asia or Europe, as with his predecessors. He would start in New Delhi and Islamabad.

Li's trip to India illustrated why an ostensibly simple set of economic goals in South Asia was so fraught with complication. The visit itself was almost called off by New Delhi before it even began, on the not unreasonable grounds that Chinese troops had set up camp in Indian territory about a month before he was due to arrive. On 15 April, thirty Chinese soldiers pitched their tents 10km inside the Line of Actual Control in Ladakh, and erected signs in English for their Indian counterparts saying "You are in Chinese side"[26] and "You've crossed the border, please go back".[27] The political firestorm set off in India by this latest manifestation of China's military assertiveness continued well after the troops had been withdrawn, which was barely two weeks before the visit. Li's message, when he arrived in New Delhi on 19 May, was perfectly sensible: that India and China's unresolved disputes in the region need not preclude a closer partnership on global issues and economic matters.[28] But it would have sounded more convincing fresh out of the recent

BRICS summit, rather than after one of the most serious border incursions in years.[29]

The economic project that he was there to sell did get a hearing, the first time that it had been taken up at such high levels of government on the two sides.[30] The so-called "Southern Silk Road" or "BCIM economic corridor" would link Yunnan province in China's south-west to India's north-east and the Bangladeshi port of Chittagong, via northern Myanmar.[31] The proposal had been kicking around for years, and a Kunming-Calcutta car rally had recently been staged to demonstrate that the route was no longer just a theoretical one.[32] But while the Chinese, Burmese, and Bangladeshis were enthusiastic, the Indians were still cautious. There were some concerns that this would be yet a further contributor to India's huge bilateral trade deficit with China, unleashing another flood of cheap Chinese goods.[33] There were security concerns too. New Delhi has long been worried about the military advantages that could accrue to China from the build up of infrastructure around its borders, one of the reasons that India's own transport networks in these areas have been so underdeveloped.[34] And when it came to the strategic economic geography of connecting India's northeast with southeast Asia, New Delhi was not at all sure that it wanted China in the lead. When Li stated in his speech to the Indian Council of World Affairs that "No country can choose its neighbours, and a distant relative may not be as helpful as a near neighbour. China and India should not seek cooperation from afar with a ready partner at hand," the Indians had their doubts.[35] Moreover, while the target of Li's remarks was the United States, another Chinese adversary "from afar" was drawing the attention of the Indian leadership. Not long after Li's departure, his counterpart Manmohan Singh was off to Tokyo. There he would finalize a deal to acquire Japanese nuclear technology and equipment, and push ahead with plans for various Japanese-backed "industrial corridors"—Delhi-Mumbai and Chennai-Bangalore—that New Delhi found a great deal more congenial than the BCIM.[36]

Li Keqiang would find a far warmer welcome on the next leg of his trip. The Pakistanis were well aware that they were the necessary add-on to his South Asian tour this time rather than the main event. With the political transition after Pakistan's elections still underway, what would ordinarily have been an extensive bonanza of MOUs and joint agreements instead had to proceed with more modest preparation. Li arrived to a grand reception nonetheless. JF-17 jets accompanied his plane as it entered Pakistani air space,[37] and Pakistan's "entire civil and military leadership" was waiting to greet him on his arrival at Chaklala airbase in Rawalpindi.[38] Here, the Chinese prime minister's talk of a new economic corridor was rapturously received, the departing President Zardari responding to his proposal with the statement that "today is one of the happiest days of my life".[39] After years of featuring more regularly in the fantasies of geostrategists than in realities on the ground, the long-talked-about Xinjiang-Gwadar connection looked as if it was getting a new lease on life. When Li sat down with Nawaz Sharif and his advisers, barely a week after the election, the modalities of the plan were one of the main subjects of discussion, and its most ambitious element—a new railway—featured prominently in Sharif's inaugural speech as Prime Minister on 5 June.[40] "This is a game changer," he declared, "it will change the fate of Pakistan."[41]

There was plenty more too: China was ready to do its bit for Pakistan's energy crisis, with everything from new hydro-electric dams and coal-fired power stations to the next phase of civil nuclear cooperation on the table. China was in the process of exporting its first 1000MW reactor, which, unlike the smaller reactors at Chashma, could actually start to make a dent in Pakistan's energy needs.[42] It also appeared that, for once, Pakistan had caught a lucky break. On the eve of Li's visit, a bomb was detonated in Karachi's affluent Clifton neighbourhood. The 10kg home-made bomb, filled with ballbearings and bolts, was packed in a metallic bucket and placed inside a sack by the roadside.[43] The target was a van of Chinese engineers who were heading to work at the port and regularly passed by the spot close to the harbour. But while one of the detonators went off, causing a small explosion, the bomb itself misfired. It was a near miss. "If the 10-kilo bomb had exploded, it would have caused much destruction in an area of 25 to 30 metres, engulfing the vehicles of the delegation and destroying oil tankers parked there," said bomb disposal squad official Ghulam Mustafa in a statement to the press.[44] It would have been a catastrophic start for the two new prime ministers, and the fact that it ended up as little more than a minor item in the local press was a huge relief. But Pakistan's luck didn't hold for long.

Bordering on China, Gilgit-Baltistan is considered the safest province in Pakistan, largely free from the terrorist attacks that have plagued other regions. It is one of the few parts of the country that have continued to attract foreign tourists, most of them mountaineers drawn by the densest concentration of high peaks in the world. While the majority of visitors were driven away by Pakistan's burgeoning security threats, Islamabad airport still thronged with groups in conspicuous climbing apparel waiting for the packed morning flights to Skardu and Gilgit. Thirteen of the world's tallest thirty mountains lie within a span of barely a hundred miles, where the Hindu Kush meets the Karakoram and the Himalayas. One of the most fearsome peaks is Nanga Parbat, known as the "killer mountain", a name that took on another meaning early on the morning of 24 June.[45] The killers in question were on a carefully planned operation. Dressed as paramilitary police, the gunmen had hiked for at least eighteen hours to reach their target, one of the high-altitude base camps frequented by climbers. They would later claim to be from a new branch of the Pakistani Taliban, Jundul Hafsa, established specifically to target foreigners.[46] They found ten of them at the camp, who were dragged out of their tents, tied up and executed. Among the dead were two Chinese nationals and one Chinese-American. Another Chinese climber, Zhang Jingchuan, who had served four years in the PLA, managed to escape.[47] Five Russians, a Ukrainian, and a Pakistani guide (who was believed by the killers to be a Shia) also died in the attack. But the timing—squarely between Li Keqiang's visit and Nawaz Sharif's return trip—immediately prompted suspicions from Chinese officials that damaging the China-Pakistan relationship itself was the real political motivation. The Chinese ambassador in Islamabad was quickly on the phone to the new Interior Minister, Chaudry Nisar: "He asked whether Chinese tourists were the target," the minister explained to the press.[48] The embassy would later call on Pakistan to "severely punish" the attackers, an echo of the language used around the time of the Red Mosque assault.[49] The Pakistani foreign ministry stated that it was an attempt "to disrupt the growing relations of Pakistan with China and other friendly countries".[50]

The attack was the single worst on foreigners in Pakistan since the Marriott Hotel bombing in 2008. And its location was a warning: not only did it demonstrate that even China's projects in supposedly calm parts of the country could no longer be viewed as secure, but it was in close proximity to many of the proposed new hydro-electric dams, as well as the mammoth rebuilding job underway on the Karakoram

Highway. The Pakistani investigators who were hunting the perpetrators in the weeks after the attack were shot dead in Chilas, a small town along the KKH near where the killers were believed to be hiding.[51] The same faction of the Pakistani Taliban claimed responsibility. It was a worrying encroachment on territory that may have experienced deadly outbursts of sectarian violence in the past,[52] but was known more for being a Taliban "home away from home"than a live zone of militant operations.[53] For China, nowhere in Pakistan could fully be trusted.

Nawaz Sharif arrived in Beijing on 3 July. The choreography was not always seamless. In his meeting with Li Keqiang at the Great Hall of the People, with television cameras rolling, Sharif struggled to remember the China-Pak relationship mantras, requiring his brother, Shahbaz, to mouth them to him: "Higher than the…?" "Himalayas".[54] But the trip was a world removed from Zardari's ill-fated 2008 visit. He had been sent packing to the IMF after his request for a large bailout was dismissed out of hand. Nawaz Sharif would come home with promises of substantial new Chinese investment. The economic corridor would be a "game changer" not just for Pakistan but for the whole region, he claimed.[55] Pakistan's Planning Minister, Ahsan Iqbal, and Sharif's Foreign Affairs Adviser, Tariq Fatemi, had been sent out ahead to sell the message to the Chinese that the new government was different.[56] Above all, it would ensure that projects were delivered. A special "China cell" was being set up in the prime minister's office committed to that single task—"The cell will oversee the execution of all such development projects in order to steer the country out of its crisis," Nawaz Sharif announced.[57] "The country does not need civil servants and concerned officials who cannot ensure the completion of development projects."[58] His aides briefed the press that Sharif "did all he could to offset a perception among Chinese financial and investment circles that Pakistan is only good for signing MoUs and then sleeping over them." "Write to me directly on my e-mail," he told Chinese business leaders, and "we will get back to you in 24 hours…And see to it that hiccups are removed within 7 days."[59] The Chinese weren't enthralled but they believed that they had someone to work with now. "The PPP government was hopeless. And with Zardari we always had to check that the money was going to Pakistan, not to Switzerland. Nawaz isn't so much better but he can at least get things done."[60] For China, the line about the PML-N that "their real ideology is managerialism" was a major point of appeal.[61]

But there was caution on Beijing's part too. Yes, they were willing to move ahead, but they had some reservations. "The strategic decision to expand investments in Pakistan has been made, by the political leadership and the military, but there are still real practical difficulties," one Chinese official explained.[62] "Above all, security." "If terrorist attacks like the one last month continue, the corridor will be impossible to realise," said another former official.[63] They would tread carefully—there were motorways to build and industrial parks to develop before any grandiose $18 billion railway plans were put into motion. "We still think the railway line is ridiculous," one Chinese expert remarked after the visit, "but that's not to say it won't happen… We and the Pakistanis just have a different sense of what 'long term' means for these projects."[64] The major unknown quantity was whether the new political dispensation in Pakistan could make a better job of securing peace than its predecessor. Certainly, the Sharifs' base in the Punjab had been suspiciously untroubled by terrorist incidents, an achievement that many believed was due to a willingness to strike deals with militant groups operating in the south of the province, such as the electoral alliance formed with Lashkar-e-Jhangvi[65] and the financial contributions provided to Jamaat-ud-Dawa, Lashkar-e-Taiba's parent organization.[66] But Nawaz Sharif's strategy for dealing with them from the prime minister's office was unclear. His proposed peace talks with the Pakistani Taliban[67] may have been motivated by no more than the need for a political gesture before mobilizing public opinion behind a military operation.[68] To the Chinese, the means didn't matter. They were happy to see the new government kill off, buy off, or settle with whoever it had to, if that helped to stabilize the country. And while they waited to see what happened, they were willing to make some significant early gestures of economic support.

On 26 November 2013, at a site just outside Karachi, Nawaz Sharif attended the groundbreaking ceremony for one of the largest energy projects in the country. After nearly a year of rumours, the next phase of Sino-Pakistani nuclear cooperation was now definitively moving ahead. Other projects, such as a coal venture in Sindh and a new set of hydro-electric plants, would deliver the more immediate energy fix. The Thar coal project alone should add 6,000MW of capacity within ten years.[69] But the nuclear plants had an additional political frisson. In their meetings with Pakistani officials, the Chinese had been apprehensive about when and how they should announce this latest mega-project, given the international sensitivities. Now it was a fact on the ground. Two 1,100 MW reactors would be built by the China National Nuclear Corporation at a cost of nearly $10 billion, $6.5 billion of which was being financed by Chinese loans.[70] Each of them would add more generating capacity than all the working reactors in Pakistan combined, and Sharif announced that several more would follow. Chinese investment, he said, was "the only way" that the country could overcome its energy shortage.[71] Even critics of the smaller 300MW reactors at Chashma, who argued that they had more to do with political symbolism than practicality, admitted that the new round could make a real difference.[72] This was not the only significance of the move. It was the first time that the Chinese nuclear industry had built a power plant on this scale outside the country. If successful, it promised to be the first of a wave of nuclear exports from China. The crucial technology for the reactors, the AP-1000 pressure vessels, had been transferred by the US nuclear power company Westinghouse, as part of an agreement that involved the firm in the dramatic take-off of China's nuclear infrastructure.[73] Because the pressure vessel was now "indigenous" Chinese technology, the only remaining obstacle to the export of the reactors had been removed: Beijing's flaunting of objections from the Nuclear Suppliers Group over its nuclear cooperation with Pakistan could not be deterred by US legal obstacles to the use of American components. Some NSG members had acquiesced to the Chashma plants on the premise that they were the last piece of the "grandfathered" Sino-Pak nuclear cooperation.[74] The new reactors, and the promise of many more to come, blew up the tacit compromise completely. Pakistan now effectively had a China-sized exemption to the NSG rules, and the showcase was a set of nuclear plants next to Pakistan's largest and most chaotic city.[75]

There was one last transition to be completed in 2013. The most powerful position in Pakistan, that of Chief of Army Staff, would be changing hands at the end of November, and before that the outgoing Chief had a valedictory trip to make. General Kayani had last visited China at the beginning of 2012, and it was his meetings with the Chinese leadership rather than those of President Zardari that had defined the parameters of the bilateral relationship for the remainder of the two men's terms in office.[76] Kayani's trip came after a turbulent year. 2011 had seen a little too much international interest in China-Pakistan relations for Beijing's taste, as Islamabad flirted openly with the idea of making a political break with the Americans in the aftermath of the Abbottabad raid.[77] China had not enjoyed the scrutiny that this placed on interactions between the two sides that would previously have been considered routine, from fighter jet sales to simple professions of mutual friendship. It was a throwback to an era that they thought had long been put behind them. With the Party Congress in China due in late 2012, and elections in Pakistan in early 2013 coming up too, it was preferable that there should be a quiet period in the relationship. Kayani made sure that the geopolitical rumblings out of Rawalpindi abated,[78] a task made much easier by the fact that US-Pakistan relations had stabilized, and the absence of any more Bin-Laden-scale surprises.[79] Defence cooperation between China and Pakistan rolled forward again without raising any eyebrows, and even the takeover of Gwadar port by Chinese companies proceeded without much fuss. The one awkward subject during Kayani's January 2012 visit was a bilateral agreement that the Chinese were pressing on Pakistan over its handling of the East Turkistan "separatist threat". The content itself was uncontroversial but the fact that so much time still needed to be spent on the Uighur issue was embarrassing, the single black mark against Kayani in Beijing's eyes during his long tenure as army chief. As it turned out, his final visit to China would be dogged by the very same issue.

Kayani's visit in late October was supposed to be a final courtesy call. A relatively light agenda[80] touched on plans for an upcoming joint military exercise, as well as some regional issues, such as Afghanistan's prospects and the recent tensions with India on the Line of Control.[81] The next round of heavy lifting would be undertaken with the new civilian government and with Kayani's successor, Raheel Sharif. But he would not receive a gentle send-off. On 28 October, the day of Kayani's arrival, an SUV crashed through the crowds in Tiananmen Square and burst into flames by one of the stone bridges at the north side of the square. Two tourists were killed, thirty-eight people were injured, and black smoke was left billowing in front of the iconic portrait of Mao Zedong that hangs over the entrance to the Forbidden City. With the passengers in the 4x4 also losing their lives, Chinese officials had no hesitation about labelling the incident a suicide attack.[82] It took place barely a few hundred metres from the seat of government in Zhongnanhai. The *modus operandi*—a low-tech vehicular attack with primitive explosives—immediately signalled its provenance in Xinjiang. And the protagonists turned out to be a Uighur family from a location close to the Pakistani border.[83]

Like clockwork, China's top security official, Meng Jianzhu, blamed ETIM, which he allusively referred to as "based in Central and West Asia".[84] This was a vaguer formulation than that of the Xinjiang officials who were willing to accuse Pakistan by name. Chinese scholars, including one of those who had been in the CICIR delegation that met Mullah Omar, linked the attack to the upcoming 2014 transition in Afghanistan, claiming that this was likely to result in "a tougher security situation amid increased penetration of extremists".[85] Accounts suggested that the attackers may actually have been motivated by the demolition of a mosque in their home village.[86] But the facts were not necessarily the most important thing. The Turkistan Islamist Party gleefully claimed responsibility for the "jihadi operation" and warned of future attacks in China's capital.[87] And the most damning narrative would be hard to shake off—that a Pakistan-based Uighur separatist group masterminded a successful suicide attack in the most visible location in China during the valedictory visit of Pakistan's army chief. If the timing was embarrassing for Kayani, who had to sit down with China's minister for public security the very next day, it certainly demonstrated Pakistan's centrality to Beijing's concerns. A Chinese foreign ministry spokesman described Uighur terrorists as "the most direct and real threat to our security".[88] That threat was now unavoidably linked in the eyes of China's military and political establishment with militancy across the region, Afghanistan's future, and the stability of Pakistan itself.

The Tiananmen Square attack was only the start. Within the next few months, China was shaken by a series of incidents that brought the menace of terrorism from its previous confines in the country's remote northwest to its urban centres. The most shocking attack, on 1 March 2014, saw a group of eight black-clad, knife-wielding men and women stab 29 people to death in Kunming railway station, scenes darkly reminiscent of the Chechen-style assaults that few imagined would ever be seen in China. When Xi Jinping made his first presidential trip to Xinjiang a couple of months later, he called for "nets spread from the earth to the sky" to defend against terrorism. The Chinese security services were almost immediately embarrassed by their inability to prevent another bomb and knife attack from taking place, at Urumqi railway station, on the final day of his visit. It was the worst sequence of terrorist violence that China has faced in its modern history.

There were immediate repercussions for Pakistan, although not for the major economic projects, which if anything were now even more important for China's domestic security agenda. Li's visit to South Asia was due to be followed in September 2014 by Xi himself, armed with near-final plans for the Silk Road Economic Belt, Maritime Silk Road, BCIM Economic Corridor, and—most importantly for Islamabad—the China-Pakistan Economic Corridor. While political infighting would result in an embarrassing delay to Xi's Pakistan visit, the one thing that the Sharif government, the Pakistani army, and Imran Khan agreed on was the value of a relationship with China that now promised to deliver tens of billions of dollars in investment, the new saviour of the Pakistani economy. But, at the same time, the urgency of Chinese calls to crack down on Uighur militants in their North Waziristan base had grown. Whether or not they were directly responsible for any of the attacks, Beijing believed that the propaganda operation being conducted out of FATA was itself helping to instigate the wave of violence. As the drumbeat of Chinese pressure intensified, the Pakistani army finally obliged, Raheel Sharif embarking on the campaign that his predecessor had resisted for so long. The army's North Waziristan operation involved tens of thousands of troops and the displacement of nearly half a million people. It was triggered by an array of factors: an IMU attack on Karachi airport; the breakdown of the government's talks with the Pakistani Taliban; and the need to consolidate Pakistan's borders before the U.S. withdrawal from Afghanistan. But, in an echo of the Red Mosque raid seven years earlier, there was also an irate China to consider, the one country whose requests few Pakistani army chiefs are comfortable turning down.

The most obvious security issues that Beijing faces are to its east. Strategic competition with the United States largely plays out in the Asia Pacific. China's historical rivalries are with its East Asian neighbours. The greatest risk of China becoming embroiled in a war is over its maritime disputes in the South China and East China Seas. These are the main testing grounds for China's capacity and intentions as a great power. But they are also contests of choice, typically occurring at a time and manner of Beijing's choosing. Shifts in the economic and military balance of power in the Asia Pacific have so far moved inexorably in China's favour. It is Beijing's impatience, its assertiveness, that is the greatest risk to China's rising power. In China's western neighbourhood, by contrast, it has been Beijing's caution and its unwillingness to try to steer developments in a direction consonant with Chinese interest, that pose the greater problem.

Xinjiang looks more and more like an Achilles heel, a vulnerability that is growing increasingly exposed as China's rise continues. Even if the Pakistani army's campaign succeeds in the narrow objective of displacing Uighur and IMU fighters from Pakistan itself, the problems for China in this respect continue to mount. Attacks in Xinjiang have become virtually a weekly occurrence. And Uighur militants, by now well networked across the jihadi world during their years in North Waziristan, have been appearing as far afield as Iraq and Syria fighting with the so-called Islamic State. Where Osama Bin Laden and Mullah Omar judiciously weighed the risks of taking China on as an enemy, the newer generation of militants, whether the TTP or ISIS, have had no such qualms. And unlike Beijing's carefully calibrated escalations in East Asia, the threats emerging in its west have caught it looking seriously unprepared.

The factors that are driving one form of Chinese assertiveness in East Asia are hence forcing a different response in South, South-West, Central Asia and beyond, to the Middle East. As a power in its near seas, China looks uncomfortably like a bully. As a land power, it looks like a potential anchor for a region that has struggled to break out of a set of vicious and debilitating rivalries. In the maritime realm, China is contesting the control of islands and overlapping exclusive economic zones with multiple claimants. Its land borders, by contrast, are almost entirely settled. The sole major outstanding dispute is with India and even India is likely to derive advantage from a greater Chinese willingness to address the security issues that stretch out from Xinjiang's western borders.[89] Over the last decade, Beijing has sat passively watching developments in the region that are inimical to its strategic interests. Now sitting on the sidelines no longer looks like the most prudent approach.

The coming years present a potent constellation of threats but also an opportunity to shift the balance of incentives in the region to ensure that they don't recur. One part of the task is economic: the grand trade and infrastructure projects that can integrate the region more closely with the East Asian growth phenomenon. Beijing hopes to unleash forces of trade, finance, and economic opportunity that have never had the chance to compete with the seemingly ineluctable logic of the region's security rivalries. Yet the politics rely on Pakistan. Beijing needs a political settlement in Afghanistan, a stable relationship between Pakistan and India, and a settled security situation in Pakistan itself. China can dangle very large financial carrots that might help to persuade different actors there that the strategic trade-offs are worthwhile. It can invest its considerable diplomatic capacities. But the crucial decisions will be made in Islamabad and Rawalpindi—and it is already clear that they will require some pushing from Beijing if they are going to come out the way it would like.

Yet for China, Pakistan's importance in the longer term goes well beyond its central position in the volatile politics of its western neighbourhood. While the United States' position as the pre-eminent global power is augmented by a decades-old alliance system that spans the Atlantic and the Pacific, and commands hundreds of overseas military installations that span the globe, Beijing can count its reliable friends on the fingers of one hand. The North Koreans have proved to be truculent and resentful, and are a standing risk to Chinese strategic interests in North-East Asia. The Burmese junta decided that China's overweening role was too much to put up with, preferring political reform and an opening to the West to the risk of becoming a Chinese satrapy. Authoritarian affinity and a common cause in resisting Western hegemony have not yet eradicated the deep-seated mutual suspicion in the Russia-China relationship. From Iran to Sudan, Zimbabwe to Laos and Cambodia, so many of China's other supposedly close relationships are fragile, reversible, and overly contingent on the continuation in power of a specific regime. Pakistan is the only friendship China has that has been tested out over decades, commands deep support from across the political spectrum and institutions of state, and has a base of public support that is so high that it is a striking outlier in any opinion survey of how China is perceived abroad.

For the last couple of decades none of this added up to much more than an interesting footnote in Chinese foreign policy. Beijing was wedded to a non-aligned stance that dismissed alliance politics as "cold war thinking". Outside its immediate neighbourhood, China's primary interest was in advancing economic relationships, and Beijing had neither the inclination nor the capacity to send the PLA to help protect its citizens or its companies in far-flung places. This has now changed. The sheer scale of China's economy has expanded its global footprint, provided the means to pay for a far larger and more advanced military, and driven rising expectations from the public at home. Once a trading power, China has become an investing power too, with far greater exposure to the countries where its people and projects are present.

EPILOGUE: THE DRAGON MEETS THE LION

Once a defensive military power with horizons that did not extend far beyond Taiwan, China has now had nearly a decade of preparing the PLA for "new historic missions" across the world.[90] For these reasons alone, it is not a surprise that Beijing is carefully weighing up which countries it can trust to facilitate the global projection of Chinese power in the years to come. A "string of pearls" of ports and pipelines is all very well but which host governments will be politically ambivalent in a crisis and which military partners can it count on? Who would help China break Western embargoes if it found itself embroiled in a war in East Asia, and who would leave it in the lurch? Which intelligence agencies can it trust to penetrate the networks of transnational terrorism that are eyeing Chinese targets across the globe? Beijing would prefer to have a longer list of candidates, but when it evaluates whom it can consistently expect to find in its camp, there is a single name that recurs. As one Chinese expert stated: "If China decides to develop formal alliances, Pakistan would be the first place we would turn. It may be the only place we could turn".[91] China undoubtedly has its fears about the country's long-term future. The challenge of dealing with a country that is both the greatest source of China's terrorist threat and the crucial partner in combating it, is challenging to navigate. Pakistan cannot match the trade and commercial prospects of its larger, more economically successful neighbour. But friendship, the one commodity that Pakistan can offer China more convincingly than any other country, matters far more to Beijing than it used to. As a result, the China-Pakistan axis is almost ready to step out of the shadows.

NOTE ON SOURCING

The biggest challenge in the research process for this book was finding reliable sources. As the introduction indicates, the relationship spans areas of genuine sensitivity. Having previously conducted work on other delicate Chinese relationships—such as its ties with North Korea, Iran, Sudan, Myanmar, Zimbabwe, and Cuba—I found the level of care taken over the divulging of information notably higher when it came to dealing with Pakistan. The circumspection is explained partly because it is the only relationship in Chinese foreign policy that is essentially led by the PLA, with the significant additional involvement of the Chinese intelligence services. These are not institutions that are especially interested in handing over details to foreigners about an important bilateral security relationship. Although I was able to meet, for instance, the PLA's Pakistan handlers, military intelligence officers who had run China's Afghanistan operations, PSB officers in charge of counter-terrorism strategy in Xinjiang, and ministry of state security agents who had dealt with Taliban leaders, they were not necessarily keen to reveal many details. It is easy enough to have general discussions about Sino-Pak relations, but beyond things become more delicate. Matters of sensitivity included not only the predictable contemporary issues but various historical matters that remain contentious, from China's involvement in the 1971 war to China's support for the *mujahideen* in the 1980s. Certain topics covered in the text are a little delicate for other parties too—the subject of Sino-US Cold War defence and intelligence cooperation, for instance, is still not readily discussed.

Despite some of these challenges, over time the iterative process of interviews that I undertook for the book yielded what I believe to be accurate versions of many of the crucial events described. I was able to meet people over a number of years, test many different accounts out against each other, and work out whose stories checked out against subsequent, verifiable events. Interview-based research processes can be problematic—if the interviews are conducted on a one-off basis, and thinly spread, it is possible to assemble some juicy tidbits and quotes but it can be difficult to determine the veracity of many of the claims. I think I was at least able to mitigate this problem. Most of the topics covered in the book benefited from the perspectives of multiple parties: officials from different sides, "watchers" close to the official processes in the countries in question, and outside observers with access to their own sources of information. It generally became clear who genuinely knew what they were talking about, whose analysis was borne out, who was able to provide independent corroboration, and who was reliant on the same source for their information. Given how thin the literature is on some of the crucial subjects, and the difficulties in getting access to archives, there was really no viable alternative to this research method.

On many subjects, my presumption tended normally towards scepticism, but many of the claims that seemed sensational-sounding when they were first presented to me proved to be entirely well-founded. I heard a number of stories about Chinese access to the US stealth helicopter while I was in Islamabad and Abbottabad in the weeks after the Osama Bin Laden raid, all of which turned out to be true. The same went for various accounts of meetings between Chinese intelligence officers and Taliban representatives that I first heard in New Delhi, and were subsequently verified by Chinese, Pakistani, Afghan, and US officials. Sino-Pakistani civil nuclear cooperation consistently proved to be on a grander scale than many people had expected, but I had good sources who kept me accurately informed throughout the evolution of the process from the latest Chashma plants to the new round of reactors in Karachi.

I was greatly assisted by a number of colleagues in China, Pakistan, Afghanistan, India, the United States and Europe, many of whom I was dealing with in the course of my day-to-day work at the German Marshall Fund of the United States on issues other than the subject matter of the book. My work at GMF enabled me to travel regularly to all of the countries in question, including extensive side-trips outside the major cities, and to meet people at an array of conferences and seminars in other locations. Some of the most useful material was as likely to come from a brief chat over coffee at a workshop in Paris as it was in a formal sit-down interview in Lahore. As far as possible I tried to visit the locations described, from the Red Mosque and the house in F-8 from which the Chinese "acupuncturists" were kidnapped to the market in Peshawar where the Chinese "academic" was shot, from the length of the Karakoram Highway to Kabul and Kashgar. Since I was travelling independently, safety considerations precluded some trips that would have been useful, particularly in Afghanistan.

The greater part of the book is based on interviews and exchanges conducted between July 2008 and September 2013. Between July 2008 and November 2011 these were part of my ongoing research, and after that the material was gathered specifically for the purposes of the book. Given the subject matter and the nature of the research process, I have felt obliged to conceal the names of the individuals. While this is standard practice for a lot of publications on contemporary Chinese policy issues, it is evidently undesirable. The community working on these issues directly is very small and I have been grateful that people have been so candid with me. Without this blanket approach of anonymity, it would not, in some cases, be very difficult for well-informed readers to work out who they are. In addition, particularly for the interviews conducted before the book was planned, there was a reasonable presumption on the part of most interviewees that they would not be named, even when the rules of attribution had not been explicitly agreed. Unless stated otherwise, I have also ensured that there are at least two, separate reliable sources for all the interview-based claims, both for the purposes of accuracy and to ensure that none of the material can be traced to a single individual. Wherever possible, I used additional written sources that verified or repeated the claims. The interviews were conducted in English.

Although the interview process was at the heart of the research, it has naturally relied also on an extensive range of written sources. The early years of the China-Pakistan relationship are actually very well covered, particularly in works by Pakistani authors, such as Anwar Syed's *China and Pakistan: Diplomacy of an Entente Cordiale*[1] and F.S. Aijazuddin's *From a Head, Through a Head, To a Head: the Secret Channel between the U.S. and China through Pakistan.*[2] The relationship is also dealt with extensively in other treatments of the period, such as Mahnaz Ispahani's

Roads and Rivals: The Political Uses of Access in The Borderlands of Asia,[3] Altaf Gauhar's *Ayub Khan: Pakistan's First Military Ruler,*[4] and Muhammad Mumtaz Khalid's two-volume *History of the Karakoram Highway.*[5] For the period after the 1970s, aside from a couple of essay collections—*China-Pakistan Strategic Cooperation: Indian Perspectives*[6] and the very recent Chinese volume, *A Model of State-to-State Relations: Retrospects and Prospects of the China-Pakistan Ties since 1951*[7]—the material becomes more scattered, and the China-Pakistan relationship is largely addressed in the sidelines of other subjects, such as the China-India relationship or Pakistan's nuclear history. Some of these treatments, such as John Garver's seminal studies, are excellent, and provide essential reference points for any examination of the subject.[8] There are also individual chapters and articles of considerable value, whether on the overall relationship, such as Riaz Mohammad Khan's "Pakistan-China Relations: An Overview"[9] and Ye Hailin's "China-Pakistan Relationship: All Weathers, But Maybe Not All-Dimensional",[10] or on important individual themes, such as Ziad Haider's "Sino-Pakistan Relations and Xinjiang's Uighurs"[11] or Fazal-ur Rehman's "China-Pakistan Economic Relations".[12] More recently, the challenge has been balancing the analysis of what had previously been a relationship defined by its South Asian framework with the growing influence that terrorism, the take-off of militancy in the region, and developments in Afghanistan and Pakistan's border regions have started to exert. Some experts, such as Yitzak Shichor, have worked on this angle for a long time, and other researchers such as Raffaello Pantucci have gathered very interesting new material that not only looks at the Xinjiang-Central Asia-Afghanistan-Pakistan nexus but extends it to look at the role of Uighurs in transnational networks as far afield as Syria.[13]

The Chinese material is of mixed quality. Some studies are disappointing collections of platitudes. There are any number of highly misleading descriptions of the history of Sino-Pakistani nuclear cooperation that are contradicted even by semi-official Pakistani accounts. But there is also increasingly good source material emerging here too, whether on key historical moments, such as Cheng Xiaohe's archive-based account of China's role in the 1965 war, "China's Aid toward Pakistan in the India-Pakistan War II";[14] frank assessments of current priorities in the region, such as Hu Shisheng's "Afghan Reconstruction: Regional Challenges";[15] or the broader strategic context, such as Wang Jisi's now widely-cited "Westward: China's Rebalancing Geopolitical Strategy".[16] The detailed translations of the Chinese-language sources were provided by Zhao Yuxi.

The book has also drawn on the significant existing literature on some of the better trodden topics. The subject of China-Pakistan nuclear cooperation is well covered by the cluster of excellent books around the A.Q. Khan network, such as Gordon Corera's *Shopping For Bombs*,[17] by studies from the likes of Mark Hibbs on the civil nuclear side, and Evan Medeiros on China's proliferation practices, and by the context provided in works such as George Perkovich's *India's Nuclear Bomb: the Impact on Global Proliferation*.[18] The counter-terrorism section pulls together much of the existing research on Xinjiang, such as S. Fredrick Starr's *Xinjiang: China's Muslim Borderland*,[19] and on Central Asia and Afghanistan, such as Ahmed Rashid's *Jihad: The Rise of Military Islam in Central Asia*;[20] and sources on individual operations, such as the accounts provided in the *Long War Journal*. It goes without saying that I have also benefited from the defining works on Pakistan by Stephen Cohen and on Afghanistan by Barnett Rubin. Some important new books also came out while this one was being written, including Feroz Khan's *Eating Grass: the Making of the Pakistani Bomb*,[21] Gary Bass's *The Blood Telegram: Nixon, Kissinger, and a Forgotten Genocide*,[22] and Daniel Markey and Hussain Haqqani's studies of US-Pakistan relations. Much of the rest of the work has been a filleting process, extracting the China-related snippets from an assortment of other archives, memoirs, monographs and media reports. I sometimes benefited as much from an afternoon sifting through former diplomats' memoirs in Saeed Book Bank in Islamabad or Shah M books in Kabul as I did from my official interviews.

Versions of much of the material in this text have been tested out through various seminars, unpublished conference papers, and critiques of earlier publications. These have included articles for GMF, such as "Afghanistan-Pakistan: Bringing China (back) in";[23] for the *Washington Quarterly*, "China's Caution on Afghanistan/Pakistan";[24] and for *Foreign Policy*, "Why is China Talking to the Taliban?"[25] and "China's Afghan Moment".[26] Papers on Chinese contingency planning prepared for presentations at the Brookings Institution and the Council on Foreign Relations, on China's counterterrorism policy for Sciences Po, and on "China and Instability in South Asia" for CSIS all benefited considerably from the associated workshops, and informed the relevant sections of the text.

Despite the growing interest in the subject and the increasing accessibility of the information, the number of people working on the subject, particularly those undertaking on-the-ground research, has not grown that much larger in the past six years (indeed, one member of that small group, Alexandros Petersen, tragically lost his life in the January 2014 Kabul restaurant attack). This remains a serious challenge in the process of developing a set of robust and detailed studies in what is still a thinly covered field. For many topics covered in this book, while I have been able to take a first cut, there is a huge amount of work still to be done.

NOTES

PROLOGUE: IN THE SHADOW OF THE RED MOSQUE

1. The title is owed to "In the Shadow of Lal Masjid", *China Matters*, 7 Nov. 2007, http://chinamatters.blogspot.com/2007/11/in-shadow-of-lal-masjid.html, last accessed 27 Jan. 2014.

2. Aijazuddin, F.S., *From A Head, Through A Head, To A Head: The Secret Channel between the US and China through Pakistan*, Karachi: Oxford University Press, 2000, p. 20.

3. For an excellent compilation of all the detailed reporting in the Pakistani press, see: Nur Al Haq, "Lal Masjid Crisis", *IPRI Factfile*, 2007, http://ipri-pak.org/factfiles/ff90.pdf, last accessed 27 Jan. 2014.

4. Syed Mohsin Naqbi, "Hostages freed after raid on 'brothel'", CNN, 23 Jun. 2007, http://edition.cnn.com/2007/WORLD/asiapcf/06/23/pakistan.raid/index.html?eref=rss_world, last accessed 27 Jan. 2014.

5. Minxin Pei, "Party and the Patriot", *Indian Express*, 21 Jul. 2012, http://www.gmfus.org/archives/party-and-the-patriot/, last accessed 27 Jan. 2014.

6. Shakeel Anjum, "Lal Masjid cleric free Chinese", *The News*, 24 Jun. 2007, http://archive.thenews.com.pk/TodaysPrintDetail.aspx?ID=8648&Cat=13&dt=6/16/2007, last accessed 23 Jan. 2014.

7. "Pakistan GDP Growth Rate 1951–2009", Data Source: Federal Bureau of Statistics, Government of Pakistan, http://upload.wikimedia.org/wikipedia/commons/2/2b/Pakistan_gdp_growth_rate.svg, last accessed 22 Dec. 2013.

8. Aasif Inam, "Foreign Direct Investment in Pakistan Telecommunication Sector", Pakistan Telecommunication Authority Federal Bureau of Statistics, Government of Pakistan, http://www.itu.int/ITU-D/finance/work-cost-tariffs/events/tariff-seminars/Korea-07/presentations/FDI_Aasif_Inam.pdf, last accessed 23 Jan. 2014.

NOTES

9. "Record-breaking spree at KSE on better earnings expectations", *Daily Times*, 27 Dec. 2007, http://archives.dailytimes.com.pk/business/27-Dec-2007/record-breaking-spree-at-kse-on-better-earnings-expectations, last accessed 23 Jan. 2014; "KSE Stock Market", *Wiki Invest*, http://www.wikinvest.com/wiki/KSE_Stock_Market, last accessed 23 Jan. 2014.

10. Steve Coll, "The Back Channel", *New Yorker*, 2 Mar. 2009, http://www.newyorker.com/reporting/2009/03/02/090302fa_fact_coll, last accessed 22 Jan. 2014.

11. Ahmed Rashid, "Taliban Temptation", *Far Eastern Economic Review*, 11 Mar. 1999, p. 29.

12. Anne Kornblut, "Encounters: Jon Stewart and Pervez Musharraf", *New York Times*, 26 Sep. 2006, http://www.nytimes.com/2006/09/26/us/politics/26pfun.html?_r=0, last accessed 22 Jan. 2014.

13. Schmidle, Nicholas S., *To Live or to Perish Forever: Two Tumultuous Years in Pakistan*, USA: Henry Holt and Company, 2009, p. 91.

14. Lieven, Anatol, *Pakistan: A Hard Country*, New York: Public Affairs, 2011, p157.

15. Amelie Blom, "Changing Religious Leadership in Contemporary Pakistan: The Case of the Red Mosque", in Bolognani, Marta and Stephen M. Lyon (eds.), *Pakistan and Its Diaspora: Multidisciplinary Approaches*, New York: Palgrave, 2011; Syed Shoaib Hasan, "Profile: Islamabad's Red Mosque", BBC News, 27 Jul. 2007, http://news.bbc.co.uk/2/hi/6503477.stm, last accessed 27 Jan. 2014.

16. Ibid.

17. Ibid. p. 113.

18. Graham Usher, "Red Mosque: Endgame for Musharraf?", *The Nation*, 30 Jul. 2007, http://www.thenation.com/article/red-mosque-endgame-musharraf#, last accessed 25 Jan. 2014.

19. "Obituary: Abdul Rashid Ghazi", BBC News, 10 Jul. 2007, http://news.bbc.co.uk/2/hi/south_asia/6281228.stm, last accessed 27 Jan. 2014; "Maulana Abdul Rashid Ghazi freed on my intervention: Ejaz", *Pak Tribune*, http://www.paktribune.com/news/print.php?id=174827, last accessed 27 Jan. 2014; Hussain, Zahid, *The Scorpion's Tail: The Relentless Rise of Islamic Militants in Pakistan—and How it Threatens America*, New York: Free Press, 2010, p. 113.

20. Ibid. p. 114.

21. Syed Saleem Shahzad, "Pakistan: Trouble in the Mosque", *Asia Times*, 12 Apr. 2007, http://www.atimes.com/atimes/South_Asia/ID12Df03.html, last accessed 27 Jan. 2014.

22. Zhang Cheng, "Jiang Yili, from a scholar to a diplomat", China Radio International, 3 Oct. 2010, http://english.cri.cn/4406/2010/03/10/2401s555552.htm, last accessed 23 Jan. 2014.

23. Syed Irfan Raza, "Chinese hostages freed", *Dawn*, 23 Jun. 2007, http://www.dawn.com/news/253217/chinese-hostages-freed, last accessed 23 Jan. 2014.

24. Ibid.;"All 9 Hostages Held in Pakistani Capital Released", China Radio International, 23 Jun. 2007, http://english.cri.cn/2947/2007/06/23/176@241684.htm, last accessed 27 Jan. 2014.

25. Shakeel Anjum, "Lal Masijd cleric free Chinese", *Dawn*, 24 Jun. 2007, http://archive.thenews.com.pk/TodaysPrintDetail.aspx?ID=8648&Cat=13&dt=6/16/2007, last accessed 23 Jan. 2014.

26. Syed Irfan Raza, "Chinese hostages freed", *Dawn*, 23 Jun. 2007, http://www.dawn.com/news/253217/chinese-hostages-freed, last accessed 23 Dec. 2013, Ibid.

27. Shakeel Anjum, "Lal Masjid cleric free Chinese", *The News*, 24 Jun. 2007, http://archive.thenews.com.pk/TodaysPrintDetail.aspx?ID=8648&Cat=13&dt=6/16/2007, last accessed 23 Jan. 2014

28. Ibid.

29. Syed Irfan Raza, "Chinese hostages freed", *Dawn*, 24 Jun. 2007, http://www.dawn.com/news/253217/chinese-hostages-freed, last accessed 23 Jan. 2014.

30. Ibid.

31. "Editorial: Lal Masjid's damage to Pak-China Relations", *Daily Times*, 29 Jun. 2007, http://archives.dailytimes.com.pk/editorial/29-Jun-2007/editorial-lal-masjid-s-damage-to-pak-china-relations, last accessed 13 Dec. 2013.

32. "Pakistan told to do more to protect Chinese workers", AAJ News, 27 Jun., 2007, http://www.aaj.tv/2007/06/pakistan-told-do-more-to-protect-chinese-workers/, last accessed 12 Dec. 2013.

33. Mathieu Duchâtel, "The Old Friend and the Three Evils: China's Policy towards Pakistan", presentation at the 23rd Conference of the Association of Chinese Political Studies, Endicott College, Boston, 30–31 Jul., 2010.

34. B. Raman, "How China Forced Musharraf To Move", *Outlook India*, 4 Jul. 2007, http://www.outlookindia.com/article.aspx?235015, last accessed 20 Jan. 2014.

35. Author interviews in Lahore, Islamabad, Brussels, Washington DC, December 2008–June 2013.

36. Pervez Musharraf, "Address to the Nation: Declaration of Emergency", speaking on national TV, 3 Nov. 2007, video (in Urdu) and English translation available at Manan Ahmed, "The General Speaks", *Informed Comment: Global Affairs*, 4 Nov. 2007. Note that the official printed text of the speech differs from that delivered on television. The source used here is a translation of the video.

37. Al Haq, Nur, "Lal Masjid Crisis", *Islamabad Policy Research Institute Fact File*, 2007, p. 90, http://ipripak.org/factfiles/ff90.pdf, last accessed 27 Jan. 2014.

38. High estimates are given by, for instance, Schmidle, Nicholas S., *To Live or to Perish Forever: Two Tumultuous Years in Pakistan*, USA: Henry Holt and Company, 2009, p. 151; and other press reporting from the time, such as: "300 confirmed dead in Lal Masjid Operation", *Pak Tribune*, 12 Jul. 2007, http://paktribune.com/news/300-confirmed-dead-in-Lal-Masjid-Operation-183843.html, last accessed 23 Dec. 2013; "103 people killed in Lal Masjid operation", *Pakistan Today*, 20 Apr. 2013, http://www.pakistantoday.com.pk/2013/04/103-people-killed-in-lal-masjid-operation-report/, last accessed 27 Jan. 2014.

39. Singh, R.S.N., *The Military Factor in Pakistan*, India: Lancer Publishers, 2008, p. 426.

40. "Three Chinese killed in Pakistan", *China Daily*, 9 Jul. 2007, http://www.chinadaily.com.cn/china/2007–07/09/content_5421741.htm, last accessed 25 Jan. 2014; http://news.bbc.co.uk/2/hi/south_asia/6282574.stm

41. Luo Zhaohui quoted in "Mosque is Pakistan's 'internal matter'", *China Daily*, 18 Jul. 2007, http://www.chinadaily.com.cn/cndy/2007–07/18/content_5438233.htm, last accessed 24 Jan. 2014.

42. "Hectic efforts under way for release of Chinese Nationals", *Pak Tribune*, 4 Sep. 2008, http://www.paktribune.com/news/print.php?id=205296, last accessed 24 Jan. 2014.

43. Author interview in Peshawar, Jun.2013.

44. Akbar Nasir Khan, "Analyzing Suicide Attacks in Pakistan", *Conflict and Peace Studies*, Vol. 3, No. 4, Oct.-Dec. 2010, https://www.academia.edu/386901/Analysing_Suicide_Attacks_in_Pakistan, last accessed 27 Jan. 2014.

45. Hussain, Zahid, *The Scorpion's Tail: The Relentless Rise of Islamic Militants in Pakistan—And How it Threatens America*, Free Press, 2010, p. 120.

46. Ibid. p. 118.

47. "Editorial: 60 Miles from Islamabad", *New York Times*, 26 April 2009, http://www.nytimes.com/2009/04/27/opinion/27mon1.html, last accessed 22 Jan. 2014.

48. Author interview in Washington DC, Apr. 2010.

INTRODUCTION

1. Douglas Paal, 'China and the East Asian Security Environment: Complementarity and Competition', in Vogel, Ezra, *Living with China: U.S./China Relations in the Twenty First Century*, Norton, 1997, p. 113; Mohan Malik,

'The China Factor in the India-Pakistan Conflict', *Parameters*, Spring 2003, p. 62.

2. Ashley Tellis, "New Delhi, Washington: Who Gets What?", *Times of India*, 30 Jan. 2010, http://articles.timesofindia.indiatimes.com/2010–01–30/india/28119085_1_global-community-robert-d-blackwill-kashmir/2, last accessed 23 Jan. 2014.

3. Amir Mir, "China seeks military bases in Pakistan", *Asia Times*, 26 October, 2011 and Saurabh Shukla, "China plans military base in Northern Pakistan, says report". *India Today*, 24 Jan, 2012.

4. Amir Karim Tantray, "Pakistan govt leases land in Gilgit to China", *Hindustan Times*, 24 March, 2012.

5. Selig S. Harrison, "China's Discreet Hold on Pakistan's Northern Borderlands", *International Herald Tribune*, 26 Aug, 2010.

6. Albright, David, *Peddling Peril: How the Secret Nuclear Trade Arms America's Enemies*, New York: Free Press, 2010, p. 48.

1. A FRIENDSHIP FORGED BY WAR

1. Gauhar, Altaf, *Ayub Khan: Pakistan's First Military Ruler*, Lahore: Oxford University Press, 1993, p. 345.

2. Rakesh Krishan Simha, "1971 War: How Russia Sank Nixon's Gunboat Diplomacy", *Russia and India Report*, 20 Dec. 2011, http://indrus.in/articles/2011/12/20/1971_war_how_russia_sank_nixons_gunboat_diplomacy_14041.html, last accessed 22 Jan. 2014.

3. Akhund, Iqbal, *Memoirs of a Bystander: A Life in Diplomacy*, Karachi: Oxford University Press, 2000, p. 197.

4. Bass, Gary J., *The Blood Telegram: Nixon, Kissinger, and a Forgotten Genocide*, New York: Knopf, 2013, p. 290.

5. Telegram reprinted in Hamoodur Rahman Commission, Supplementary Report, 23 Oct. 1974, p. 108, http://www.pppusa.org/Acrobat/Hamoodur%20Rahman%20Commission%20Report.pdf, last accessed 22 Jan. 2014.

6. Akhund, Iqbal, *Memoirs of a Bystander: A Life in Diplomacy*, Karachi: Oxford University Press, 2000, p. 197.

7. Bass, *The Blood Telegram*, p. 174.

8. National Security Council note on the Anderson Papers, requested by Henry Kissinger, 6 Jan. 1972, http://www2.gwu.edu/~nsarchiv/NSAEBB/NSAEBB79/BEBB45.pdf, last accessed 27 Jan. 2014.

9. Kissinger, Henry, *The White House Years*, London: Phoenix Press, 1979, p. 907.

10. Ibid.

11. *Foreign Relations of the United States, 1969–1976, Volume XI, South Asia Crisis, 1971, Document 179*, U.S. State Department Archive, Washington, DC, 4 Nov. 1971, http://history.state.gov/historicaldocuments/frus1969–76v11/d179, last accessed 26 Jan. 2014.
12. Bass, *The Blood Telegram*, p. 239.
13. "Conversation Between President Nixon and his Assistant for National Security Affairs (Kissinger)", U.S. State Department Archive, Washington, DC, 6 Dec. 1971, *Foreign Relations, 1969–1976, Volume E-7, Documents on South Asia, 1969–1972*, http://2001–2009.state.gov/r/pa/ho/frus/nixon/e7/48535.htm, last accessed 27 Jan. 2014.
14. "Conversation Among President Nixon, the President's Assistant for National Security Affairs (Kissinger), and Attorney General Mitchell", U.S. State Department Archive, Washington DC, 6 Dec. 1971, *Foreign Relations, 1969–1976, Volume E-7, Documents on South Asia, 1969–1972*, http://2001–2009.state.gov/r/pa/ho/frus/nixon/e7/48537.htm, last accessed 27 Jan. 2014.
15. Kux, Dennis, *The United States and Pakistan 1947–2000: Disenchanted Allies*, Washington, DC: Woodrow Wilson Centre Press, 2001, p. 202.
16. Kissinger, *The White House Years*, 1979, p. 910.
17. Bass, *The Blood Telegram*, p. 254.
18. Kissinger, *The White House Years*, p. 910.
19. Ibid.
20. Bass, *The Blood Telegram*, p. 308.
21. Akhund, *Memoir of a Bystander*, p. 200.
22. Ibid. p. 202.
23. Syed, Anwar Hussain, *China & Pakistan: Diplomacy of an Entente Cordiale*, London: Oxford University Press, 1974, p. 152.
24. Khan, Sultan M., *Memories & Reflections of a Pakistani Diplomat*, Oxford: The Alden Press, 1998, p. 344.
25. Ibid. p. 308.
26. Ibid. p. 347.
27. Pande, Aparna, *Explaining Pakistan's Foreign Policy: Escaping India*, New York: Routledge, 2011, p. 124.
28. Syed, *China & Pakistan*, p. 151.
29. Sisson, Richard and Leo E. Rose, *War and Secession: Pakistan, India, and the Creation of Bangladesh*, Berkeley: University of California Press, 1990, p. 252.
30. Bass, *The Blood Telegram*, p. 239.
31. Sisson and Rose, *War and Secession*, p. 251.
32. Ibid. p. 252.
33. Ibid. p. 199.

34. Bass, *The Blood Telegram*, p. 305.
35. Prasad, S.N., *Official History of the 1971 India Pakistan War*, History Division, Ministry of Defence, Government of India, New Delhi, 1992, p. 117, p. 278; Bass, *The Blood Telegram*p. 94.
36. CIA assessments cited in Bass, *The Blood Telegram*, p. 259 and p. 292; U.S. Defense Intelligence Agency, "Sino-Indian Border Troops Dispositions" [sic], 15 Jun. 1971, cited in Bass, *The Blood Telegram*, p. 314.
37. Khan, *Memories & Reflections*, p. 373.
38. Ibid. p. 378.
39. Ibid. p. 379.
40. Sisson and Rose, *War and Secession*, p. 233.
41. Prasad, *Official History*, p. 670.
42. Macfarquhar, Roderick and Michael Schoenhals, *Mao's Last Revolution*, Cambridge, MA: Harvard University Press, 2009, p. 353.
43. Khan, *Memories & Reflections*, p. 345.
44. Vertzberger, Yaacov Y.I., *China's Southwestern Strategy: Encirclement and Counterencirclement*, New York: Praeger, 1985, p. 54.
45. Syed, *China & Pakistan*, p. 152.
46. Sisson and Rose, *War and Secession*, p. 216.
47. Khan, *Memories & Reflections*, p. 307.
48. Ibid. p. 306.
49. Khan, Riaz Mohammad, "Pakistan-China Relations: An Overview", *Pakistan Horizon*, Vol. 64, No. 4, Oct. 2011, p. 12.
50. Syed, *China & Pakistan*, p. 149.
51. Khan, *Memories & Reflections*, p. 307.
52. Nawaz, Shuja, *Crossed Swords: Pakistan, Its Army, and the Wars Within*, Karachi: Oxford University Press, 2008, p. 305.
53. Bass, *The Blood Telegram*, p. 310.
54. Sisson and Rose, *War and Secession*, p. 251.
55. Wuthnow, Joel, *Chinese Diplomacy and the UN Security Council: Beyond the Veto*, Oxford and New York: Routledge, 2013, p. 17.
56. Editorial, *Dawn*, 4 Feb. 1972.
57. Syed, *China & Pakistan*, p. 109.
58. Khan, *Memories & Reflections*, pp. 162–3.
59. Nawaz, *Crossed Swords*, p. 194.
60. Wolpert, Stanley, *Zulfi Bhutto of Pakistan: His Life and Times*, New York: Oxford University Press, 1993, p. 89.
61. Khan, Gohar Ayub, *Glimpses Into the Corridors of Power*, Karachi: Oxford University Press, 2007, p. 320.
62. Garver, John W., *Protracted Contest: Sino-Indian Rivalry in the Twentieth Century*, Seattle: University of Washington Press, 2001, p. 201.

63. Dixit, J.N., *India-Pakistan in War and Peace*, New York: Routledge, 2002, p. 147.
64. Syed, *China & Pakistan*, pp. 110–12.
65. Gupta, Bhabani Sen, *The Fulcrum of Asia: Relations Among China, India, Pakistan and the U.S.S.R*, New York: Pegasus, 1970, p. 213.
66. Ibid.
67. Cheng, Xiaohe, "China's Aid toward Pakistan in the India-Pakistan War II", *Diplomacy Commentary*, No. 3, 2012, p. 77.
68. Ibid. p. 81.
69. Khan, *Glimpses*, p. 99.
70. Gauhar, *Ayub Khan*, pp. 352–3.
71. Author interview, Islamabad, May 2013.
72. Author interview, Beijing, February 2014; interviewee drew on the Chinese Foreign Ministry Archive.
73. Vertzberger, *China's Southwestern Strategy*, p. 43.
74. "War Diplomacy, Cease-fire and Tashkent", UN Efforts-Restricted, Chapter XI, 1965, p. 312, http://www.bharat-rakshak.com/LAND-FORCES/Army/History/1965War/PDF/1965Chapter11.pdf, last accessed 26 Jan. 2014.
75. Kux, *The United States and Pakistan*, p. 165.
76. Levy, Adrian and Catherine Scott-Clark, *Nuclear Deception: The Dangerous Relationship between the United States and Pakistan*, New York: Walker & Company, 2007, p. 61.
77. Banerjee, Purnendu Kumar, "China in India and Pakistan", speech to the United States Congress, Congressional Record, Washington, DC, 13 Jun. 1966, p. 12961–12964.
78. Ibid.
79. Kux, *The United States and Pakistan*, p. 91.
80. John W. Garver, "China's Decision for War with India in 1962", in Alastair Iain Johnston and Robert S. Ross (eds), *New Directions in The Study of China's Foreign Policy*, Stanford, CA: Stanford University Press, 2006, p. 92.
81. Dunham, Mikel, *Buddha's Warriors*, New York: Tarcher, 2004, p. 198.
82. "Agreement (with exchange of notes) on trade and intercourse between Tibet Region of China and India", signed in Peking, 29 Apr. 1954, full text available in United Nations Treaty Series, vol. 299, United Nations, p. 57–81, https://treaties.un.org/doc/publication/unts/volume%20299/v299.pdf, last accessed 27 Jan. 2014.
83. Khan, Mohammed Ayub, "India as a Factor in Sino-Pakistani Relations", *International Studies*, New Delhi, 9, No. 3, Jan. 1963, p. 292. As one illustrative account from the late 19th century has it, "it was a point of etiquette in his savage Court, on certain occasions, for a Wazir to ask in the Thum's presence 'Who is the greatest king of the East?' and for another flatterer to

reply 'Surely, the Thum of Hunza; unless perhaps it be the Khan of China; for those without doubt are the greatest'": in Edward F. Knight, *Where Three Empires Meet: A Narrative of Recent Travel in Kashmir, Western Tibet, Gilgit, and the Adjoining Countries*, New York: Longmans, 1893, p. 349.

84. Ibid. p. 350.
85. Mohammed Ayub Khan, "Pakistan Perspective", *Foreign Affairs*, Jul. 1960; Alastair Lamb, "Crisis in Kashmir, 1947–1966", *Modern Asia Studies*, London: Routledge & Kegan Paul, 1966.
86. Mohammed Ayub Khan, "Pakistan Perspective", *Foreign Affairs*, Jul. 1960.
87. Syed, *China & Pakistan*, p. 61.
88. Ibid. p. 75.
89. John W. Garver, "China's Decision", p. 95.
90. Garver, *Protracted Contest*, p. 57.
91. Ispahani, Mahnaz Z., *Roads and Rivals: The Political Uses of Access in The Borderlands of Asia*, Ithaca, NY: Cornell University Press, 1989, p. 170.
92. Garver, John W., *Protracted Contest: Sino-Indian Rivalry in the Twentieth Century*, Seattle: University of Washington Press, 2001, pp. 100–02.
93. John W. Garver, "China's Decision for War with India in 1962", in Alastair Lain Johnston and Robert S. Ross (eds), *New Directions in The Study of China's Foreign Policy*, Stanford, CA: Stanford University Press, 2006, p. 117.
94. Frankel, Francine R. and Harry Harding, *The India-China Relationship: What the United States Needs to Know*, New York: Columbia University Press, 2004, p. 30.
95. Garver, *Protracted Contest*, p. 57.
96. Perkovich, George, *India's Nuclear Bomb: The Impact on Global Proliferation*, Los Angeles: University of California Press, 1999, p. 46.
97. Riedel, Bruce, *Avoiding Armageddon: America, India and Pakistan to the Brink and Back*, Washington, DC: Brookings Institution Press, 2013, p. 62.
98. Cited in Ibid.
99. Galbraith, John Kenneth, *Ambassador's Journal*, Boston: Houghton Mifflin Company, 1969, p. 434.
100. Khan, Gohar Ayub, *Glimpses Into the Corridors of Power*, Karachi: Oxford University Press, 2007, p. 50.
101. Gauhar, Altaf, *Ayub Khan: Pakistan's First Military Ruler*, Lahore: New York: Oxford University Press, 1993, p. 202.
102. Ibid. p. 241.
103. Ibid. p. 239.
104. Ibid. p. 213.
105. Wolpert, Stanley, *Zulfi Bhutto of Pakistan: His Life and Times*, Oxford University Press, 1993, p. 64.

106. Ibid. p. 65.
107. Gauhar, *Ayub Khan*, Lahore: Oxford University Press, 1993, pp. 237–40.
108. Fravel, Taylor M., *Strong Borders, Secure Nation: Cooperation and Conflict in China's Territorial Disputes*, New Jersey: Princeton University Press, 2009, p. 106.
109. Gauhar, *Ayub Khan*, p. 235.
110. Fravel, *Strong Borders*, p. 116.
111. Ibid. pp. 118–19.

2. NUCLEAR FUSION

1. Quoted in M. Taylor Fravel and Evan S. Medeiros, "China's Search for Assured Retaliation: The Evolution of Chinese Nuclear Strategy and Force Structure", *International Security*, Vol. 35, No. 2, Fall 2010, p. 61.
2. Chidanand Rajghatta, "AQ Khan blows the whistle on Pakistan", *Economic Times*, 20 Sep. 2009, http://articles.economictimes.indiatimes.com/2009–09–20/news/27661296_1_uf6-china-in-enrichment-technology-aqkhan, last accessed 27 Jan. 2014.
3. "PRC envoy: China hopes to develop good bilateral ties", *Hindustan Times*, 26 Feb. 1999.
4. Corera, Gordon, *Shopping for Bombs: Nuclear Proliferation, Global Insecurity, and the Rise and Fall of the A.Q. Khan Network*, London: C. Hurst & Co., pp. 221–22; Levy, Adrian and Catherine Scott-Clark, *Nuclear Deception: The Dangerous Relationship between the United States and Pakistan*, New York: Walker & Company, 2007, pp. 383–4; Joby Warrick and Peter Slevin, "Libyan arms designs traced back to China", *Washington Post*, 15 Feb. 2004; David Albright and Corey Hinderstein, "Unraveling the A Q Khan and Future Proliferation Networks", *Washington Quarterly*, Vol. 28, No. 2, Spring 2005, p. 32.
5. Albright, David, *Peddling Peril: How the Secret Nuclear Trade Arms America's Enemies*, New York: Free Press, 2010, p. 49.
6. Khan, Feroz H., *Eating Grass: The Making of The Pakistani Bomb*, Stanford, CA: Stanford University Press, 2012, p. 439.
7. David Albright and Corey Hinderstein, "Uncovering the Nuclear Black Market: Working Toward Closing Gaps in the International Nonproliferation Regime", Institute for Science and International Security, 2004, http://www.isis-online.org/publications/southasia/nuclear_black_market.html, last accessed 22 Jan. 2014.
8. David Albright quoted in Warrick and Slevin, "Libyan arms designs traced back to China".
9. Corera, *Shopping for Bombs*, p. 222.

10. Warrick and Slevin, "Libyan arms designs traced back to China".
11. Corera, *Shopping for Bombs*, pp. 176–94.
12. "New Documents Spotlight Reagan-era Tensions over Pakistani Nuclear Program", National Security Archive Electronic Briefing Book No. 377, 27 Apr. 2012, http://www2.gwu.edu/~nsarchiv/nukevault/ebb377/, last accessed 27 Jan. 2014; "The United States and Pakistan's Quest for the Bomb", National Security Archive Electronic Briefing Book No. 333, 21 Dec. 2010, http://www2.gwu.edu/~nsarchiv/nukevault/ebb333/, last accessed 27 Jan. 2014.
13. Levy and Scott-Clark, *Nuclear Deception*, p. 384.
14. Corera, *Shopping for Bombs*; Levy and Scott-Clark, *Nuclear Deception*; Albright, *Peddling Peril*.
15. Khan, *Eating Grass*, p. 171.
16. Cloughey, Brian, *War, Coups and Terror, Pakistan's Army in Years of Turmoil*, Huddersfield: Pen and Sword, 2008, p. 164.
17. Author interviews in Islamabad, Jun. 2013; Washington, Apr.-May 2013.
18. Author interviews in Beijing, Islamabad, and Lahore, 2008–2013.
19. Khan, Riaz Mohammad, *Afghanistan and Pakistan: Conflict, Extremism, and Resistance to Modernity*, Karachi: Oxford University Press, 2010, p. 346.
20. Treaty of Friendship, Cooperation and Good-Neighborly Relations between the People's Republic of China and the Islamic Republic of Pakistan, 2005.
21. Khan, Sultan M., *Memories & Reflections of a Pakistani Diplomat*, Oxford: The Alden Press, 1997, p. 181.
22. Ibid. p. 182.
23. Ibid. p. 183.
24. Zulfikar Ali Bhutto, "If I am Assassinated", Supreme Court of Pakistan Criminal Appeal No. 11 of 1978, p. 233, http://pt.slideshare.net/yawik/if-iamassassinatedbyshaheedbhutto-23982975, last accessed 18 Nov. 2013.
25. Yasser Latif Hamdani, "Zulfi Bhutto and Chairman Mao Tse Tung", *Friday Times*, 11–17 Mar. 2011, http://www.thefridaytimes.com/11032011/page30.shtml, last accessed 18 Nov. 2013.
26. Agha Shahi, quoted in Levy and Scott-Clark, *Deception: Pakistan, the United States, and the Secret Trade in Nuclear Weapons*, New York: Walker Publishing, 2010, p. 61.
27. Khan, *Eating Grass*, p. 60; Syed, Anwar Hussain, *China & Pakistan: Diplomacy of an Entente Cordiale*, London: Oxford University Press, 1974, p. 10.
28. Ibid. p. 7.
29. "Chinese Policy and Practices Regarding Sensitive Nuclear Transfers", Special National Intelligence Estimate, Director of Central Intelligence (USA), 20 Jan. 1983, declassified 30 May 2012, http://digitalarchive.wilsoncenter.org/document/116893, last accessed 18 Nov. 2013.

30. Lewis, John Wilson and Xue Litai, *China Builds the Bomb*, Stanford, CA: Stanford University Press, 1988, p. 35.
31. Ibid. p. 61.
32. Ibid. p. 99.
33. Ibid. p. 160.
34. Corera, *Shopping for Bombs*, p. 45.
35. Medeiros, Evan, *Reluctant Restraint: The Evolution of China's Nonproliferation Policies and Practices, 1980–2004*, Stanford, CA: Stanford University Press, 2007, p. 17.
36. Ali, Mahmud, *U.S.-China Cold War Collaboration, 1971–1989*, Oxford: Routledge, 2005, p. 137.
37. Khan, Feroz H., *Eating Grass*, p. 171.
38. Jeffrey R. Smith and Joby Warrick, "Pakistani nuclear scientist's accounts tell of Chinese proliferation", *Washington Post*, 13 Nov. 2009, http://www. washingtonpost.com/wp-dyn/content/article/2009/11/12/ AR2009111211060.html, last accessed 27 Jan. 2014.
39. Lewis and Litai, *China Builds the Bomb*, p. 54.
40. Levy and Scott-Clark, *Deception*, p. 35.
41. Jeffrey R. Smith and Joby Warrick, "Pakistani nuclear scientist's accounts".
42. Ibid.
43. Ibid.
44. Khan, *Eating Grass*, p. 152.
45. Levy and Scott-Clark, *Deception*, pp. 100–01.
46. Levy and Scott-Clark, *Nuclear Deception*, p. 101; Corera, *Shopping for Bombs*, p. 45.
47. Khan, *Eating Grass*, p. 156.
48. Levy and Scott-Clark, *Deception*, p. 85.
49. Peter Lavoy, "Islamabad's Nuclear Posture: Its Premises and Implementation", in Henry D. Sokoloski, "Pakistan's Nuclear Future: Worries Beyond War", Carlisle, PA: Strategic Studies Institute, U.S. Atmy War College, Jan. 2008, http://www.strategicstudiesinstitute.army.mil/pdffiles/pub832.pdf, last accessed 22 Jan. 2014.
50. Khan, *Eating Grass*, p. 157.
51. Corera, *Shopping for Bombs*, p. 44.
52. R. Jeffrey Smith, "US aides see troubling trend in China-Pakistan nuclear ties", *Washington Post*, 1 Apr. 1996.
53. Corera, *Shopping for Bombs*, p. 46.
54. "US Embassy Pakistan Cable 15696 to State Department, 'Pakistan Nuclear Issue: Meeting with General Zia'", 17 Oct. 1982, History and Public Policy Program Digital Archive State Department Mandatory Declassification Review release. Obtained and contributed by William Burr and included

in NPIHP Research Update #6. http://digitalarchive.wilsoncenter.org/document/114254, last accessed 18 Nov. 2013.

55. Coll, Steve, *Ghost Wars: The Secret History of the CIA, Afghanistan, and Bin Laden, from the Soviet Invasion to September 10, 2001*, London: Penguin Books, 2004, p. 51.

56. U.S. Department of Defense Cable 06242 to State Department, Meeting between Secretary of Defense Harold Brown and Vice Premier Deng Xiaoping, Secretary of Defense, 8 Jan. 1980, https://www.documentcloud.org/documents/347015-doc-3–1–31–80.html, last accessed 18 Nov. 2013.

57. Kux, Dennis, *The United States and Pakistan, 1947–2000: Disenchanted Allies*, Washington, DC: Woodrow Wilson Center Press, 2001, p. 259.

58. U.S. Department of State Memorandum of Conversation, RG 59, Records of Henry Kissinger, Entry 5403, Box 5, Nodis Memoranda of Conversations, 31 Oct. 1974, http://2001–2009.state.gov/r/pa/ho/frus/nixon/e8/97002.htm, last accessed 18 Nov. 2013.

59. Ali, Mahmud, *U.S.-China*, p. 81.

60. Ibid. pp. 82–3.

61. Ibid. p. 137.

62. Akhund, Iqbal, *Memoirs of a Bystander: A Life in Diplomacy*, Karachi: Oxford University Press, 2000, p. 238; when I have raised this quote, and topic, with Michael Pillsbury he has stated that information around the subject remains classified.

63. Mann, James, *About Face: A History of America's Curious Relationship with China, from Nixon to Clinton*, New York: Knopf, 1998, p. 73–4.

64. *Foreign Relations of the United States, 1969–1976: Volume XVIII, China, 1973–1976, Document 124*, U.S. Department of State, Office of the Historian, 21 Oct. 1975, http://history.state.gov/historicaldocuments/frus1969–76v18/d124, last accessed 14 Feb. 2014.

65. Mann, *About Face*, pp. 74–5; Ali, *U.S.-China*, 2005, p. 142.

66. Ali, *U.S.-China*, p. 142.

67. Fravel and Medeiros, "China's Search", p. 54.

68. Tyler, Patrick, *A Great Wall: Six Presidents and China: An Investigative History*, New York: A Century Foundation Book, 1999, p. 285.

69. Michael Pillsbury, "U.S.-Chinese Military Ties?", *Foreign Policy*, No. 20, Autumn 1975, p. 58.

70. "China Policy and the National Security Council", National Security Council Project Oral History Roundtables, Ivo H. Daalder and I.M. Destler (moderators); Shakira Edwards and Josh Pollack (rapporteurs), 4 Nov. 1999.

71. Tyler, *A Great Wall*, pp. 284–5.

72. US Department of Commerce, "US-China Relations", Washington, DC, Aug. 1995, in Ali, *U.S.-China*, p. 251.

73. Tyler, *A Great Wall*, pp. 284–5.

74. Jeffrey T. Richelson, "The Wizards of Langley: The CIA's Directorate of Science and Technology" in Jeffreys-Jones, Rhodri and Christopher M. Andrew (eds), *Eternal Vigilance? 50 Years of the CIA*, Newbury Park: Frank Cass and Company, 1997, p. 94.

75. Gates, Robert M., *From the Shadows: The Ultimate Insider's Story of Five Presidents and How They Won the Cold War*, New York: Simon & Schuster, 2007, p. 123; Bob Woodward, *Veil: The Secret Wars of the CIA, 1981–1987*, New York: Simon & Schuster, 2005, pp. 63–4.

76. Gates, *From the Shadows*, p. 123.

77. James A. Gregor, "The People's Republic of China as a Western Security Asset", *Air University Review*, Jul.-Aug. 1983, http://www.airpower.max-well.af.mil/airchronicles/aureview/1983/jul-aug/gregor.html, last accessed 22 Jan. 2014.

78. "Risk Assessment of the Sale of the e69", Central Intelligence Agency, Memorandum for Frank Carlucci, Document number CIA-RD84B000 49R001604090013–3, approved for release 14 Jun. 2007. http://s3.docu-mentcloud.org/documents/347031/doc-15-a-11–8–82.txt, last accessed 23 Jan. 2014.

79. Ibid.

80. Albright, David and Paul Brannan and Andrea Scheel Stricker, "Self-Serving Leaks from the A.Q. Khan Circle", Institute for Science and International Security, 9 Dec. 2009, http://isis-online.org/isis-reports/detail/self-serving-leaks-from-the-a.q.-khan-circle/20, last accessed 27 Jan. 2014.

81. Jeffrey Lewis, "China's New Centrifuge Plants", *Arms Control Wonk*, 17 Sep. 2013, http://lewis.armscontrolwonk.com/archive/6826/chinas-new-centrifuge-plants, last accessed 18 Nov. 2013.

82. "Nuclear Weapons Systems in China", Defense Intelligence Agency, Defense Estimative Brief, 24 Apr. 1984, http://www2.gwu.edu/~nsarchiv/news/19990527/01–01.htm, last accessed 18 Nov. 2013.

83. Ibid.

84. Mann, *About Face*, p. 140.

85. Corera, *Shopping for Bombs*, p. 45.

86. Khan, *Eating Grass*, p. 175.

87. Author interviews in Islamabad, Jun. 2013.

88. "Pakistan Derives its First "Hatf" Missiles from Foreign Space Rockets", *The Risk Report*, Vol. 1, No. 8, Oct. 1995.

89. Khan, *Eating Grass*, p. 238.

90. Ibid.

91. Ibid. p. 240.

92. Vikram Sood in Hsin-Huang Michael Hsiao and Cheng-Yi Lin, *The Rise*

of China: Beijing's Strategies and Implications for the Asia-Pacific, London: Routledge, 2009, p. 242.

93. Levy and Scott-Clark, Deception, p. 258.
94. Khan, Eating Grass, p. 238.
95. Ibid. p. 239.
96. John W. Garver, "Future of the Sino-Pakistani Entente Cordiale", in Michael R. Chambers, South Asia in 2020: Future Strategic Balances and Alliances, Carlisle, PA: U.S. Army War College, 2002, p. 22; 405.
97. "Shaheen-II/Hatf-6/Ghaznavi", Strategic Security Project, 10 Mar. 2004, http://www.fas.org/nuke/guide/pakistan/missile/shaheen-2.htm,   last accessed 18 Nov. 2013.
98. Jeffrey Lewis, "Pakistan's Nuclear Artillery", Arms Control Wonk, 12 Dec. 2011, http://lewis.armscontrolwonk.com/archive/4866/pakistans-nuclear-artillery, last accessed 18 Nov. 2013.
99. Levy and Scott-Clark, Deception, p. 249.
100. Jeffrey R. Smith, "Chinese missile launchers sighted in Pakistan," Washington Post, 6 Apr. 1991.
101. Mann, About Face, p. 271.
102. Shirley A. Kan, "China and Proliferation of Weapons of Mass Destruction and Missiles: Policy Issues", CRS Report for Congress, Congressional Research Office, 7–5700, 23 Dec. 2009, p. 3.
103. Reed, Thomas C. and Danny B. Stillman, The Nuclear Express: A Political History of the Bomb and Its Proliferation, Minneapolis: Zenith Press, 2009, p. 252.
104. Shirley A. Kan, "China and Proliferation of Weapons of Mass Destruction and Missiles: Policy Issues", CRS Report for Congress, Congressional Research Office, 7–5700, 23 Dec. 2009, p. 5.
105. Levy and Scott-Clark, Deception, p. 173.
106. Ottaway, David B., The King's Messenger: Prince Bandar bin Sultan and America's Tangled Relationship with Saudi Arabia, New York: Walker Publishing Company, 2008, p. 69.
107. Ibid. p. 70.
108. Ibid.; Bin Sultan, Khaled, Desert Warrior: A Personal View of the Gulf War by the Joint Forces Commander, London: HarperCollins, 1995, pp. 139–41.
109. Ibid. p. 145.
110. Khan, Eating Grass, p. 383.
111. See for instance, citations in Levy and Catherine Deception, pp. 173, 225–6 and Lynch, Thomas, Crisis Stability and Nuclear Exchange Risks on the Subcontinent: Major Trends and the Iran Factor, Institute for National Strategic Studies, National Defense University Press, November 2013.

112. Ottaway, *The King's Messenger*, p. 230; "Saudi Arabia Special Weapons", Global Security, http://www.globalsecurity.org/wmd/world/saudi/, last accessed 23 Jan. 2014.

113. Tariq Butt, "Nawaz visits Kahuta nuclear labs for the fourth time", *The News*, 5 Oct. 2013, http://www.thenews.com.pk/Todays-News-2–206358-Nawaz-visits-Kahuta-nuclear-labs-for-the-fourth-time, last accessed 27 Jan. 2014.

114. Ottaway, *The King's Messenger*, p. 230.

115. "Saudi nuclear weapons 'on order' from Pakistan", BBC News, 6 Nov. 2013, http://www.bbc.co.uk/news/world-middle-east-24823846, last accessed 27 Jan. 2014.

116. Gary Samore quoted in Ibid.

117. Jeff Stein, "CIA helped Saudis in secret Chinese missile deal", *Newsweek*, 29 Jan. 2014, http://www.newsweek.com/exclusive-cia-helped-saudis-chinese-missile-deal-227283#.UuoRJKq3YmA.twitter, last accessed 2 Feb. 2014.

118. Jeffrey Lewis, "Saudi Missile Claims", *Arms Control Wonk*, 8 Jun. 2010, http://lewis.armscontrolwonk.com/archive/2761/china-and-saudi-bms, last accessed 18 Nov. 2013.

119. Ottaway, *The King's Messenger*, p. 231.

120. Kamran Khan, "Pakistanis say they are studying U.S. missile, Tomahawk was recovered after raid on camps in Afghanistan", *Washington Post*, 28 Aug. 1998.

121. Sanger, David E., *Confront and Conceal: Obama's Secret Wars and Surprising Use of American Power*, New York: Crown Publishing, 2012, p. 102; Mark Mazzetti, "U.S. aides believe China examined stealth copter", *New York Times*, 14 Aug. 2011, http://www.nytimes.com/2011/08/15/world/asia/15copter.html, last accessed 2 Feb. 2014.

122. "Saving the F-16 program", U.S. State Department Cable, *The Hindu*, 30 May 2011, http://www.thehindu.com/news/the-india-cables/the-cables/197576-saving-the-f16-program/article2059826.ece, last accessed 22 Jan. 2014.

123. Perkovich, *India's Nuclear Bomb*, p. 108.

124. Cohen, Stephen P., *Pakistan Army*, Los Angeles: University of California Press, 1984, p. 153.

125. Tellis, Ashley and C. Christine Fair and Jamison Jo Melby, *Limited Conflicts under the Nuclear Umbrella: Indian and Pakistani Lessons from the Kargil Crisis*, Santa Monica, CA: RAND, 2001, p. 48–9.

126. Tom Hundley, "Pakistan and India: Race to the End", *Foreign Policy*, 5 Sep. 2012, http://www.foreignpolicy.com/articles/2012/09/05/race_to_the_end, last accessed 22 Jan. 2014.

127. Michael Krepon, "Pakistan's Nuclear Strategy and Deterrence Stability", Stimson Center, Dec. 2012, p. 9, http://www.stimson.org/images/uploads/research-pdfs/Krepon_-_Pakistan_Nuclear_Strategy_and_Deterrence_Stability.pdf, last accessed 27 Jan. 2014.

128. "Wikileaks: US on Indian Army's Cold Start Doctrine", U.S. State Department Cable, 26 Feb. 2010, released by NDTV, http://www.ndtv.com/article/wikileaks-india-cableswikileaks-us-on-indian-army-s-cold-start-doctrine-69859

129. Michael Krepon, "Pakistan's Nuclear Strategy and Deterrence Stability", Stimson Center, Dec. 2012, p. 9, http://www.stimson.org/images/uploads/research-pdfs/Krepon_-_Pakistan_Nuclear_Strategy_and_Deterrence_Stability.pdf, last accessed 27 Jan. 2014.

130. Quoted in David O. Smith, "The US Experience With Tactical Nuclear Weapons: Lessons For South Asia", Stimson Centre, 4 Mar. 2013, p. 32, http://www.stimson.org/images/uploads/research-pdfs/David_Smith_Tactical_Nuclear_Weapons.pdf, last accessed 27 Jan. 2014.

131. Shashank Joshi, "Pakistan's Tactical Nuclear Nightmare: Déjà vu?", *Washington Quarterly*, Summer 2013, p. 165, http://csis.org/files/publication/TWQ_13Summer_Joshi.pdf, last accessed 27 Jan. 2014.

132. Michael Krepon, "The Arms Crawl that Wasn't", *Arms Control Wonk*, 2 Nov. 2011, http://krepon.armscontrolwonk.com/archive/3265/the-arms-crawl-that-wasnt, last accessed 27 Jan. 2014.

3. RE-HYPHENATING INDIA

1. Reproduced in Dixit, J.N., *India-Pakistan in War and Peace*, New York: Routledge, 2002, pp. 148–9.

2. Jiang Zemin, "Carrying Forward Generations of Friendly and Good-Neighbourly Relations and Endeavouring Towards a Better Tomorrow for All", Address to the Pakistani Senate, Dec. 1996, reproduced in Noor ul-Haq, *China-Pakistan Relations: A Profile of Friendship*, available at http://www.ipripak.org/factfiles/ff60.shtml, last accessed 23 Jan. 2014.

3. Li Keqiang, "Seize the New Opportunities in India-China Cooperation", speech at the Indian Council of World Affairs, 21 May 2013, available at, http://www.ipripak.org/factfiles/ff60.shtml, last accessed 23 Jan. 2014.

4. Riaz Mohammad Khan, "Pakistan-China Relations: An Overview" in "60 Years Of Pakistan-China Relations", *Pakistan Horizon*, Vol. 64, No. 4, Oct. 2011; Masood Khalid, "Pakistan-China relations: an exemplary friendship", *Daily Times*, 22 May 2013, http://archives.dailytimes.com.pk/editorial/22-May-2013/view-pakistan-china-relations-an-exemplary-friendship-masood-khalid, last accessed 27 Jan. 2014.

5. Eisenman, Joshua, Eric Heginbotham and Derek Mitchell, *China and the Developing World: Beijing's Strategy for the Twenty-First Century*, Armonk, NY: M.E. Sharpe/East Gate Books, 2007, p. 146; Murray Scot Tanner, Kerry B. Dumbaugh and Ian M. Easton, "Distracted Antagonists, Wary Partners: China and India Assess their Security Relations", CNA China Studies, Sep. 2011, pp. 9–12, http://www.cna.org/sites/default/files/research/Distracted%20Antagonists%2C%20Wary%20Partners%20D0025816%20A1.pdf, last accessed 27 Jan. 2014.

6. Garver, John W., *Protracted Contest: Sino-Indian Rivalry in the Twentieth Century*, Seattle: University of Washington Press, 2001, p. 6.

7. Robert S. Ross, "The 1995–1996 Taiwan Strait Confrontation Coercion, Credibility, and the Use of Force", *International Security*, 25:2, Fall 2000, p. 1, http://ppe.wiki.hci.edu.sg/file/view/ross3.pdf, last accessed 27 Jan. 2014.

8. Scott, David, *China Stands Up: The PRC and the International System*, New York: Routledge, 2007, p. 86.

9. "China makes nuclear pledge as it signs border deal with India", Agence France Presse, 29 Nov. 1996.

10. Jiang Zemin, Address to the Pakistani Senate, Dec. 1996.

11. Garver, *Protracted Contest*, p. 231.

12. Then US ambassador to Pakistan Thomas Simons Jr., quoted in Aparna Pande, *Explaining Pakistan's Foreign Policy: Escaping India*, New York: Routledge, 2011, p. 128.

13. Author interviews in Islamabad, Jun. 2013.

14. Perkovich, George, *India's Nuclear Bomb: The Impact on Global Proliferation*, Los Angeles: University of California Press, 1999, p. 191.

15. Tellis, Ashley, *India as a New Global Power: An Action Agenda for the United States*, Washington, DC: Carnegie Endowment for International Peace, 2005, p. 50.

16. Jayshree Bajoria and Esther Pan, "The U.S.-India Nuclear Deal", Council on Foreign Relations, 5 Nov. 2010, http://www.cfr.org/india/us-india-nuclear-deal/p9663, last accessed 20 Nov. 2013.

17. Indrani Bagchi, "Austria, Ireland against NSG waiver for India", *Times of India*, 6 Sep. 2008, http://articles.timesofindia.indiatimes.com/2008–09–06/india/27892506_1_proliferation-full-civil-nuclear-cooperation-global-nuclear-commerce, last accessed 27 Jan. 2014; R. Jeffrey Smith and Joby Warrick, "What Happens in Vienna …", *Arms Control Wonk*, 12 Sep. 2008, http://lewis.armscontrolwonk.com/archive/2039/what-happened-friday-night, last accessed 27 Jan. 2014.

18. Author interviews in Washington, Jun. 2013.

19. Rice, Condoleezza, *No Higher Honor: A Memoir of My Years in Washington*, New York: Random House, 2012, p. 698.

20. Clark T. Randt, Jr. "Ambassador Presses MFA AFM Liu On Nuclear Suppliers Group Draft Exception For India", U.S. State Department Cable, 3 Sep. 2008, https://www.wikileaks.org/plusd/cables/08BEIJING3401_a.html, last accessed 26 Jan. 2014.

21. Siddarth Varadarajan, "Inscrutable Chinese Behaviour at NSG Meet in Vienna", *Mainstream Weekly*, Vol. XLVI, No. 40, 20 Sep. 2008, http://www.mainstreamweekly.net/article940.html, last accessed 26 Jan. 2014.

22. "Indo-US Nuclear Deal at the Nuclear Suppliers Group", seminar report, Institute of Peace Conflict Studies, 17 Sep. 2008, http://www.ipcs.org/seminar/india/indo-us-nuclear-deal-at-the-nuclear-suppliers-group-619.html, last accessed 26 Jan. 2014.

23. Siddarth Varadarajan, "Inscrutable Chinese Behaviour at NSG Meet in Vienna", *Mainstream Weekly*, Vol. XLVI, No. 40, 20 September 2008, http://www.mainstreamweekly.net/article940.html, last accessed 26 Jan. 2014.

24. "China showing 'flexibility' on border talks with India", *Times of India*, 29 Sep. 2008; Harsh V. Pant, "China and India: A Rivalry Takes Shape", *E-Notes*, Foreign Policy Research Institute, Jun. 2011, p. 5, http://www.fpri.org/enotes/201106.pant.china_india.pdf, last accessed 27 Jan. 2014.

25. Somini Sengupta and Mark Mazzetti, "Atomic club votes to end restrictions on India", *New York Times*, 6 Sep. 2008, http://www.nytimes.com/2008/09/07/world/asia/07india.html?pagewanted=all, last accessed 27 Jan. 2014.

26. "India conveys unhappiness to China over its role in NSG", *Outlook India*, 8 Sep. 2008, http://news.outlookindia.com/items.aspx?artid=606511, 27 Jan. 2014.

27. Author interviews in Beijing, 2005–08.

28. Author interviews in Beijing, 2005–06.

29. Tellis, *India as a New Global Power*, p. 25; Robert D. Blackwill, "A new deal for New Delhi", *Wall Street Journal*, 21 March 2005, http://belfercenter.hks.harvard.edu/publication/1403/new_deal_for_new_delhi.html, last accessed 27 Jan. 2014.

30. Tellis, *India as a New Global Power*, p. 9.

31. Lora Saalman, "Divergence Similarity and Symmetry in Sino-Indian Threat Perceptions", *Journal of International Affairs*, Spring/Summer 2011, Vol. 64, No. 2, pp. 187 and 190.

32. Shyam Saran, "Is India's Nuclear Deterrent Credible?" (Speech at the India Habitat Centre, New Delhi, 24 Apr. 2013), http://southasiamonitor.org/detail.php?type=pers&nid=4987, last accessed 26 Jan. 2014.

33. Ananth Krishnan, "India, China renew push to bridge deficit ahead of trade talks", *The Hindu*, 27 Oct. 2012, http://www.thehindu.com/business/Economy/india-china-renew-push-to-bridge-deficit-ahead-of-trade-talks/article4038531.ece, last accessed 27 Jan. 2014.

34. "Copenhagen brought change of climate in Sino-India ties: Ramesh", *The Hindu*, 11 Apr. 2010, http://www.thehindu.com/news/national/article39 4433.ece, last accessed 27 Jan. 2014.

35. Paul Blustein, "The Nine-Day Misadventure of the Most Favoured Nations", Brookings Institution, Jul. 2008, http://www.brookings.edu/~/media/Research/Files/Articles/2008/12/05%20trade%20blustein/1205_trade_blustein.PDF, last accessed 27 Jan. 2014.

36. Cited in Samudra Manthan and Raja Mohan, *Sino-Indian Rivalry in the Indo-Pacific*, Carnegie Endowment for International Peace, loc, 485/6659 [IPAD 3rd Generation; MD366LL/A version]; Jalal Alamgir, *India's Open-Economy Policy: Globalism, Rivalry, Continuity*, Routledge, 2009, p. 58.

37. Brahma Chellaney, "Border-talks charade", *Mail Today*, 29 Nov. 2013, http://chellaney.net/2013/11/28/border-talks-charade/, last accessed 26 Jan. 2014.

38. Author interviews in Beijing, 2004–2013.

39. Zhang Feng, "China's New Thinking on Alliances", *Survival*, Oct.-Nov. 2012, http://www.iiss.org/en/publications/survival/sections/2012–23ab/survival—global-politics-and-strategy-october-november-2012-fda3/54–5–09-zhang-dd4b, last accessed 20 Nov. 2013.

40. Ashley Tellis, "The Merits of Dehyphenation: Explaining U.S. Success in Engaging India and Pakistan", *Washington Quarterly*, Autumn 2008, https://csis.org/files/publication/twq08autumntellis.pdf, last accessed 20 Dec. 2013.

41. Sarah Parnass, "Hillary Clinton urges India to lead in China's neighbourhood", *ABC News*, 20 Jul. 2011, http://abcnews.go.com/blogs/politics/2011/07/hillary-clinton-urges-india-to-lead-in-chinas-neighborhood/, last accessed 20 Dec. 2013.

42. Zhao Suisheng, Chinese Foreign Policy: Pragmatism and Strategic Behaviour, Armonk, NY: M.E. Sharpe/East Gate Books, 2004, p. 189.

43. "China is threat No. 1, says Fernandes", *Hindustan Times*, 3 May 1998.

44. Perkovich, *India's Nuclear Bomb*, p. 419.

45. Atal Bihari Vajpayee, then Prime Minister of India, in a letter to Bill Clinton, then-U.S. President, reproduced in "Nuclear anxiety; Indian's letter to Clinton on the nuclear testing", *New York Times*, 13 May 1998, http://www.nytimes.com/1998/05/13/world/nuclear-anxiety-indian-s-letter-to-clinton-on-the-nuclear-testing.html, last accessed 27 Jan. 2014.

46. Erik Eckholm, "China is 'seriously concerned' but restrained in its criti-

cisms", *New York Times*, 13 May 1998, http://www.nytimes.com/1998/05/13/world/nuclear-anxiety-reaction-china-seriously-concerned-but-restrained-its-criticism.html, last accessed 27 Jan. 2013.

47. Justin Jin, "China, gloves off, attacks India", Reuters, 14 May 1998.
48. "India's nuclear tests show fear of China", *Wall Street Journal*, 15 May 1998.
49. Li Wenyun, "India: nuclear tests condemned, lobbying suffers setbacks", *People's Daily*, 28 Jun. 1998.
50. Author interview with former Chinese official in Beijing, Jan. 2009.
51. "Pakistani envoy sees eye to eye with China", Reuters, 19 May 1998.
52. Stephen Kinzer, "China may give Pakistan defense assurances, averting A-tests", *New York Times*, 19 May 1998, http://www.nytimes.com/1998/05/19/world/china-may-give-pakistan-defense-assurances-averting-a-tests.html, last accessed 27 Jan. 2014.
53. Quoted under condition of anonymity in Elisabeth Rosenthal, "Chinese delegation seems to deny Pakistan a nuclear umbrella", *New York Times*, 21 May 1998, http://www.nytimes.com/1998/05/21/world/chinese-delegation-seems-to-deny-pakistan-a-nuclear-umbrella.html, last accessed 27 Jan. 2014.
54. John Cherian, "Diplomatic Fallout", *Frontline*, Vol. 15, No. 12, 6–19 Jun. 1998.
55. "Pakistan evens nuclear account: Sharif", *China Daily*, 29 May 1998.
56. "U.N. Security Council 'deplores' Pakistan's tests", CNN, 29 May 1998, http://edition.cnn.com/WORLD/asiapcf/9805/29/un.pakistan/index.html, last accessed 27 Jan. 2014.
57. Ibid.
58. Quoted in "Monitoring Nawaz Sharif's speech", BBC News, 28 May 1998, http://news.bbc.co.uk/2/hi/world/monitoring/102445.stm, last accessed 27 Jan. 2014.
59. "US-China Joint Statement On South Asia", statement issued by Presidents Bill Clinton and Jiang Zemin, Beijing, official White House text, 27 Jun. 1998, http://www.acronym.org.uk/proliferation-challenges/nuclear-weapons-possessors/china/us-china-joint-statement-south-asia-june-1998, last accessed 23 Jan. 2014.
60. Feroz Khan, Peter R. Lavoy and Christopher Clary, "Pakistan's Motivations and Calculations for the Kargil Conflict", in Peter Lavoy (ed.), *Asymmetric Warfare in South Asia: The Causes and Consequences of the Kargil Conflict*, New York: Cambridge University Press, 2009, p. 64–91; Shuja Nawaz, *Crossed Swords: Pakistan, Its Army and the Wars Within*, Karachi: Oxford University Press, 2008, p. 507–514.
61. Lavoy, Peter (ed.), Asymmetric Warfare, p. 85.
62. Sardar F.S. Lod, "Indian Air Force In Kargil Operations", *Defence Notes*,

Jan. 2000, http://www.Defencejournal.Com/2000/Jan/Indian-Airforce.
Htm, last accessed 26 Jan. 2014.

63. Ganguly, Sumit, *Nuclear Proliferation in South Asia: Crisis Behaviour and the Bomb*, New York: Routledge, 2009, p. 124; Arthur Max, "Indian air-strikes in Kashmir to continue", Associated Press, 30 May 1999, http://news.google.com/newspapers?nid=1988&dat=19990530&id=nkYiAAAA IBAJ&sjid=pKwFAAAAIBAJ&pg=2444,2575222, last accessed 27 Jan. 2014.

64. Hasahn-Askari Rizvi, "The Lessons of Kargil as Learned by Pakistan", in Peter Lavoy (ed.), *Asymmetric Warfare*, p. 344.

65. Ritu Sarin, "India gave Kargil tapes to Sharif a week before release", *Indian Express*, 25 Oct. 1999.

66. Sukumar Muralidharan, "High Stakes, Hardening Positions", *Frontline*, Vol. 16, Issue 13, 19 Jun.—2 Jul. 1999, http://www.hindu.com/fline/fl1613/16131250.htm, last accessed 27 Jan. 2014.

67. Dixit, J.N., *India-Pakistan in War and Peace*, New York: Routledge, 2002, p. 66.

68. "South Asia Tiger Hill—how important is it?", BBC News, 4 Jul. 1999, http://news.bbc.co.uk/1/hi/world/south_asia/385826.stm, last accessed 27 Jan. 2014.

69. Judith Miller and James Risen, "United States is worried about an increased threat of nuclear conflict over Kashmir", *New York Times*, 8 Aug. 2000, http://www.nytimes.com/2000/08/08/world/united-states-worried-about-increased-threat-nuclear-conflict-over-kashmir.html?pagewanted=all&src=pm, last accessed 27 Jan. 2014.

70. Abdul Naeem, "Kargil: Lessons Learned on Both Sides", in Ashley Tellis, C. Christine Fair and Jamison Jo Melby (eds), *Limited Conflicts*, p. 30.

71. Abbas Rashid, "Raising the ante in Kashmir", *The News*, 2 Jul. 1999.

72. Ibid.

73. Aziz, Sartaz, *Between Dreams And Realities: Some Milestones in Pakistan's History*, Karachi: Oxford University Press, 2010, p. 268.

74. Bruce Riedel, "American Diplomacy and the 1999 Kargil Summit at Blair House", in Peter Lavoy (ed.), *Asymmetric Warfare*, p. 134.

75. Hasahn-Askari Rizvi, "The Lessons of Kargil as Learned by Pakistan", in Peter Lavoy (ed.), *Asymmetric Warfare*, p. 344.

76. Ibid. p. 137.

77. Author interviews with European and US officials in Beijing and Washington, DC, Sep. 2010, and former Chinese officials in Beijing, Nov. 2012.

78. Zhang Qiyue, Chinese foreign ministry spokesperson, quoted in "Respect LoC, says China", *The Tribune*, 7 Jul. 1999, http://www.tribuneindia.com/1999/99jul07/world.htm#5, last accessed 27 Jan. 2014.

79. Bostrom, Nick and Milan M. Cirkovic, *Global Catastrophic Risks*, Oxford: Oxford University Press, 2008, p. 392.
80. Steven Coll, "The stand-off", *New Yorker*, 13 Feb. 2006, http://www.newyorker.com/archive/2006/02/13/060213fa_fact_coll, last accessed 27 Jan. 2014.
81. Ibid.
82. Nayak, Polly and Michael Krepon, *U.S. Crisis Management in South Asia's Twin Peaks Crisis*, Stimson Center Report, 2002, p. 21 and 26, http://www.stimson.org/images/uploads/research-pdfs/USCrisisManagement.pdf, last accessed 23 Jan. 2014.
83. U.S. official quoted in Polly Nayak and Michael Krepon, *U.S. Crisis Management in South Asia's Twin Peaks Crisis*, Stimson Center Report, 2002, p. 21 and 26, http://www.stimson.org/images/uploads/research-pdfs/USCrisisManagement.pdf, last accessed 23 Jan. 2014.
84. "Chinese special envoy calls on the Foreign Minister", Foreign Ministry of Pakistan, Press Release, 29 Dec. 2008.
85. Narayan Lakshman, "China blocked U.N. sanctions against terror group at Pakistan's behest", *The Hindu*, 7 Dec. 2010, http://www.thehindu.com/news/international/article936090.ece, last accessed 27 Jan. 2014.
86. Author interviews in Beijing, Sep. and Nov. 2010.
87. Cited in Levy, Adrian, *The Siege: Three Days of Terror Inside the Taj*, Viking, loc. 2694 [IPAD 3rd Generation; MD366LL/A version].
88. Bill Roggio, "UN declares Jamaat-ud-Dawa a terrorist front group", *Long War Journal*, 11 Dec. 2008, http://www.longwarjournal.org/archives/2008/12/un_declares_jamaatud.php, last accessed 27 Jan. 2014.
89. Jonathan S. Landay, "UN adds Pakistani militants to terrorist watch list", *Christian Science Monitor*, 12 Dec. 2008, http://www.csmonitor.com/World/Asia-South-Central/2008/1212/p25s03-wosc.html, last accessed 27 Jan. 2014.
90. See for instance, Mohan Malik, "The China Factor in the India-Pakistan Conflict", Carlisle, PA: Strategic Studies Institute, U.S. Army War College, 2003, http://strategicstudiesinstitute.army.mil/pubs/parameters/Articles/03spring/malik.pdf, last accessed 26 Jan. 2013.
91. Author interviews in Beijing, Feb. 2014.
92. Sean Lucas, "China Enters the Nuclear Suppliers Group: Positive Steps in the Global Campaign against Nuclear Weapons Proliferation", *Nuclear Threat Initiative*, 1 Nov. 2004, http://www.nti.org/analysis/articles/china-enters-nuclear-suppliers-group/, last accessed 27 Jan. 2014.
93. G. Balachandran, "India and NSG: Approaches to Indian Membership", Institute for Defence Studies and Analyses, 23 May 2013, http://www.idsa.in/issuebrief/IndiaandNSG_gbalachandran_230513, last accessed 27 Dec. 2013.

94. Mark Hibbs, "The Future of the Nuclear Suppliers Group", Washington, DC: Carnegie Endowment for International Peace, 2011, p. 23, http://carnegieendowment.org/files/future_nsg.pdf, last accessed 27 Dec. 2013.
95. Mark Hibbs, "Pakistan Deal Signals China's Growing Nuclear Assertiveness", Washington, DC: Carnegie Endowment for International Peace, 27 Apr. 2010, http://carnegieendowment.org/2010/04/27/pakistan-deal-signals-china-s-growing-nuclear-assertiveness/4su?reloadFlag=1, last accessed 27 Dec. 2013.
96. Elisabeth Bumiller and Carlotta Gall, "Bush says Pakistan cannot expect nuclear deal like one with India", *New York Times*, 4 May 2006, http://www.nytimes.com/2006/03/04/international/asia/04cnd-pakistan.html?hp&ex=1141534800&en=fd6e253a355720de&ei=5094&partner=homepage, last accessed 27 Jan. 2014.
97. "Musharraf says to seek more nuclear power plants with Chinese help", AAJ News, 10 Apr. 2008, http://www.aaj.tv/2008/04/musharraf-says-to-seek-more-nuclear-power-plants-with-chinese-help/, last accessed 27 Jan. 2014.
98. K.J.M. Varma, "U.S. Lashes Pakistan-China Atomic Deal", *NTI*, 21 Mar. 2011 http://www.nti.org/gsn/article/us-lashes-pakistan-china-atomic-deal/, last accessed 25 Jan. 2014.
99. Chris Buckley, "China confirms two nuclear reactors for Pakistan", Reuters, 21 Sep. 2010, http://www.reuters.com/article/2010/09/21/china-pakistan-nuclear-idAFTOE68K05X20100921, last accessed 27 Dec. 2013.
100. Author interviews in Beijing, Jan. 2010.
101. Chris Buckley, "China firms join controversial Pakistan nuclear push", Reuters, 24 Jun. 2010, http://in.reuters.com/article/2010/06/24/china-pakistan-nuclear-idINTOE65N02E20100624, last accessed 27 Jan. 2014.
102. "Maßnahmen zur Stärkung der Non-Proliferation und nuklearen Exportkontrolle (Measures to Strengthen Nuclear Non-Proliferation and Export Control)", German Federal Government Journal of Record, June, 2011.
103. Author interviews in Beijing, Washington, DC and Brussels, Jun. 2012–Dec. 2012.
104. Author interviews in Washington, DC, Oct. and Nov. 2010; Raja Mohan, "Don't Blame it on China", *Indian Express*, 17 Oct. 2013, http://archive.indianexpress.com/news/dont-blame-it-on-china/1183657/0, last accessed 27 Jan. 2014.
105. "China defends deal to build 1000 MW nuclear plant for Pakistan", *Economic Times*, 25 Mar. 2013, http://articles.economictimes.indiatimes.com/2013–10–16/news/43107332_1_china-and-pakistan-chashma-chinese-foreign-ministry, last accessed 27 Jan. 2014.

106. Author interviews in Washington, DC, Oct. and Nov. 2010.
107. Author interviews in Beijing, Sep. 2010 and Washington, DC, Nov. 2010.
108. Author interviews in Islamabad and Beijing, Jun. 2011.
109. Author interviews in New Delhi, Mar. 2010; Lora Saalman, "Divergence Similarity and Symmetry in Sino-Indian Threat Perceptions", *Journal of International Affairs*, Spring/Summer 2011, Vol. 64, No. 2, p. 173, http://carnegieendowment.org/files/Divergence_Similarity_and_Symmetry_in_Sino-Indian_Threat_Perceptions.pdf, last accessed 27 Jan. 2014.
110. Nickles, David P. and Adam Howard (eds), *Foreign Relations of the United States, 1977–1980, Volume XIII, China*, Office of the Historian, U.S. State Department, Bureau of Public Affairs, 2013, p. 1100.
111. Sana Hashim, "India's Concern Over China-Pakistan Nuclear Nexus", New Delhi: Centre for Air Power Studies, Oct. 2013, http://capsindia.org/files/documents/CAPS_Infocus_SH2.pdf, last accessed 27 Dec. 2013; "Pakistan promised missile armed Chinese UAVs", 5 Dec. 2012, available at, http://pakistanchinarelations.wordpress.com/2012/12/05/pakistan-promised-missile-armed-chinese-uavs/, last accessed 24 Jan. 2014.
112. Selig S. Harrison, "China's discreet hold on Pakistan's northern borderlands", *International Herald Tribune*, 26 Aug. 2010, http://www.nytimes.com/2010/08/27/opinion/27iht-edharrison.html, last access 27 Jan. 2014.

4. THE CHINESE WAR ON TERROR

1. Author interview with Pakistani expert in Islamabad, Jun. 2011.
2. Pope, Hugh, *Sons of the Conquerors: The Rise of the Turkic World*, London: Duckworth Publishers/Overlook Press, 2006, p. 166.
3. "China to further strengthen ties with Pakistan", *The Nation*, 6 Apr. 2010, http://www.nation.com.pk/politics/06-Apr-2010/China-to—further-strengthen-ties-with-Pakistan, last accessed 27 Jan. 2014.
4. Thomas Johnson and Chris Mason, "Understanding the Taliban and Insurgency in Afghanistan", Calhoun Institutions Archive of the Naval Postgraduate School, Winter 2007, Elsevier Limited, p. 73, http://hdl.handle.net/10945/30471, last accessed 27 Jan. 2014.
5. Rashid, Ahmed, *Taliban: Militant Islam, Oil and Fundamentalism in Central Asia*, New Haven: Yale University Press, p. 201.
6. Josy Joseph, "Harkat-ul-Mujahideen helped Osama bin Laden during Pak stay", *Times of India*, 25 Jun. 2011, http://articles.timesofindia.indiatimes.com/2011–06–25/india/29702395_1_hum-global-jihad-kashmiri-militant-group, last accessed 27 Jan. 2014.
7. "Maulana Fazlur Rehman arrives in Beijing", *Awaz*, 5 Apr. 2010 http://www.awaztoday.com/News_Maulana-Fazlur-Rehman-arrives-in-Beijing_1_4933_Political-News.aspx, last accessed 27 Jan. 2014.

8. Syed Saleem Shahzad, "Taliban's call for jihad answered in Pakistan", *Asia Times*, 16 Jun. 2006, http://www.atimes.com/atimes/South_Asia/HF16D f01.html, last accessed 27 Jan. 2014.

9. "Jamaat-e-Islami, Chinese Communist Party ink MoU", *The News*, 17 Feb. 2009, http://www.thenews.com.pk/TodaysPrintDetail.aspx?ID=163116& Cat=6&dt=2/16/2009, last accessed 27 Jan. 2014.

10. Zulfiqar Ali, "Pakistan's Jamaat-i-Islami to preach Islam in China", *Dawn*, 4 Apr. 2009, http://www.dawn.com/news/937790/pakistan-s-jamaat-i-islami-to-preach-islam-in-china, last accessed 27 Jan. 2014.

11. Ibid.

12. Yitzhak Shichor, "Great Wall of Steel: Military and Strategy in Xinjiang", in S. Frederick Starr (ed.), *Xinjiang: China's Muslim Borderland*, London: M.E. Sharpe, 2004, p. 145.

13. "Two Uighurs handed 10 years for UAE bomb plot", Reuters, 1 Jul. 2010, http://www.arabnews.com/node/349165, last accessed 27 Jan. 2014.

14. Raffaello Pantucci, "Uyghurs Convicted in East Turkestan Islamic Movement", *Terrorism Monitor*, Vol. 8, Issue 29, 22 Jul. 2010, http://www.jamestown.org/single/?no_cache=1&tx_ttnews[tt_news]=36656#.UucOojo1hMs, last accessed 27 Jan. 2014.

15. Hassan Hassan, "Revealed: the plot to blow up DragonMart", *The National*, 9 Jul. 2010, http://www.thenational.ae/news/uae-news/courts/revealed-the-plot-to-blow-up-dragonmart, last accessed 27 Jan. 2014.

16. Raffaello Pantucci, "Uyghurs Convicted in East Turkestan Islamic Movement", *Terrorism Monitor*, Vol. 8, Issue 29, 22 Jul. 2010, http://www.jamestown.org/single/?no_cache=1&tx_ttnews[tt_news]=36656#.UucOo jo1hMs, last accessed 27 Jan. 2014.

17. Hassan Hassan, "Uighur terrorists jailed for DragonMart bomb plot", *The National*, 1 Jul. 2010, http://www.thenational.ae/news/uae-news/courts/uighur-terrorists-jailed-for-dragonmart-bomb-plot, last accessed 27 Jan. 2014.

18. Hassan Hassan, "Revealed: the plot to blow up DragonMart", 9 Jul. 2010, *The National*, http://www.thenational.ae/news/uae-news/courts/revealed-the-plot-to-blow-up-dragonmart, last accessed 2 Feb. 2014.

19. Hassan Hassan, "Uighur terrorists jailed for DragonMart bomb plot", *The National*, 1 Jul. 2010, http://www.thenational.ae/news/uae-news/courts/uighur-terrorists-jailed-for-dragonmart-bomb-plot, last accessed 27 Jan. 2014.

20. Lattimore, Owen, *Inner Asian Frontiers of China*, New York: American Geographical Society, 1940, p. 171.

21. James A. Millward and Peter Perdue, "Political Histories and Strategies of Control", in Starr (ed.), *Xinjiang*, pp. 77–85.

22. Dillon, Michael, *Xinjiang: China's Muslim Far Northwest*, London: Routledge, 2009, p. 77.

23. For a detailed analysis of how Xinjiang was affected by the Cultural Revolution, see Millward and Perdue, pp. 94–8.

24. James A. Millward, "Violent Separatism in Xinjiang: A Critical Assessment", East-West Center, Policy Studies 6, 2005, p. 7, http://www.eastwestcenter. org/fileadmin/stored/pdfs/PS006.pdf, last accessed 27 Jan. 2014.

25. Rémi Castets, "The Uyghurs in Xinjiang—The Malaise Grows", *China Perspectives*, Issue 49, Sep.-Oct. 2003, http://chinaperspectives.revues. org/648#tocto1n6, last accessed 2 Feb. 2014.

26. Dru C. Gladney, "The Chinese Program of Development and Control, 1978–2001", in Starr (ed.), *Xinjiang*, p. 109.

27. Ziad Haider, "Sino-Pakistan Relations and Xingiang's Uighurs", *Asian Survey*, Vol. XLV, 4, University of California Press, July/August 2005, p. 525, http://www.stimson.org/images/uploads/research-pdfs/XINJIANG. pdf, last accessed 27 Jan. 2014.

28. Ibid.; see also: Alessandro Rippa, "From Uyghurs to Kashgari", *The Diplomat*, Dec. 20 2013, http://thediplomat.com/2013/12/from-uyghurs-to-kashgari/ last accessed 13 Feb. 2014.

29. Yitzhak Shichor, "Great Wall of Steel: Military and Strategy in Xinjiang", in Starr (ed.), *Xinjiang*, p. 144; Ziad Haider, "Sino-Pakistan Relations and Xingiang's Uighurs", *Asian Survey*, Vol. XLV, 4, University of California Press, July/August 2005, p. 525, http://www.stimson.org/images/uploads/ research-pdfs/XINJIANG.pdf, last accessed 27 Jan. 2014; Rippa, "From Uyghurs to Kashgari".

30. Millward, "Violent Separatism", p. 9.

31. Fravel, M. Taylor, *Strong Borders, Secure Nation: Cooperation and Conflict in China's Territorial Disputes*, New Jersey: Princeton University Press, 2008, p. 155.

32. See (on new transport links) John W. Garver, "China's Influence in Central and South Asia: Is it Increasing?" in David Shambaugh (ed.), *Power Shift: China and East Asia's New Dynamics*, Los Angeles: University of California Press, p. 215.

33. Matthew Oresman, "Repaving the Silk Road: China's Emergence in Central Asia", in Joshua Eisenmann, Eric Heginbotham and Derek Mitchell (eds), *China and the Developing World: Beijing's Strategy for the Twenty-First Century*, New York: M.E. Sharpe, 2007, p. 77.

34. Elizabeth Van Wie Davis, "Uyghur Muslim Ethnic Separatism in Xinjiang", China Asia-Pacific Center for Security Studies, January 2008, p. 4, http:// www.dtic.mil/cgi-bin/GetTRDoc?AD=ADA493744, last accessed 26 Jan. 2014.

35. Leavitt, Sandra Ruth, "Persuasion, Coercion, and Neglect: Understanding State Policy and the Mobilization of Muslim Minorities in Asia", PhD Dissertation, Georgetown University, 2008, p. 134.

36. Starr (ed.), *Xinjiang*, p. 15.

37. Reed, J. Todd and Diana Raschke, *The ETIM: China's Islamic Militants and the Global Terrorist Threat*, Washington, DC: Library of Congress, 2010, p. 77.

38. Brent Hierman, "The Pacification of Xinjiang: Uighur Protest and the Chinese State, 1988–2002", *Problems of Post-Communism*, May/June 2007, http://www.academia.edu/329476/The_Pacification_of_Xinjiang_Uighur_Protest_and_the_Chinese_State_1988–2002, last accessed 23 Jan. 2014.

39. Julie R. Sirrs, Sirrs, J., *The Taliban's Foreign Fighters: A Report Prepared for the Committee for a Free Afghanistan*, Washington: Committee for a Free Afghanistan, 21 January 2001, pp. 1–8.

40. Ibid.

41. Daniel Klaidman, *Kill or Capture: The War on Terror and the Soul of the Obama Presidency*, Boston: Houghton Mifflin Harcourt, 2012, p. 98.

42. See, for instance, "The terrorist nature of 'east Turkestan' separatists", *China Daily*, 23 Jul. 2009, http://www.chinadaily.com.cn/china/2009–07/23/content_8466072.htm, last accessed 27 Jan. 2014; "China cites East Turkistan Islamic Movement terrorist threat", *Global Times*, 1 Nov. 2013, http://www.globaltimes.cn/content/821971.shtml#.Uuozxz1dV2o, last accessed 30 Jan. 2014; or "World Uyghur Congress behind Xinjiang violence: expert", *China Daily*, 7 Jul. 2009, http://www.chinadaily.com.cn/china/2009–07/07/content_8389647.htm, last accessed 2 Feb. 2014.

43. Dillon, *Xinjiang*, p. 58.

44. James A. Millward and Nabijan Tursun, "Political History and Strategies of Control, 1884–1978", in Starr (ed.), *Xinjiang*, p. 97.

45. Ibid.

46. Castets, "The Uyghurs".

47. See, for instance, Justin Rudelson and William Jankowiak, "Acculturation and Resistance: Xinjiang Identities in Flux", in Starr (ed.), *Xinjiang*, pp. 316–17; Millward, "Violent Separatism", p. 28; Acharya, Arabinda, Rohan Gunaratna and Wang Pengxin, *Ethnic Identity and National Conflict in China*, New York: Palgrave Macmillan, 2010, p. 49; Bovingdon, Gardner, *The Uyghurs: Strangers in Their Own Land*, New York: Columbia University Press, 2010, pp. 60, 66, 123–5; Dillon, *Xinjiang*, pp. 63–5; and, for good measure, http://en.wikipedia.org/wiki/Baren_Township_riot

48. Castets, "The Uyghurs ".

49. Millward, "Violent Separatism", p. 12.

50. Bovingdon, *The Uyghurs*, p. 124.

51. Millward, "Violent Separatism", p. 28.
52. Castets, "The Uyghurs".
53. "'East Turkistan' Terrorist Forces Cannot Get Away With Impunity", PRC State Council Information Office, 21 Jan. 2002, http://www.china.org.cn/english/2002/Jan/25582.htm, last accessed 27 Jan. 2014.
54. Reed, J. Todd and Diana Raschke, *The ETIM: China's Islamic Militants and the Global Terrorist Threat*, Washington, DC: Library of Congress, 2010, p. 39.
55. Ibid. p. 38.
56. Author interviews in Peshawar, June 2013.
57. Reed and Raschke, *The ETIM*, p. 48.
58. Ibid.
59. Acharya, Gunaratna and Pengxin, *Ethnic Identity*, p. 55.
60. B. Raman, "Explosions in Xinjiang", South Asia Analysis Group, Paper no. 1232, 27 Jan. 2005, http://web.archive.org/web/20070927194700/http://www.saag.org/papers13/paper1232.html, last accessed 2 Feb. 2014.
61. Reed and Raschke, *The ETIM*, p. 48.
62. "'East Turkistan' Terrorist Forces Cannot Get Away With Impunity", PRC State Council Information Office, 21 Jan. 2002, http://www.china.org.cn/english/2002/Jan/25582.htm, last accessed 27 Jan. 2014.
63. Murad Batal Al-shishani, "Journal of the Turkistan Islamic Party Urges Jihad in China", *Terrorism Monitor*, 10 Apr. 2009, http://www.freerepublic.com/focus/news/2227307/posts, last accessed 27 Jan. 2014.
64. Rashid, Ahmed, *Jihad: The Rise of Militant Islam in Central Asia*, New York: Penguin Group, 2003, p. 142.
65. Ibid. p. 9 and p. 142; Enze Han, *Contestation and Adaptation: The Politics of National Identity in China*, Oxford University Press, 2013, p. 61.
66. Ahmed Rashid, "They're only sleeping", *New Yorker*, 14 Jan. 2002, http://www.newyorker.com/archive/2002/01/14/020114fa_FACT, last accessed 27 Jan. 2014.
67. Rashid, *Jihad*, pp. 145–8.
68. Ibid. p. 204.
69. Chung Chien-peng, "Confronting Terrorism and Other Evils in China: All Quiet on the Western Front?", *China and Eurasia Foreign Quarterly*, Vol. 4, No. 2, May 2006, p. 77.
70. Rebecca Louise Nadin, "China and the Shanghai 5/Shanghai Cooperation Organization: 1996–2006, A Decade on the New Diplomatic Frontier", PhD Dissertation, University of Sheffield, 2007, http://ethos.bl.uk/OrderDetails.do?uin=uk.bl.ethos.443900, last accessed 27 Jan. 2014.
71. Rashid, *Jihad*, pp. 70–71.
72. Cohen, Stephen P., *The Idea of Pakistan*, Washington, DC: Brookings Institution Press, 2004, p. 104.

73. Rubin, Barnett, *Afghanistan in the Post-Cold War Era*, New York: Oxford University Press, 2013, p. 366.

74. Nawaz, Shuja, *Crossed Swords: Pakistan, Its Army and the Wars Within*, Karachi: Oxford University Press, 2008, p. 206.

75. "Jamaat Secretary General gets death for war crimes in Bangladesh", *Tehelka Daily*, 17 Jul. 2013, http://www.tehelka.com/jamaat-secretary-general-gets-death-for-war-crimes-in-bangladesh/, last accessed 27 Jan. 2014.

76. John W. Garver, *Protracted Contest: Sino-Indian Rivalry in the Twentieth Century*, Seattle: University of Washington Press, 2001, p. 95; Lintner, Bertil, *Great Game East: India, China and the Struggle for Asia's Most Volatile Frontier*, New Delhi: Harpers Today, 2012, pp. 147–159 and pp. 336–43.

77. Lintner, *Great Game East*, p. 149.

78. Ibid. p. 342.

79. Ibid. p. xi.

80. Ibid. pp. 336–9; Garver, *Protracted Contest*, p. 94.

81. Lintner, *Great Game East*, p. xii.

82. Garver, *Protracted Contest*, p. 94.

83. "Unravelling Chittagong arms haul mystery", Policy Research Group, 1 Oct., 2010, http://policyresearchgroup.com/regional_weekly/hot_topics/unravelling_chittagong_arms_haul_mystery.html, last accessed 20 Nov. 2013; *Jane's Intelligence Review*, 1 May 2004 and 1 August 2004, referenced in Lintner, *Great Game East*, pp. 344–5.

84. Coll, Steve, *Ghost Wars: The Secret History of the CIA, Afghanistan and Bin Laden*, London: Penguin, 2004, p. 66; also see a more extensive treatment of the episode in Chapter 6, "Tea with the Taliban".

85. George Garner, "The Afghan Taliban and Pakistan's 'Strategic Depth'", *Bellum* (a project of the *Stanford Review*), 17 May 2010, http://bellum.stanfordreview.org/?p=2184, last accessed 2 Feb. 2014.

86. Jamal, Arif, *Shadow War: The Untold Story of Jihad in Kashmir*, New York: Melville House Printing, 2009, p. 108–110.

87. Ibid.

88. Ibid.

89. Coll, *Ghost Wars*, p. 227.

90. Ibid.

91. Ibid. p. 221.

92. Nawaz, *Crossed Swords*, p. 360; Jamal, *Shadow War*, pp. 139–51.

93. Jayshree Bajoria and Eben Kaplan, "The ISI and Terrorism: Behind the Accusations", Council on Foreign Relations, 4 May. 2011, http://www.cfr.org/pakistan/isi-terrorism-behind-accusations/p11644, last accessed 2 Feb. 2014.

94. Rashid, *Taliban*, p. 129.

95. Ghosh, Partha Sarathy, *Cooperation and Conflict in South Asia*, Delhi: Manohar Publishers, 1995, p. 26.

96. Haqqani, Hussain, *Pakistan: Between Mosque and Military*, Washington, DC: Carnegie Endowment for International Peace, 2005, pp. 148–52.

97. Bennett-Jones, Owen, *Pakistan: Eye of the Storm*, New Haven: Yale University Press, 2003, p. 259.

98. Adiran Hänni and Lukas Hegi, "The Pakistani Godfather: The Inter-Services Intelligence and the Afghan Taliban 1994–2010", *Small Wars Journal*, 2 Apr. 2013, http://smallwarsjournal.com/jrnl/art/the-pakistani-godfather-the-inter-services-intelligence-and-the-afghan-taliban-1994–2010, last accessed 2 Feb. 2014.

99. Rashid, *Jihad*, pp. 187–8.

100. Ibid. p. 188.

101. Haqqani, Hussain, *Pakistan: Between Mosque and Military*, Washington, DC: Carnegie Endowment for International Peace, 2005, p. 171.

102. Castets, "The Uyghurs".

103. Ziad Haider, "Sino-Pakistan Relations and Xingiang's Uighurs", *Asian Survey*, Vol. XLV, 4, University of California Press, July/August 2005, p. 541, http://www.stimson.org/images/uploads/research-pdfs/XIN-JIANG.pdf, last accessed 27 Jan. 2014.

104. Author interviews in Islamabad, Jun. 2011.

105. Ziad Haider, "Sino-Pakistan Relations and Xinjiang's Uighurs", *Asian Survey*, Vol. XLV, 4, University of California Press, July/August 2005, p. 535, http://www.stimson.org/images/uploads/research-pdfs/XIN-JIANG.pdf, last accessed 27 Jan. 2014.

106. Sadia Fayaz, "China's Xinjiang Problem and Pakistan", *The Dialogue*, Vol. 7, No. 3, Jul-Sep. 2012, p. 249. http://www.qurtuba.edu.pk/thedialogue/The%20Dialogue/7_3/Dialogue_July_September2012_235–254.pdf, last accessed 27 Jan. 2014.

107. Ziad Haider, "Sino-Pakistan Relations", p. 536.

108. Author interviews in Beijing and Islamabad, 2008–2013.

109. Shirley A. Khan, "U. S.-China Counterterrorism Cooperation: Issues for U. S. Policy", Congressional Research Service, 7 May 2009, p. 25.

110. Author interviews in Beijing and Islamabad, 2008–2013.

111. See, for instance, Rashid, *Jihad*, p. 141.

112. Yitzhak Shichor, "Great Wall of Steel", in Starr (ed.), Xinjiang:, p. 145.

113. See Chapter 6, "Tea with the Taliban".

114. Author interviews in Beijing, Nov. 2008.

115. "Bin Ladin Charges U.S. involvement in China Bombings", Islamabad, The Muslim in English, 15 Mar. 1997, pp. 1–11; "New Analysis: Bin Laden: Dissident Turns Pan-Islamist", *The Observer* in "Compilation of

Usama Bin Laden Statements 1994–January 2004", FBIS Report, Jan. 2004, p. 39, http://www.fas.org/irp/world/para/ubl-fbis.pdf, last accessed 22 Dec. 2013.

116. Rashid, *Jihad*, p. 204.
117. Millward, "Violent Separatism".
118. "'East Turkistan' Terrorist Forces Cannot Get Away With Impunity", PRC State Council Information Office, 21 Jan. 2002, http://www.china.org. cn/english/2002/Jan/25582.htm, last accessed 27 Jan. 2014.
119. "China hails US decision to put ETIM on terror list", *People's Daily*, 28 Aug. 2002, http://www.china.org.cn/english/international/40575.htm, last accessed 27 Jan. 2014; Colin Mackerras, "Xinjiang and the War Against Terrorism", in Simon Shen (ed.), *China and Antiterrorism*, New York: Nova Science Publishers, 2007, p. 100.
120. Willy Wo-Lap Lam, "China welcomes separatists' terror tag", CNN, 12 Sep. 2002, http://edition.cnn.com/2002/WORLD/asiapcf/east/09/12/ china.xinjiang/index.html, last accessed 27 Jan. 2014.
121. "JTF GTMO Detainee Assessment", U.S. Department of Defense Joint Task Force Guantanamo Memorandum for Commander of the United States Southern Command, 22 Jun. 2007, http://wikileaks.org/gitmo/ pdf/ch/us9ch-000219dp.pdf, last accessed 27 Jan. 2014.
122. "Bin Laden's associate Juma Namangani killed, assert Taleban", *Pravda. Ru*, 10 Nov. 2001, http://english.pravda.ru/news/hotspots/conflicts/20–11–2001/27958–0/, last accessed 27 Jan. 2014.
123. Rashid, *Taliban*, p. 243.
124. "East Turkistan' terrorist killed", *China Daily*, 24 Dec. 2003, http://www. chinadaily.com.cn/en/doc/2003–12/24/content_293163.htm, last accessed 20 Nov. 2013.
125. "Competing Perceptions of PRC Activities", U.S. State Department Cable, 12 Dec. 2009, wikileaks.org/cable/2009/12/09BEIJING3287.html, last accessed 20 Nov. 2013.
126. "China: Uighur group added to U.S. list of terrorist organizations", EurasiaNet, 31 Aug. 2002, http://www.eurasianet.org/departments/ insight/articles/eav090102.shtml, last accessed 20 Nov. 2013.
127. Ben Blanchard, "Chinese government concerned about Hizb ut-Tahrir in Xinjiang", Reuters, 31 Jul. 2008, http://enews.fergananews.com/articles/2434, last accessed 2 Feb. 2014.
128. Author interviews in Beijing, Jan. 2009.
129. Edward Wong, "Warning of attacks on Olympics is said to be linked to Muslim separatist group", *New York Times*, 9 Aug. 2008, http://www. nytimes.com/2008/08/10/sports/olympics/10uighurs.html, last accessed 20 Nov. 2013.

130. "Our Blessed Jihad in Yunan" (video), TIP Voice of Islam Information Center, 23 Jul. 2008 quoted in "IntelCenter: Islamic party threatens Olympic Games", CBS News, 25 Jul. 2008, http://www.cbsnews.com/8301–502684_162–4295655–502684.html, last accessed 20 Nov. 2013.

131. Raffaello Pantucci, "A Post-Mortem Analysis of Turkistani Amir Emeti Yakuf: A Death that Sparked More Questions than Answers", *Terrorism Monitor*, Vol. 3, Issue 10, 1 Nov. 2012, http://mlm.jamestown.org/single/?tx_ttnews%5Btt_news%5D=40043&tx_ttnews%5BbackPid%5D=551&cHash=e13aadc198482b3c8c34129c423af1f6#.UubQVJH0AUs, last accessed 20 Nov. 2013.

132. "Two dead in China 'terror' raid", BBC News, 18 Feb. 2008, http://news.bbc.co.uk/2/hi/asia-pacific/7251517.stm, last accessed 20 Nov. 2013.

133. Liu Shaoyong, then-President of China Southern Airlines, in an interview with Phoenix TV, quoted in Richard Spencer, "The plane incident and the Uighur girl", *Telegraph*,11 Mar. 2008, http://blogs.telegraph.co.uk/news/richardspencer/3614711/The_plane_incident_and_the_Uighur_girl_/, last accessed 2 Feb. 2014; "China says 19-year-old woman confessed to terror plot on plane", *New York Times*, 27 Mar. 2008, http://www.nytimes.com/2008/03/27/world/asia/27iht-china.1.11467307.html?_r=0, last accessed 20 Nov. 2013.

134. Praveen Swami, "China's mid-air terror trail leads to Pakistan", *The Hindu*, 22 Mar. 2008, http://www.hindu.com/2008/03/22/stories/2008032254581200.htm, last accessed 4 Feb. 2014.

135. Unidentified Chinese official, quoted in the *Global Times* and reproduced in "China: Plane incident a 'terror act'", *USA Today*, 13 Mar. 2008, http://usatoday30.usatoday.com/news/world/2008–03–13-china-terror_N.htm, last accessed 20 Nov. 2013.

136. Elizabeth Van Wie Davis, "China confronts its Uyghur threat", *Asia Times*, 18 Apr. 2008, http://www.atimes.com/atimes/China/JD18Ad01.html, last accessed 14 Feb. 2014.

137. Pallavi Aiyar, "Musharraf bolsters China-Pakistan bond", *Asia Times*, 24 Apr. 2008, http://www.atimes.com/atimes/China/JD24Ad01.html, last accessed 14 Feb. 2014; Nirupama Subramanian, "All eyes on Musharraf's China visit", *The Hindu*, 8 Apr. 2008, http://www.thehindu.com/todays-paper/tp-international/all-eyes-on-musharrafs-china-visit/article1235331.ece, last accessed 14 Feb. 2014.

138. "Olympic Torch hits China-friendly Pakistan", CBS News, 16 Apr. 2008, http://www.cbsnews.com/news/olympic-torch-hits-china-friendly-pakistan/, last accessed 14 Feb. 2014.

139. Andrew Jacobs, "Ambush in China raises concerns as Olympics near", *New York Times*, 5 Aug. 2008, http://www.nytimes.com/2008/08/05/world/asia/05china.html?pagewanted=all, last accessed 20 Nov. 2013.

140. Edward Wong, "Attack in West China kills 3 security officers", *New York Times*, 12 Aug. 2008, http://www.nytimes.com/2008/08/13/sports/olympics/13china.html?_r=0, last accessed 27 Jan. 2014.

141. Austin Ramzy, "China's restive Xinjiang region hit by renewed violence", *Time*, 29 Feb. 2012, http://world.time.com/2012/02/29/chinas-restive-xinjiang-region-hit-by-renewed-violence/, last accessed 27 Jan. 2014; "Group of axe-wielding men attack market place in Xinjian", *Telegraph*, 29 Feb. 2012, http://www.telegraph.co.uk/news/worldnews/asia/china/9112502/Group-of-axe-wielding-men-attack-market-place-in-Xinjiang.html, last accessed 27 Jan. 2014.

142. Author interviews in Beijing, Aug. 2011.

143. Liu Yong, "Uighur group claims bus attacks, threatens Olympics", *China Digital Times*, 25 Jul. 2008, http://chinadigitaltimes.net/2008/07/uighur-group-claims-china-bus-attacks-threatens-olympics/, last accessed 20 Nov. 2013.

144. Tania Branigan, "China knife attach and explosions leave several dead", *Guardian*, 31 Jul. 2011, http://www.theguardian.com/world/2011/jul/31/china-knife-attack-several-dead, last accessed 20 Nov. 2013.

145. Sui-lee Wee, "China boosts security in Xinjiang after the attacks", Reuters, 2 Aug. 2011, http://in.reuters.com/article/2011/08/02/idINIndia-58582720110802, last accessed 1 Feb. 2014; "China: 10 dead in blast and stabbing rampage", Sky News, 31 Jul. 2011, http://news.sky.com/story/871018/china-10-dead-in-blast-and-stabbing-rampage, last accessed 27 Jan. 2014.

146. Jacob Zenn, "Insurgency in Xinjiang Complicates Chinese-Pakistani Relations", *Terrorism Monitor*, Vol. 10, Issue 8, 20 Apr. 2012, http://www.freerepublic.com/focus/f-news/2875031/posts, last accessed 27 Jan. 2014.

147. Kamran Yousaf, "Looking towards East: Spy chief on a mission to Beijing", *Express Tribune*, 1 Aug. 2011, http://tribune.com.pk/story/221259/cias-pakistan-chief-leaves-country/, last accessed 27 Jan. 2014.

148. Shohret Hoshur (reporter), Mamatjan Juma (translator), and Joshua Lipes (writer), "Pakistan deports Uyghurs", Radio Free Asia, 10 Aug. 2011, http://www.rfa.org/english/news/uyghur/pakistan-08102011175506.html/, last accessed 14 Feb. 2014.

149. Chi-Chi Zhang, "Muslim militant group claims western China attacks", Associated Press, 8 Sep. 2011, http://news.yahoo.com/muslim-militant-group-claims-western-china-attacks-070833873.html, last accessed 14 Feb. 2014.

150. Author interviews in Beijing, Aug. 2011.

151. Ananth Krishnan, "Pakistan link to Xinjiang attacks questioned", *The Hindu*, 11 Aug. 2011, http://www.thehindu.com/todays-paper/tp-inter-

national/pakistan-link-to-xinjiang-attacks-questioned/article2344990.ece, last accessed 14 Feb. 2014.

152. Amir Mir, "China absolves Pakistan of Kashgar attacks", *The News*, 12 Oct. 2011, http://www.thenews.com.pk/TodaysPrintDetail.aspx?ID=9484& Cat=13, last accessed 27 Jan. 2014.

153. Brian Spegele, "China points finger at Pakistan again", *Wall Street Journal*, 7 Mar. 2012, http://online.wsj.com/news/articles/SB100014240529702 04781804577266952254783484, last accessed 20 Nov. 2013. "Evidence shows Rebiya Kadeer behind Urumqi riot: Chinese gov't", Xinhua, 9 Jul. 2009, http://news.xinhuanet.com/english/2009–07/09/content_1167 6293.htm, last accessed 20 Nov. 2013.

154. Jane Macartney, "Riot police battle protesters as China's Uighur crisis escalates", *The Times*, 7 Jul. 2009, http://www.thetimes.co.uk/tto/news/world/ asia/article2610804.ece, last accessed 27 Jan. 2014.

155. "Chinese question police absence in ethnic riots", *New York Times*, 18 Jul. 2009, http://www.nytimes.com/2009/07/18/world/asia/18xinjiang.html? pagewanted=all&_r=0, last accessed 27 Jan. 2014.

156. "Evidence shows Rebiya Kadeer behind Urumqi riot: Chinese gov't", Xinhua, 8 Jul. 2007, http://news.xinhuanet.com/english/2009–07/09/ content_11676293.htm, last accessed 20 Nov. 2013.

157. "Urumqi party chief, Xinjiang police chief sacked", Xinhua, 5 Sep. 2009, http://news.xinhuanet.com/english/2009–09/05/content_12001223.htm, last accessed 2 Feb. 2014.

158. Gordon Fairclough, "Xinjiang official removed in China", *Wall Street Journal*, 25 Apr. 2010, http://online.wsj.com/news/articles/SB10001424 052748704627704575203353627235946, last accessed 2 Feb. 2014.

159. "Hu skips G8 over China unrest", Al Jazeera, 8 Jul. 2009, http://www. aljazeera.com/news/asia-pacific/2009/07/200978581162184.html, last accessed 22 Nov. 2013.

160. "Turkey attacks China 'genocide'", BBC News, 10 Jul. 2009, http://news. bbc.co.uk/2/hi/asia-pacific/8145451.stm, last accessed 22 Nov. 2013

161. Author interviews in Beijing, Aug. 2009.

162. Saad Abedine, "Al Qaeda tells China's Uyghurs to prepare for holy war", CNN, 8 Oct. 2008, http://edition.cnn.com/2009/WORLD/asiapcf/ 10/08/china.uyghur.threat/, last accessed 22 Nov. 2013.

163. Malcolm Moore, "China Pleads for understanding as al-Qaeda vows revenge over Uighur deaths", *Telegraph*, 14 Jul. 2009, http://www.telegraph.co.uk/news/worldnews/asia/china/5826040/China-pleads-for-understanding-as-al-Qaeda-vows-revenge-over-Uighur-deaths.html, last accessed 2 Feb. 2014.

164. Mohammad Afridi, spokesman of a TTP faction, quoted in "Tehreek-e-

Taliban Pakistan claims responsibility for killing Chinese tourist", Reuters, 2 Mar. 2012, http://tribune.com.pk/story/344297/tehreek-e-taliban-pakistan-claims-responsibility-for-killing-chinese-tourist/, last accessed 22 Nov. 2013.

165. "Wang Gang meets Pakistani JUI delegation", International Department Central Committee of CPC, 6 Apr. 2010, http://www.idcpc.org.cn/english/reports/2010/100406–2.htm, last accessed 2 Feb. 2014.

166. Rashid, *Taliban*, p. 90.

167. Rashid, Ahmed, *Descent into Chaos: The U.S. and the Disaster in Pakistan, Afghanistan, and Central Asia*, London: Penguin, 2009, p. 276.

168. "Pak Oppn leader's home comes under rocket attack", *DNA India*, 21 Apr. 2007, http://www.dnaindia.com/world/report-pak-oppn-leader-s-home-comes-under-rocket-attack-1092300, last accessed 22 Nov. 2013.

169. Arif Jamal, "Pakistani Taliban Widen the Civil War—Against Fellow Deobandis", 14 Apr. 2011, *Terrorism Monitor*, Vol. 9, Issue 15, http://www.refworld.org/docid/4dad7e982.html, last accessed 22 Nov. 2013.

170. Manzoor Ali and Qaiser Butt, "Charsadda strike: Second attack targets Maulana Fazlur Rehman", *Express Tribune*, 1 Apr. 2011, http://tribune.com.pk/story/140320/blast-in-charsadda-kills-8-injures-25/, last accessed 22 Nov. 2013.

171. Senior Pakistani security official speaking on condition of anonymity, quoted in Mazhar Tufail, "ANP, JUI leaders now prime Taliban targets", *The News*, 26 May, 2011, http://www.thenews.com.pk/Todays-News-2–49191-ANP-JUI-leaders-now-prime-Taliban-targets, last accessed 22 Nov. 2013.

172. Jane Perlez, "Onetime Taliban handler dies in their hands", *New York Times*, 24 Jan. 2011, http://www.nytimes.com/2011/01/25/world/asia/25pakistan.html, last accessed 22 Dec. 2013; Karin Brulliard, "In Pakistan, ex-spy Khalid Khawaja's killing is surrounded by mystery", *Washington Post*, 3 May 2010, http://www.washingtonpost.com/wp-dyn/content/article/2010/05/02/AR2010050202801.html, last accessed 2 Feb. 2014.

173. "Pak-China rapidly boosting economic, cultural cooperation", *The News Tribe*, 29 May 2013, http://www.thenewstribe.com/2013/03/29/pak-china-rapidly-boosting-economic-cultural-cooperation/, last accessed 27 Nov. 2013.

174. Alessandro Rippa, "From Uyghurs to Kashgari".

175. Author interviews in Islamabad, and Lahore, Jun. 2009, Peshawar, June 2013.

176. Ismail Khan, "The game is up for Uzbeks", *Dawn*, 5 Apr. 2007, http://www.dawn.com/news/240842/the-game-is-up-for-uzbeks, last accessed 15 Jan. 2014.

177. Holly Fletcher and Jayshree Bajoria, "The East Turkestan Islamic Movement (ETIM)", Council on Foreign Relations, 31 Jul. 2008, http://www.cfr. org/china/east-turkestan-islamic-movement-etim/p9179, last accessed 15 Jan. 2014.
178. Author interviews in Beijing, Nov. 2012.
179. Author interviews in Islamabad and Lahore, Jun. 2009.
180. Author interview in Beijing, 2009.
181. Author interviews in Washington, DC, Feb. 2012.
182. Author interviews in Beijing, Aug. 2009.
183. Author interviews, 2012, location withheld.
184. Author interview in Beijing, February 2014.
185. Warikoo, K., "The Xinjiang Issue" in Marlene Laruelle and Sebastian Peyrouse (eds), *Mapping Central Asia: Indian Perceptions and Strategies*, Farnham: Ashgate, 2011, p. 226.

5. THE TRADE ACROSS THE ROOF OF THE WORLD

1. Khalid, Muhammad Mumtaz, *History of the Karakoram Highway, Vol. II*, Rawalpindi: Hamza, 2009, p. 5.
2. Nisar Baluch quoted in Robert D. Kaplan, *Monsoon: The Indian Ocean and the Future of American Power*, New York: Random House, 2011, p. 124.
3. Musharraf, Pervez, *In The Line Of Fire: A Memoir*, New York: Free Press, 2006, p. 189.
4. Li Zhisui, *The Private Life of Chairman Mao: The Memoirs of Mao's Personal Physician*, London: Random House, 1996, p. 503.
5. Leese, Daniel, *Mao Cult: Rhetoric and Ritual in China's Cultural Revolution*, New York: Cambridge University Press, 2011, p. 220.
6. "Keke mangguo enqing shen—Xinxin xiangzhi hongtaiying. Mao zhuxi zengsong zhengui liwu de teda xixun zhuankai yihou" (Every mango is full of deep kindness—every heart longs for the red sun: the time after the incredibly happy news had spread), *People's Daily*, 8 Aug. 1968.
7. Adam Yuet Chau, "Mao's Travelling Mangoes: Food as Relic in Revolutionary China", *Past and Present*, 2010, Supplement 5, p. 263.
8. Ibid.
9. Ibid.
10. Farooq Baloch, "New Destination: Pakistani mangoes to be sold in Walmart China", *Express Tribune*, 19 Aug. 2012, http://tribune.com.pk/story/423993/ new-destination-pakistani-mangoes-to-be-sold-in-walmart-china/, last accessed: 26 Jan. 2014.
11. Ibid.
12. Ibid.

13. Sahid Shah, "Pakistani mangoes lose markets to China, India", *The News*, 26 Jul. 2012, http://www.thenews.com.pk/Todays-News-3–122724-Pakistani-mangoes-lose-markets-to-China-India, last accessed 26 Jul. 2012.

14. "Pakistan fails to achieve mango export target", *The News*, 13 Oct. 2012, http://www.thenews.com.pk/Todays-News-3–137176-Pakistan-fails-to-achieve-mango-export-target, last accessed 26 Jan. 2014.

15. Human Yusuf, "Mango mania", Latitude Blog, *New York Times*, 31 Jul. 2012, http://latitude.blogs.nytimes.com/2012/07/31/the-mango-pakistans-king-of-fruits-may-not-meet-expectations/, last accessed 27 Jan. 2014.

16. Cited in, among others, Ahmad Faruqui, "A Blueprint for Pakistan's Economic Revival", *IPRIPAK*, Winter 2002, http://ipripak.org/journal/winter2002/ablueprintforpak.shtml, last accessed 27 Jan 2014.

17. Trade data from the International Monetary Fund (IMF) direction of trade statistic (DOTS), Chinese National Bureau of Statistics (NBS), and World Trade Organization (WTO) statistics database.

18. Ibid.

19. Ibid.

20. Data from the State Bank of Pakistan (SBP).

21. Shahid Yusuf, "Can Chinese FDI Accelerate Pakistan's Growth?", International Growth Centre, 4 Feb. 2013, p. 2, http://www.theigc.org/publications/working-paper/can-chinese-fdi-accelerate-pakistan%E2%80%99s-growth, last accessed 26 Jan. 2014.

22. Fazlur Rehman, "Pakistan-China Trade and Investment Relations", Institute of Strategic Studies Islamabad, 2011, p. 3, http://www.issi.org.pk/publication-files/1299822989_45060000.pdf, last accessed 23 Dec. 2013.

23. Khan, Riaz Mohammad, *Afghanistan and Pakistan: Conflict, Extremism, and Resistance to Modernity*, Karachi: Oxford University Press, 2010, p. 11.

24. Christopher Tang, "Beyond India: the Utility of Sino-Pakistani Relations in Chinese Foreign Policy, 1962–1965", CWIHP Working Paper #64 http://www.wilsoncenter.org/sites/default/files/CWIHP_WP_64_Beyond%20India_The_Utility_of_Sino_Pakistani_Relations_in_Chinese_Foreign_Policy.pdf p6–7

25. Jane Perlez, "Rebuffed by China, Pakistan may seek I.M.F. aid", *New York Times*, 18 Oct. 2008, http://www.nytimes.com/2008/10/19/world/asia/19zardari.html?ref=asia, last accessed 26 Jan. 2014.

26. Charles Wolf Jr., Xiao Wang and Eric Warner (eds), *China's Foreign Aid and Government-Sponsored Investment Activities: Scale, Content, Destinations and Implications*, Santa Monica, CA: RAND, 2013, http://www.rand.org/content/dam/rand/pubs/research_reports/RR100/RR118/RAND_RR118.pdf, last accessed 11 Dec. 2013.

27. Ye Hailin, "China-Pakistan Relationship: All-Weathers, But Maybe Not

All-Dimensional", in Kristina Zetterlund (ed.), *Pakistan—Consequences of Deteriorating Security in Afghanistan*, Stockholm: Swedish Defence Research Agency, 2009, p. 117.

28. Ibid. p. 109.

29. Vertzberger, Yaacov Y.I., *China's Southwestern Strategy: Encirclement and Counterencirclement*, New York: Praeger, 1985, pp. 94–5.

30. Author's interviews, Islamabad, Jun. 2011 and Jun. 2013.

31. Fazlur Rehman paraphrased in "Pakistan-China Economic Relations with Special Focus on Thar Coal, Kashgar Special Economic Zone and Gwadar Sea Port", Islamabad Policy Research Institute conference report, 13 Mar. 2013, p. 6, http://ipripak.org/conf/pcer.pdf, last accessed 26 Jan. 2014.

32. Xu Lin, "Top 10 fastest-growing provincial economies in China 2012", 22 Feb. 2013, http://www.china.org.cn/top10/2013–02/22/content_28027035.htm, last accessed 26 Jan. 2014.

33. "China-Pakistan FTA", China FTA Network, http://fta.mofcom.gov.cn/topic/enpakistan.shtml, last accessed 26 Jan. 2014.

34. Wolf, Wang and Warner (eds), *China's Foreign Aid*.

35. Author's interviews, Islamabad, Jun. 2013.

36. Jim O'Neill, Dominic Wilson, Roopa Purushothaman and Anna Stupnytska, "How Solid are the BRICs?", Global Economics Paper No. 134, Goldman Sachs, 1 Dec. 2005, http://www.sdnbd.org/sdi/issues/economy/BRICs_3_12–1–05.pdf, last accessed 27 Jan. 2014.

37. World Development Indicators, World Bank, http://data.worldbank.org/indicator/NY.GDP.MKTP.KD.ZG/countries/PK?display=graph, last accessed 27 Jan. 2014.

38. Pakistani growth rates went into free fall from 2006, reaching lows of under 2% in 2008 and then again in 2010. Figures recovered somewhat in 2012, hitting around 4%. Source: World Development Indicators, World Bank, http://data.worldbank.org/indicator/NY.GDP.MKTP.KD.ZG/countries/PK?display=graph, last accessed 27 Jan. 2014.

39. Author interviews in Beijing, Nov. 2008.

40. Ispahani, Mahnaz, *Roads and Rivals: The Political Uses of Access in the Borderlands of Asia*, Ithaca, NY: Cornell University Press, 1989, p. 191.

41. "Memo signed to Initiate China-Pakistan Highway renovation", Xinhua, available on the Chinese government's official web portal, 8 Jul. 2006, http://www.gov.cn/misc/2006–07/08/content_330955.htm, last accessed 27 Jan. 2014.

42. "Raja to launch $282m KKH re-alignment project", *Pak Observer*, 28 Sep. 2012, http://pakobserver.net/201209/28/detailnews.asp?id=175713, last accessed 2 Feb. 2014.

43. "Gojal: Karakoram Highway reconstruction to be completed in 2014",

Pamir Times, 16 Feb. 2013, http://pamirtimes.net/2013/02/17/gojal-kara-koram-highway-repair-and-expansion-to-be-completed-in-2014/, last accessed 26 Jan. 2014.

44. Author interviews in Islamabad, Jun. 2013.
45. Author interviews in Islamabad, Jun. 2011.
46. Imtiaz Ahmad, "Gwadar awaits Chinese takeover", *Hindustan Times*, 27 Feb. 2013, http://www.hindustantimes.com/world-news/gwadar-awaits-chinese-takeover/article1–1018585.aspx, last accessed 26 Jan. 2014.
47. Ibid.
48. Kaplan, *Monsoon*, p. 74.
49. Author interviews in Islamabad, Jun. 2013.
50. Kemp, Geoffrey, *The East Moves West: India, China, and Asia's Growing Presence in the Middle East*, Washington, DC: Brookings Institution Press, 2010, p. 25.
51. Zahid Ali Khan, "China's Gwadar and India's Chahbahar: an Analysis of Sino-India Geo-strategic and Economic Competition", *Strategic Studies*, Winter 2012 & Spring 2013, Vol. XXXII & XXXIII, No. 4 & 1, http://www.issi.org.pk/publication-files/1379479541_87064200.pdf/, last accessed 26 Jan 2014.
52. "Gwadar go ahead…", *World Cargo News*, Apr. 2002, http://www.worldcargonews.com/htm/n20020401.518943.htm, last accessed 2 Feb. 2014.
53. Ziad Haider, "Baluchis, Beijing, and Pakistan's Gwadar Port", *Georgetown Journal of International Affairs*, Winter 2005, Vol. 6, No. 1, http://journal.georgetown.edu/wp-content/uploads/6.1-Haider.pdf, last accessed 26 Jan. 2014.
54. "China may take over Gwadar port from Singaporean firm", *Express Tribune*, 1 Sep. 2012, http://tribune.com.pk/story/429443/china-may-take-over-gwadar-port-from-singaporean-firm/, last accessed 26 Jan. 2014.
55. Zahid Ali Khan, "China's Gwadar".
56. "Rs16.3bn released for Gwadar port project", *Dawn*, 1 Jun. 2005, http://www.dawn.com/news/141662/rs16–3bn-released-for-gwadar-port-project, last accessed 2 Feb. 2014.
57. Aiza Azam, "Gwadar: from slumber to strategic hub", *Youlin Magazine*, 30 Jul. 2012, http://www.youlinmagazine.com/article/gwadar-from-slumber-to-strategic-hub/mzi=, last accessed 26. Jan 2014.
58. "Makran Coastal Highway Project (MCHP)", Frontier Works Organisation of Pakistan, http://www.fwo.com.pk/index.php?option=com_k2&view=item&id=176:makran-coastal-highway-project-mchp, last accessed 2 Feb. 2014.
59. Musharraf, Pervez, "Address at the inauguration of Gwadar Deep Seaport", 20 Mar. 2007, http://presidentmusharraf.wordpress.com/2008/01/07/gwadar-deep-seaport/, last accessed 26 Jan. 2014.

60. "Gwadar Port", Business Recorder, 22 Feb. 2013, http://www.brecorder. com/editorials/0/1156300/, last accessed 26 Jan. 2014.

61. Syed Fazl-e-Haider, "China calls halt to Gwadar refinery", *Asia Times*, 14 Aug. 2009, http://www.atimes.com/atimes/South_Asia/KH14Df02. html, last accessed 26 Jan 2014.

62. "Development of Gwadar Port road linkages NHA's top priority", *The News*, 17 Feb. 2009, http://archive.thenews.com.pk/TodaysPrintDetail.aspx?ID =162987&Cat=2&dt=2/17/2009, last accessed 12 Dec. 2013.

63. John Garver, "Development of China's Overland Transportation Links with Central, South-west and South Asia", *China Quarterly*, No. 185, Mar. 2006, pp. 1–22.

64. Syed Fazl-e-Haider, "China calls halt".

65. Imtiaz Ahmad, "Gwadar awaits Chinese takeover", *Hindustan Times*, 27 Feb. 2013, http://www.hindustantimes.com/world-news/gwadar-awaits-chinese-takeover/article1-1018585.aspx, last accessed 27 Jan. 2014.

66. Syed Fazl-e-Haider, "China set to run Gwadar port as Singapore quits", *Asia Times*, 5 Sep. 2012, http://www.atimes.com/atimes/China_Business/ NI05Cb01.html, last accessed 26 Jan. 2014.

67. Author interviews in Islamabad, Jun. 2010.

68. Syed Fazl-e-Haider, "China set to run".

69. Ziad Haider, "Baluchis, Beijing".

70. Author interviews in Islamabad, Jun. 2013.

71. Frédéric Grare, "Pakistan: The Resurgence of Baluch Nationalism", Washington, DC: Carnegie Endowment for International Peace, 2007, http://carnegieendowment.org/files/CP65.Grare.FINAL.pdf, last accessed 3 Jan. 2014.

72. "Chinese, Pakistanis back at work in Gwadar", Reuters, 7 May 2004

73. "6 rockets fired near Gwadar airport", *Dawn*, 22 May 2005, http://www. dawn.com/news/394288/6-rockets-fired-near-gwadar-airport, last accessed 23 Nov. 2013.

74. "Rocket fired on PC Hotel Gwadar", *Daily Times*, 7 Jul. 2010, http://www. dailytimes.com.pk/default.asp?page=2010%EF%BF%BD7%EF%BF%B D7story_7–7–2010_pg7_4, last accessed 18 Nov. 2014.

75. "Chinese camp in Pakistan attacked", *Shanghai Daily*, 18 Nov. 2005, http:// www.shanghaidaily.com/art/2005/11/16/214203/Chinese_camp_in_ Pakistan_attacked.htm, last accessed 23 Nov. 2013.

76. "Chinese workers feared dead in Pakistan bombing", Associated Press, 19 Jul. 2007, http://www.chinadaily.com.cn/china/2007–07/19/con-tent_5439706.htm, last accessed 27 Jan. 2014.

77. Declan Walsh, "Chinese company will run strategic Pakistani port", *New York Times*, 31 Jan. 2013, http://www.nytimes.com/2013/02/01/world/

asia/chinese-firm-will-run-strategic-pakistani-port-at-gwadar.html?_r=0, last accessed 27 Jan. 2014.

78. Gabe Collins and Andrew Erickson, "Still a pipedream: Pakistan-to-China Rail Corridor is not a substitute for maritime transport", *China SignPost*, No. 13, 22 Dec. 2010, http://www.chinasignpost.com/2010/12/still-a-pipedream-a-pakistan-to-china-rail-corridor-is-not-a-substitute-for-maritime-transport/, last accessed 13 Dec. 2013.

79. John Lee and Charles Horner, "China faces barriers in the Indian Ocean", *Asia Times*, 10 Jan. 2014, http://www.atimes.com/atimes/China/CHIN-02-100114.html, last accessed 27 Jan. 2014.

80. James Holmes, U.S. Naval War College, quoted in "How important is Gwadar port for China?", *Asian Warrior*, Jun. 2013, http://www.asianwarrior.com/2013/06/how-important-is-gwadar-port-for-china.html#. Uu3UkXmQePE, last accessed 2 Feb. 2014.

81. Farhan Bokhari and Kathrin Hille, "Pakistan turns to China for naval base", *Financial Times*, 22 May 2011, http://www.ft.com/intl/cms/s/0/3914 bd36–8467–11e0-afcb-00144feabdc0.html, last accessed 27 Jan. 2014.

82. "Gwadar port integral to China maritime expansion", *Express Tribune*, 17 Feb. 2013, http://tribune.com.pk/story/508607/gwadar-port-integral-to-china-maritime-expansion/, last accessed 27 Jan. 2014.

83. Indranil Banerjee, "The Indian Navy At War: 1971 Blockade From The Seas", SAPRA India, http://www.bharat-rakshak.com/Navy/History/1971 war/Banerjee.Html, last accessed 27 Jan. 2014.

84. "Naval Moves Pose Pyschological Threat to Pakistan", *Stratfor*, 23 May 2002, http://www.freerepublic.com/focus/news/688524/posts, last accessed 27 Jan. 2014.

85. Abdul Majeed and Anwar Kamal, *Gwadar: Integrated Development Vision*, Government of Baluchistan, Pakistan and IUCN, Pakistan, 2007, p. 1, http://cmsdata.iucn.org/downloads/pk_gwadar_idv.pdf, last accessed 13 Dec. 2013.

86. "Navy to build base in Gwadar", *Daily Times*, 19 Apr. 2004.

87. Author interviews in Beijing, 2004–2011.

88. Leslie Hook, "Chinese oil interests attacked in Libya", *Financial Times*, 24 Feb. 2011, http://www.ft.com/intl/cms/s/0/eef58d52–3fe2–11e0–811f-00144feabdc0.html#axzz2nMSvVMji, last accessed 12 Dec. 2013.

89. "In Libya, mass evacuation of foreigners continues", VOA News, 22 Feb. 2011, http://www.voanews.com/content/us-other-nations-send-ferries-planes-to-libya-for-evacuations-116720514/135452.html, last accessed 27 Jan. 2014.

90. "269 Chinese nationals arrive in Khartoum from Libya", *Xinhua*, 27 Feb. 2011, http://news.xinhuanet.com/english2010/china/2011–02/27/c_1375 2794.htm, last accessed 27 Jan. 2014.

91. "Missile frigate Xuzhou transits Suez Canal, to arrive off Libya: China's first operational deployment to Mediterranean addresses Libya's evolving security situation", *China SignPost*, 27 Feb. 2011, http://www.chinasignpost.com/wp-content/uploads/2011/02/China-SignPost_26_Further-analysis-of-Chinas-Libya-deployment_20110227.pdf, last accessed 13 Dec. 2013.

92. Andrew Erickson and Austin Strange, "No Substitute for Experience: Chinese Antipiracy Operations in the Gulf of Aden", U.S. Naval War College, *China Maritime Study*, No. 10, Nov. 2013, p. 139.

93. Gabe Collins and Andrew S. Erickson, "Implications of China's Military Evacuation of Citizens from Libya", *China Brief*, Vol. 11, Issue 4, 10 Mar. 2011, http://www.jamestown.org/programs/chinabrief/single/?tx_ttnews%5Btt_news%5D=37633&tx_ttnews%5BbackPid%5D=25&cHash=c1302a9ecaddfc23450fb6ec13a98136#.Uu3eBHmQePE, last accessed 14 Jan. 2014.

94. Author interviews in Beijing, May 2011.

95. "Suspicions on China's taking over of Gwadar port are groundless", *People's Daily*, 20 Feb. 2013, http://english.peopledaily.com.cn/90883/8137013.html, last accessed 27 Jan. 2014.

96. Author interviews in Beijing, Feb. 2014.

97. Li Boqiang, director of the China Center for Energy Economics Research at Xiamen University, quoted in Hao Zhou, "China to run Pakistani port", *Global Times*, 1 Feb. 2013, http://www.globaltimes.cn/content/759538.shtml, last accessed 27 Jan. 2014.

98. Khalid, *History*, p. 14.

99. Ibid. p. 59.

100. Ibid. p. 22.

101. Ibid. p. 282.

102. Ibid. pp. 282–85.

103. Ibid. p. 273.

104. "Convention between Great Britain, China and Tibet", Reproduced for the Islamabad Policy Research Institute *Fact File*, 3 Jul. 1914, http://www.ipripak.org/factfiles/ff43.shtml, last accessed 2 Feb. 2014.

105. Khalid, *History*, p. 383.

106. Ispahani, *Roads and Rivals*, p. 201.

107. Ibid. p. 22.

108. Barry Naughton, "The Third Front: Defence Industrialisation in the Chinese Interior", *China Quarterly*, No. 115, Sep. 1988, pp. 351–86, http://journals.cambridge.org/action/displayAbstract?fromPage=online&aid=3546864, last accessed 24 Jan. 2014.

109. Khalid, *History*, p. 14.

110. Syed, Anwar Hussain, *China & Pakistan: Diplomacy of an Entente Cordiale*, London: Oxford University Press, 1974, p. 93–6; Kux, Dennis, *The United States and Pakistan 1947–2000: Disenchanted Allies*, Washington, DC: Woodrow Wilson Centre Press, 2001, p. 143.

111. Khalid, *History*, p. xvii.

112. "Pakistan buys 55% of China's arms exports", *Hindustan Times*, 19 Mar. 2013, http://www.hindustantimes.com/world-news/pakistan-buys-55-of-china-s-arms-exports/article1-1028561.aspx, last accessed 13 Dec. 2013.

113. Guy Martin, "Pakistan and China to jointly market Al Khalid tank", Defence Web, 9 Nov. 2012, http://www.defenceweb.co.za/index.php?option=com_content&view=article&id=28466:pakistan-and-china-to-jointly-market-al-khalid-tank&catid=112:ideas-2012&Itemid=254, last accessed 27 Jan. 2014.

114. Bates, Gill and Evan S. Medeiros, *Chinese Arms Exports: Policy, Players and Process*, Carlisle, PA: U.S. Army War College Strategic Studies Institute, Aug. 2000, p. 45, http://www.fas.org/nuke/guide/china/doctrine/chinarms.pdf, last accessed 27 Jan. 2014.

115. Yezid Sayigh, "Arms Production in Pakistan and Iran: the Limits of Self-reliance", in Eric H. Arnett (ed.), *Military Capacity and the Risk of War: China, India, Pakistan and Iran*, New York: Oxford University Press, 1997, p. 168.

116. "JF-17 Thunders: Pakistan to get 50 Chinese jets in six months", *Express Tribune*, 21 May 2011, http://tribune.com.pk/story/173009/jf-17-thunders-pakistan-to-get-50-chinese-stealth-jets-in-six-months/, last accessed 21 May 2011.

117. "PN gets F-22P frigate", *The Nation*, 18 Apr. 2013, http://www.nation.com.pk/karachi/18-Apr-2013/pn-gets-f-22p-frigate, last accessed 27 Jan. 2014.

118. "Sino-Pak defence cooperation: Pakistan Navy inducts first fast attack craft", *Express Tribune*, 24 Apr. 2012, http://tribune.com.pk/story/369112/sino-pak-defence-cooperation-pakistan-navy-inducts-first-fast-attack-craft/, last accessed 27 Jan. 2014.

119. Mulvenon, James, *Soldiers of Fortune: The Rise and Fall of the Chinese Military-Business Complex, 1978–1998*, Armonk, NY: M.E. Sharpe/East Gate Books, 2001, p. 118.

120. Ilaina Jonas and Jeffrey Goldfarb, "China Mobile to buy Paktel in first overseas deal", Reuters, 22 Jan. 2007, http://www.reuters.com/article/2007/01/22/paktel-chinamobile-idUSL2278866820070122, last accessed 27 Jan. 2014.

121. "Wrong key fumble for China Mobile in Pakistan", *Caixin*, 23 May 2011, http://english.caixin.com/2011-05-23/100262335.html, last accessed 27 Jan. 2014.

122. "Pakistan's Wapda, China's Sinohydro for Civil Works sign a contract worth Rs26.053 billion", *Nihao-Salam*, 10 Sep. 2013, http://www.nihao-salam.com/news-detail.php?id=NDUyNg%3D%3D, last accessed 27 Jan. 2014.

123. "China's Three Gorges Corp ready to invest $15b in Pakistan", *China Daily*, 7 Apr. 2013, http://www.chinadaily.com.cn/bizchina/2011–04/07/content_12287700.htm, last accessed 27 Jan. 2014.

124. Muhammad Anis, "Nawaz to visit Neelum-Jhelum hydropower project today", *The News*, 19 Jun. 2013, http://www.thenews.com.pk/Todays-News-13–23602-Nawaz-to-visit-Neelum-Jhelum-hydropower-project-today, last accessed 27 Jan. 2014.

125. "MCC continues to undertake the Saindak project in Pakistan", MCC China, 20 May 2011, http://www.mccchina.com/ENGLISH/ShowArticle.asp?ArticleID=9096, last accessed 27 Jan. 2014.

126. Tom Wright and Jeremy Page, "China pullout deals blow to Pakistan", *Wall Street Journal*, 30 Sep. 2011, http://online.wsj.com/news/articles/SB10001424052970203405504576600671644602028, last accessed 27 Jan. 2014.

127. "Wrong key fumble for China Mobile in Pakistan", *Caixin*, 23 May 2011, http://english.caixin.com/2011–05–23/100262335.html, last accessed 27 Jan. 2014.

128. Khalid Mustafa, "Neelum-Jhelum project also hits finance snags", *The News*, 12 Aug. 2012, http://www.thenews.com.pk/Todays-News-3–126061-Neelum-Jhelum-project-also-hits-finance-snags, last accessed 16 Jan. 2014.

129. Grare, "Pakistan: The Resurgence".

130. "Waking up to the war in Balochistan", BBC News, 29 Feb. 2012, http://www.bbc.co.uk/news/world-asia-17182978, last accessed 16 Jan. 2014.

131. "Hydroelectric Power Plants in Pakistan", Power Plants Around the World, http://www.industcards.com/hydro-pakistan.htm, last accessed 2 Feb. 2014.

132. Ibid.

133. Mansur Khan Mahsud, *The Battle for Pakistan: Militancy and Conflict in South Waziristan*, Washington, DC: New America Foundation, Apr. 2010, http://www.operationspaix.net/DATA/DOCUMENT/4799~v~The_Battle_for_Pakistan___Militancy_and_Conflict_in_South_Waziristan.pdf, last accessed 17 Jan. 2014.

134. "Two Chinese engineers kidnapped in Pakistan", *China Daily*, 9 Oct. 2004, http://www.chinadaily.com.cn/english/doc/2004–10/09/content_380846.htm, last accessed 16 Jan. 2014.

135. "One hostage killed, another freed", *China Daily*, 14 Oct. 2004, http://

www.chinadaily.com.cn/english/doc/2004–10/14/content_382469.htm, last accessed 27 Jan. 2014.

136. Rahimullah Yusufzai, "What really happened…", *Newsline*, 7 Nov. 2004, http://www.newslinemagazine.com/2004/11/what-really-happened/, last accessed 27 Jan. 2014.

137. Amir Mir, "Last Abdullah Mehsud", Raman's Pashtun Belt Database, 4 Aug. 2007, http://ramanspashtunbeltdatabase.blogspot.com/2008/01/late-abdullah-mehsud.html, last accessed 16 Jan. 2014.

138. Yusufzai, "What really happened…".

139. Ibid.

140. "Work on Gomal Zam dam to resume soon", *Dawn*, 4 Apr. 2005, http://www.dawn.com/news/240758/work-on-gomal-zam-dam-to-resume-soon, last accessed 27 Jan. 2014.

141. Rahimullah Yusufzai, "What really happened…".

142. "Chinese workers shot in Pakistan", BBC News, 9 Jul. 2007, http://news.bbc.co.uk/2/hi/south_asia/6282574.stm, last accessed 27 Jan. 2014.

143. "Liaison committee for Chinese security being formed", *Daily Times*, 10 Jul. 2007, http://archive.is/Ddgv7, last accessed 27 Jan. 2014.

144. Author interviews in Islamabad, Aug. 2009.

145. Author interviews in Islamabad, Jun. 2011 and Beijing, Jan. 2011.

146. "Chinese Embassy in Pakistan raises vigilance to protect local Chinese", CCTV, 27 Oct. 2009, http://english.cctv.com/program/worldwide-watch/20091027/101719.shtml, last accessed 27 Jan. 2014.

147. Ibid.

148. Author interviews in Islamabad, Jun. 2011.

149. Author interviews in Beijing, Oct. 2008–Jan. 2013.

150. Author interviews in Beijing, Oct. 2008.

151. Jane Perlez, "Rebuffed by China".

152. Author interview in Washington, Nov. 2008.

153. Author interviews in Beijing, Oct. 2008.

154. "China may raise issue of missing engineers with COAS", *Pakistan Tribune*, 24 Sep. 2008, http://www.paktribune.com/news/print.php?id=206042, last accessed 27 Jan. 2014.

155. "Taliban claims kidnap of two Chinese in Pakistan", Reuters, 2 Sep. 2008, http://www.reuters.com/article/2008/09/02/us-pakistan-china-idUSISL20463320080902, last accessed 27 Jan. 2014.

156. Pamela Constable, "Islamic law instituted in Pakistan's Swat Valley", *Washington Post*, 17 Feb. 2009, http://articles.washingtonpost.com/2009–02–17/world/36797348_1_pakistani-army-swat-valley-afghan-taliban, last accessed 27 Jan. 2014.

157. J.T. Quigley, "Commander behind Malala Attack: the Next Pakistani

Taliban Leader", *The Diplomat*, 7 Nov. 2013, http://thediplomat.com/2013/11/commander-behind-malala-attack-the-next-pakistani-taliban-leader/, last accessed 27 Jan. 2014.

158. Miatthia Gebauer, "Pakistan's Swat Valley: in the realm of Mullah Fazlullah", *Spiegel*, 22 Nov. 2007, http://www.spiegel.de/international/world/pakistan-s-swat-valley-in-the-realm-of-mullah-fazlullah-a-518962.html, last accessed 27 Jan. 2014.

159. Author interview in Peshawar, Jun. 2013.

160. Author interviews in Beijing, Oct. 2008.

161. "Pakistani Taliban militants free Chinese engineer", *New York Times*, 5 Nov. 2009, http://www.nytimes.com/2009/02/15/world/asia/15iht-pakistan.1.20193519.html, last accessed 27 Jan. 2014.

162. Ibid.

163. "Pakistan govt frees 20 Taliban militants as a goodwill gesture", *Times of India*, 20 Mar. 2009, http://articles.timesofindia.indiatimes.com/2009–03–20/pakistan/28033613_1_taliban-militants-taliban-prisoners-muslim-khan, last accessed 27 Jan. 2014.

164. "China may raise issue of missing engineers with COAS", *Pak Tribune*, http://www.paktribune.com/news/print.php?id=206042, last accessed 23 Jan. 2014.

165. Bruce Riedel, "The Battle for Pakistan", *Yale Global*, 2 Jun. 2011, http://yaleglobal.yale.edu/content/battle-pakistan, last accessed 26 Jan. 2014.

166. B. Raman, "Another boss for ISI", *Outlook India*, 30 Sep. 2008, http://www.outlookindia.com/printarticle.aspx?238542, last accessed 23 Jan. 2014.

167. "Pasha replaces Taj as ISI chief", *The Nation*, 30 Sep. 2008, http://www.nation.com.pk/Politics/30-Sep-2008/Pasha-replaces-Taj-as-ISI-chief, last accessed 26 Jan. 2014.

168. Author interviews in Beijing, Oct. 2008.

169. Quoted in Mathieu Duchâtel, "China's Policy Towards Pakistan And Stability In South Asia", presentation at the Asia-Pacific Security Forum, Europe Institute for Asian Studies, Brussels, 10–11 Sep. 2010, p. 14.

170. Bill Roggio, "Taliban Assault Team Attacks Pakistani Navy Base", *Long War Journal*, 22 May 2011, http://www.longwarjournal.org/archives/2011/05/pakistani_navy_base.php, last accessed 27 Jan. 2014.

171. Ibid.

172. "Chinese woman, local companion shot dead", *The News*, 28 Feb. 2012, http://www.thenews.com.pk/article-37475-Chinese-woman, last accessed 27 Jan. 2014.

173. "Chinese woman was intelligence operative", *Pak Observer*, 3 Mar. 2013

174. Tom Wright and Jeremy Page, "China pullout deals blow to Pakistan",

Wall Street Journal, 30 Sep. 2011, http://www.freerepublic.com/focus/f-news/2785832/posts, last accessed 27 Jan. 2014.

175. Text of agreement in the China-Pakistan treaty of "friendship, cooperation and good neighbourly relations", quoted in Naveed Ahmad, "Pakistan China sign historic defense pact", ISN Security Watch, 6 Apr. 2005, http://www.isn.ethz.ch/Digital-Library/Articles/Detail/?lng=en&id=107574, last accessed 27 Jan. 2014.

176. Author interviews in Beijing, Oct. 2008–Dec. 2012.

6. TEA WITH THE TALIBAN

1. Karen DeYoung, "China says it's ready to cooperate with U.S.", *Washington Post*, 21 Sep. 2013, http://www.washingtonpost.com/world/national-security/china-says-its-ready-to-cooperate-with-us/2013/09/20/add6ed0e-225a-11e3-a358–1144dee636dd_story.html, last accessed 27 Jan. 2014.

2. Ben Farmer, "Hamid Karzai government under fire for oil deal with company run by cousin", *Telegraph*, 20 Jun. 2012, http://www.telegraph.co.uk/news/worldnews/asia/afghanistan/9344450/Hamid-Karzai-government-under-fire-for-oil-deal-with-company-run-by-cousin.html, last accessed 27 Jan. 2014.

3. Farhan Reza, "Afghan minister, 7 others die in plane crash near Karachi", *Daily Times*, 25 Feb. 2003, http://www.dailytimes.com.pk/print.asp?page=2003%5C02%5C25%5Cstory_25–2–2003_pg1_7, last accessed 27 Jan. 2014; "Petition—Seeking Answers to the Disappearance of Mr. Mohamadi and the Deaths of His Colleagues", *e-Ariana*, 23 Jul. 2003, http://www.e-ariana.com/ariana/eariana.nsf/allArticles/E10DE4ABF5A387C487256D6B005759A0?OpenDocument, last accessed 20 Nov. 2013.

4. "Assassination attempt in Afghanistan latest of several", CNN, 5 Sep. 2002, http://edition.cnn.com/2002/WORLD/asiapcf/central/09/05/afghan.recent.attacks/, last accessed 27 Jan. 2014.

5. Masuda Anna Mohamadi, un-named submission to *Kabul Reconstructions*, 31 Mar. 2003, http://www.kabul-reconstructions.net/images/masuda8.pdf, last accessed 27 Jan. 2014.

6. Maqbool Ahmed, "SHC moved to amend law limiting compensation at Rs 39,500", *Daily Times*, 7 Apr. 2006, http://www.dailytimes.com.pk/print.asp?page=2006%5C04%5C07%5Cstory_7–4–2006_pg7_24, last accessed 27 Jan. 2014.

7. Author interviews in Washington, DC, Jan. 2013.

8. Ron Synovitz, "China: Afghan investment reveals larger strategy", Radio Free Europe, 29 May 2008, http://www.rferl.org/content/article/1144514.html, last accessed 27 Jan. 2014.

9. Alikuzai, Hamid Wahed, *A Concise History of Afghanistan in 25 Volumes:* Volume 1, Bloomington, IN: Trafford Publishing, 2013, p. 707.

10. "Aynak Information Package: Part I Introduction", Afghanistan Geological Survey (AGS) and British Geological Survey (BGS), 2005, p. 3, http://www.bgs.ac.uk/afghanminerals/docs/tenders/Aynak/PartI_Aynak_Information_Package.pdf, last accessed 27 Jan. 2014.

11. "Al Qaeda aims at the American Homeland", National Commission on Terrorist Attacks Upon the United States, http://govinfo.library.unt.edu/911/report/911Report_Ch5.htm, last accessed 9 Dec. 2013.

12. "Chinese embassy in Kabul reopened", Xinhua, 6 Feb. 2002, http://news.xinhuanet.com/english/2002–02/06/content_270885.htm, last accessed 27 Jan. 2014.

13. Yeager, James R., *The Aynak Copper Tender: Implications for Afghanistan and the West*, Tucson: Skyline Laboratories and Assayers, Oct. 2009, p. 5.

14. Zhao Jianfei, "A long march to Kabul", *Caijing Magazine*, 7 Jan. 2008, available in *MCC Times*, http://www.mcc.com.cn/MCCZZ/mcctimes010.pdf, last accessed 19. Nov. 2013.

15. Michael Wines, "China willing to spend big on Afghan commerce", *New York Times*, 29 Dec. 2009, http://www.nytimes.com/2009/12/30/world/asia/30mine.html?pagewanted=all, last accessed 27 Jan. 2014.

16. Ibid.

17. Erica S. Downs, "China Buys into Afghanistan", *SAIS Review*, Vol. XXXII, No. 2, Summer-Fall 2012, pp. 65–84.

18. Steven A. Zyck, "The Role of China in Afghanistan's Economic Development & Reconstruction", *Afghanistan In Transition*, Mar. 2012, https://www.cimicweb.org/cmo/afg/Documents/Economic/Role_of_China_in_Afghanistan_Economy_Development.pdf, last accessed 26 Jan. 2014.

19. "Aynak Copper: Details Of Winning Chinese Bid Remain Elusive", U.S. State Department Cable, 27 Nov. 2007, https://www.wikileaks.org/plusd/cables/07KABUL3933_a.html, last accessed 27 Jan. 2014.

20. Joshua Partlow, "Afghan minister accused of taking bribe", *Washington Post*, 18 Nov. 2009, http://www.washingtonpost.com/wp-dyn/content/article/2009/11/17/AR2009111704198.html, last accessed 27 Jan. 2014.

21. "Comparative Table of Bidding Companies for (AYNAK Copper Mine)", Ministry of Mines and Petroleum, http://mom.gov.af/Content/files/List%20of%20Companies%20for%20Aynak.pdf, last accessed 26 Jan. 2014; "Chinese Firm Again Frontrunner For Major Afghan Mining Contract", U.S. State Department cable, 7 Nov. 2009, https://www.wikileaks.org/plusd/cables/09KABUL3574_a.html, last accessed 2 Feb. 2014.

22. Emmanuel Huntzinger, "Aynak Copper Mine: Opportunities and Threats

for Development from a Sustainable Business Perspective", Integrity Watch Afghanistan, Jan. 2008, https://www.cimicweb.org/cmo/Afghanistan/ Crisis%20Documents/Economic%20Stabilization/Recent%20 Publications/Aynak%20Copper%20Mine%20Report%20IWA.pdf, last accessed 27 Jan. 2014.

23. Ibid.
24. Author interviews, Kabul, Aug. 2010; William Dalrymple, "A Deadly Triangle; Afghanistan, Pakistan and India", *The Brookings Essay*, 25 Jun. 2013, http://www.brookings.edu/research/essays/2013/deadly-triangle-afghanistan-pakistan-india-c, last accessed 9 Dec. 2013.
25. "China wins major Afghan project", BBC News, 20 Nov. 2007, http://news.bbc.co.uk/2/hi/south_asia/7104103.stm, last accessed 27 Jan. 2014.
26. Robert D. Kaplan, "Beijing's Afghan gamble", *New York Times*, 6 Oct. 2009, http://www.nytimes.com/2009/10/07/opinion/07kaplan.html, last accessed 27 Jan. 2014.
27. Quoted in Richard Weitz, "Why China free-riding is OK", *Diplomat*, 12 Aug. 2011, http://thediplomat.com/2011/08/why-chinas-free-riding-ok/, last accessed 18 Nov. 2013.
28. Stuart Burns, "US Troops Protecting Chinese Mine Workers Against Taliban", *Metal Miner*, 10 Nov. 2009, http://agmetalminer.com/2009/11/10/us-troops-protecting-chinese-workers-against-taliban/, last accessed 27 Jan. 2014.
29. Author interviews, Kabul, Aug. 2010 and Feb. 2012.
30. "Karzai meets Chinese leaders amid security concerns", *The Hindu*, 28 Sep. 2013, http://www.thehindu.com/todays-paper/tp-international/karzai-meets-chinese-leaders-amid-security-concerns/article5178048.ece, last accessed 27 Jan. 2014.
31. Zhao Huasheng, "China and Afghanistan: China's Interest, Stances and Perspectives", Washington, DC: Centre for Strategic and International Studies, Mar. 2012, p. 2, http://csis.org/files/publication/120322_Zhao_ChinaAfghan_web.pdf, last accessed 26 Jan. 2014.
32. Russell Hsiao and Glen E. Howard, "China Builds Closer Ties to Afghanistan through Wakhan Corridor", Jamestown Foundation, China Brief, Vol. 10, Issue 1, 7 Jan. 2010, http://www.jamestown.org/single/?no_cache=1&tx_ttnews%5Btt_news%5D=35879&tx_ttnews%5BbackPid%5D=7&cHash=8aeb0ffe75#.UuWXrZH0CqQ, last accessed 26 Jan. 2014.
33. Alikuzai, *A Concise History*, Volume 1, p. 638.
34. Morgan, Gerald, *Anglo-Russian Rivalry in Central Asia: 1810–1895*, New York: Routledge, 1981, p. 200.
35. Rasanayagam, Angelo, *Afghanistan: A Modern History*, New York: I.B. Tauris, 2005, p. 10.

36. Author interviews, Kabul, Aug. 2010 and Beijing, Jul. 2009.
37. Vertzberger, Yaacov, *China's Southwestern Strategy: Encirclement and Counterencirclement*, New York: Praeger Publishers, 1985, pp. 107–8.
38. Ibid. pp. 108–111.
39. Ibid. p. 111–14 and 119–22.
40. Ibid. p. 125.
41. Wiegand, Krista Eileen, *Enduring Territorial Disputes: Strategies of Bargaining, Coercive Diplomacy and Settlement*, London: University of Georgia Press, 2011, p. 268.
42. "Afghan land annexed", *The Age*, 6 Nov. 1980, http://news.google.com/newspapers?nid=1300&dat=19801106&id=m_pUAAAAIBAJ&sjid=iJID AAAAIBAJ&pg=4869,2783378, last accessed 20 Nov. 2013.
43. Amstutz, J. Bruce, *The First Five Years of Soviet Occupation*, Honolulu: University Press of the Pacific, 2002, p. 416.
44. *Foreign Relations of the United States, 1977–1980: Volume XIII, China*, Document 290, U.S. Department of State, Office of the Historian, 7 Jan.1980, http://history.state.gov/historicaldocuments/frus1977–80v13/d290, last accessed 18 Nov. 2013.
45. Chinque, S., *News from Xinhua News Agency, Volumes 594–620*, 1980, p. 114.
46. Gates, Robert, *From the Shadows: The Ultimate Insider's Story of Five Presidents and How They Won the Cold War*, New York: Simon & Schuster, 1996, p. 146.
47. James Mulvenon, "Chen Xiaogong: A Political Biography", *China Leadership Monitor*, No. 22, Oct. 2013, p. 1, http://media.hoover.org/sites/default/files/documents/CLM22JM.pdf, last accessed 18 Nov. 2013.
48. Rubin, Barnett R., *The Fragmentation of Afghanistan: State Formation and Collapse in the International System*, New Haven: Yale University Press, 2002, p. 197.
49. Yousaf, Mohammad and Mark Adkin, *Afghanistan, The Bear Trap: The Defeat of a Superpower*, Barnsley: Leo Cooper/Pen and Sword Books, 2001, p. 150.
50. Ibid. p. 85.
51. Mohan Malik, "Dragon On Terrorism: Assessing China's Tactical Gains And Strategic Losses Post-September 11", Carlisle, PA: U.S. Army Strategic Studies Institute, Oct. 2002, p. 11, http://www.Strategicstudiesinstitute. Army.Mil/Pdffiles/Pub57.Pdf, last accessed 27 Jan. 2014.
52. Quoted in Vivek Katju, "The many roads to Kabul", *The Hindu*, 15 Oct. 2013, http://www.thehindu.com/opinion/lead/the-many-roads-to-kabul/article5234525.ece, last accessed 27 Jan. 2014.
53. Faligot, Roger, *Les services secrets chinois: de Mao aux JO* (The Chinese Secret Service: From Mao to the Olympic Games), Paris: Nouveau Monde Editions, 2008, pp. 382–5.

54. Vogel, Ezra F., *Deng Xiaoping and the Transformation of China*, Cambridge, MA: Harvard University Press, 2011, p. 539.

55. Steve Coll, "In CIA's covert Afghan War, where to draw the line was key", *Washington Post*, 20 Jul. 1992.

56. Coll, Steve, *Ghost Wars: The Secret History of the CIA, Afghanistan and Bin Laden*, London: Penguin, 2004, p. 66.

57. Steve Coll, "In CIA's".

58. Author interviews, Washington, DC, Feb. 2013.

59. Rubin, *The Fragmentation*, p. 197.

60. Yousaf and Adkin, *Afghanistan, The Bear Trap*, p. 84 and p. 109.

61. Author interviews, Kabul, Aug. 2010 and Islamabad 2011.

62. Amin Tarzi, "Afghanistan: new foreign minister steps out of obscurity", RFE/RL, 20 Apr. 2006, http://www.rferl.org/content/article/1067792. html, last accessed 9 Dec. 2013; "Historical Overview of the Marxist Revolutionary Movement in Afghanistan and the Afghanistan Liberation Organization (ALO)", http://a-l-o.maoism.ru/historical.htm, last accessed 27 Jan. 2014.

63. Ibid.

64. James Mulvenon, "Chen Xiaogong: A Political Biography", *China Leadership Monitor*, No. 22, Oct. 2013, p. 2, http://media.hoover.org/sites/default/files/documents/CLM22JM.pdf, last accessed 18 Nov. 2013.

65. Kaplan, Robert D., *Soldiers of God: With Islamic Warriors in Afghanistan and Pakistan*, New York: Vintage Departures, 2001, p. 39.

66. Coll, "In CIA's".

67. Coll, *Ghost Wars*, p. 11.

68. Ibid., p. 150; Diego Cordovez and Selig S. Harrison, *Out of Afghanistan: The Inside Story of the Soviet Withdrawal*, New York: Oxford University Press, 1995, p. 196.

69. Cordovez and Harrison, Ibid.

70. Yousaf and Adkin, *Afghanistan, The Bear Trap*, p. 181.

71. Steve Coll, "In CIA's".

72. Hatch, Orrin, *Square Peg: Confessions of a Citizen-Senator*, New York: Basic Books, 2003, p. 102.

73. Coll, *Ghost Wars*, p. 150.

74. Mann, James, *About Face: A History of America's Curious Relationship with China, from Nixon to Clinton*, New York: Knopf, 1998, p. 139.

75. Yousaf and Adkin, *Afghanistan, The Bear Trap*, p. 181.

76. Ibid., p. 182.

77. Keller, Bill, "Last Soviet soldiers leave Afghanistan", *New York Times*, 16 Feb. 1989, http://partners.nytimes.com/library/world/africa/021689afghan-laden.html, last accessed 27 Jan. 2014.

78. "Afghan gardeners and driver await return of Chinese ambassador", *People's Daily*, 17 Dec. 2001, http://english.peopledaily.com.cn/200112/17/eng20011217_86859.shtml, last accessed 27 Jan. 2014.
79. Ibid.
80. Ahmed, Rashid, *Taliban: Islam, Oil and the New Great Game in Central Asia*, London: I.B.Tauris & Co. 2002, p. 58.
81. Ibid. p. 49.
82. "Security Council Tightens Sanctions against Taliban and Al-Qaeda", UN News Centre, 30 Jan. 2004, http://www.un.org/apps/news/story.asp?NewsID=9630&Cr=qaida&Cr1=taliban#.UqXeu9JDt28, last accessed 9 Dec. 2013.
83. Reed, J. Todd and Diana Raschke, *The ETIM: China's Islamic Militants and the Global Terrorist Threat*, Washington, DC: Library of Congress, 2010, p. 71.
84. LeVine, Steve, *The Oil and the Glory: The Pursuit of Empire and Fortune on the Caspian Sea*, New York: Random House, 2007, p. 307.
85. Rashid, *Taliban*, p. 202.
86. Ahmed Rashid, "Taliban temptation", *Far Eastern Economic Review*, 11 Mar. 1999.
87. "Taliban, China sign defence pact: Chinese scientists allowed access to US cruise missiles", *Frontier Post*, 12 Dec. 1998, http://www.afghanistannews-center.com/news/1998/december/dec12c1998.htm, last accessed 27 Jan. 2014; John Hooper, "Claims that China paid Bin Laden to see cruise missiles", *Guardian*, 20 Oct. 2001, http://www.theguardian.com/world/2001/oct/20/china.afghanistan, last accessed 27 Jan. 2014; "How China is advancing its military reach", BBC News, 18 Jan. 2012, http://www.bbc.co.uk/news/world-asia-16588557, last accessed 27 Jan. 2014.
88. Mohan Malik, "Dragon on Terrorism", p. 8.
89. Tara Shankar Sahay, "Taliban-China deal puzzles diplomats", Rediff, 12 Feb. 1999, http://www.rediff.com/news/1999/feb/12tali.htm, last accessed 19 Nov. 2013.
90. "Afghan foreign minister fails to meet Tang", Agence France Presse, 25 Jul. 2000, http://www.afghanistannewscenter.com/news/2000/july/jul26f2000.html, last accessed 27 Jan. 2014.
91. "Taliban envoy meets Chinese Foreign Ministry official", IRNA, 25 Jul. 2000, http://www.afghanistannewscenter.com/news/2000/july/jul26f2000.html, last accessed 2 Feb. 2014.
92. John W. Garver, "Future of the Sino-Pakistani Entente Cordiale", in Michael R. Chambers (ed.), *South Asia in 2020: Future Strategic Balances and Alliances,* Carlisle, PA: U.S. Army War College, 2002, p. 434.
93. Zaif, Abd al-Salam, *My Life With the Taliban*, New York: Columbia University Press, 2010, p. 135.

94. Yusufzai, Rahimulla Yusufzai, "Chinese scholars leaving for Kabul, Kandahar today", *The News*, 21 Nov. 2000, http://www.afghanistannewscenter.com/news/2000/november/nov21p2000.htm; last accessed 27 Jan. 2014.

95. Munawar Hasan, "Taliban team to visit China to boost trade", *The Nation*, 21 Nov. 2000, http://www.afghanistannewscenter.com/news/2001/july/jul4p2001.html, last accessed 27 Jan. 2014.

96. Bergen, Peter, *The Longest War: The Enduring Conflict between America and Al-Qaeda*, London: Free Press, 2011, p. 188.

97. Zaeef, *My Life*, p. 135.

98. Ibid.

99. "Security Council imposes wide new measures against Taliban authorities in Afghanistan, demands action on terrorism", UN Security Council press release SC/6979, 19 Dec. 2000, http://www.un.org/News/Press/docs/2000/20001219.sc6979.doc.html, last accessed 27 Jan. 2014.

100. Mohan Malik, "Dragon On Terrorism".

101. Abu Mus'ab al-Suri, "The Call to Global Islamic Resistance", quoted in Brian Fishman, "Al-Qaeda and the Rise of China: Jihadi Geopolitics in a Post-Hegemonic World", *Washington Quarterly*, Summer 2011, http://csis.org/files/publication/twq11summerfishman.pdf, last accessed 26 Jan. 2014.

102. Rashid, Ahmed, *Jihad: The Rise of Militant Islam in Central Asia*, New York: Penguin Group, 2003, p. 176 and p. 204.

103. Zaeef, *My Life*, p. 126.

104. Munawar Hasan, "Taliban team".

105. John Pomfret, "China strengthens ties with Taliban by signing economic deal," *International Herald Tribune*, 13 Sep. 2001, http://www.propagandamatrix.com/china_economic_deal_taliban.html, last accessed 27 Jan. 2014.

106. Funabashi, Yoichi, *The Peninsular Question: A Chronicle of the Second Korean Nuclear Crisis*, Washington, DC: Brookings Institution Press, 2007, pp. 266–7.

107. Author interviews in Washington, DC, Nov. 2008.

108. "FBI office opened in US embassy in Beijing", *People's Daily*, 25 Oct. 2002, http://english.peopledaily.com.cn/200210/24/eng20021024_105 622.shtml, last accessed 27 Jan. 2014.

109. Swaine, Michael D., *America's Challenge: Engaging a Rising China in the Twenty-First Century*, Washington, DC: Carnegie Endowment for International Peace, 2011, p. 231.

110. Cockburn, Andrew, *Rumsfeld: His Rise, Fall and Catastrophic Legacy*, New York: Scribner, 2007, p. 125.

111. Ibid.

112. Shirley A. Khan, "China-U.S. Aircraft Collision Incident of April 2001: Assessments and Policy Implications", CRS Report for Congress, Updated 10 Oct. 2001, https://www.fas.org/sgp/crs/row/RL30946.pdf, last accessed 26 Jan. 2014.

113. Musharraf, Pervez, *In The Line Of Fire: A Memoir*, New York: Free Press, 2008, p. 204–06.

114. Author interviews, Islamabad, Jun. 2013.

115. Willy Wo-Lap Lam, "Smoke Clears over China's U.S. Strategy", CNN, 26 Sep. 2001, http://edition.cnn.com/2001/WORLD/asiapcf/east/09/25/willy.column/, last accessed 19 Nov. 2013.

116. Pollpeter, Kevin, *U.S.-China Security Management: Assessing the Military-to-Military Relationship*, Santa Monica, CA: RAND Corporation, 2004, p. 31; John W. Garver, "China's Influence in Central and South Asia: Is it Increasing?", in David Shambaugh (ed.), *Power Shift: China and East Asia's New Dynamics*, Los Angeles: University of California Press, 2005, p. 215.

117. "U.S. 'threatened to bomb' Pakistan", BBC News, 22 Sep. 2006, http://news.bbc.co.uk/2/hi/world/south_asia/5369198.stm, last accessed 27 Jan. 2014; see also the denials of this account in Daniel Markey, *No Exit From Pakistan: America's Tortured Relationship with Islamabad*, loc. 3243 of 7903, 2013, New York: Cambridge University Press, [IPAD 3rd Generation; MD366LL/A version].

118. Fazlur Rehhman, "Pakistan's Evolving Relations with China, Russia, and Central Asia", *Acta Slavica Iaponica*, No. 16, Slavic Research Center, 25 Jun. 2007, p. 215.

119. Author interviews in Islamabad, Jun. 2013, and Beijing, Dec. 2012.

120. "President Jiang Zemin had a telephone conversation with Pakistani President Pervez Musharraf", Embassy of the People's Republic of China in the Kingdom of Saudi Arabia, 2 Feb. 2001, http://sa.china-embassy.org/eng/zt/fdkbzy/t154518.htm, last accessed 20 Nov. 2013.

121. Khan, Riaz Mohammad, *Afghanistan and Pakistan: Conflict, Extremism, and Resistance to Modernity*, Karachi: Oxford University Press, 2010, p. 199.

122. Daniel Korski and John Fox, "Can China Save Afghanistan?", European Council on Foreign Relations, 29 Sep. 2008, http://www.ecfr.eu/content/entry/can_china_save_afghanistan/, last accessed 20 Nov. 2013.

123. "First Fiber Optic Network in Afghanistan", Wadsam.com, 2 Dec. 2012, http://www.wadsam.com/first-fiber-optic-network-in-afghanistan-798/, last accessed 27 Jan. 2014.

124. Sean Cronin, "Chinese Contractor Snags Afghan Road building Work",

ENR: Engineering News-Record, Vol. 251, Issue 22, 22 Dec. 2003, p. 16, http://connection.ebscohost.com/c/articles/11634154/chinese-contractor-snags-afghan-roadbuilding-work, last accessed 20 Nov. 2013.

125. Peter Wonacott, "Afghan road project shows bumps in drive for stability", *Wall Street Journal*, 17 Aug. 2009, http://online.wsj.com/news/articles/SB125046546672735403, last accessed 20 Nov. 2013.

126. "China to repair Kabul hospital", *China Daily*, 16 Jul. 2002, http://www.china.org.cn/english/Life/36999.htm, last accessed 20 Nov. 2013.

127. "China-built hospital helps Afghan war victims in Kandahar", *Afghan Voice Agency*, 2 Feb. 2013, http://avapress.com/vdcjmoei.uqea8z29fu.html, last accessed 20 Nov. 2013.

128. Farid Behbud, "China-funded irrigation project helps boost farming in Afghanistan", *Xinhua*, 8 Jan. 2012, http://news.xinhuanet.com/english/indepth/2012–01/08/c_131348931.htm, last accessed 20 Nov. 2013.

129. "Kabul zoo gets lions, bears from China", Associated Press, 3 Oct. 2002, http://cjonline.com/stories/100302/usw_zoo.shtml, last accessed 20 Nov. 2013.

130. "Lion of Kabul roars his last", BBC News, 26 Jan. 2002, http://news.bbc.co.uk/2/hi/south_asia/1783910.stm, last accessed 27 Jan. 2014.

131. Alisa Tang, "Chinese prostitutes imported to Afghanistan", *USA Today*, 14 Jun. 2008, http://usatoday30.usatoday.com/news/world/2008–06–14–2605427433_x.htm, last accessed 20 Nov. 2013.

132. Rashid, Ahmed, *Descent into Chaos: The U.S. and the Disaster in Pakistan, Afghanistan, and Central Asia*, London: Penguin Books, 2009, pp. 240–42.

133. Ibid. p. 242.

134. Bruce Riedel, *Pakistan, Taliban and the Afghan Quagmire*, Washington, DC: Brookings Institution, 24 Aug. 2013, http://www.brookings.edu/research/opinions/2013/08/26-pakistan-influence-over-afghan-taliban-riedel, last accessed 27 Jan. 2014.

135. David Rhode, "Taliban officials tell of plans to grind down the Americans", *New York Times*, 12 Sep. 2003, http://www.nytimes.com/2003/09/12/international/asia/12TALI.html, last accessed 27 Jan. 2014.

136. Gilles Dorronsoro, *The Taliban's Winning Strategy in Afghanistan*, Washington, DC: Carnegie Endowment for International Peace, Jul. 2009, http://carnegieendowment.org/files/taliban_winning_strategy.pdf, last accessed 27 Jan. 2014.

137. Riedel, *Pakistan, Taliban*.

138. C.J. Chivers, "Central Asians call on U.S. to set a timetable for closing bases", *New York Times*, 6 Jul. 2005, http://www.nytimes.com/2005/07/06/international/asia/06kazakhstan.html, last accessed 27 Jan. 2014.

139. Kimberly Marten, "Understanding the Impact of the K2 Closure", PONARS Policy Memo, No. 401, Dec. 2005; Alexander Cooley, *Base Politics: Democratic Change and the U.S. Military Overseas*, Ithaca, NY: Cornell University Press, 2008, pp. 230–32.

140. Author interviews, Kabul, Aug. 2010.

141. "China still meeting with Taliban", *Free Republic*, 10 Sep. 2002, http://www.freerepublic.com/focus/f-news/747598/posts, last accessed 27 Jan. 2014.

142. Author interviews, Washington, DC, Feb. 2012 and Beijing, Sep. 2012.

143. Zhao Huasheng, *China and Afghanistan: China's Interest, Stances and Perspectives*, Washington, DC: Centre for Strategic and International Studies, Mar. 2012, http://csis.org/files/publication/120322_Zhao_ChinaAfghan_web.pdf, last accessed 24 Jan. 2014.

144. Paul Danahar, "Taleban 'getting Chinese arms'", BBC News, 3 Sep. 2007, http://news.bbc.co.uk/2/hi/south_asia/6975934.stm, last accessed 27 Jan. 2014.

145. "Chinese weapons reaching Taliban", *One India News*, 4 Sep. 2007, http://news.oneindia.in/2007/09/04/chinese-weapons-reaching-taliban.html, last accessed 9 Dec. 2013.

146. Author interviews, Peshawar, Jun. 2013, and Washington, DC, May 2013.

147. Donor Financial Review, Islamic Republic of Afghanistan Ministry of Finance, Report 1388, Nov. 2009, p. 38, http://www.undp.org.af/Publications/KeyDocuments/Donor'sFinancialReview%20ReportNov2009.pdf, last accessed 27 Jan. 2014.

148. Author interview in Kabul, Aug. 2010.

149. Peter Wonacott, "Afghan road project shows bumps in drive for stability", *Wall Street Journal*, 17 Aug. 2009, http://online.wsj.com/news/articles/SB125046546672735403, last accessed 27 Jan. 2014.

150. Author interviews in Kabul, Aug. 2010.

151. Ibid.

152. Bernard Smith, "Afghan hospital in coma for poor workmanship", Al Jazeera, 3 Oct. 2012, http://www.aljazeera.com/indepth/features/2012/10/201210210243520232.html, last accessed 27 Jan. 2014.

153. "Chinese prostitutes arrested in Kabul 'restaurant' raids", *Independent*, 10 Feb. 2006, http://www.independent.co.uk/news/world/asia/chinese-prostitutes-arrested-in-kabul-restaurant-raids-466118.html, last accessed 26 Jan. 2014.

154. Author interviews in Kabul, Aug. 2010.

155. "Eleven Chinese workers killed in Afghan attack", *China Daily*, 10 Jun. 2004, http://www.chinadaily.com.cn/english/doc/2004–06/10/content_338324.htm, last accessed 27 Jan. 2014.

156. Keith B. Richburg, "As Taliban makes comeback in Kunduz Province, war spreads to Northern Afghanistan", *Washington Post*, 19 Mar. 2010, http://www.washingtonpost.com/wp-dyn/content/article/2010/03/18/AR2010031805399.html, last accessed 27 Jan. 2014.

157. Michael Moran, "The 'Airlift of Evil'", Council on Foreign Relations, 29 Nov. 2001, http://www.cfr.org/pakistan/airlift-evil/p10301, last accessed 9 Dec. 2013.

158. "Mystery surrounds attack on road workers", *China Daily*, 13 Jun. 2004, http://www.chinadaily.com.cn/english/doc/2004–06/13/content_338972.htm, last accessed 27 Jan. 2014.

159. Qin Yuding, "Bodies of slain workers brought home", *China Daily*, 14 Jun. 2004, http://www.chinadaily.com.cn/english/doc/2004–06/14/content_339316.htm, last accessed 2 Feb. 2014.

160. Gen. Mohammed Daoud, Kunduz military, paraphrased in Amir Shah, "10 Arrested in Afghan Killing of Chinese", Associated Press, 13 Jun. 2004.

161. Rashid, *Taliban*, pp. 184–7.

162. "Hizb-i-Islami Gulbuddin (HIG)", Institute for the Study of War, http://www.understandingwar.org/hizb-i-islami-gulbuddin-hig, last accessed 20 Nov. 2013.

163. Syed Saleen Shahzad, "The new Afghan jihad is born", *Asia Times*, 7 Sep. 2002, http://www.atimes.com/atimes/Central_Asia/DI07Ag02.html, last accessed 27 Jan. 2014.

164. Mohammad Shezad, "Interview with Gulbuddin Hekmatyar", *Sikh Spectrum*, Issue 17, Aug. 2004.

165. Author interviews, Kabul, Aug. 2010.

166. Ibid.

167. Author interviews, Kabul, Feb. 2012.

168. Michelle Nichols, "Ancient relics will delay huge Afghan copper mine", Reuters, 5 Dec. 2010, http://www.reuters.com/article/2010/12/05/afghanistan-mcc-relics-idAFSGE6B401B20101205, last accessed 27 Jan. 2014.

169. Alexandros Petersen, "China's strategy in Afghanistan", *The Atlantic*, 21 May 2013, http://www.theatlantic.com/china/archive/2013/05/chinas-strategy-in-afghanistan/276052/, last accessed 27 Jan. 2014.

170. Missy Ryan and Susan Cornwell, "U.S. says Pakistan's ISI supported Kabul embassy attack", Reuters, 22 Sep. 2011, http://www.reuters.com/article/2011/09/22/us-usa-pakistan-idUSTRE78L39720110922, last accessed 27 Jan. 2014.

171. Eric Schmitt and Alissa J. Rubin, "Afghanistan assaults signal evolution of a militant foe", *New York Times*, 16 Apr. 2012, http://www.nytimes.com/2012/04/17/world/asia/afghan-assaults-signal-evolution-of-haqqani-network.html, last accessed 27 Jan. 2014.

172. Author interviews in Beijing, Feb. 2010.

173. Author interviews in Kabul, Feb. 2012.

174. "Chinese Firm Re-Thinks Afghan Mining Contract After Difficulties Of The Aynak Copper Mine Project", U.S. State Department Cable, 10 Dec. 2009, http://www.cablegatesearch.net/cable.php?id=09BEIJING3295, last accessed 27 Jan. 2014.

175. Jessica Donati and Mirwais Harooni, "Chinese halt at flagship mine imperils Afghan future", Reuters, 27 Sep. 2012, http://uk.reuters.com/article/2012/09/27/uk-afghanistan-aynak-idUKBRE88Q0XL20120927, last accessed 27 Jan. 2014.

176. Author interviews in Kabul, Aug. 2010.

177. "MCC reports $1.16b losses in 2012", *China Daily*, 31 Jan. 2013, http://usa.chinadaily.com.cn/business/2013–01/31/content_16192147.htm, last accessed 27 Jan. 2014.

178. Donati and Harooni, "Chinese halt".

179. Erica S. Downs, "China Buys into Afghanistan", *SAIS Review*, Vol. XXXII. No. 2, Summer-Fall 2012, p. 65; "China gets approval for Afghanistan oil exploration bid", BBC News, 27 Dec. 2011, http://www.bbc.co.uk/news/business-16336453, last accessed 27 Jan. 2014.

180. Matthew Rosenberg, "U.S. cuts off Afghan firm", *Wall Street Journal*, 8 Dec, 2010, http://online.wsj.com/news/articles/SB100014240527487 04447604576007653943186130, last accessed 27 Jan. 2014.

181. "Warlord, Inc. Extortion and Corruption Along the U.S. Supply Chain in Afghanistan, Report of the Majority Staff, U.S. House of Representatives", Jun. 2010.

182. Aram Roston, "How the US army protects its trucks—by paying the Taliban", *Guardian*, 13 Nov. 2009, http://www.theguardian.com/world/2009/nov/13/us-trucks-security-taliban, last accessed 27 Jan. 2014.

183. "Popal, Ahmad Rateb Ratib", Afghan Bios, Record 1985 of 2857, http://www.afghan-bios.info/index.php?option=com_afghanbios&id=60&task=view&total=2854&start=1984&Itemid=2, last accessed 27 Jan. 2014.

184. Ibid.

185. Letter from Dana Rohrabacher, Chairman of the House Committee on Foreign Affairs, to Leon E. Panetta, Secretary of Defense, 31 Oct. 2012, Washington, DC, http://rohrabacher.house.gov/sites/rohrabacher.house.gov/files/documents/rep._rohrabacher_to_secretary_panetta_oct._31.pdf, last accessed 27 Jan. 2014.

186. Dexter Filkins, "Convoy guards in Afghanistan face an inquiry", *New York Times*, 6 Jun. 2010, http://www.nytimes.com/2010/06/07/world/asia/07convoys.html?pagewanted=all, last accessed 27 Jan. 2014.

187. Author interviews, Kabul, Aug. 2010.

188. Simon Clark, "Karzai's Afghanistan, poisoned by heroin habit, seeks investors", Bloomberg, 21 Mar. 2005, http://www.bloomberg.com/apps/new s?pid=newsarchive&sid=azmMmdBu2edg, last accessed 27 Jan. 2014.

189. Hamid Shalizi, "China's CNPC begins oil production in Afghanistan", Reuters, 21 Oct. 2012, http://uk.reuters.com/article/2012/10/21/uk-afghanistan-oil-idUKBRE89K07Y20121021, last accessed 27 Jan. 2014.

190. Alexandros Petersen, "Afghanistan Has What China Wants", *Foreign Policy*, 18 Apr. 2013, http://southasia.foreignpolicy.com/posts/2013/04/18/afghanistan_has_what_china_wants, last accessed 27 Jan. 2014.

191. Sayed Salahuddin, "Why can't Afghanistan tackle corruption?", Reuters, 8 Sep. 2011, http://www.reuters.com/article/2010/09/08/us-afghanistan-corruption-analysis-idUSTRE6871KP20100908, last accessed 27 Jan. 2014.

192. Hamid Shalizi, "Afghans say former warlord meddling in China oil deal", Reuters, 11 Jun. 2012, http://www.reuters.com/article/2012/06/11/us-afghanistan-dostum-idUSBRE85A15W20120611, last accessed 27 Jan. 2014.

193. "Gen Dostum accused of 'undermining national interest'", TOLO News, 10 Jun. 2012, http://www.tolonews.com/en/afghanistan/6525-gen-dostum-accused-of-undermining-national-interest, last accessed 27 Jan. 2014.

194. "China is a trust-worthy friend: Gen Dostum", *Daily Outlook Afghanistan*, 14 Jun. 2012, http://outlookafghanistan.net/national_detail.php?post_id=4590, last accessed 27 Jan. 2014.

195. Jessica Donati, "Missing refinery deal halts landmark China-Afghan oil project", Reuters, 18 Aug. 2013, http://www.reuters.com/article/2013/08/18/afghanistan-china-idUSL4N0GJ05G20130818, last accessed 27 Jan. 2014.

196. Jessica Donati, "From New York heroin dealer to Afghanistan's biggest oil man", *Reuters*, 7 Jul. 2014, http://www.reuters.com/article/2014/07/07/afghanistan-energy-idUSL4N0OS1R620140707, last accessed 7 Jul. 2014.

197. "1.5 billion barrels of oil, and no takers", Wall Street Cheat Sheet, 29 Sep. 2013, http://wallstcheatsheet.com/stocks/1-5-billion-barrels-of-oil-and-no-takers.html/, last accessed 27 Jan. 2014; Jessica Donati, "Small firms seek to move in on Afghanistan's vast mineral wealth", Reuters, 22 Sep. 2013, http://www.reuters.com/article/2013/09/22/us-afghanistan-mines-idUSBRE98L08G20130922, last accessed 27 Jan. 2014.

198. Maeva Bambuk, "Chinese investor suspends contract with Afghan gov't", CCTV, 23 Sep. 2013, http://english.cntv.cn/program/asiatoday/20130923/105249.shtml, last accessed 27 Jan. 2014.

199. Jessica Donati, "Indian firms seek to renegotiate $10.8 billion Afghan iron ore deal: Kabul official", Reuters, 29 Oct. 2013, http://www.reuters.com/

article/2013/10/29/us-afghanistan-mines-idUSBRE99S08J20131029, last accessed 27 Jan. 2014.

200. Javed Noorani, Integrity Watch Afghanistan, quoted in Jessica Donati, "Landmark Chinese copper deal with Afghanistan at risk", Reuters, 27 Aug. 2013, http://www.reuters.com/article/2013/08/27/afghanistan-mines-idUSL6N0GS1ZB20130827, last accessed 27 Jan. 2014.

201. Author interviews in Washington, Brussels and Beijing, 2008–2012.

202. Jonathon Burch and Myra Macdonald, "China takes higher-profile role in Afghan diplomacy-diplomats", Reuters, 3 Nov. 2011, http://in.reuters.com/article/2011/11/02/idINIndia-60281020111102, last accessed 27 Jan. 2014.

203. Author interviews in Washington, Jan. 2012.

204. Quoted on the condition of anonymity in Jonathon Burch and Myra Macdonald, "China takes higher-profile role in Afghan diplomacy-diplomats", Reuters, 3 Nov. 2011, http://in.reuters.com/article/2011/11/02/idINIndia-60281020111102, last accessed 27 Jan. 2014.

205. Ibid.

206. "China, Afghanistan, Pakistan agree to enhance cooperation", Xinhua, 12 Oct. 2013, http://news.xinhuanet.com/english/china/2013–12/10/c_132957176.htm, last accessed 27 Jan. 2014; Ananth Krishnan, "China, Russia, Pak. Discuss Afghanistan situation", The Hindu, 4 Apr. 2013, http://www.thehindu.com/news/international/china-russia-pak-discuss-afghanistan-situation/article4577718.ece, last accessed 27 Jan. 2014.

207. Ananth Krishnan, "India, China, Russia hold talks on Afghan issue", The Hindu, 17 Jan. 2014, http://www.thehindu.com/news/international/world/india-china-russia-hold-talks-on-afghan-issue/article5583356.ece, last accessed 27 Jan. 2014; Harsh V. Pant, "China reaches to India on Afghanistan", Observer Research Foundation, 8 Jan. 2014, http://orfonline.org/cms/sites/orfonline/modules/analysis/AnalysisDetail.html?cmaid=61496&mmacmaid=61497, last accessed 27 Jan. 2014.

208. Author interviews in Beijing and Washington, DC, 2012–13.

209. "Top Chinese official makers landmark Afghan visit", Agence France Presse, 23 Sep. 2012, http://www.google.com/hostednews/afp/article/ALeqM5iHVQRfyXMpcjXEGKPgiwiYkq1tVA?docId=CNG.3af9f6348c0359a862a5d1618b77fb24.2e1, last accessed 27 Jan. 2014; Andrew Small, "China's Afghan Moment", Foreign Policy, 3 Oct. 2012, http://www.foreignpolicy.com/articles/2012/10/03/chinas_afghan_moment, last accessed 27 Jan. 2014.

210. Author interviews in Beijing, Feb. 2014.

211. Author interviews in Beijing, Oct. 2012.

7. LORD, MAKE THEM LEAVE—BUT NOT YET

1. Deng Xiaoping quoted in David P. Nickles, Adam Howard and Office of the Historian, U.S. State Department, *Foreign Relations of the United States, 1977–1980, Volume XIII, China*, Washington, DC: Bureau of Public Affairs, 2013, p. 1060, http://static.history.state.gov/frus/frus1977–80v13/pdf/frus1977–80v13.pdf, last accessed 27 Jan. 2014.

2. Aubrey Carlson, "SRAP Holbrooke's April 15 dinner with Chinese foreign minister Yang Jiechi", U.S. State Department Cable, 20 Apr. 2009, https://www.wikileaks.org/plusd/cables/09BEIJING1046_a.html, last accessed 27 Jan. 2014.

3. Stockholm China Forum, Shanghai, Feb. 2014.

4. Karachi Islam report quoted in Bill Roggio, "Al Qaeda Appoints New Leader of Forces in Pakistan's Tribal Areas", *Long War Journal*, 9 May 2011, http://www.longwarjournal.org/archives/2011/05/al_qaeda_appoints_ne_2.php, last accessed 27 Jan. 2014.

5. Bill Roggio, "Turkistan Islamic Party Leader Thought Killed in US Drone Strike", *Long War Journal*, 25 Aug. 2012, http://www.longwarjournal.org/archives/2012/08/turkistan_islamic_pa_1.php, last accessed 27 Jan. 2014.

6. Edward Wong, "Warning of attacks on Olympics is said to be linked to Muslim separatist group", *New York Times*, 9 Aug. 2008, http://www.nytimes.com/2008/08/10/sports/olympics/10uighurs.html, last accessed 27 Jan. 2014; "A Post-Mortem Analysis of Turkistani Amir Emeti Yakuf: A Death that Sparked More Questions than Answers", Jamestown Foundation *Militant Leadership Monitor*, Vol. 3, Issue 10, 31 Oct. 2012, http://mlm.jamestown.org/single/?tx_ttnews%5Btt_news%5D=40043&tx_ttnews%5BbackPid%5D=551&cHash=e13aadc198482b3c8c34129c423af1f6#.Uu78fnddXgU, last accessed 2 Feb. 2014.

7. Edward Wong, "Chinese separatists tied to Norway bomb plot", *New York Times*, 9 Jul. 2010, http://www.nytimes.com/2010/07/10/world/asia/10uighur.html, last accessed 27 Jan. 2014.

8. "China identifies 8 alleged "East Turkistan" terrorists", *Xinhua*, 21 Oct. 2008

9. Bill Roggio, "Chinese Terrorist Leader Abdul Haq al Turkistani is Dead: Pakistani Interior Minister", *Long War Journal*, 7 May 2010, http://www.longwarjournal.org/archives/2010/05/chinese_terrorist_le.php, last accessed 27 Jan. 2014.

10. Ibid.

11. Bill Roggio, "6 Uzbeks Killed in North Waziristan Drone Strike", *Long War Journal*, 29 Jul. 2012, http://www.longwarjournal.org/archives/2012/07/six_uzbeks_killed_in.php, last accessed 27 Jan. 2014.

12. Bill Roggio, "Zawahiri Eulogizes Abu Yahya al Libi", *Long War Journal*, 11 Sep. 2012, http://www.longwarjournal.org/threat-matrix/archives/2012/09/zawahiri_eulogizes_abu_yahya_a.php, last accessed 27 Jan. 2014.

13. Bill Roggio, "U.S. Airstrike Killed 15 Turkistan Islamic Party Fighters in Afghanistan", *Long War Journal*, 23 Jan. 2010, http://www.longwarjournal.org/archives/2010/01/us_airstrike_killed_1.php, last accessed 27 Jan. 2014.

14. "Pakistan kills Uighur independence fighter", Al Jazeera, 23 Dec. 2003, http://www.aljazeera.com/archive/2003/12/200849145930813927.html, last accessed 27 Jan. 2014.

15. Bill Roggio, "US Drones Kill 4 Turkistan Islamic Party Fighters in Pakistan Strike", *Long War Journal*, 31 Aug. 2013, http://www.longwarjournal.org/archives/2013/08/us_drones_kill_4_tur.php, last accessed 27 Jan. 2014.

16. Ibid.

17. Takir Khan, "North Waziristan: Gul Bahadur's aide killed in clash with rivals", *Express Tribune*, 22 Aug. 2011, http://tribune.com.pk/story/236757/north-waziristan-gul-bahadurs-aide-killed-in-clash-with-rivals/, last accessed 27 Jan. 2014.

18. Charlie Szrom, "The Survivalist of North Waziristan: Hafiz Gul Bahadur Biography and Analysis", *Critical Threats*, 6 Aug. 2009, http://www.criticalthreats.org/pakistan/survivalist-north-waziristan-hafiz-gul-bahadur-biography-and-analysis, last accessed 27 Jan. 2014.

19. Pakistani official quoted on condition of anonymity in Faran Bokhari, "Death of a militant a victory for China?", CBS News, 1 Mar. 2010, http://www.cbsnews.com/news/death-of-militant-a-victory-for-china/, last accessed 27 Jan. 2014.

20. Zhao Huasheng, "China and Afghanistan: China's Interests, Stances and Perspectives", Washington, DC: Centre for Strategic and International Studies, Mar. 2012, p. 4, http://csis.org/files/publication/120322_Zhao_ChinaAfghan_web.pdf, last accessed 27 Jan. 2014.

21. Author interviews in Washington, DC, Feb. 2013.

22. Nickles, Howard and Office of the Historian, U.S. State Department, *Foreign Relations*, p. 446.

23. Kux, Dennis, *The United States and Pakistan 1947–2000: Disenchanted Allies*, Washington, DC: Woodrow Wilson Centre Press, 2001, p. 308–10.

24. Suettinger, Robert L., *Beyond Tiananmen: The Politics of U.S.-China Relations 1989–2000*, Washington, DC: Brookings Institution Press, 2003, p. 67.

25. Tyler, Patrick, *A Great Wall: Six Presidents and China: An Investigative History*, New York: A Century Foundation Book, 1999, p. 399; Kux, *The United States and Pakistan*, pp. 308–33.

26. Douglas Paal, "China and the East Asian Security Environment: Complementarity and Competition", in Vogel, Ezra, *Living with China: U.S./China*

Relations in the Twenty First Century, New York: W.W. Norton, 1997, p. 113; Mohan Malik, "The China Factor in the India-Pakistan Conflict", *Parameters*, Spring 2003, p. 62.

27. Suettinger, *Beyond Tiananmen*, pp. 139–41.
28. Author interviews in Washington, DC, Nov. 2008.
29. Polly Nayak and Michael Krepon, "US Crisis Management in South Asia's Twin Peaks Crisis", Stimson Center, pp. 27–8, http://www.stimson.org/images/uploads/research-pdfs/USCrisisManagementFull.pdf, last accessed 23 Jan. 2014.
30. Jane Perlez, "Rebuffed by China, Pakistan may seek I.M.F. aid", *New York Times*, 18 Oct. 2008, http://www.nytimes.com/2008/10/19/world/asia/19zardari.html, last accessed 23 Jan. 2014.
31. Swaine, Michael D., *America's Challenge: Engaging a Rising China in the Twenty-First Century*, Washington, DC: Carnegie Endowment for International Peace, 2011, p. 133.
32. Author interview in Washington, DC, Dec. 2011.
33. Jonathan S. Landay, "Insurgencies spread in Afghanistan and Pakistan", McClatchy Newspapers, 3 Feb. 2008, http://www.mcclatchydc.com/2008/02/03/26133/insurgencies-spread-in-afghanistan.html, last accessed 27 Jan. 2014; Sanger, David E., *The Inheritance: The World Obama Confronts and the Challenges to American Power*, London: Bantam Press, 2009, pp. 232–42.
34. "Pakistan facing financial crisis", Al Jazeera, 30 Sep. 2008, http://www.aljazeera.com/news/asia/2008/09/200892885733125929.html, last accessed 27 Jan. 2014; "Pakistan under martial law", CNN, 4 Nov. 2007, http://edition.cnn.com/2007/WORLD/asiapcf/11/03/pakistan.emergency/, last accessed 27 Jan. 2014; James Traub, "The lawyers' crusade", *New York Times*, 1 Jun. 2008, http://www.nytimes.com/2008/06/01/magazine/01PAKISTAN-t.html?pagewanted=print&_r=0, last accessed 27 Jan. 2014.
35. Mark Mazzetti and Eric Schmitt, "Afghan strikes by Taliban get Pakistan help, U.S. aides say", *New York Times*, 26 Mar. 2009, http://www.nytimes.com/2009/03/26/world/asia/26tribal.html?gwh=1851E9AE244BBF6B4F942C533DF96188&gwt=pay, last accessed 27 Jan. 2014.
36. Foon Rhee, "Obama: Afghanistan, not Iraq, should be focus", *Boston Globe*, 15 Jul. 2008, http://www.boston.com/news/politics/politicalintelligence/2008/07/obama_afghanist.html, last accessed 27 Jan. 2014.
37. Elizabeth Williamson and Peter Spiegel, "Obama says Afghan war 'of necessity'", *Wall Street Journal*, 17 Aug. 2009, http://online.wsj.com/news/articles/SB125054391631638123, last accessed 27 Jan. 2014.
38. Author interviews in Beijing, Nov. 2008.

39. Barnett Rubin and Ahmed Rashid, "From Great Game to Grand Bargain", *Foreign Affairs*, November/December 2008, http://www.foreignaffairs.com/articles/64604/barnett-r-rubin-and-ahmed-rashid/from-great-game-to-grand-bargain, last accessed 26 Jan. 2014.

40. Dune Lawrence, "U.S., China military talks deepen on Pakistan, Sedney says", Bloomberg, 28 Feb. 2009, http://www.bloomberg.com/apps/news?pid=newsarchive&sid=a4B6GAO4lgUE, last accessed 26 Jan. 2014; author interviews, Washington, DC, Dec. 2008, February 2009.

41. Author interviews in Beijing, Jun. 2009.

42. Author interviews in Washington, DC, Mar.-Dec. 2009.

43. Author interviews in Beijing, Jun. 2009.

44. Ibid.

45. Craig Whitlock, "China rebuffed U.S. request to open route for Afghanistan war supplies, cables ahow", *Washington Post*, 2 Jul. 2011, http://www.washingtonpost.com/national/national-security/china-rebuffed-us-request-to-open-route-for-afghanistan-war-supplies-cables-show/2011/06/30/AG8cdYvH_story.html, last accessed 26 Jan. 2014.

46. Ivan Watson, "Taliban claims victory near Islamabad", CNN, 22 Apr. 2009, http://www.cnn.com/2009/WORLD/asiapcf/04/22/pakistan.taliban/, last accessed 26 Jan. 2014.

47. Zahid Hussain, "Taliban move closer to Islamabad", *Wall Street Journal*, 23 Apr. 2009, http://online.wsj.com/news/articles/SB124041153700943789, last accessed 26 Jan. 2014.

48. Author interviews in Beijing, Jun. 2009.

49. Author interviews in Washington, DC, Feb. 2010.

50. David E. Sanger, "Pakistan strife raises U.S. doubt on nuclear arms", *New York Times*, 3 May. 2009, http://www.nytimes.com/2009/05/04/world/asia/04nuke.html, last accessed 26 Jan. 2014.

51. Author interviews in Beijing, Dec. 2011.

52. For discussion on contingencies in China's neighbourhood, see Paul Stares, "Managing Instability on China's Periphery", Council on Foreign Relations, 16 Sep. 2011, p. 41, http://www.cfr.org/thinktank/cpa/asia_security.html, last accessed 27 Jan. 2014; Daniel Markey, "Pakistan Contingencies", Council on Foreign Relations, May 2011, pp. 41–59.

53. Interviews in Beijing and Washington, 2008–10.

54. Bruce W. Bennett, "Preparing for the Possibility of a North Korean Collapse", Santa Monica, CA: Rand Corporation, 2013, http://www.rand.org/content/dam/rand/pubs/research_reports/RR300/RR331/RAND_RR331.pdf, last accessed 27 Jan. 2014.

55. Drew Thompson, "Border Burdens: China's Response to the Myanmar Refugee Crisis", Centre for the National Interest, 2009, http://cftni.org/

Thompson-Border-Burdens-China-Security-2009.pdf, last accessed 2 Feb. 2014.

56. Stephen Chen, "Ministerial edict warns of nuclear emergencies", *South China Morning Post*, 21 Oct. 2009, http://www.scmp.com/article/696025/ministerial-edict-warns-nuclear-emergencies, last accessed 26 Jan. 2014.

57. Author interviews in Beijing, Mar. 2009 and Sep. 2009.

58. Narayan Lakshman, "China blocked U.N. sanctions against terror group at Pakistan's behest", *The Hindu*, 7 Dec. 2010, http://www.thehindu.com/news/international/article936090.ece, last accessed 2 Feb. 2014.

59. Ahmed Rashid, "Beware Pakistan's small nuclear weapons", *Financial Times*, 22 Oct. 2013, http://blogs.ft.com/the-a-list/2013/10/22/beware-pakistans-small-nuclear-weapons/#axzz2reL95KAj, last accessed 26 Jan. 2014; Sanger, *The Inheritance*, p. 179.

60. Author interviews in Beijing, Mar. 2010.

61. Myra MacDonald, "Attack in Rawalpindi: are Pakistan's militant groups uniting?", Reuters, 10 Oct. 2009, http://blogs.reuters.com/pakistan/2009/10/10/attack-in-rawalpindi-are-pakistans-militant-groups-uniting/, last accessed 23 Jan. 2014.

62. "Pakistan: Troops end attack on Karachi naval air base", BBC, 23 May 2011, http://www.bbc.co.uk/news/world-south-asia-13495127, last accessed 2 Feb. 2014.

63. Asad Kharal and Salman Siddiqui, "PNS Mehran investigation: former navy commander arrested in Lahore", *Express Tribune*, 31 May 2011, http://tribune.com.pk/story/178747/pns-mehran-investigation-former-navy-commander-arrested-in-lahore/, last accessed 23 Jan. 2014.

64. "Taliban claim attack on Minhas base; nine militants killed", *Dawn*, 16 Aug. 2012, http://www.dawn.com/news/742608/militants-attack-pakistani-air-base-at-kamra, last accessed 23 Jan. 2014.

65. Declan Walsh, "Militants attack Pakistani Air Force base", *New York Times*, 16 Aug. 2012, http://www.nytimes.com/2012/08/17/world/asia/pakistani-air-force-base-with-nuclear-ties-is-attacked.html, last accessed 24 Jan. 2014.

66. Author interview in Beijing, Mar. 2009.

67. Jeffrey Goldberg and Marc Ambinder, "The ally from hell", *The Atlantic*, 28 Oct. 2011, http://www.theatlantic.com/magazine/archive/2011/12/the-ally-from-hell/308730/, last accessed 24 Jan. 2014.

68. Author interviews in Washington, DC, Nov. 2012.

69. Author interviews in Beijing, Feb. 2014.

70. "China, Pakistan joint military exercise concludes", *People's Daily*, 19 Dec. 2006, http://english.people.com.cn/200612/19/eng20061219_333837.html, last accessed 24 Jan. 2014.

71. Mathieu Duchâtel, "The Old Friend and the Three Evils: China's Policy

towards Pakistan", paper prepared for 23rd Conference of the Association of Chinese Political Studies, Endicott College, Boston, 30 Jul.—1 Aug. 2010, p. 11.

72. "Pak-China joint exercise Friendship 2006 continues", *Pak Tribune*, 14 Dec. 2006, http://www.paktribune.com/news/print.php?id=163082, last accessed 24 Jan. 2014.

73. Declan Walsh, "In hiding, Bin Laden had four children and five houses", *New York Times*, 29 Mar. 2012, http://www.nytimes.com/2012/03/30/world/asia/on-run-bin-laden-had-4-children-and-5-houses-a-wife-says.html?pagewanted=all, last accessed 2 Feb. 2014.

74. Mark Mazzetti, "How a single spy helped turn Pakistan against United States", *New York Times*, 14 Apr. 2013, http://www.nytimes.com/2013/04/14/magazine/raymond-davis-pakistan.html?pagewanted=all&gwh=64CB3FDF640B3A8A39C770D7521FFBCF&gwt=pay, last accessed 2 Feb. 2014.

75. Alex Spillius, "CIA suicide bomber 'worked with bin Laden allies'", *Telegraph*, 7 Jan. 2010, http://www.telegraph.co.uk/news/worldnews/northamerica/usa/6944280/CIA-suicide-bomber-worked-with-bin-Laden-allies.html, last accessed 2 Feb. 2014.

76. Jane Perlez, "Pakistan's chief of army fights to keep his job", *New York Times*, 15 Jun. 2011, http://www.nytimes.com/2011/06/16/world/asia/16pakistan.html?pagewanted=all, last accessed 24 Jan. 2014.

77. Jane Perlez, "China gives Pakistan 50 fighter jets", *New York Times*, 19 May 2011, http://www.nytimes.com/2011/05/20/world/asia/20pakistan.html, last accessed 24 Jan. 2014.

78. Farhan Bokhari, "Pakistan turns to China for naval base", *Financial Times*, 30 June 2011, http://www.ft.com/intl/cms/s/0/3914bd36–8467–11e0-afcb-00144feabdc0.html#axzz2rbXPHMKc, last accessed 27 Jan. 2014.

79. "Pakistani PM hails China as his country's best friend", BBC News, 17 May 2011, http://www.bbc.co.uk/news/world-south-asia-13418957, last accessed 27 Jan. 2014.

80. James Lamont and Farhan Bokhari, "China and Pakistan: an alliance is built", *Financial Times*, 30 Jun. 2011, http://www.ft.com/intl/cms/s/0/417a48c4-a34d-11e0-8d6d-00144feabdc0.html, last accessed 27 Jan. 2014; Sebastien Blanc, "China-Pakistan alliance strengthened post bin Laden", AFP, 15 May 2011, http://www.google.com/hostednews/afp/article/ALeqM5gg3VbghEVKFnXDP7NJbT7L2O9QMg?docId=CNG.dd035276a74a1dfc4910aded0e7a6b3b.b71, last accessed 27 Jan. 2014.

81. Author interviews in Islamabad and Beijing, Jun. 2011.

82. Author interviews in Beijing, May 2011.

83. Markey, Daniel, *No Exit from Pakistan: America's Tortured Relationship with*

Islamabad, New York: Cambridge University Press, 2013, loc. 5465 of 7903 [IPAD 3rd Generation; MD366LL/A version].

84. Zia Khan, "Eastern Alliance: Pakistan lobbying for defence pact with China", *Express Tribune*, 27 Sep. 2011, http://tribune.com.pk/story/261311/eastern-alliance-pakistan-lobbying-for-defence-pact-with-china/, last accessed 24 Jan. 2014.
85. Author interviews in Beijing, Feb. 2014.
86. Sergei DeSilva-Ranasinghe, "China refutes Gwadar naval base conjecture", *Jakarta Post*, 13 Jun. 2011, http://www.thejakartapost.com/news/2011/06/13/china-refutes-gwadar-naval-base-conjecture.html, last accessed 27 Jan. 2014.
87. Author interviews in Paris, May 2011.
88. "Bin Laden raid: China 'viewed US helicopter wreckage'", BBC News, 15 Aug. 2011, http://www.bbc.co.uk/news/world-south-asia-14527170, last accessed 24 Jan. 2014; Sanger, David E., *Confront and Conceal: Obama's Secret Wars and Surprising Use of American Power*, New York: Crown Publishing, 2012, 2012, p. 102.
89. Author interviews in Washington, Nov. 2010.
90. Author interviews in Washington, Jun. 2010.
91. "Karl Eikenberry, Obama's man in Afghanistan", CNN, 12 Nov. 2009, http://www.cnn.com/2009/POLITICS/11/12/eikenberry.profile/index.html?eref=rss_latest, last accessed 27 Jan. 2014.
92. Author interviews in Kabul, Aug. 2010.
93. Ibid.
94. Author interviews in London, Brussels, Washington and Beijing, Sep. 2008—Dec. 2010.
95. "Full text of Chinese FM's remarks at London Conference on Afghanistan", *Global Times*, 28 Jan. 2010, http://www.globaltimes.cn/china/diplomacy/2010-01/502104.html, last accessed 27 Jan. 2014.
96. Author interviews in Beijing and Washington, Jun. 2009.
97. Aubrey Carlson, "SRAP Holbrooke's April 15 dinner with Chinese foreign minister Yang Jiechi", U.S. State Department Cable, 20 Apr. 2009, https://www.wikileaks.org/plusd/cables/09BEIJING1046_a.html, last accessed 27 Jan. 2014.
98. See previous chapter for additional details.
99. "The Enhanced Partnership with Pakistan Act", USAID, 16 Dec. 2013, http://www.usaid.gov/pk/about/klb.html, last accessed 27 Jan. 2014.
100. Aubrey Carlson, "China standing by on Afghanistan and Pakistan", U.S. State Department Cable, 9 Mar. 2009, https://www.wikileaks.org/plusd/cables/09beijing606_a.html2009, last accessed 27 Jan. 2014.
101. See Woodward, Bob, *Obama's Wars*, New York: Simon & Schuster, 2010 for the blow-by-blow account.

102. "Remarks by the President in Address to the Nation on the Way Forward in Afghanistan and Pakistan", The White House, Office of the Press Secretary, 1 Dec. 2009, http://www.whitehouse.gov/the-press-office/remarks-president-address-nation-way-forward-afghanistan-and-pakistan, last accessed 27 Jan. 2014.

103. Author interviews in Kabul, Aug. 2010; Beijing, Jul. 2010 and Dec. 2009.

104. Author interviews in Beijing, Nov. 2011.

105. "Action Request On U.S.-China Joint Assistance To Afghanistan", U.S. State Department Cable, 22 Jan. 2010, https://www.wikileaks.org/plusd/cables/10STATE6320_a.html, last accessed 27 Jan. 2014.

106. Author interviews in Beijing, Nov. 2011; "U.S.-China Strategic and Economic Dialogue 2011 Outcomes of the Strategic Track", U.S. State Department, Office of the Spokesman, 10 May 2011, http://www.state.gov/r/pa/prs/ps/2011/05/162967.htm, last accessed 26 Jan. 2014.

107. "List of U.S.-China Cooperative Projects", U.S. State Department Media Note, Office of the Spokesperson, 22 Jan. 2014, http://www.state.gov/r/pa/prs/ps/2014/01/220530.htm, last accessed 27 Jan. 2014.

108. Richard Weitz, "Global Insights: China Ponders U.S. Withdrawal from Afghanistan", World Politics Review, 6 Sep. 2011, http://www.worldpoliticsreview.com/articles/9910/global-insights-china-ponders-u-s-withdrawal-from-afghanistan, last accessed 26 Jan. 2014.

109. Author interviews in Beijing, Nov. 2011.

110. Jonathon Burch and Myra MacDonald, "China takes higher-profile role in Afghan diplomacy—diplomats", Reuters, 3 Nov. 2011, http://in.reuters.com/article/2011/11/02/idINIndia-60281020111102, last accessed 26 Jan. 2014.

111. Author interviews in Washington, DC, Jan. 2012.

112. Iftikhar Firdous, "24 soldiers killed in NATO attack on Pakistan check post", Express Tribune, 26 Nov. 2011, http://tribune.com.pk/story/297979/nato-jets-attack-checkpost-on-pak-afghan-border/, last accessed 26 Jan. 2014.

113. Author interviews in Washington, DC, Jan. 2012.

114. "SCO admits Afghanistan as observer", Dawn, 7 Jun. 2012, http://www.dawn.com/news/724732/sco-admits-afghanistan-as-observe, last accessed 27 Jan. 2014.

115. "China, Afghanistan in strategic partnership", China Daily, 8 Jun. 2012, http://www.chinadaily.com.cn/china/2012–06/08/content_15489241.htm, last accessed 27 Jan. 2014.

116. "China's security chief makes surprise visit to Afghan capital", Bloomberg, 23 Sep. 2012, http://www.bloomberg.com/news/2012–09–23/china-s-security-chief-makes-surprise-visit-to-afghanistan-1-.html, last accessed 27 Jan. 2014.

117. "China, Russia and India hold talks on Afghanistan", *Xinhua*, 16 Jan. 2014, http://news.xinhuanet.com/english/china/2014–01/16/c_12601 7891.htm, last accessed 27 Jan. 2014.
118. "India, China to hold first dialogue on Afghanistan", *Times of India*, 17 Apr. 2013, http://articles.timesofindia.indiatimes.com/2013–04–17/ india/38615480_1_first-ever-dialogue-close-ally-pakistan-xinjiang, last accessed 27 Jan. 2014.
119. Author interviews in Beijing, Kabul and Washington, DC, 2012–13.
120. Author interviews in Washington, DC, Feb. 2012.
121. Author interviews in Beijing, Feb. 2014.
122. Ibid.
123. Author interviews in Beijing and Washington, DC, 2012–13.
124. Matthew Rosenberg, "Karzai told to dump U.S.", *Wall Street Journal*, 27 Apr. 2011, http://online.wsj.com/news/articles/SB10001424052748 7047293045762870410940358 16, last accessed 27 Jan. 2014.
125. Ibid.
126. Chidanand Rajghatta, "Pak tries to outflank US and India in Kabul with China card", *Times of India*, 28 Apr. 2011, http://articles.timesofindia. indiatimes.com/2011–04–28/us/29482082_1_yousuf-raza-gilani-afghan-president-hamid-karzai-shuja-pasha, last accessed 27 Jan. 2014.
127. Author interviews in Islamabad, Jun. 2013.
128. Author interviews in Beijing, Oct. 2012; Zhao Huasheng, "China and Afghanistan", p. 4.
129. Author interviews in Kabul, Feb. 2012.
130. Author interviews in Beijing, Feb. 2014.
131. Kenneth Lieberthal, "The American Pivot to Asia", *Foreign Policy*, 21 Dec. 2011, http://www.foreignpolicy.com/articles/2011/12/21/the_american_pivot_to_asia, last accessed 26 Jan. 2014.
132. Hillary Clinton, "America's Pacific Century", *Foreign Policy*, 11 Oct. 2011, http://www.foreignpolicy.com/articles/2011/10/11/americas_pacific_century, last accessed 26 Jan. 2014.
133. Ryan Lizza, "The consequentialist", *New Yorker*, 2 May 2011, http://www.newyorker.com/reporting/2011/05/02/110502fa_fact_lizza?currentPage=all, last accessed 26 Jan. 2014.
134. Zhou Jinghao, "US containment frays China's nerves", *Global Times*, 25 Nov. 2013, http://www.globaltimes.cn/content/827508.shtml, last accessed 26 Jan. 2014.
135. Author interviews in Beijing, Jan. 2012–Dec. 2012.
136. Wang Jisi, "Westward: China's Rebalancing Geopolitical Strategy", International and Strategic Studies Report 73, Center for International and Strategic Studies at Peking University, 2012, pp. 6–7.

137. Ibid. p. 6.
138. Author interviews in Beijing, Dec. 2012.
139. Author interviews in Beijing, Dec. 2012, and Washington, DC, Sept. 2013.

EPILOGUE: THE DRAGON MEETS THE LION

1. Tariq Fatemi, "Chinese prime minister's visit", *The Express Tribune*, 21 May 2013, http://tribune.com.pk/story/552398/chinese-prime-ministers-visit/, last accessed 26 Jan. 2014.
2. Author interviews in Beijing and Islamabad, 2008–13.
3. Author interviews in Islamabad, May 2013.
4. "PML-N dominates Punjab, PTI rule K-P, PPP hold Sindh", *The Express Tribune*, 12 May 2013, http://tribune.com.pk/story/548201/pml-n-dominates-punjab-pti-rule-k-p-ppp-hold-sindh/, last accessed 30 Nov. 2013.
5. Bruce Riedel, "Nawaz Sharif, Pakistan's comeback kid", *The Daily Beast*, 14 May 2013, http://www.thedailybeast.com/articles/2013/05/14/nawaz-sharif-pakistan-s-comeback-kid.html, last accessed 26 Jan. 2014.
6. Nawaz Sharif and Shahbaz Sharif, "Victory Speech, Election 2013", Lahore, 11 May 2013.
7. Faran Bokhari and Victor Mallet, "Nawaz Sharif takes steps to revive Pakistan's economy", *Financial Times*, 13 May 2013, http://www.ft.com/intl/cms/s/0/374bc1a6-bbe8-11e2-a4b4-00144feab7de.html#axzz2lr7lLTWA, last accessed 27 Nov. 2013.
8. Author interviews in Beijing, 2008–13.
9. Paul Bonnicelli, "Pakistan's Third Chance with Sharif", *Foreign Policy*, 20 May 2013, http://shadow.foreignpolicy.com/posts/2013/05/20/pakistans_third_chance_with_sharif, last accessed 26 Jan. 2013; Mira Sethi, "Watch the Throne", *The Caravan*, 1 Apr. 2013, http://caravanmagazine.in/reportage/watch-throne, last accessed 27 Jan. 2014.
10. "Nawaz Sharif's PML-N leads, Imran Khan's PTI 2nd" Ibnlive.in.com, http://ibnlive.in.com/news/pakistan-polls-live-nawaz-sharifs-pmln-leads-imran-khans-pti-2nd/391076-56.html, last accessed 27 Nov. 2013.
11. Ananth Krishnan, "China reaches out to Imran Khan amid stability fears", *The Hindu*, 2 Nov. 2011, http://www.thehindu.com/news/international/china-reaches-out-to-imran-khan-amid-stability-fears/article2591996.ece, last accessed 26 Jan. 2014.
12. Zahir Shah Sherazi, "No enmity with the Taliban, says PTI CM-designate", *Dawn*, 17 Mar. 2013, http://www.dawn.com/news/1027360/no-enmity-with-the-taliban-says-pti-cm-designate, last accessed 7 Nov. 2013.
13. "A landmark decision for Balochistan and the monumental challenges

ahead", *The Balochhal*, 3 Jun. 2013, http://thebalochhal.com/2013/06/03/editorial-a-landmark-decision-for-balochistan-and-the-monumental-challenges-ahead/, last accessed 27 Nov. 2013.

14. One of the more striking examples of Pakistan's proliferation of new media outlets is the increased number and independence of television channels. In the year 2000, Pakistan had only three television channels, all of which were state-owned. By 2012, that number had increased to 89. See Huma Yusuf and Enrys Schoemaker, "The media of Pakistan: Fostering inclusion in a fragile democracy?", *BBC Media Action*, Policy Briefing #9, September 2013.

15. Declan Walsh, "Pakistani court widens role, atirring fears for stability", *New York Times*, 22 Jan. 2012, http://www.nytimes.com/2012/01/23/world/asia/pakistan-high-court-widens-role-and-stirs-fears.html?pagewanted=all, last accessed 26 Jan. 2014.

16. Author interview in Washington, DC, Jun. 2013.

17. "China's 'princelings' wield sway to shape politics", *New York Times*, 13 Nov. 2012, http://www.nytimes.com/2012/11/14/world/asia/chinas-princelings-wield-influence-to-shape-politics.html?pagewanted=all, last accessed 20 Jan. 2014.

18. "Shadow of former president looms over China's new leaders", CNN, 16 Nov. 2012, http://edition.cnn.com/2012/11/15/world/asia/china-leadership-reaction-cheng-li/, last accessed 26 Jan. 2014.

19. "Everybody who loves Mr [sic] Xi, say yes", *The Economist*, 16 Nov. 2013, http://www.economist.com/news/china/21589869-communist-party-calls-wide-ranging-economic-reforms-and-gives-itself-new-tools-implement, last accessed 26 Jan. 2014.

20. "Accumulated Regional Domestic Product", Chinese National Bureau of Statistics (NBS), data collected in 2012.

21. "China president opens Turkmenistan gas pipeline", BBC, 14 Dec. 2009, http://news.bbc.co.uk/2/hi/asia-pacific/8411204.stm, last accessed 26 Jan. 2014.

22. "China-Kazakhstan pipeline starts to pump oil", *China Daily*, 15 Dec. 2005, http://www.chinadaily.com.cn/english/doc/2005–12/15/content_503709.htm, last accessed 26 Jan. 2014.

23. Keith Bradsher, "Hauling new treasure along the Silk Road", *New York Times*, 20 Jul. 2013, http://www.nytimes.com/2013/07/21/business/global/hauling-new-treasure-along-the-silk-road.html?pagewanted=all&_r=1&, last accessed 21 Jul. 2013.

24. "Promote Friendship Between Our People and Work Together to Build a Bright Future", Speech by Xi Jinping, Nazarbayev University, Astana, Kazakhstan, 7 September 2013, http://www.fmprc.gov.cn/mfa_eng/wjb_

663304/zzjg_663340/dozys_664276/gjlb_664280/3180_664322/3182_664326/t1078088.shtml, last accessed 25 May 2014.

25. Ding Qingfen, Xue Chaohua and Chen Jia, "Western program new engine for growth", *China Daily*, 20 Aug. 2013, http://usa.chinadaily.com.cn/china/2013–08/20/content_16905696.htm, last accessed 27 Nov. 2013.

26. "PLA banner in Ladakh says 'You are in China' but Govt insists no intrusion", *India Today*, 29 Apr. 2013, http://indiatoday.intoday.in/story/chinese-troops-put-up-another-tent-in-ladakh/1/268364.html, last accessed 3 Feb. 2014.

27. Manoj Joshi, "Making sense of the Depsang incursion", *The Hindu*, 7 May 2013, http://www.thehindu.com/opinion/op-ed/making-sense-of-the-depsang-incursion/article4689838.ece, last accessed 27 Nov. 2013.

28. Li Keqiang, Written Address at New Delhi Airport, 19 May 2013, http://www.fmprc.gov.cn/eng/topics/lkqipsg/t1043366.shtml, last accessed 26 Jan. 2014.

29. "BRICS and Africa: Partnership for Development, Integration and Industrialisation", eTHekwini Declaration, Fifth BRICS Summit, 27 Mar. 2013, http://www.brics5.co.za/fifth-brics-summit-declaration-and-action-plan/, last accessed 26 Jan. 2014.

30. Ananth Krishnan, "BCIM corridor gets push after first official-level talks in China", *The Hindu*, 21 Dec. 2013, http://www.thehindu.com/news/international/world/bcim-corridor-gets-push-after-first-officiallevel-talks-in-china/article5483848.ece, last accessed 26 Jan. 2014.

31. Harun ur Rashid, "BCIM Economic Corridor: A Giant Step Towards Integration," Institute for Peace and Conflict Studies, Article #4172, 12 Nov. 2013, http://www.ipcs.org/article/india/bcim-economic-corridor-a-giant-step-towards-integration-4172.html, last accessed 26 Jan. 2014.

32. Sudha Mahalingam, "Kolkata-Kunming rally begins", *The Hindu*, 23 Feb. 2013, http://www.thehindu.com/news/international/kolkatakunming-rally-begins/article4446805.ece, last accessed 26 Jan. 2014.

33. Puyam Rakesh Singh, "Opening northeast for BCIM corridor large challenge for India", *Global Times*, 28 Oct. 2013, http://www.globaltimes.cn/content/820856.shtm, last accessed 26 Jan. 2014.

34. Rajagopalan, Rajeswari Pillai and Rahul Prakesh, "Sino-Indian Border Infrastructure: an Update", Observer Research Foundation, Occasional Paper #42, May 2013, pp. 10–21, http://www.observerindia.com/cms/sites/orfonline/modules/occasionalpaper/attachments/Occasional42_13691368 36914.pdf, last accessed 26 Jan. 2014.

35. Li Keqiang, "Seize the New Opportunities in China-India Strategic Cooperation", *Indian Review of Global Affairs*, 22 May 2013, http://www.irgamag.com/resources/interviews-documents/item/2851-seize-the-new-

opportunities-in-china-india-strategic-cooperation, last accessed 18 Nov. 2013.

36. "India, Japan to build industrial corridor", *Times of India*, 13 Dec. 2006, http://articles.timesofindia.indiatimes.com/2006-12-13/india/27787427_ 1_industrial-corridor-freight-corridor-japan-india-policy-dialogue, last accessed 18 Nov. 2013.

37. "Six Thunder jets escort Premier Li Keqiang's plane in Pakistan", SinaEnglish, 23 Mar. 2013, http://english.sina.com/china/p/2013/0522/592832.html, last accessed 26 Jan. 2014.

38. Sumera Khan, "Enter the dragon: China offers help to end Pakistan's energy woes", *Express Tribune*, 23 May 2013, http://tribune.com.pk/story/553246/ enter-the-dragon-china-offers-help-to-end-pakistans-energy-woes/, last accessed 26 Jan. 2014.

39. Ibid.

40. Shabhaz Rana, "Building on ties: new premier indicates plans to link Gwadar with China", *Express Tribune*, 6 Jun. 2013, http://tribune.com.pk/ story/559370/building-on-ties-new-premier-indicates-plan-to-link-gwadar-with-china/ last accessed 12 Feb. 2014.

41. Quoted in "PM's address to the nation: Nawaz Sharif dreams to make Pakistan an 'Asian Tiger'", *Express Tribune*, 19 Aug. 2013, http://tribune. com.pk/story/592284/pms-address-to-the-nation-nawaz-sharif-dreams-to-make-pakistan-an-asian-tiger/, last accessed 18 Nov. 2013.

42. "China says its nuclear reactor gets first foreign contract", *Times of India*, 20 Apr. 2013, http://articles.timesofindia.indiatimes.com/2013-04-20/ china/38692640_1_china-national-nuclear-corporation-reactor-earlier-nuclear-power-plants, last accessed 27 Nov. 2013.

43. "Chinese engineers escape bomb attack in Clifton", *Dawn*, 22 May. 2013, http://dawn.com/news/1012910/chinese-engineers-escape-bomb-attack-in-clifton, last accessed 18 Nov. 2013.

44. Ibid.

45. "Facing down the Taliban on the Himalayas' killer mountain", 5 Jan. 2014, *The Guardian*, http://www.theguardian.com/world/2014/jan/05/taliban-himalayas-mountain-nanga-parbat-climbers, last accessed 27 Jan. 2014.

46. Farooq Ahmed Khan, "Taliban say their Jundul Hafsa unit carried out killings", *Dawn*, 24 Jun. 2013, http://www.dawn.com/news/1020309/otaliban-say-their-jundul-hafsa-unit-carried-out-killings-ojundullah-also-claims-responsibility-terroris, last accessed 26 Jan. 2014; Zarar Khan, "Taliban kill 10 Foreign climbers, Pakistani guide", *USA Today*, 23 Jun. 2013, http:// www.usatoday.com/story/news/world/2013/06/23/pakistan-mountain-climbers-shot/2449809/, last accessed at 20 Nov. 2013.

47. Jamal Shahid, "Chinese mountaineer narrates dramatic escape", *Dawn*, 29 Jun. 2013, http://www.dawn.com/news/1021528/chinese-mountaineer-narrates-dramatic-escape, last accessed 20 Nov. 2013.

48. Haq Nawaz Khan and Tim Craig, "Taliban kills foreign climbers in Pakistan", *Washington Post*, 23 Jun. 2013, http://www.washingtonpost.com/world/taliban-kills-foreign-climbers/2013/06/23/a811ea4c-dbef-11e2-a484-7b7f79cd66a1_story.html, last accessed 26 Jan. 2014.

49. "China condemns violent attack in Pakistan-administered Kashmir", *People's Daily*, 24 Jun. 2013, http://english.peopledaily.com.cn/90883/8295751.html, last accessed 26 Jan. 2014.

50. Salman Masood and Declan Walsh, "Militants kill 10 climbers in Himalyas of Pakistan", *New York Times*, 23 Jun. 2013, http://www.nytimes.com/2013/06/24/world/asia/gunmen-kill-climbers-in-northern-pakistan.html?_r=0, last accessed 18 Nov. 2013.

51. "Nanga Parbat investigators shot dead in Chilas", *Express Tribune*, 7 Aug. 2013, http://tribune.com.pk/story/587534/terror-in-gilgit-baltistan-nanga-parbat-investigators-shot-dead-in-chilas/, last accessed 18 Nov. 2013.

52. Salam Masood, "Pakistani Taliban kill 22 Shiites in bus attack", *New York Times*, 16 Aug. 2012; Farman Ali, "Sectarian Violence: Jundallah claims responsibility for Kohistan bus attack", *Express Tribune*, 28 Feb. 2012.

53. Tom Hussain, "Karachi, Besham choice home bases for Afghan Taliban", *The News*, 17 Sept. 2011, http://www.thenews.com.pk/TodaysPrintDetail.aspx?ID=68140&Cat=2, last accessed 18 Nov. 2013; Rina Saeed Khan, "Why I hate Chilas", *Dawn*, http://www.dawn.com/news/1022046/why-i-hate-chilas/1, last accessed 18 Nov. 2013.

54. "Nawaz Sharif fails to speak English", YouTube.com, uploaded Jul. 2013, http://www.youtube.com/watch?v=0lWVvmnzbyk, last accessed 21 Jul. 2013.

55. "Kashagar-Gwadar project a "game changer" for whole region: Sharif", *Dawn*, 7 Jul. 2013, http://dawn.com/news/1023486/kashgar-gwadar-project-a-game-changer-for-whole-region-sharif, last accessed 26 Jan. 2014.

56. "Ahsan Iqbal discusses trade, energy with Chinese minister", *Dawn*, 26 Jun. 2013, http://www.dawn.com/news/1020852/ahsan-iqbal-discusses-trade-energy-with-chinese-minister, last accessed 26 Jan. 2014.

57. "Speeding up development: Nawaz to induct 'China cell' into PM's office", *Express Tribune*, 8 Jul. 2013, http://tribune.com.pk/story/573934/speeding-up-development-nawaz-to-induct-china-cell-into-pms-office/, last accessed 26 Jan. 2014.

58. Ibid.

59. Rana Jawad, "Chinese firms ready to invest billions of dollars in Pakistan", *The News*, 5 Jul. 2013, http://www.thenews.com.pk/Todays-News-13–

23889-Chinese-firms-ready-to-invest-billions-of-dollars-in-Pakistan, last accessed 6 Jul. 2013.

60. Author interviews, Beijing, Feb. 2014.
61. Lieven, Anatol, *Pakistan: A Hard Country*, New York: Public Affairs, 2011, p. 245.
62. Ibid.
63. Author interview in Washington, DC, Jun. 2013.
64. Ibid.
65. Feisal H. Naqvi, "An unholy alliance", *Express Tribune*, 25 Feb. 2013, http://tribune.com.pk/story/512400/an-unholy-alliance/, last accessed 26 Jan. 2014.
66. "Pakistan's Punjab Government allocates funds for JuD centre", *The Hindu*, 18 Jun. 2013, http://www.thehindu.com/news/international/south-asia/pakistans-punjab-government-allocates-funds-for-jud-centre/article4826052.ece, last accessed 26 Jan. 2014; "Why Pakistan is desperate for Lashkar-e-Taiba's friendship", *First Post*, 21 Jun. 2013, http://www.firstpost.com/world/why-pakistan-is-desperate-for-lashkar-e-taibas-friendship-893349.html, last accessed 26 Jan. 2014.
67. "Nawaz Sharif calls for Taliban talks", *Dawn*, 21 May. 2013, http://www.dawn.com/news/1012539/nawaz-sharif-calls-for-taliban-talks, last accessed 26 Jan. 2014.
68. Interviews in Islamabad, May 2013.
69. "Thar coal: MoU to set up 6,000MW power plants", *Express Tribune*, 16 Aug. 2013, http://www.dawn.com/news/1058719/karachi-operation-to-continue-until-objectives-met-sharif, last accessed 3 Feb. 2014.
70. Mehreen Zahra-Malik, "China commits $6.5 billion for Pakistani nuclear project", Reuters, 24 Dec. 2013, http://www.reuters.com/article/2013/12/24/us-pakistan-china-nuclear-idUSBRE9BN06220131224, last accessed 27 Dec. 2013.
71. "Karachi operation to continue until objectives met: Sharif", *Dawn*, 26 Nov. 2013, http://www.dawn.com/news/1058719/pm-in-karachi-inaugurates-coastal-power-project, last accessed 23 Jan. 2014.
72. Author interviews in Islamabad, Jun. 2013.
73. Lucy Hornby and Ed Crooks, "China set to supply components to US nuclear power plants", *Financial Times*, 30 Oct. 2013, http://www.ft.com/intl/cms/s/0/e8a83158-4164-11e3-9073-00144feabdc0.html#axzz2orTTeMHv, last accessed 23 Jan. 2014.
74. Author interviews in Beijing, May 2011.
75. A.H. Nayyar, Pervez Hoodbhoy and Zia Mian, "Nuclear Karachi", *Dawn*, 16 Dec. 2013, http://www.dawn.com/news/1074169/nuclear-karachi, last accessed 23 Jan. 2014.
76. Sikander Shaheen, "Kayani off to China to buttress defence ties", *Nation*,

5 Jan. 2012, http://www.nation.com.pk/national/05-Jan-2012/kayani-off-to-china-to-buttress-defence-ties, last accessed 26 Jan. 2014.

77. "As ties with U.S. sour Islamabad turns to Beijing", *Express Tribune*, 28 Apr. 2011, http://tribune.com.pk/story/158245/as-ties-with-us-sour-islamabad-turns-to-beijing/, last accessed 26 Jan. 2014.

78. Author interviews in Beijing, Mar. 2012, and Islamabad, Jun. 2013.

79. Katherine Houreld, "U.S., Pakistan ties fully repaired: Pakistan foreign minister", Reuters, 28 Nov. 2012, http://www.reuters.com/article/2012/11/28/us-pakistan-usa-idUSBRE8AR0R320121128, last accessed 26 Jan. 2014.

80. "Kayani in China: Army chief discusses LoC, Afghanistan issues", *Express Tribune*, 29 Oct. 2013, http://tribune.com.pk/story/623957/kayani-in-china-army-chief-discusses-loc-afghanistan-issues/, last accessed 26 Jan. 2014.

81. Sikander Shaheen, "Kayani meets top Chinese leadership", *The Nation*, 29 Oct. 2013, http://www.nation.com.pk/national/29-Oct-2013/kayani-meetstop-chinese-leadership, last accessed 26 Jan. 2014.

82. Benjamin Kang Lim and Ben Blanchard, "China suspects Tiananmen crash a suicide attack", Reuters, 29 Oct. 2013, http://www.reuters.com/article/2013/10/29/us-china-tiananmen-idUSBRE99S02R20131029, last accessed 26 Jan. 2014.

83. Jeremy Page, "China says Tiananmen crash was terrorism", *Wall Street Journal*, 30 Oct. 2013, hhttp://online.wsj.com/news/articles/SB10001424052702303618904579167181737377834, last accessed 26 Jan. 2014.

84. "China names Islamic group as 'supporter' of Tiananmen attack", AFP, 1 Nov. 2013, http://au.news.yahoo.com/thewest/a/19638547/china-names-islamic-group-as-supporter-of-tiananmen-attack/, last accessed 26 Jan. 2014.

85. Zhang Yunbi, "Cooperation needed in terror fight", *China Daily*, 4 Nov. 2013, http://usa.chinadaily.com.cn/epaper/2013–11/04/content_17079272.htm, last accessed 26 Jan. 2014.

86. Andrew Jacobs, "Tiananmen attack linked to police raid on a mosque in Xinjiang", *New York Times*, 7 Nov. 2013, http://sinosphere.blogs.nytimes.com/2013/11/07/tiananmen-attack-linked-to-police-raid-on-a-mosque-in-xinjiang/?smid=tw-share&_r=0, last accessed 26 Jan. 2014.

87. "Islamist group calls Tiananmen attack 'jihadi operation': SITE", Reuters, 23 Nov. 2013, http://www.reuters.com/article/2013/11/23/us-china-attack-claim-idUSBRE9AM0B520131123, last accessed 26 Jan. 2014.

88. "China cites East Turkistan Islamic Movement terrorist threat", Xinhua, 1 Nov. 2013, http://news.xinhuanet.com/english/china/2013–11/01/c_132852165.htm, last accessed 26 Jan. 2014.

89. The other unsettled issue, with Bhutan, is effectively a subsidiary of the India border problem.

90. See James Mulvenon, Chairman Hu and the PLA's 'New Historic Missions', China Leadership Monitor, no. 27.

91. Author interviews in Beijing, Feb 2014.

NOTE ON SOURCING

1. Syed, Anwar Hussain, *China & Pakistan: Diplomacy of an Entente Cordiale*, London: Oxford University Press, 1974.

2. Aijazuddin, F.S., *From A Head, Through A Head, To A Head: The Secret Channel between the U.S. and China through Pakistan*, Karachi: Oxford University Press, 2000.

3. Ispahani, Mahnaz Z., *Roads and Rivals: The Political Uses of Access in The Borderlands of Asia*, Ithaca, NY: Cornell University Press, 1989.

4. Gauhar, Altaf, *Ayub Khan: Pakistan's First Military Ruler*, Lahore: Oxford University Press, 1993.

5. Khalid, Muhammad Mumtaz, *History of the Karakoram Highway, Volumes I and II*, Rawalpindi: Hamza, 2009.

6. Singh, Swaran, *China-Pakistan Strategic Cooperation: India Perspectives*, New Delhi: Manohar Publishers, 2007.

7. Du Youkang, *A Model of State-to-State Relations: Retrospects and Prospects of the China-Pakistan Ties since 1951*, Beijing: Current Affairs Press, 2012.

8. Garver, John W., *Protracted Contest: Sino-Indian Rivalry in the Twentieth Century*, Seattle: University of Washington Press, 2001.

9. Khan, Riaz Mohammad, "Pakistan-China Relations: An Overview", *Pakistan Horizon*, Vol. 64, No. 4, October 2011.

10. Ye Hailin, "China-Pakistan Relationship: All-Weathers, But Maybe Not All-Dimensional", in Zetterlund, Kristina (ed.), *Pakistan—Consequences of Deteriorating Security in Afghanistan*, Stockholm: Swedish Defence Research Agency, 2009.

11. Ziad Haider, "Sino-Pakistan Relations and Xingiang's Uighurs', Asian Survey, Vol. XLV, 4, University of California Press, July/August 2005, http://www.stimson.org/images/uploads/research-pdfs/XINJIANG.pdf, last accessed 2 Feb. 2014.

12. Fazlur Rehman, "Pakistan-China Economic Relations Opportunities and Challenges", Institute of Strategic Studies, 2006, http://www.issi.org.pk/old-site/ss_Detail.php?datald=390, last accessed 2 Feb. 2014.

13. See a number of the articles at: http://raffaellopantucci.com

14. Cheng Xiaohe, "China's Aid toward Pakistan in the India-Pakistan War II", *Diplomacy Commentary*, No. 3, 2012.

15. Hu Shisheng, "Afghan Reconstruction: Regional Challenges", CICIR Institute of South, South East Asian and Oceania Studies, 2012, http://d.

wanfangdata.com.cn/periodical_xdgjgx-e2012z1004.aspx, last accessed 2 Feb. 2014.

16. Wang Jisi, "Marching Westwards: The Rebalancing of China's Geostrategy", *International and Strategic Studies Report*, Centre for International and Strategic Studies, Peking University, No. 73, 7 Oct. 2012.

17. Corera, *Gordon, Shopping for Bombs: Nuclear Proliferation, Global Insecurity, and The Rise and Fall of the A.Q. Khan Network*, London: C. Hurst & Co., 2006.

18. Perkovich, George, *India's Nuclear Bomb: The Impact on Global Proliferation*, Los Angeles: University of California Press, 1999.

19. Starr, S. Frederick (ed.), *Xinjiang: China's Muslim Borderland*, New York: M. E. Sharpe, 2004.

20. Rashid, Ahmed, *Jihad: The Rise of Militant Islam in Central Asia*, New York: Penguin Group, 2003.

21. Khan, Feroz H., *Eating Grass: The Making of The Pakistani Bomb*, Stanford, CA: Stanford University Press, 2012.

22. Bass, Gary, *The Blood Telegram: Nixon, Kissinger, and a Forgotten Genocide*, New York: Knopf, 2013.

23. Andrew Small, "Afghanistan-Pakistan: Bringing China (back) in", GMF Transatlantic Take, 23 Oct. 2009, http://blog.gmfus.org/2009/10/23/afghanistan-pakistan-bringing-china-back-in/, last accessed 2 Feb. 2014.

24. Andrew Small, "China's Caution on Afghanistan-Pakistan", *Washington Quarterly*, Vol. 33, Issue 3, 2010, http://www.tandfonline.com/doi/abs/10.1080/0163660X.2010.492343#.UvUMkHddX8k, last accessed 2 Feb. 2014.

25. Andrew Small, "Why is China Talking to the Taliban?", *Foreign Policy*, 21 Jun. 2013, http://www.foreignpolicy.com/articles/2013/06/20/why_is_china_talking_to_the_taliban, last accessed 2 Feb. 2014.

26. Andrew Small, "China's Afghan Moment", *Foreign Policy*, 3 Oct. 2012, http://www.foreignpolicy.com/articles/2012/10/03/chinas_afghan_moment, last accessed 2 Feb. 2014.

BIBLIOGRAPHY

Acharya, Arabinda, Rohan Gunaratna and Wang Pengxin, *Ethnic Identity and National Conflict in China*, New York: Palgrave Macmillan, 2010.

Ahmad, Naveed, "Pakistan China sign historic defense pact", ISN Security Watch, 6 Apr. 2005, http://www.isn.ethz.ch/Digital-Library/Articles/Detail/? lng=en&id=107574, last accessed 27 Jan. 2014.

Aijazuddin, F.S., *From a Head, Through a Head, To a Head: The Secret Channel between the U.S. and China through Pakistan*, Karachi: Oxford University Press, 2000.

Akhund, Iqbal, *Memoirs of a Bystander: A Life in Diplomacy*, Karachi: Oxford University Press, 2000.

Al Haq, Nur, "Lal Masjid Crisis", Islamabad Policy Research Institute Fact File, 2007, http://ipripak.org/factfiles/ff90.pdf, last accessed 27 Jan. 2014.

——— "Indo-China Relations: Convention between Great Britain, China and Tibet", Reproduced in the Islamabad Policy Research Institute Fact File, 3 Jul. 1914, http://www.ipripak.org/factfiles/ff43.shtml, last accessed 2 Feb. 2014.

——— "China-Pakistan Relations: A Profile of Friendship", http://www.ipripak.org/factfiles/ff60.shtml, last accessed 23 Jan. 2014.

Albright, David, *Peddling Peril: How the Secret Nuclear Trade Arms America's Enemies*, New York: Free Press, 2010.

Albright, David and Corey Hinderstein, "Uncovering the Nuclear Black Market: Working Toward Closing Gaps in the International Nonproliferation Regime", Institute for Science and International Security, 2004, http://www.isis-online.org/publications/southasia/nuclear_black_market.html, last accessed 22 Jan. 2014.

Albright, David and Corey Hinderstein, "Unraveling the A Q Khan and Future Proliferation Networks", *Washington Quarterly*, Vol. 28, No. 2, Spring 2005.

Albright, David, Paul Brannan and Andrea Scheel Stricker, "Self-Serving Leaks from the A.Q. Khan Circle", *Institute for Science and International Security*, 9 Dec. 2009, http://isis-online.org/isis-reports/detail/self-serving-leaks-from-the-a.q.-khan-circle/20, last accessed 27 Jan. 2014.

Albright, David, Frans Berkhout and William Walker, *World Inventory of Plutonium and Highly Enriched Uranium*, Oxford: Oxford University Press, 1993.

Alamgir, Jalal, *India's Open-Economy Policy: Globalism, Rivalry, Continuity*, Routledge, 2009.

Ali, Mahmud, *U.S.-China Cold War Collaboration, 1971–1989*, Oxford: Routledge, 2005.

Alikuzai, Hamid Wahed, *A Concise History of Afghanistan in 25 Volumes: Volume 1*, Bloomington, IN: Trafford Publishing, 2013.

Al-shishani, Murad Batal, "Journal of the Turkistan Islamic Party Urges Jihad in China", *Terrorism Monitor*, 10 Apr. 2009, http://www.freerepublic.com/focus/news/2227307/posts, last accessed 27 Jan. 2014.

Amstutz, J. Bruce, *The First Five Years of Soviet Occupation*, Honolulu: University Press of the Pacific, 2002.

Arnett, Eric (ed.), *Military Capacity and the Risk of War: China, India, Pakistan and Iran*, New York: Oxford University Press, 1997.

Bajoria, Jayshree and Eben Kaplan, "The ISI and Terrorism: Behind the Accusations", Council on Foreign Relations, 4 May 2011, http://www.cfr.org/pakistan/isi-terrorism-behind-accusations/p11644, last accessed 2 Feb. 2014.

Bajoria, Jayshree and Esther Pan, "The U.S.-India Nuclear Deal", Council on Foreign Relations, 5 Nov. 2010, http://www.cfr.org/india/us-india-nuclear-deal/p9663, last accessed 20 Nov. 2013.

Balachandran, G., "India and NSG: Approaches to Indian Membership", Institute for Defence Studies and Analyses, 23 May 2013, http://www.idsa.in/issuebrief/IndiaandNSG_gbalachandran_230513, last accessed 27 Dec. 2013.

Banerjee, Indranil, "The Indian Navy At War: 1971 Blockade From The Seas", SAPRA India, http://www.bharat-rakshak.com/Navy/History/1971war/Banerjee.Html, last accessed 27 Jan. 2014.

Bass, Gary J., *The Blood Telegram: Nixon, Kissinger, and a Forgotten Genocide*, New York: Knopf, 2013.

Bates Gill and Evan Medeiros, *Chinese Arms Exports: Policy, Players and Process*, Carlisle, PA: Army War College Strategic Studies Institute, Aug. 2000, http://www.fas.org/nuke/guide/china/doctrine/chinarms.pdf, last accessed 27 Jan. 2014.

Baxter, Craig (ed.), *Diaries of Field Marshal Mohammad Ayub Khan 1966–1972*, London: Oxford University Press, 2007.

BIBLIOGRAPHY

Bell, Imogen, *Eastern Europe, Russia and Central Asia 2003*, London: Taylor and Francis, 2002.

Bennett, Bruce W., "Preparing for the Possibility of a North Korean Collapse", RAND, 2013, http://www.rand.org/content/dam/rand/pubs/research_reports/RR300/RR331/RAND_RR331.pdf, last accessed 27 Jan. 2014.

Bennett-Jones, Owen, *Pakistan: Eye of the Storm*, New Haven: Yale University Press, 2003.

Bergen, Peter, *The Longest War: The Enduring Conflict between America and Al-Qaeda*, New York: Free Press, 2011.

Bidwal, Praful and Achin Vanalk, *New Nukes: India, Pakistan and Global Nuclear Disarmament*, Oxford: Signal Books, 2000.

Bin Sultan, Khaled, *Desert Warrior: A Personal View of the Gulf War by the Joint Forces Commander*, London: HarperCollins, 1995.

Blom, Amelie, "Changing Religious Leadership in Contemporary Pakistan: The Case of the Red Mosque", in Bolognani, Marta and Stephen M. Lyon (eds), *Pakistan and Its Diaspora: Multidisciplinary Approaches*, New York: Palgrave, 2011.

Blustein, Paul, "The Nine-Day Misadventure of the Most Favoured Nations", Washington, DC: Brookings Global Economy and Development Program, Jul. 2008, http://www.brookings.edu/~/media/Research/Files/Articles/2008/12/05%20trade%20blustein/1205_trade_blustein.PDF, last accessed 27 Jan. 2014.

Bolognani, Marta and Stephen M. Lyon (eds), *Pakistan and Its Diaspora: Multidisciplinary Approaches*, New York: Palgrave, 2011.

Bonnicelli, Paul, "Pakistan's Third Chance with Sharif", *Foreign Policy*, 20 May 2013, http://shadow.foreignpolicy.com/posts/2013/05/20/pakistans_third_chance_with_sharif, last accessed 26 Jan. 2013.

Bostrom, Nick and Milan M. Cirkovic, *Global Catastrophic Risks*, Oxford: Oxford University Press, 2008.

Bovingdon, Gardner, *The Uyghurs: Strangers in Their Own Land*, New York: Columbia University Press, 2010.

Castets, Rémi, "The Uyghurs in Xinjiang—The Malaise Grows", *China Perspectives*, Issue 49, Sep.-Oct. 2003, http://chinaperspectives.revues.org/648#tocto1n6, last accessed 2 Feb. 2014.

Chambers, Michael R., *South Asia in 2020: Future Strategic Balances and Alliances*, Carlisle, PA: U.S. Army War College, 2002.

Chau, Adam Yuet, "Mao's Travelling Mangoes: Food as Relic in Revolutionary China", *Past and Present*, 2010, Supplement 5.

Cheng, Xiaohe, "China's Aid toward Pakistan in the India-Pakistan War II', *Diplomacy Commentary*, No. 3, 2012.

Cherian, John, "Diplomatic Fallout", *Frontline*, Vol. 15, No. 12, 6–19 Jun. 1998.

Chinque, S., *News from Xinhua News Agency*, Vol. 594–620, 1980.

Choudhury, G.W., *India, Pakistan, Bangladesh, and the Major Powers: Politics of a Divided Subcontinent*, New York: The Free Press, 1975.

Chung Chien-peng, "Confronting Terrorism and Other Evils in China: All Quiet on the Western Front?", *China and Eurasia Foreign Quarterly*, Vol. 4, No. 2, May 2006.

Clinton, Hillary, "America's Pacific Century", *Foreign Policy*, 11 Oct. 2011, http://www.foreignpolicy.com/articles/2011/10/11/americas_pacific_century, last accessed 26 Jan. 2014.

Cloughey, Brian, *War, Coups and Terror, Pakistan's Army in Years of Turmoil*, Huddersfield: Pen and Sword, 2008.

Cockburn, Andrew, *Rumsfeld: His Rise, Fall, and Catastrophic Legacy*, New York: Simon & Schuster, 2007.

Cohen, Stephen P., *The Pakistan Army*, Los Angeles: University of California Press, 1984.

———— *The Idea of Pakistan*, Washington, DC: Brookings Institution Press, 2004.

———— *The Future of Pakistan*, Washington, DC: Brookings Institution Press, 2011.

Coll, Steve, *Ghost Wars: The Secret History of the CIA, Afghanistan, and Bin Laden, from the Soviet Invasion to September 10, 2001*, London: Penguin Books, 2004.

Collins, Gabe and Andrew S. Erickson, "Implications of China's Military Evacuation of Citizens from Libya", *China Brief*, Vol. 11, Issue 4, 10 Mar. 2011, http://www.jamestown.org/programs/chinabrief/single/?tx_ttnews%5Btt_news%5D=37633&tx_ttnews%5BbackPid%5D=25&cHash=c1302a9ecaddfc23450fb6ec13a98136#.Uu3eBHmQePE, last accessed 14 Jan. 2014.

Cooley, Alexander, *Base Politics: Democratic Change and the U.S. Military Overseas*, Ithaca, NY: Cornell University Press, 2008.

Cordovez, Diego and Selig S. Harrison, *Out of Afghanistan: The Inside Story of the Soviet Withdrawal*, New York: Oxford University Press, 1995.

Corera, Gordon, *Shopping for Bombs: Nuclear Proliferation, Global Insecurity, and the Rise and Fall of the A.Q. Khan Network*, London: C. Hurst & Co., 2006.

Cronin, Sean, "Chinese Contractor Snags Afghan Road Building Work", *ENR: Engineering News-Record*, Vol. 251, Issue 22, 22 Dec. 2003, http://connection.ebscohost.com/c/articles/11634154/chinese-contractor-snags-afghan-roadbuilding-work, last accessed 20 Nov. 2013.

Dalrymple, William, "A Deadly Triangle; Afghanistan, Pakistan and India", *The Brookings Essay*, 25 Jun. 2013, http://www.brookings.edu/research/essays/2013/deadly-triangle-afghanistan-pakistan-india-c, last accessed 9 Dec. 2013.

BIBLIOGRAPHY

Dillon, Michael, *Xinjiang: China's Muslim Far Northwest*, London: Routledge, 2009.

Dixit, J.N., *India-Pakistan in War and Peace*, New York: Routledge, 2002.

Dorronsoro, Gilles, "The Taliban's Winning Strategy in Afghanistan", Washington, DC: Carnegie Endowment for International Peace, Jul. 2009, http://carnegieendowment.org/files/taliban_winning_strategy.pdf, last accessed 27 Jan. 2014.

Downs, Erica S., "China Buys into Afghanistan", *SAIS Review*, Vol. XXXII, No. 2, Summer-Fall 2012.

Du, Youkang, *A Model of State-to-State Relations: Retrospects and Prospects of the China-Pakistan Ties since 1951*, Beijing: Current Affairs Press, 2012.

Duchâtel, Mathieu, "The Old Friend and the Three Evils: China's Policy towards Pakistan", paper prepared for 23rd Conference of the Association of Chinese Political Studies, Endicott College, Boston, 30 Jul.—1 Aug. 2010.

————"China's Policy Towards Pakistan And Stability In South Asia", Asia-Pacific Security Forum, Europe Institute for Asian Studies, Brussels, 10–11 September 2010.

Dunham, Mikel, *Buddha's Warriors*, New York: Tarcher, 2004.

Eftimiades, Nicholas, *Chinese Intelligence Operations*, Annapolis, MD: Naval Institute Press, 1994.

Eisenman, Joshua, Eric Heginbotham and Derek Mitchell, *China and the Developing World: Beijing's Strategy for the Twenty-First Century*, Armonk, NY: M.E. Sharpe/East Gate Books, 2007.

Erickson, Andrew and Austin Strange, "No Substitute for Experience: Chinese Antipiracy Operations in the Gulf of Aden", U.S. Naval War College, *China Maritime Study*, No. 10, November 2013.

Faligot, Roger, *Les services secrets chinois: de Mao à nos jours*, Paris: Nouveau Monde, 2010.

Faruqui, Ahmad, "A Blueprint for Pakistan's Economic Revival", *IPRIPAK*, Winter 2002, http://ipripak.org/journal/winter2002/ablueprintforpak.shtml, last accessed 27 Jan. 2014.

Fayaz, Sadia, "China's Xinjiang Problem and Pakistan", *The Dialogue*, Vol. 7, No. 3, Jul.-Sep. 201, http://www.qurtuba.edu.pk/thedialogue/The%20 Dialogue/7_3/Dialogue_July_September2012_235–254.pdf, last accessed 27 Jan. 2014.

Feigenbaum, Evan A. and Robert A. Manning, "The Tale Of Two Asias", Foreign Policy, 31 Oct. 2012, http://www.foreignpolicy.com/Articles/2012/10/30/A_Tale_Of_Two_Asias, last accessed 26 Jan. 2014.

Fletcher, Holly and Jayshree Bajoria, "The East Turkestan Islamic Movement (ETIM)", Council on Foreign Relations, 31 Jul. 2008, http://www.cfr.org/china/east-turkestan-islamic-movement-etim/p9179, last accessed 15 Jan. 2014.

Frankel, Francine R., and Harry Harding, *The India-China Relationship: What the United States Needs to Know*, New York: Columbia University Press, 2004.

Fravel, Taylor M., *Strong Borders, Secure Nation: Cooperation and Conflict in China's Territorial Disputes*, New Jersey: Princeton University Press, 2009.

Fravel, M. Taylor and Evan S. Medeiros, "China's Search for Assured Retaliation: The Evolution of Chinese Nuclear Strategy and Force Structure", *International Security*, Vol. 35, No. 2, Fall 2010.

Funabashi, Yoichi, *The Peninsular Question: A Chronicle of the Second Korean Nuclear Crisis*, Washington, DC: Brookings Institution Press, 2007.

Galbraith, John Kenneth, *Ambassador's Journal*, Boston: Houghton Mifflin Company, 1969.

Ganguly, Sumit, *Nuclear Proliferation in South Asia: Crisis Behaviour and the Bomb*, New York: Routledge, 2009.

Garner, George, "The Afghan Taliban and Pakistan's 'Strategic Depth'", *Bellum* (A project of the *Stanford Review*), 17 May 2010, http://bellum.stanfordreview.org/?p=2184, last accessed 2 Feb. 2014.

Garver, John W., *Protracted Contest: Sino-Indian Rivalry in the Twentieth Century*, Seattle: University of Washington Press, 2001.

———— "China's Decision for War with India in 1962", in Alastair Iain Johnston and Robert S. Ross (eds), *New Directions in The Study of China's Foreign Policy*, Stanford, CA: Stanford University Press, 2006.

———— "Development of China's Overland Transportation Links with Central, South-west and South Asia", *China Quarterly*, No. 185, March 2006.

Gates, Robert, *From the Shadows: The Ultimate Insider's Story of Five Presidents and How They Won the Cold War*, New York: Simon & Schuster, 1996.

Gauhar, Altaf, *Ayub Khan: Pakistan's First Military Ruler*, Lahore: Oxford University Press, 1993.

Gladney, Dru C., "The Chinese Program of Development and Control, 1978–2001", in S. Frederick Starr (ed.), *Xinjiang: China's Muslim Borderland*, London: M.E. Sharpe, 2004.

Grare, Frédéric, "Pakistan: The Resurgence of Baluch Nationalism", Washington, DC: Carnegie Endowment for International Peace, 2007, http://carnegieendowment.org/files/CP65.Grare.FINAL.pdf, last accessed 3 Jan. 2014.

Gregor, James, "The People's Republic of China as a Western Security Asset", *Air University Review*, Jul.-Aug. 1983, http://www.airpower.maxwell.af.mil/airchronicles/aureview/1983/jul-aug/gregor.html, last accessed 22 Jan. 2014.

Guha, Ramachandra, *India After Gandhi: The History of World's Largest Democracy*, London: Pan Macmillan, 2007.

Gupta, Bhabani Sen, *The Fulcrum of Asia: Relations among China, India, Pakistan and the U.S.S.R.*, New York: Pegasus, 1970.

Guruswamy, Mohan and Zorawar Daulet Singh, *India China Relations: The Border Issue and Beyond*, New Delhi: Viva Books Private Limited, 2009.

BIBLIOGRAPHY

Haider, Ziad, "Sino-Pakistan Relations and Xingiang's Uighurs", *Asian Survey*, Vol. XLV, 4, University of California Press, Jul./Aug. 2005, http://www.stimson.org/images/uploads/research-pdfs/XINJIANG.pdf, last accessed 27 Jan. 2014.

——— "Baluchis, Beijing, and Pakistan's Gwadar Port", *Georgetown Journal of International Affairs*, Winter 2005, Vol. 6, No. 1, http://journal.georgetown.edu/wp-content/uploads/6.1-Haider.pdf, last accessed 26. Jan. 2014.

Hailin, Ye, "China-Pakistan Relationship: All-Weathers, But Maybe Not All-Dimensional", in Zetterlund, Kristina (ed.), *Pakistan—Consequences of Deteriorating Security in Afghanistan*, Stockholm: Swedish Defence Research Agency, 2009.

Han, Enze, *Contestation and Adaptation: The Politics of National Identity in China*, New York: Oxford University Press, 2013.

Hänni, Adiran and Lukas Hegi, "The Pakistani Godfather: The Inter-Services Intelligence and the Afghan Taliban 1994–2010", *Small Wars Journal*, 2 Apr. 2013, http://smallwarsjournal.com/jrnl/art/the-pakistani-godfather-the-inter-services-intelligence-and-the-afghan-taliban-1994–2010, last accessed 2 Feb. 2014.

Haqqani, Hussain, *Pakistan: Between Mosque and Military*, Washington, DC: Carnegie Endowment for International Peace, 2005.

Hashim, Sana, "India's Concern Over China-Pakistan Nuclear Nexus", New Delhi: Centre for Air Power Studies, Oct. 2013, http://capsindia.org/files/documents/CAPS_Infocus_SH2.pdf, last accessed 27 Dec. 2013.

Hatch, Orrin, *Square Peg: Confessions of a Citizen-Senator*, New York: Basic Books, 2003.

Hibbs, Mark, "The Future of the Nuclear Suppliers Group", Washington, DC: Carnegie Endowment for International Peace, 2011, http://carnegieendowment.org/files/future_nsg.pdf, last accessed 27 Dec. 2013.

——— "Pakistan Deal Signals China's Growing Nuclear Assertiveness", Washington, DC: Carnegie Endowment for International Peace, 27 Apr. 2010, http://carnegieendowment.org/2010/04/27/pakistan-deal-signals-china-s-growing-nuclear-assertiveness/4su?reloadFlag=1, last accessed 27 Dec. 2013.

Hierman, Brent, "The Pacification of Xinjiang: Uighur Protest and the Chinese State, 1988–2002", *Problems of Post-Communism*, May/June 2007, http://www.academia.edu/329476/The_Pacification_of_Xinjiang_Uighur_Protest_and_the_Chinese_State_1988–2002, last accessed 23 Jan. 2014.

Hoodbhoy, Pervez (ed.), *Confronting the Bomb, Pakistani and Indian Scientists Speak Out*, Karachi: Oxford University Press, 2013.

Hsiao, Hsin-Huang Michael and Cheng-Yi Lin, *The Rise of China: Beijing's Strategies and Implications for the Asia-Pacific*, New York: Routledge, 2009.

Hsiao, Russell and Glen E. Howard, "China Builds Closer Ties to Afghanistan

BIBLIOGRAPHY

through Wakhan Corridor", Jamestown Foundation, *China Brief*, Vol. 10, Issue 1, 7 Jan. 2010, http://www.jamestown.org/single/?no_cache=1&tx_ttnews%5Btt_news%5D=35879&tx_ttnews%5BbackPid%5D=7&cHash=8aeb0ffe75#.UuWXrZH0CqQ, last accessed 26 Jan. 2014.

Hu, Shisheng, "Afghan Reconstruction: Regional Challenges", CICIR Institute of South, South East Asian and Oceania Studies, 2012, http://d.wanfangdata.com.cn/periodical_xdgjgx-e2012z1004.aspx, last accessed 2 Feb. 2014.

Huasheng, Zhao, "China and Afghanistan: China's interest, stances and perspectives", Washington, DC: Centre for Strategic and International Studies, Mar. 2012, http://csis.org/files/publication/120322_Zhao_ChinaAfghan_web.pdf, last accessed 26 Jan. 2014.

Hundley, Tom, "Pakistan and India: Race to the End", *Foreign Policy*, 5 Sep. 2012, http://www.foreignpolicy.com/articles/2012/09/05/race_to_the_end, last accessed 22 Jan. 2014.

Huntzinger, Emmanuel, "Aynak Copper Mine: Opportunities and Threats for Development from a Sustainable Business Perspective", Integrity Watch Afghanistan, Jan. 2008, https://www.cimicweb.org/cmo/Afghanistan/Crisis%20Documents/Economic%20Stabilization/Recent%20Publications/Aynak%20Copper%20Mine%20Report%20IWA.pdf, last accessed 27 Jan. 2014.

Hussain, Zahid, *The Scorpion's Tail: The Relentless Rise of Islamic Militants in Pakistan—And How It Threatens America*, New York: Free Press, 2010.

Ispahani, Mahnaz Z., *Roads and Rivals: The Political Uses of Access in the Borderlands of Asia*, Ithaca, NY: Cornell University Press, 1989.

Jamal, Arif, *Shadow War: The Untold Story of Jihad in Kashmir*, New York: Melville House, 2009.

——— "Pakistani Taliban Widen the Civil War—Against Fellow Deobandis", 14 April 2011, *Terrorism Monitor*, Vol 9, Issue 15, http://www.refworld.org/docid/4dad7e982.html, last accessed 27 May 2014.

Jeffreys-Jones, Rhodri, and Christopher M. Andrew (ed.), *Eternal Vigilance? 50 Years of the CIA*, Newbury Park: Frank Cass and Company, 1997.

Jisi, Wang, "Westward: China's Rebalancing Geopolitical Strategy", International and Strategic Studies Report 73, Peking University, Oct. 2012.

Johnson, Thomas, and Chris Mason, "Understanding the Taliban and Insurgency in Afghanistan", Calhoun Institutions Archive of the Naval Postgraduate School, Winter 2007, Elsevier Limited, http://hdl.handle.net/10945/30471, last accessed 27 Jan. 2014.

Johnston, Alastair Lain, and Robert S. Ross (ed.), *New Directions in the Study of China's Foreign Policy*, Stanford, CA: Stanford University Press, 2006.

Joshi, Shashank, "Pakistan's Tactical Nuclear Nightmare: Déjà vu?", *Washington Quarterly*, Summer 2013, http://csis.org/files/publication/TWQ_13Summer_Joshi.pdf, last accessed 27 Jan. 2014.

BIBLIOGRAPHY

Kan, Shirley A., *China-U.S. Aircraft Collision Incident of April 2001: Assessments and Policy Implications*, CRS Report for Congress, Updated 10 Oct. 2001, https://www.fas.org/sgp/crs/row/RL30946.pdf, last accessed 26 Jan. 2014.

———— *China and Proliferation of Weapons of Mass Destruction and Missiles: Policy Issues*, CRS Report for Congress, Congressional Research Office, 7–5700, 23 Dec. 2009.

Kaplan, Robert D., *Soldiers of God: With Islamic Warriors in Afghanistan and Pakistan*, New York: Vintage Departures, 2001.

———— *Monsoon: The Indian Oceans and the Future of American Power*, New York: Random House, 2010.

Kemp, Geoffrey, *The East Moves West: India, China, and Asia's Growing Presence in the Middle East*, Washington, DC: Brookings Institution Press, 2010.

Keqiang, Li, "Seize the New Opportunities in China-India Strategic Cooperation", *Indian Review of Global Affairs*, 22 May 2013, http://www.irgamag.com/resources/interviews-documents/item/2851-seize-the-new-opportunities-in-china-india-strategic-cooperation, last accessed 18 Nov. 2013.

Khalid, Muhammad Mumtaz, *History of the Karakoram Highway, Vol. I and II*, Rawalpindi: Hamza, 2009.

Khan, Akbar Nasir, "Analyzing Suicide Attacks in Pakistan", *Conflict and Peace Studies*, Vol. 3, No. 4, Oct.-Dec. 2010, https://www.academia.edu/386901/Analysing_Suicide_Attacks_in_Pakistan, last accessed 27 Jan. 2014.

Khan, Feroz H., *Eating Grass: The Making of the Pakistani Bomb*, Stanford, CA: Stanford University Press, 2012.

Khan, Feroz H., Peter R. Lavoy and Christopher Clary, "Pakistan's Motivations and Calculations for the Kargil Conflict', in Peter R. Lavoy (ed.), *Asymmetric Warfare in South Asia: The Causes and Consequences of the Kargil Conflict*, New York: Cambridge University Press, 2009.

Khan, Gohar Ayub, *Glimpses Into the Corridors of Power*, Karachi: Oxford University Press, 2007.

Khan, Mohammed Ayub, "Pakistan Perspective," *Foreign Affairs*, Jul. 1960.

———— "India as a Factor in Sino-Pakistani Relations", *International Studies*, New Delhi, 9, No. 3, Jan. 1963.

Khan, Riaz Mohammad, "Pakistan-China Relations: An Overview", *Pakistan Horizon*, Vol. 64, No. 4, Oct. 2011.

———— *Afghanistan and Pakistan: Conflict, Extremism, and Resistance to Modernity*, Karachi: Oxford University Press, 2010.

Khan, Sultan M., *Memories & Reflections of a Pakistani Diplomat*, Oxford: The Alden Press, 1997.

Khan, Zahid Ali, "China's Gwadar and India's Chahbahar: an Analysis of Sino-India Geo-strategic and Economic Competition", *Strategic Studies*, Winter 2012 & Spring 2013, Vol. XXXII & XXXIII, No. 4 & 1, http://www.issi.

org.pk/publication-files/1379479541_87064200.pdf/, last accessed 26 Jan. 2014.

Kissinger, Henry, *The White House Years*, London: Phoenix Press, 1979.

Klaidman, Daniel, *Kill or Capture: The War on Terror and the Soul of the Obama Presidency*, Boston: Houghton Mifflin Harcourt, 2012.

Knight, Edward F., *Where Three Empires Meet: A Narrative of Recent Travel in Kashmir, Western Tibet, Gilgit, and the Adjoining Countries*, New York: Longmans, 1893.

Korski, Daniel and John Fox, "Can China Save Afghanistan?", European Council on Foreign Relations, 29 Sep. 2008, http://www.ecfr.eu/content/entry/can_china_save_afghanistan/, last accessed 20 Nov. 2013.

Krepon, Michael, "The Arms Crawl that Wasn't", *Arms Control Wonk*, 2 Nov. 2011, http://krepon.armscontrolwonk.com/archive/3265/the-arms-crawl-that-wasn't, last accessed 27 Jan. 2014.

———— "Pakistan's Nuclear Strategy and Deterrence Stability", Stimson Center, Dec. 2012, http://www.stimson.org/images/uploads/research-pdfs/Krepon_-_Pakistan_Nuclear_Strategy_and_Deterrence_Stability.pdf, last accessed 27 Jan. 2014.

Kux, Dennis, *The United States and Pakistan 1947–2000: Disenchanted Allies*, Washington, DC: Woodrow Wilson Centre Press, 2001.

Lamb, Alastair, "Crisis in Kashmir 1947–1966", *Modern Asia Studies*, Vol. 2, Issue 2, Mar. 1968.

Langewiesche, William, *The Atomic Bazaar: The Rise of The Nuclear Poor*, London: Penguin Books, 2007.

Laruelle, Marlene and Sebastian Peyrouse (eds), *Mapping Central Asia: Indian Perceptions and Strategies*, Farnham: Ashgate, 2011.

Lattimore, Owen, *Inner Asian Frontiers of China*, New York: American Geographical Society, 1940.

Lavoy, Peter (ed.), *Asymmetric Warfare in South Asia: The Causes and Consequences of the Kargil Conflict*, New York: Cambridge University Press, 2009.

Leavitt, Sandra Ruth, "Persuasion, Coercion, and Neglect: Understanding State Policy and the Mobilization of Muslim Minorities in Asia", PhD Dissertation, Georgetown University, 2007.

Leese, Daniel, *Mao Cult: Rhetoric and Ritual in China's Cultural Revolution*, New York: Cambridge University Press, 2011.

LeVine, Steve, *The Oil and the Glory: The Pursuit of Empire and Fortune on the Caspian Sea*, New York: Random House, 2007.

Levy, Adrian, *The Siege: Three Days of Terror Inside the Taj*, London: Viking Penguin, 2013.

Levy, Adrian and Catherine Scott-Clark, *Nuclear Deception: The Dangerous Relationship between the United States and Pakistan*, New York: Walker Publishing Company, 2007.

BIBLIOGRAPHY

Levy, Adrian and Catherine Scott-Clark, *Deception: Pakistan, the United States, and the Secret Trade in Nuclear Weapons*, New York: Walker Publishing Company, 2010.

Lewis, Jeffrey, "Saudi Missile Claims", *Arms Control Wonk*, 8 Jun. 2010, http://lewis.armscontrolwonk.com/archive/2761/china-and-saudi-bms, last accessed 18 Nov. 2013.

———— "China's New Centrifuge Plants", *Arms Control Wonk*, 17 Sep. 2013, http://lewis.armscontrolwonk.com/archive/6826/chinas-new-centrifuge-plants, last accessed 18 Nov. 2013.

———— "Pakistan's Nuclear Artillery", *Arms Control Wonk*, 12 Dec. 2011, http://lewis.armscontrolwonk.com/archive/4866/pakistans-nuclear-artillery, last accessed 18 Nov. 2013.

Lewis, John Wilson and Xue Litai, *China Builds the Bomb*, Stanford, CA: Stanford University Press, 1988.

Li, Zhisui, *The Private Life of Chairman Mao: The Memoirs of Mao's Personal Physician*, London: Random House, 1996.

Lieberthal, Kenneth, "The American Pivot to Asia", *Foreign Policy*, 21 Dec. 2011, http://www.foreignpolicy.com/articles/2011/12/21/the_american_pivot_to_asia., last accessed 26 Jan. 2014.

Lieven, Anatol, *Pakistan: A Hard Country*, New York: Public Affairs, 2011.

Lintner, Bertil, *Great Game East: India, China and the Struggle for Asia's Most Volatile Frontier*, New Delhi: Harpers Today, 2012.

Lod, Sardar F.S., "Indian Air Force In Kargil Operations", *Defence Notes*, Jan. 2000, http://www.Defencejournal.Com/2000/Jan/Indian-Airforce.Htm, last accessed 26 Jan. 2014.

Lucas, Sean, "China Enters the Nuclear Suppliers Group: Positive Steps in the Global Campaign against Nuclear Weapons Proliferation", *Nuclear Threat Initiative*, 1 Nov. 2004, http://www.nti.org/analysis/articles/china-enters-nuclear-suppliers-group/, last accessed 27 Jan. 2014.

MacDonald, Myra, *Heights of Madness: One Woman's Journey in Pursuit of a Secret War*, New Delhi: Rupa & Co., 2007.

Macfarquhar, Roderick and Michael Schoenhals, *Mao's Last Revolution*, Cambridge, MA: Harvard University Press, 2009.

Mahsud, Mansur Khan, "The Battle for Pakistan: Militancy and Conflict in South Waziristan", New America Foundation, Apr. 2010, http://www.operationspaix.net/DATA/DOCUMENT/4799-v-The_Battle_for_Pakistan___Militancy_and_Conflict_in_South_Waziristan.pdf, last accessed 17 Jan. 2014.

Majeed, Abdul and Anwar Kamal, "Gwadar: Integrated Development Vision", Government of Baluchistan, Pakistan and IUCN, Pakistan, 2007, http://cmsdata.iucn.org/downloads/pk_gwadar_idv.pdf, last accessed 13 Dec. 2013.

Malik, Mohan, "Dragon on Terrorism: Assessing China's Tactical Gains and

BIBLIOGRAPHY

Strategic Losses Post-September 11", Carlisle, PA: Strategic Studies Institute, U.S. Army War College, Oct. 2002, http://www.Strategicstudiesinstitute. Army.Mil/Pdffiles/Pub57.Pdf, last accessed 27 Jan. 2014.

———— "The China Factor in the India-Pakistan Conflict", Carlisle, PA: Strategic Studies Institute, U.S. Army War College, 2003, http://strategic-studiesinstitute.army.mil/pubs/parameters/Articles/03spring/malik.pdf, last accessed 26 Jan. 2013.

Mancall, Mark, *China at the Center: 300 Year of Foreign Policy*, New York: The Free Press, 1984.

Mann, James, *About Face*, New York: Knopf, 1998.

Manthan, Samudra and Raja Mohan, *Sino-Indian Rivalry in the Indo-Pacific*, Washington, DC: Carnegie Endowment for International Peace, 485.6659 [IPAD 3rd Generation; MD366LL/A version].

Markey, Daniel, *No Exit from Pakistan: America's Tortured Relationship with Islamabad*, New York: Cambridge University Press, 2013.

Marten, Kimberly, "Understanding the Impact of the K2 Closure", *PONARS Policy Memo*, No. 401, Dec. 2005.

Medeiros, Evan, *Reluctant Restraint: The Evolution of China's Nonproliferation Policies and Practices, 1980–2004*, Stanford, CA: Stanford University Press, 2007.

Millward, James, "Violent Separatism in Xinjiang: A Critical Assessment", East-West Center, Policy Studies 6, 2005, http://www.eastwestcenter.org/fileadmin/stored/pdfs/PS006.pdf, last accessed 27 Jan. 2014.

Millward, James and Nabijan Tursun, "Political History and Strategies of Control, 1884–1978", in Frederick Starr (ed.), *Xinjiang: China's Muslim Borderland*, New York, London: M.E. Sharpe, 2004.

Mir, Amir, "Last Abdullah Mehsud", Raman's Pashtun Belt Database, 4 Aug. 2007, http://ramanspashtunbeltdatabase.blogspot.com/2008/01/late-abdul-lah-mehsud.html, last accessed 16 Jan. 2014.

Moran, Michael, "The 'Airlift of Evil'", Council on Foreign Relations, 29 Nov. 2001, http://www.cfr.org/pakistan/airlift-evil/p10301, last accessed 9 Dec. 2013.

Morgan, Gerald, *Anglo-Russian Rivalry in Central Asia: 1810–1895*, New York: Routledge, 1981.

Mulvenon, James, *Soldiers of Fortune: The Rise and Fall of the Chinese Military-Business Complex, 1978–1998*, Armonk, NY: M.E. Sharpe/East Gate Books, 2001.

———— "Chen Xiaogong: A Political Biography", *China Leadership Monitor*, No. 22, Oct. 2013, http://media.hoover.org/sites/default/files/documents/CLM22JM.pdf, last accessed 18 Nov. 2013.

Muralidharan, Sukumar, "High Stakes, Hardening Positions", *Frontline*, Vol. 16,

Issue 13, 19 Jun.—2 Jul. 1999, http://www.hindu.com/fline/fl1613/161312 50.htm, last accessed 27 Jan. 2014.

Murray, Scot Tanner, Kerry B. Dumbaugh and Ian M. Easton, "Distracted Antagonists, Wary Partners: China and India Assess their Security Relations", CNA China Studies, Sep. 2011, http://www.cna.org/sites/default/files/ research/Distracted%20Antagonists%2C%20Wary%20Partners%20D00 25816%20A1.pdf, last accessed 27 Jan. 2014.

Musharraf, Pervez, *In the Line of Fire: A Memoir*, New York: Free Press, 2006.

Nadin, Rebecca Louise, "China and the Shanghai 5/Shanghai Cooperation Organization: 1996–2006, A Decade on the New Diplomatic Frontier", PhD Dissertation, University of Sheffield, 2007, http://ethos.bl.uk/Order Details.do?uin=uk.bl.ethos.443900, last accessed 27 Jan. 2014.

Naeem, Abdul, "Kargil: Lessons Learned on Both Sides" in Ashley Tellis, C. Christine Fair and Jamison Jo Melby, *Limited Conflicts under the Nuclear Umbrella: Indian and Pakistani Lessons from the Kargil Crisis*, Santa Monica, CA: RAND, 2001.

Naughton, Barry, "The Third Front: Defence Industrialisation in the Chinese Interior", *China Quarterly*, No. 115, Sep. 1988, http://journals.cambridge. org/action/displayAbstract?fromPage=online&aid=3546864, last accessed 24 Jan. 2014.

Nawaz, Shuja, *Crossed Swords: Pakistan, Its Army, and the Wars Within*, Karachi: Oxford University Press, 2008.

Nayak, Polly and Michael Krepon, "U.S. Crisis Management in South Asia's Twin Peaks Crisis", Stimson Center, 2002, http://www.stimson.org/images/ uploads/research-pdfs/USCrisisManagement.pdf, last accessed 23 Jan. 2014.

Nickles, David P., Adam Howard and Office of the Historian U.S. State Department (eds), *Foreign Relations of the United States, 1977–1980, Volume XIII, China*, Washington, DC: Bureau of Public Affairs, 2013.

O'Neill, Jim, Dominic Wilson, Roopa Purushothaman and Anna Stupnytska, "How Solid are the BRICs?", Global Economics Paper No. 134, Goldman Sachs, 1 Dec. 2005, http://www.sdnbd.org/sdi/issues/economy/BRICs_3_12–1–05.pdf, last accessed 27 Jan. 2014.

Oresman, Matthew, "Repaving the Silk Road: China's Emergence in Central Asia", in Joshua Eisenmann, Eric Heginbotham and Derek Mitchell (eds), *China and the Developing World: Beijing's Strategy for the Twenty-First Century*, Armonk, NY: M.E. Sharpe/East Gate Books, 2007.

Ottaway, David B., *The King's Messenger: Prince Bandar bin Sultan and America's Tangled Relationship with Saudi Arabia*, New York: Walker Publishing Company, 2008.

Paal, Douglas H., "China and the East Asian Security Environment: Complementarity and Competition", in Vogel, Ezra, *Living with China: U.S.-China Relations in the Twenty First Century*, New York: W.W. Norton, 1997.

Pande, Aparna, *Explaining Pakistan's Foreign Policy: Escaping India*, New York: Routledge, 2011.

Pant, Harsh V., "China and India: A Rivalry Takes Shape", *E-Notes*, Foreign Policy Research Institute, Jun. 2011, http://www.fpri.org/enotes/201106. pant.china_india.pdf, last accessed 27 Jan. 2014.

——— "China reaches to India on Afghanistan", Observer Research Foundation, 8 Jan. 2014, http://orfonline.org/cms/sites/orfonline/modules/analysis/ AnalysisDetail.html?cmaid=61496&mmacmaid=61497, last accessed 27 Jan. 2014.

Pantucci, Raffaello, "Uyghurs Convicted in East Turkestan Islamic Movement", *Terrorism Monitor*, Vol. 8, Issue 29, 22 Jul. 2010, http://www.jamestown.org/ single/?no_cache=1&tx_ttnews[tt_news]=36656#.UucOojo1hMs, last accessed 27 Jan. 2014.

——— "A Post-Mortem Analysis of Turkistani Amir Emeti Yakuf: A Death that Sparked More Questions than Answers", *Terrorism Monitor*, Vol. 3, Issue 10, 1 Nov. 2012, http://mlm.jamestown.org/single/?tx_ttnews%5Btt_news %5D=40043&tx_ttnews%5BbackPid%5D=551&cHash=e13aadc198482b 3c8c34129c423af1f6#.UubQVJH0AUs, last accessed 20 Nov. 2013.

Perkovich, George, *India's Nuclear Bomb: The Impact on Global Proliferation*, Los Angeles: University of California Press, 1999.

Petersen, Alexandros, "Afghanistan Has What China Wants", *Foreign Policy*, 18 Apr. 2013, http://southasia.foreignpolicy.com/posts/2013/04/18/afghani-stan_has_what_china_wants, last accessed 27 Jan. 2014.

Pillsbury, Michael, "U.S.-Chinese Military Ties?", *Foreign Policy*, No. 20, Autumn 1975.

Pollpeter, Kevin, *U.S.-China Security Management: Assessing the Military-to-Military Relationship*, Santa Monica, CA: RAND Corporation, 2004.

Pope, Hugh, *Sons of the Conquerors: The Rise of the Turkic World*, London: Duckworth Publishers/Overlook Press, 2006.

Prasad, S.N., *Official History of the 1971 India Pakistan War*, History Division, Ministry of Defence, Government of India, New Delhi, 1992.

Rajagopalan, Rajeswari Pillai and Rahul Prakesh, "Sino-Indian Border Infra-structure: an Update", Observer Research Foundation, Occasional Paper #42, May 2013, http://www.observerindia.com/cms/sites/orfonline/mod-ules/occasionalpaper/attachments/Occasional42_1369136836914.pdf, last accessed 26 Jan. 2014.

Raman, B., "Explosions in Xinjiang", South Asia Analysis Group, Paper no. 1232, 27 Jan. 2005, http://web.archive.org/web/20070927194700/ http://www.saag.org/papers13/paper1232.html, last accessed 2 Feb. 2014.

——— *The Kaoboys of & R&AW: Down Memory Lane*, New Delhi: Lancer Publishers, 2007.

BIBLIOGRAPHY

Rasanayagam, Angelo, *Afghanistan: A Modern History*, New York: I.B. Tauris, 2005.

Rashid, Ahmed, "Taliban temptation", *Far Eastern Economic Review*, 11 Mar. 1999.

———— *Taliban: Militant Islam, Oil and Fundamentalism in Central Asia*, New Haven: Yale Nota Bene, 2001.

———— *Jihad: The Rise of Militant Islam in Central Asia*, New York: Penguin Group, 2003.

———— *Descent into Chaos: How the War against Islamic Extremism is Being Lost in Pakistan, Afghanistan and Central Asia*, London: Penguin Books, 2008.

Rashid, Harun ur, "BCIM Economic Corridor: A Giant Step Towards Integration," Institute for Peace and Conflict Studies, Article #4172, 12 Nov. 2013, http://www.ipcs.org/article/india/bcim-economic-corridor-a-giant-step-towards-integration-4172.html, last accessed 26 Jan. 2014.

Reed, J. Todd, and Diana Raschke, *The ETIM: China's Islamic Militants and the Global Terrorist Threat*, Washington, DC: Library of Congress, 2010.

Reed, Thomas C., and Danny B. Stillman, *The Nuclear Express: A Political History of the Bomb and Its Proliferation*, Minneapolis: Zenith Press, 2009.

Rehman, Fazlur, "Pakistan-China Trade and Investment Relations", Institute of Strategic Studies Islamabad, 2011, http://www.issi.org.pk/publication-files/1299822989_45060000.pdf, last accessed 23 Dec. 2013.

———— "Pakistan-China Economic Relations Opportunities and Challenges", Institute of Strategic Studies, Islamabad, 2006, http://www.issi.org.pk/old-site/ss_Detail.php?datald=390, last accessed 2 Feb. 2014.

———— paraphrased in "Pakistan-China Economic Relations with Special Focus on Thar Coal, Kashgar Special Economic Zone and Gwadar Sea Port", Islamabad Policy Research Institute conference report, 13 Mar. 2013, http://ipripak.org/conf/pcer.pdf, last accessed 26 Jan. 2014.

Rice, Condoleezza, *No Higher Honor: A Memoir of My Years in Washington*, New York: Random House, 2012.

Richelson, Jeffrey T., "The Wizards of Langley: The CIA's Directorate of Science and Technology", in Rhodri Jeffreys-Jones and Christopher M. Andrew (eds), *Eternal Vigilance? 50 Years of the CIA*, Newbury Park: Frank Cass and Company, 1997.

Riedel, Bruce, "American Diplomacy and the 1999 Kargil Summit at Blair House", in Peter Lavoy (ed.), *Asymmetric Warfare in South Asia: The Causes and Consequences of the Kargil Conflict*, New York: Cambridge University Press, 2009.

———— "The Battle for Pakistan", *Yale Global*, 2 Jun. 2011, http://yaleglobal.yale.edu/content/battle-pakistan, last accessed 26 Jan. 2014.

———— *Avoiding Armageddon: America, India and Pakistan to the Brink and Back*, Washington, DC: Brookings Institution Press, 2013.

BIBLIOGRAPHY

————— "Pakistan, Taliban and the Afghan Quagmire", Brookings Institution, 24 Aug. 2013, http://www.brookings.edu/research/opinions/2013/08/26-pakistan-influence-over-afghan-taliban-riedel, last accessed 27 Jan. 2014.

Roggio, Bill, "U.S. Airstrike Killed 15 Turkistan Islamic Party Fighters in Afghanistan", *Long War Journal*, 23 Jan. 2010, http://www.longwarjournal.org/archives/2010/01/us_airstrike_killed_1.php, last accessed 27 Jan. 2014.

————— "Chinese Terrorist Leader Abdul Haq al Turkistani is Dead: Pakistani Interior Minister", *Long War Journal*, 7 May 2010, http://www.longwarjournal.org/archives/2010/05/chinese_terrorist_le.php, last accessed 27 Jan. 2014.

————— "Al Qaeda Appoints New Leader of Forces in Pakistan's Tribal Areas", *Long War Journal*, 9 May 2011, http://www.longwarjournal.org/archives/2011/05/al_qaeda_appoints_ne_2.php, last accessed 27 Jan. 2014.

————— "Taliban Assault Team Attacks Pakistani Navy Base", *Long War Journal*, 22 May 2011, http://www.longwarjournal.org/archives/2011/05/pakistani_navy_base.php, last accessed 27 Jan. 2014.

————— "6 Uzbeks Killed in North Waziristan Drone Strike", *Long War Journal*, 29 Jul. 2012, http://www.longwarjournal.org/archives/2012/07/six_uzbeks_killed_in.php, last accessed 27 Jan. 2014.

————— "Turkistan Islamic Party Leader Thought Killed in US Drone Strike", *Long War Journal*, 25 Aug. 2012, http://www.longwarjournal.org/archives/2012/08/turkistan_islamic_pa_1.php, last accessed 27 Jan. 2014.

————— "Zawahiri Eulogizes Abu Yahya al Libi", *Long War Journal*, 11 Sep. 2012, http://www.longwarjournal.org/threat-matrix/archives/2012/09/zawahiri_eulogizes_abu_yahya_a.php, last accessed 27 Jan. 2014.

————— "US Drones Kill 4 Turkistan Islamic Party Fighters in Pakistan Strike", *Long War Journal*, 31 Aug. 2013, http://www.longwarjournal.org/archives/2013/08/us_drones_kill_4_tur.php, last accessed 27 Jan. 2014.

Ross, Robert S., "The 1995–1996 Taiwan Strait Confrontation Coercion, Credibility, and the Use of Force", *International Security*, 25:2, Fall 2000, http://ppe.wiki.hci.edu.sg/file/view/ross3.pdf, last accessed 27 Jan. 2014.

Rubin, Barnett R., *The Fragmentation of Afghanistan: State Formation and Collapse in the International System*, New Haven: Yale University Press, 2002.

————— *Afghanistan in the Post-Cold War Era*, New York: Oxford University Press, 2013.

Rubin, Barnett R., and Ahmed Rashid, "From Great Game to Grand Bargain", *Foreign Affairs*, November/December 2008, http://www.foreignaffairs.com/articles/64604/barnett-r-rubin-and-ahmed-rashid/from-great-game-to-grand-bargain, last accessed 26 Jan. 2014.

Saalman, Lora, "Divergence Similarity and Symmetry in Sino-Indian Threat Perceptions", *Journal of International Affairs*, Spring/Summer 2011, Vol. 64,

BIBLIOGRAPHY

No. 2, http://carnegieendowment.org/files/Divergence_Similarity_and_Symmetry_in_Sino-Indian_Threat_Perceptions.pdf, last accessed 27 Jan. 2014.

Sanger, David E., *The Inheritance: The World Obama Confronts and the Challenges to American Power*, London: Bantam Press, 2009.

———— *Confront and Conceal: Obama's Secret Wars and Surprising Use of American Power*, New York: Crown Publishing, 2012.

Saran, Shyam, "Is India's Nuclear Deterrent Credible?" (Speech at the India Habitat Centre, New Delhi, 24 Apr. 2013), http://southasiamonitor.org/detail.php?type=pers&nid=4987, last accessed 26 Jan. 2014.

Sarathy Ghosh, Partha, *Cooperation and Conflict in South Asia*, New Delhi: Manohar Publishers, 1995.

Sartaz, Aziz, *Between Dreams and Realities: Some Milestones in Pakistan's History*, Karachi: Oxford University Press, 2010.

Sayigh, Yezid, "Arms Production in Pakistan and Iran: the Limits of Self Reliance", in Eric Arnett (ed.), *Military Capacity and the Risk of War: China, India, Pakistan and Iran*, New York: Oxford University Press, 1997.

Schein, Edgar H., *Coercive Persuasion: A Socio Psychological Analysis of the "Brainwashing" of American Civilian Prisoners by the Chinese Communists*, New York: W.W. Norton and Company, 1971.

Schmidle, Nicholas S., *To Live or to Perish Forever: Two Tumultuous Years in Pakistan*, New York: Henry Holt and Company, 2009.

Schofield, Victoria, *Kashmir in Conflict: India, Pakistan and the Unending War*, New York: I.B. Tauris, 2010.

Scott, David, *China Stands Up: The PRC and the International System*, New York: Routledge, 2007.

Shahzad, Syed Saleem, *Inside Al-Qaeda and the Taliban: Beyond the Bin Laden and 9/11*, London: Pluto Press, 2011.

Shambaugh, David (ed.), *Power Shift: China and East Asia's New Dynamics*, Los Angeles: University of California Press, 2005.

Shichor, Yitzhak, "Great Wall of Steel: Military and Strategy in Xinjiang", in S. Frederick Starr (ed.), *Xinjiang: China's Muslim Borderland*, London: M.E. Sharpe, 2004.

Shen, Simon (ed.), *China and Antiterrorism*, New York: Nova Science Publishers, 2007.

Short, Philip, *Mao: A Life*, London: John Murray, 1999.

Siddiqa-Agha, *Ayesha, Pakistan's Arms Procurement and Military Buildup, 1979–99*, Lahore: Sang-e-Meel, 2003.

Simha, Rakesh Krishan, "1971 War: How Russia Sank Nixon's Gunboat Diplomacy", *Russia and India Report*, 20 Dec. 2011, http://indrus.in/articles/2011/12/20/1971_war_how_russia_sank_nixons_gunboat_diplomacy_14041.html, last accessed 22 Jan. 2014.

Singh, R.S.N., *The Military Factor in Pakistan*, India: Lancer Publishers, 2008.

Singh, Swaran, *China-Pakistan Strategic Cooperation: India Perspectives*, New Delhi: Manohar Publishers, 2007.

Sirrs, Julie R., *The Taliban's Foreign Fighters: A Report Prepared for the Committee for a Free Afghanistan*, Washington, DC: Committee for a Free Afghanistan, 21 January 2001.

Sisson, Richard and Leo E. Rose, *War and Secession: Pakistan, India, and the Creation of Bangladesh*, Berkeley, CA: University of California Press, 1990.

Small, Andrew, "Afghanistan-Pakistan: Bringing China (back) in", GMF *Transatlantic Take*, 23 Oct. 2009, http://blog.gmfus.org/2009/10/23/afghan-istan-pakistan-bringing-china-back-in/, last accessed 2 Feb. 2014.

———— "China's Caution on Afghanistan-Pakistan", *Washington Quarterly*, Vol. 33, Issue 3, 2010, http://www.tandfonline.com/doi/abs/10.1080/0163 660X.2010.492343#.UvUMkHddX8k, last accessed 2 Feb. 2014.

———— "China's Afghan Moment", *Foreign Policy*, 3 Oct. 2012, http://www.foreignpolicy.com/articles/2012/10/03/chinas_afghan_moment, last accessed 2 Feb. 2014.

———— "Why is China Talking to the Taliban?", *Foreign Policy*, 21 Jun. 2013, http://www.foreignpolicy.com/articles/2013/06/20/why_is_china_talking_to_the_taliban, last accessed 2 Feb. 2014.

Smith, David O., "The US Experience With Tactical Nuclear Weapons: Lessons For South Asia", Stimson Centre, 4 Mar. 2013, http://www.stimson.org/images/uploads/research-pdfs/David_Smith_Tactical_Nuclear_Weapons.pdf, last accessed 27 Jan. 2014.

Smith, R. Jeffrey and Joby Warrick, "What Happens in Vienna ...", *Arms Control Wonk*, 12 Sep. 2008, http://lewis.armscontrolwonk.com/archive/2039/what-happened-friday-night, last accessed 27 Jan. 2014.

Sokoloski, Henry D., "Pakistan's Nuclear Future: Worries Beyond War", Carlisle, PA: Strategic Studies Institute, U.S. Army War College, Jan. 2008, http://www.strategicstudiesinstitute.army.mil/pdffiles/pub832.pdf, last accessed 22 Jan. 2014.

Stares, Paul, "Managing Instability on China's Periphery", Council on Foreign Relations, 16 Sep. 2011, http://www.cfr.org/thinktank/cpa/asia_security.html, last accessed 27 Jan. 2014.

Starr, S. Frederick (ed.), *Xinjiang: China's Muslim Borderland*, London: M.E. Sharpe, 2004.

Suettinger, Robert L., *Beyond Tiananmen: The Politics of U.S.-China Relations 1989–2000*, Washington, DC: Brookings Institution Press, 2003.

Swaine, Michael D., *America's Challenge: Engaging a Rising China in the Twenty-First Century*, Washington, DC: Carnegie Endowment for International Peace, 2011.

Swami, Praveen, *India, Pakistan and The Secret Jihad: The Covert War in Kashmir, 1947–2004*, New York: Routledge, 2007.

Syed, Anwar Hussain, *China & Pakistan: Diplomacy of an Entente Cordiale*, London: Oxford University Press, 1974.

Tellis, Ashley, C. Christine Fair and Jamison Jo Melby, *Limited Conflicts under the Nuclear Umbrella: Indian and Pakistani Lessons from the Kargil Crisis*, Santa Monica, CA: RAND, 2001.

――― *India as a New Global Power: An Action Agenda for the United States*, Washington, DC: Carnegie Endowment for International Peace, 2005.

――― "The Merits of Dehyphenation: Explaining U.S. Success in Engaging India and Pakistan", *Washington Quarterly*, Autumn 2008, https://csis.org/files/publication/twq08autumntellis.pdf, last accessed 20 Dec. 2013.

Thompson, Drew, "Border Burdens: China's Response to the Myanmar Refugee Crisis", Centre for the National Interest, 2009, http://cftni.org/Thompson-Border-Burdens-China-Security-2009.pdf, last accessed 2 Feb. 2014.

Tyler, Patrick, *A Great Wall: Six Presidents and China: An Investigative History*, New York: A Century Foundation Book, 1999.

Van Wie Davis, Elizabeth, "Uyghur Muslim Ethnic Separatism in Xinjiang", China Asia-Pacific Center for Security Studies, Jan. 2008, http://www.dtic.mil/cgi-bin/GetTRDoc?AD=ADA493744, last accessed 26 Jan. 2014.

Vertzberger, Yaacov Y.I., *China's Southwestern Strategy: Encirclement and Counterencirclement*, New York: Praeger, 1985.

Vogel, Ezra F., *Deng Xiaoping and the Transformation of China*, Cambridge, MA: Harvard University Press, 2011.

Wayne, Martin I., *China's War on Terrorism: Counter-insurgency, Politics, and Internal Security*, New York: Routledge, 2009.

Wiegand, Krista Eileen, *Enduring Territorial Disputes: Strategies of Bargaining, Coercive Diplomacy and Settlement*, London: University of Georgia Press, 2011.

Wilcox, Wayne, *India, Pakistan and the Rise of China*, New York: Columbia University Press, 1956.

Wolf Jr, Charles, Xiao Wang and Eric Warner (eds), "China's Foreign Aid and Government-Sponsored Investment Activities: Scale, Content, Destinations and Implications", Santa Monica, CA: RAND Corporation, 2013, http://www.rand.org/content/dam/rand/pubs/research_reports/RR100/RR118/RAND_RR118.pdf, last accessed 11 Dec. 2013.

Wolpert, Stanley, *Zulfi Bhutto of Pakistan: His Life and Times*, New York: Oxford University Press, 1993.

Woodward, Bob, *Veil: The Secret Wars of the CIA, 1981–1987*, New York: Simon & Schuster, 2005.

――― *Obama's Wars*, New York: Simon & Schuster, 2010.

BIBLIOGRAPHY

Wuthnow, Joel, *Chinese Diplomacy and the UN Security Council: Beyond the Veto*, Oxford and New York: Routledge, 2013.

Yeager, James R., *The Aynak Copper Tender: Implications for Afghanistan and the West*, Tucson: Skyline Laboratories and Assayers, 2009.

Yousaf, Mohammad and Mark Adkin, *Afghanistan-The Bear Trap: The Defeat of a Superpower*, Barnsley: Leo Cooper/Pen and Sword Books, 2001.

Yusuf, Shahid, "Can Chinese FDI Accelerate Pakistan's Growth?", International Growth Centre, 4 Feb. 2013, http://www.theigc.org/publications/working-paper/can-chinese-fdi-accelerate-pakistan%E2%80%99s-growth, last accessed 26 Jan. 2014.

Zaif, Abd al-Salam, *My Life with the Taliban*, New York: Columbia University Press, 2010.

Zenn, Jacob, "Insurgency in Xinjiang Complicates Chinese-Pakistani Relations", *Terrorism Monitor*, Vol. 10, Issue 8, 20 Apr. 2012, http://www.freerepublic.com/focus/f-news/2875031/posts, last accessed 27 Jan. 2014.

Zetterlund, Kristina (ed.), *Pakistan—Consequences of Deteriorating Security in Afghanistan*, Stockholm: Swedish Defence Research Agency, 2009.

Zhang, Feng, "China's New Thinking on Alliances", *Survival*, Oct.-Nov. 2012, http://www.iiss.org/en/publications/survival/sections/2012–23ab/survival—global-politics-and-strategy-october-november-2012-fda3/54–5–09-zhang-dd4b, last accessed 20 Nov. 2013.

Zhao, Suisheng, *Chinese Foreign Policy: Pragmatism and Strategic Behaviour*, Armonk, NY: M.E. Sharpe/East Gate Books, 2004.

Zyck, Steven A., "The Role of China in Afghanistan's Economic Development & Reconstruction", *Afghanistan In Transition*, Mar. 2012, https://www.cimicweb.org/cmo/afg/Documents/Economic/Role_of_China_in_Afghanistan_Economy_Development.pdf, last accessed 26 Jan. 2014.

Official documents

Aasif Inam, "Foreign Direct Investment in Pakistan Telecommunication Sector", Pakistan Telecommunication Authority Federal Bureau of Statistics, Government of Pakistan, http://www.itu.int/ITU-D/finance/work-cost-tariffs/events/tariff-seminars/Korea-07/presentations/FDI_Aasif_Inam.pdf, last accessed 23 Jan. 2014.

Banerjee, Purnendu Kumar, "China in India and Pakistan," speech to the United States Congress, *Congressional Record*, Washington, DC, 13 June 1966.

Bhutto, Zulfikar Ali, "If I am Assassinated", Supreme Court of Pakistan Criminal Appeal No. 11 of 1978, http://www.idsa-india.org/an-nov8–3.html, last accessed 18 Nov. 2013.

Central Intelligence Agency, Memorandum for Frank Carlucci, "Risk Assessment of the Sale of the e69", Document number CIA-RD84B000 49R001604090013–3, approved for release 14 June 2007, http://s3.documentcloud.org/documents/347031/doc-15-a-11–8–82.txt, last accessed 23 Jan. 2014.

Clinton, Bill and Jiang Zemin (statements issued by), "US-China Joint Statement On South Asia", Beijing, official White House text, 27 June 1998, http://www.acronym.org.uk/proliferation-challenges/nuclear-weapons-possessors/china/us-china-joint-statement-south-asia-june-1998, last accessed 23 Jan. 2014.

"Convention between Great Britain, China and Tibet", Reproduced for the Islamabad Policy Research Institute *Fact File*, 3 Jul. 1914, http://www.ipripak.org/factfiles/ff43.shtml, last accessed 2 Feb. 2014.

Defense Intelligence Agency, "Nuclear Weapons Systems in China", Defense Estimative Brief, 24 April 1984, http://www2.gwu.edu/~nsarchiv/news/199 90527/01–01.htm, last accessed 18 Nov. 2013.

Director of Central Intelligence, "Chinese Policy and Practices Regarding Sensitive Nuclear Transfers", Special National Intelligence Estimate, 20 Jan. 1983, declassified 30 May 2012, http://digitalarchive.wilsoncenter.org/document/116893, last accessed 18 Nov. 2013.

Donor Financial Review, Islamic Republic of Afghanistan Ministry of Finance, Report 1388, Nov. 2009, p. 38, http://www.undp.org.af/Publications/Key Documents/Donor'sFinancialReview%20ReportNov2009.pdf, last accessed 27 Jan. 2014.

Embassy of the People's Republic of China in the Kingdom of Saudi Arabia, "President Jiang Zemin had a telephone conversation with Pakistani President Pervez Musharraf", 2 Feb. 2001, http://sa.china-embassy.org/eng/zt/fdkbzy/t154518.htm, last accessed 20 Nov. 2013.

Fifth BRICS Summit 26–27 March, "BRICS and Africa: Partnership for Development, Integration and Industrialisation", *eTHekwini Declaration*, 27 March 2013 http://www.brics5.co.za/fifth-brics-summit-declaration-and-action-plan/, last accessed 27 Jan. 2014.

Institute of Peace and Conflict Studies, "Indo-US Nuclear Deal at the Nuclear Suppliers Group", seminar report, 17 September 2008, http://www.ipcs.org/seminar/india/indo-us-nuclear-deal-at-the-nuclear-suppliers-group-619.html, last accessed 26 Jan. 2014.

Li Keqiang, Written Address at New Delhi Airport, 19 May 2013, http://www.fmprc.gov.cn/eng/topics/lkqipsg/t1043366.shtml, last accessed 26 Jan. 2014.

Ministry of Foreign Affairs, Islamic Republic of Afghanistan, "The First Afghanistan-China-Pakistan Trilateral Dialogue at General-Director Level Held in Beijing", 28 February 2012. Available at http://mfa.gov.af/en/news/7481.

Musharraf, Pervez, "Address at the inauguration of Gwadar Deep Seaport", 20 March 2007. Available at http://presidentmusharraf.wordpress.com/2008/01/07/gwadar-deep-seaport.

BIBLIOGRAPHY

———— "Address to Nation: Declaration of Emergency", Our Leader-Musharraf, 3 Nov. 2007, http://presidentmusharraf.wordpress.com/2007/06/02/musharraf-3-nov-emergency/, last accessed 25 Jan. 2014.

National Commission on Terrorist Attacks Upon the United States, "Al Qaeda Aims at the American Homeland", http://govinfo.library.unt.edu/911/report/911Report_Ch5.htm, last accessed 9 Dec. 2013.

National Security Archive, "The United States and Pakistan's Quest for the Bomb", The National Security Archive Electronic Briefing Book No. 333, 21 December 2010, http://www2.gwu.edu/~nsarchiv/nukevault/ebb333/, last accessed 27 Jan. 2014.

———— "New Documents Spotlight Reagan-era Tensions over Pakistani Nuclear Program", National Security Archive Electronic Briefing Book No. 377, Posted 27 April 2012, http://www2.gwu.edu/~nsarchiv/nukevault/ebb377/, last accessed 27 Jan. 2014.

National Security Council note on the Anderson Papers, requested by Henry Kissinger, 6 Jan. 1972, http://www2.gwu.edu/~nsarchiv/NSAEBB/NSAEBB79/BEBB45.pdf, last accessed 27 Jan. 2014.

"New Analysis: Bin Laden: Dissident Turns Pan-Islamist", *The Observer* in "Compilation of Usama Bin Laden Statements 1994–January 2004", FBIS Report, Jan. 2004, http://www.fas.org/irp/world/para/ubl-fbis.pdf, last accessed 22 Dec. 2013.

"Promote Friendship Between Our People and Work Together to Build a Bright Future", Speech by Xi Jinping, Nazarbayev University, Astana, Kazakhstan, 7 September 2013, http://www.fmprc.gov.cn/mfa_eng/wjb_663304/zzjg_663340/dozys_664276/gjlb_664280/3180_664322/3182_664326/t1078088.shtml, last accessed 25 May 2014.

Rahman, Hamoodur Rahman Commission, Supplementary Report, 23 Oct. 1974, http://www.pppusa.org/Acrobat/Hamoodur%20Rahman%20Commission%20Report.pdf, last accessed 22 Jan. 2014.

Rohrabacher, Dana (Letter from) to the Chairman of the House Committee on Foreign Affairs, to Leon E. Panetta, Secretary of Defense, 31 Oct. 2012, http://rohrabacher.house.gov/sites/rohrabacher.house.gov/files/documents/rep._rohrabacher_to_secretary_panetta_oct._31.pdf, last accessed 27 Jan. 2014.

Schajee, "Pakistan GDP Growth Rate 1951–2009", Data Source: Federal Bureau of Statistics, Government of Pakistan, http://upload.wikimedia.org/wikipedia/commons/2/2b/Pakistan_gdp_growth_rate.svg, last accessed 22 Dec. 2013.

Sharif, Nawaz and Shahbaz Sharif, "Victory Speech, Election 2013", Lahore, 11 May 2013.

UN Security Council press release SC/6979, "Security Council imposes wide new measures against Taliban authorities in Afghanistan, demands action on

terrorism", 19 Dec. 2000, http://www.un.org/News/Press/docs/2000/200
01219.sc6979.doc.html, last accessed 27 Jan. 2014.

United Nations Treaty Series, vol. 299, United Nations. Available at https://
treaties.un.org/doc/publication/unts/volume%20299/v299.pdf

U.S. Department of Defense Cable 06242 to State Department, Meeting
between Secretary of Defense Harold Brown and Vice Premier Deng
Xiaoping, Secretary of Defense, 8 January 1980, https://www.document-
cloud.org/documents/347015-doc-3-1-31-80.html, last accessed 18 Nov.
2013.

U.S. Department of Defense Joint Task Force, "JTF GTMO Detainee Assessment", Guantanamo Memorandum for Commander of the United States
Southern Command, 22 June 2007, http://wikileaks.org/gitmo/pdf/ch/
us9ch-000219dp.pdf, last accessed 27 Jan. 2014.

U.S. Department of State Memorandum of Conversation, RG 59, Records of
Henry Kissinger, Entry 5403, Box 5, Nodis Memoranda of Conversations,
31 October 1974, http://2001–2009.state.gov/r/pa/ho/frus/nixon/e8/97002.
htm, last accessed 18 Nov. 2013.

U.S. Department of State Office of the Historian, *Foreign Relations of the
United States, 1977–1980: Volume XIII, China, Document 290*, U.S.
7 Jan.1980, http://history.state.gov/historicaldocuments/frus1977–80v13/
d290, last accessed 14 Feb. 2014.

U.S. Embassy Pakistan Cable 15696 to State Department, "Pakistan Nuclear
Issue: Meeting with General Zia'" October 17, 1982, History and Public
Policy Program Digital Archive State Department Mandatory Declassification
Review release. Obtained and contributed by William Burr and included in
NPIHP Research Update #6, http://digitalarchive.wilsoncenter.org/docu-
ment/114254, last accessed 18 Nov. 2013.

U.S. State Department Archive, "Foreign Relations of the United States,
1969–1976, Volume XI, South Asia Crisis, 1971, Document 179",
U.S. State Department Archive, Washington DC, 4 Nov. 1971,
http://history.state.gov/historicaldocuments/frus1969–76v11/d179, last accessed 26 Jan. 2014.

———— "Conversation Between President Nixon and his Assistant for National
Security Affairs (Kissinger), Washington, December 6, 1971, 6:14–6:38
p.m.", Foreign Relations, 1969–1976, Volume E-7, Documents on South
Asia, 1969–1972. Available at http://2001–2009.state.gov/r/pa/ho/frus/
nixon/e7/48535.htm

U.S. State Department, Office of the Spokesman, "U.S.-China Strategic and
Economic Dialogue 2011 Outcomes of the Strategic Track'" 10 May 2011,
http://www.state.gov/r/pa/prs/ps/2011/05/162967.htm, last accessed 26 Jan.
2014.

U.S. State Department Cable, "Action Request On U.S.-China Joint Assistance

To Afghanistan", 22 January 2010. Available at https://www.wikileaks.org/plusd/cables/10STATE6320_a.html

U.S. State Department Cable, Aubrey Carlson, "China Standing by on Afghanistan and Pakistan", 9 March 2009. Available at https://www.wikileaks.org/plusd/cables/09beijing606_a.html

U.S. State Department Cable, Aubrey Carlson, "SRAP Holbrooke's April 15 dinner with Chinese Foreign Minister Yang Jiechi", 20 April 2009, https://www.wikileaks.org/plusd/cables/09BEIJING1046_a.html, last accessed 27 Jan. 2014.

U.S. State Department Cable, "Aynak Copper: Details Of Winning Chinese Bid Remain Elusive", 27 Nov. 2007, https://www.wikileaks.org/plusd/cables/07KABUL3933_a.html, last accessed 27 Jan. 2014.

U.S. State Department Cable, "Chinese Firm Again Frontrunner For Major Afghan Mining Contract", 7 Nov. 2009, https://www.wikileaks.org/plusd/cables/09KABUL3574_a.html, last accessed 2 Feb. 2014.

U.S. State Department Cable, "Chinese Firm Re-Thinks Afghan Mining Contract After Difficulties Of The Aynak Copper Mine Project", 10 Dec. 2009, http://www.cablegatesearch.net/cable.php?id=09BEIJING3295, last accessed 27 Jan. 2014.

U.S. State Department Cable, Clark T. Randt, Jr., "Ambassador Presses MFA AFM Liu On Nuclear Suppliers Group Draft Exception For India", 3 Sep. 2008, https://www.wikileaks.org/plusd/cables/08BEIJING3401_a.html, last accessed 26 Jan. 2014.

U.S. State Department Cable, "Competing Perceptions of PRC Activities", U12 Dec. 2009, wikileaks.org/cable/2009/12/09BEIJING3287.html, last accessed 20 Nov. 2013.

U.S. State Department Media Note, "List of U.S.-China Cooperative Projects", Office of the Spokesperson, 22 Jan. 2014, http://www.state.gov/r/pa/prs/ps/2014/01/220530.htm, last accessed 27 Jan. 2014.

White House, Office of the Press Secretary, "Remarks by the President in Address to the Nation on the Way Forward in Afghanistan and Pakistan", 1 Dec. 2009, http://www.whitehouse.gov/the-press-office/remarks-president-address-nation-way-forward-afghanistan-and-pakistan, last accessed 27 Jan. 2014.

Wikileaks, "Ambassador Presses Mfa Afm Liu On Nuclear Suppliers Group Draft Exception For India", 3 September 2008. Available at Http://www.Wikileaks.Org/Plusd/Cables/08beijing3401_A.Html

World Development Indicators, World Bank, http://data.worldbank.org/indicator/NY.GDP.MKTP.KD.ZG/countries/PK?display=graph, last accessed 27 Jan. 2014.

ACKNOWLEDGEMENTS

This book could not have been written without the help of a great number of friends, family, colleagues, supporters, and sources.

I would first like to thank my colleagues at the German Marshall Fund of the United States, especially on the Asia team, who gave me the time and space to complete the manuscript over the last year amid all the day-to-day demands of a busy think-tank, and were a tremendous source of ideas, contacts, and practical assistance. I am hugely indebted to Craig Kennedy for all his support and advice over the years, and to Dan Twining for our fantastic partnership on the Asia program. Other colleagues at GMF have also been a great help. Dhruva Jaishankar read sections of the manuscript and opened many doors in New Delhi—the opportunity to discuss these topics with K. Subrahmanyam and Brajesh Mishra in the same day was particularly memorable. Yuxi Zhao was a phenomenal research assistant, tracing sources, translating material, cross-checking footnotes, and tracking down every imaginable book and article. Sophie Dembinski worked tirelessly through late nights and weekends on editing, footnoting, and trouble-shooting in the final stages of the writing process. Wenxin Lin and Charles Goodyear helped with the glossary and acronyms. Louise Langeby was a valued travelling companion and intellectual partner in Pakistan. My bosses at GMF— Ian Lesser, Enders Wimbush, and Ivan Vejvoda—gave me the backing I needed at different stages in the process. And I'm also grateful to my other colleagues on the Asia program—Sharon Stirling-Woolsey and Dan Kliman—and to many in GMF's Brussels office, including Corinna Horst and the late, still-missed Ron Asmus.

ACKNOWLEDGEMENTS

Many of the trips, seminars and conferences that fed into the work also took place under the auspices of GMF and its partners. Most important of these has been the Stockholm China Forum, generously supported by the Swedish Ministry for Foreign Affairs, and jointly managed with my friend and collaborator Borje Ljunggren. GMF's Pakistan Paris workshops, organized with Frederic Grare during his time at the French Ministry of Defence, were also a very helpful input. The earliest work I did on the subject was sparked by comments at a GMF event by Bob Zoellick, without which I might never have embarked on this research in the first place. Under the leadership of Craig Kennedy, and now Karen Donfried, GMF has been a wonderful home for me for the past eight years and continues to go from strength to strength.

In Pakistan, Hamayoun Khan was always exceptionally kind with his time and his contacts during my visits to Islamabad; he knows Sino-Pakistani relations exceptionally well, and without his insights my understanding of the subject would have been much poorer. I would also like to convey my appreciation to Mirwais Nab—his analysis of Sino-Afghan relations and broader strategic issues, and his helpful introductions, were invaluable, from the days when we were both living in Beijing, through his stint in Kabul, and now in Washington, DC. A number of other still-serving government officials and others with official affiliations in China, Pakistan, Afghanistan, India, the United States, the EU, the UK, France, and Germany have been very generous with their time and advice, most of whom I am unable to thank by name here. Without their willingness to share information and analysis, a book of this nature would have been extremely difficult to write.

I have also benefited enormously from the work of the still-relatively-small gang of individuals working on these topics in Europe and the United States. Given some of the research challenges involved, it is very helpful that it is such a mutually supportive group. On the US side, Evan Feigenbaum is the person whose thinking on the field of East Asia, South Asia, and Central Asia I have appreciated learning from most over the years, and I'm still hugely grateful for all his support and advice. I benefited greatly from being able to join a number of sessions at the Council on Foreign Relations organized by Dan Markey, who also gave me very helpful pointers after reading an early draft of the manuscript, and whose own research on the emerging issues in this field is some of the most interesting new material out there. David Sedney was a font of wisdom on Chinese policy and the strategic picture in the whole region. Barney Rubin's recent work on Sino-US collaboration in Afghanistan and Pakistan has been hugely valuable, as have the roundtables that Jeff Payne has put together at NDU. In Europe, Raff Pantucci has been a constant source of tips, ideas and excellent analysis across a range of the issues covered in this book. Mathieu Duchatel produced some great work on Sino-Pakistani relations that I drew on during his time at Centre Asie. I met one of the European experts who has been doing some of the best work on the ground in Xinjiang and Pakistan, Alessandro Rippa, in Karimabad as the result of a tweet about tunnels while on my way up the KKH… I'm also grateful to Isaac Stonefish at *Foreign Policy* and Alex Lennon at the *Washington Quarterly* for publishing some of the more widely-circulated pieces I wrote on these subjects. April Rabkin was a great partner for my first visit to Afghanistan and Eva Gross was the biggest source of encouragement for getting out there in the first place. Emma Graham-Harrison kindly shared many of her Kabul contacts with me, and Jon Boone helpfully put me in contact with fixers in Peshawar and Gilgit. In Beijing (where we still hope he will return), Chris Buckley has been a regular sounding board and source of insight for an array of China-related developments over the last decade.

As the book has come towards its later stages, I have been grateful to the various people who have helped to improve and promote it. Tanvi Madan put together a tremendously helpful workshop at Brookings, drawing on some of the chapter drafts, that pulled in many of the leading Sinologists and South Asia hands from around town, and was chaired and very generously introduced by Stephen Cohen. Ziad Haider, whose work on China and Pakistan I had admired long before I started to work in this area, was my counterpart at that event and at a number of others since—his comments and analysis have been extremely helpful and I am well aware that he could have written a better book on the subject himself. I'm also grateful to David Ignatius and Maleeha Lodhi, who took part in a session at Brussels Forum that was partly a preview for the book. The two anonymous peer reviewers also provided comments that were very helpful indeed.

This book came about thanks to the initiative of Michael Dwyer at Hurst—the day I received his intriguing voicemail message was the first point at which I considered turning my research on this subject into a monograph. I am very grateful for his approaching me with the idea and

ACKNOWLEDGEMENTS

patiently shepherding me through the whole publishing process, as well as everyone else at Hurst.

The single person who has done more than anyone else to help bring the book into existence is Amy Studdart, who was involved in so many elements of the conception and execution of the whole project that they are too extensive to list—I really cannot thank her enough for her support. Mark Leonard gave me my first break in the world of foreign policy and has been a great friend and mentor ever since. His advice on all sorts of aspects on this book was invaluable. Stephanie Kleine-Ahlbrandt has been my collaborator over the last eight years of working on Chinese foreign policy and I have benefited constantly from all her insights and intelligence. Kirsty McNeill went closely through the draft text, made a running set of jokes about Gwadar, and was a wonderful friend throughout. Very special thanks are also owed to Zoe Flood, who went through multiple iterations of the book, transformed the quality of the text, and was a constant source of support and ideas from the earliest plans to the very final stages. I received many other kind offers of help from friends over the course of working on the book, not all of which I took up, but were always greatly appreciated—as was everyone's forbearance during some of the most intense phases of the process.

Finally, my family have been an amazing source of advice and support throughout, as always. Without their love and their backing, none of this would have been possible.

INDEX

INDEX

INDEX

INDEX

INDEX

INDEX

INDEX